WITNESS FOR THE PROSECUTION
AND SELECTED PLAYS

AGATHA CHRISTIE

The ABC Murders
The Adventure of the
 Christmas Pudding
After the Funeral
And Then There Were None
Appointment with Death
At Bertram's Hotel
The Big Four
The Body in the Library
By the Pricking of My Thumbs
Cards on the Table
A Caribbean Mystery
Cat Among the Pigeons
The Clocks
Crooked House
Curtain: Poirot's Last Case
Dead Man's Folly
Death Comes as the End
Death in the Clouds
Death on the Nile
Destination Unknown
Dumb Witness
Elephants Can Remember
Endless Night
Evil Under the Sun
Five Little Pigs
4.50 from Paddington
Hallowe'en Party
Hercule Poirot's Christmas
Hickory Dickory Dock
The Hollow
The Hound of Death
The Labours of Hercules
The Listerdale Mystery
Lord Edgware Dies
The Man in the Brown Suit
The Mirror Crack'd from Side
 to Side
Miss Marple's Final Cases
The Moving Finger
Mrs McGinty's Dead
The Murder at the Vicarage
Murder in Mesopotamia
Murder in the Mews
A Murder is Announced
Murder is Easy
The Murder of Roger Ackroyd
Murder on the Links
Murder on the Orient Express
The Mysterious Affair at Styles

The Mysterious Mr Quin
The Mystery of the Blue Train
Nemesis
N or M?
One, Two, Buckle My Shoe
Ordeal by Innocence
The Pale Horse
Parker Pyne Investigates
Partners in Crime
Passenger to Frankfurt
Peril at End House
A Pocket Full of Rye
Poirot Investigates
Poirot's Early Cases
Postern of Fate
Problem at Pollensa Bay
Sad Cypress
The Secret Adversary
The Secret of Chimneys
The Seven Dials Mystery
The Sittaford Mystery
Sleeping Murder
Sparkling Cyanide
Taken at the Flood
They Came to Baghdad
They Do It With Mirrors
Third Girl
The Thirteen Problems
Three Act Tragedy
Towards Zero
While the Light Lasts
Why Didn't They Ask Evans?

*Novels under the Nom de Plume of
'Mary Westmacott'*
Absent in the Spring
The Burden
A Daughter's A Daughter
Giant's Bread
The Rose and the Yew Tree
Unfinished Portrait

*Books under the name of
Agatha Christie Mallowan*
Come Tell me How You Live
Star Over Bethlehem

Autobiography
Agatha Christie: An Autobiography

Plays
The Mousetrap and Selected Plays

The____ gripping plays____ the undisputed Queen of Crime, here put____ for the first time in book form, provide yet more evidence of her mastery of the detective thriller. Agatha Christie's talents as a playwright are equal to her skills as a novelist and reading her plays, with their ingenious plots and colourful cast of characters, is every bit as pleasurable.

Witness For the Prosecution had a long stage run in both London and New York, where it won the New York Drama Critics Circle Award for best foreign play, an unprecedented honour for a thriller. It was also made into a highly successful film directed by Billy Wilder, and nominated for six Academy Awards. In *Towards Zero*, which Christie adapted from her novel, a psycopath homes in on his unsuspecting victims in a seaside house, high on a cliff overlooking the Devonshire River Tern. *Verdict* is an original play of which the author said, 'I still think it is the best play I have written with the exception of *Witness For the Prosecution*'. *Go Back For Murder* was adapted by Christie from her novel *Five Little Pigs*.

Agatha Christie dramatised many of her own ____ and frequently devised new twists of plot and ____cter to surprise and enthrall her audience.

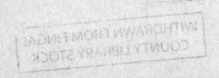

AGATHA CHRISTIE

WITNESS FOR THE PROSECUTION
&
SELECTED PLAYS

HarperCollins*Publishers*

HarperCollins*Publishers*
77–85 Fulham Palace Road,
Hammersmith, London W6 8JB

This paperback edition 1995
3

First published in Great Britain by
HarperCollins*Publishers* 1993

Witness For The Prosecution copyright
1954 by Agatha Christie

Towards Zero copyright 1957 by
Agatha Christie and Gerald Verner

Verdict © 1958 by Agatha Christie Ltd

Go Back For Murder © 1960 by Agatha Christie Ltd

ISBN 0 00 649045 X

Set in Baskerville

Printed and bound in Great Britain by
Clays Ltd, St Ives plc

CONTENTS

Witness for the Prosecution   1
Towards Zero   93
Verdict   175
Go Back for Murder   257

WITNESS FOR
THE PROSECUTION

Produced by Peter Saunders at The Winter Garden Theatre, London, on 28th October 1953, with the following cast of characters:

(in the order of their appearance)

GRETA, typist to Sir Wilfrid	*Rosalie Westwater*
CARTER, Sir Wilfrid's Chief Clerk	*Walter Horsbrugh*
MR MAYHEW, a solicitor	*Milton Rosmer*
LEONARD VOLE	*Derek Blomfield*
SIR WILFRID ROBARTS, QC	*David Horne*
INSPECTOR HEARNE	*David Raven*
PLAIN-CLOTHES DETECTIVE	*Kenn Kennedy*
ROMAINE	*Patricia Jessel*
CLERK OF THE COURT	*Philip Holles*
MR JUSTICE WAINWRIGHT	*Percy Marmont*
ALDERMAN	*Walter Horsbrugh*
MR MYERS, QC	*D.A. Clarke-Smith*
COURT USHER	*Nicolas Tannar*
COURT STENOGRAPHER	*John Bryning*
WARDER	*Denzil Ellis*
THE JUDGE'S CLERK	*Muir Little*
1ST BARRISTER	*George Dudley*
2ND BARRISTER	*Jack Bulloch*
3RD BARRISTER	*Lionel Gadsden*
4TH BARRISTER	*John Farries Moss*
5TH BARRISTER	*Richard Coke*
6TH BARRISTER	*Agnes Fraser*
1ST MEMBER OF THE JURY	*Lauderdale Beckett*
2ND MEMBER OF THE JURY	*Iris Fraser Foss*
3RD MEMBER OF THE JURY	*Kenn Kennedy*
A POLICEMAN	*David Homewood*

DR WYATT, a police surgeon	*Graham Stuart*
JANET MACKENZIE	*Jean Stuart*
MR CLEGG, a laboratory assistant	*Peter Franklin*
THE OTHER WOMAN	*Rosemary Wallace*

The play directed by Wallace Douglas

Décor by Michael Weight

Suggestions for reducing the cast to ten men and five
women will be found on page 370

SYNOPSIS OF SCENES

ACT I

The Chambers of Sir Wilfrid Robarts, QC. Afternoon

ACT II

The Central Criminal Court, London – better known as
the Old Bailey. Six weeks later. Morning

ACT III

SCENE 1   The chambers of Sir Wilfrid Robarts, QC.
The same evening
SCENE 2   The Old Bailey. The next morning

During Act III, Scene 2, the lights are lowered to
denote the passing of one hour.

AUTHOR'S NOTE

I have great faith in the ingenuity of amateurs and repertory companies to devise means of reducing the very large cast of *Witness for the Prosecution* in order to make it possible to perform, and my suggested means of reducing the cast is probably only one of many.

As there are a large number of non-speaking parts, it may well be that local amateurs can be used, or members of the audience be invited on to the stage, and I believe that this would be greatly to the benefit of the play rather than lose the spectacle of a lot of people in the court scene.

Although GRETA never appears at the same time as 'The Other Woman', i.e. the strawberry blonde in the final scene, this part should *not* be doubled, as the audience will think it is 'plot' — which, of course, it isn't.

The play has given me enormous enjoyment in writing, and I do hope that the repertory companies who do it will derive the same pleasure from it. Good luck.   AGATHA CHRISTIE

CARTER	Can double the Judge
INSPECTOR HEARNE	Can double Policeman at end of last act
PLAIN-CLOTHES DETECTIVE	Can be doubled by Warder
CLERK OF THE COURT	This part can be combined with Court Usher
ALDERMAN	Can be dispensed with
COURT STENOGRAPHER	Can be dispensed with
JUDGE'S CLERK	Can be dispensed with
SIX BARRISTERS	Four can be dispensed with
THREE MEMBERS OF THE JURY	These can be dispensed with and the 'taking of the oath' and 'returning the verdict' can be done by a voice 'off'
MR MYERS, QC	Can double Plain-Clothes Detective

ACT ONE

SCENE: *The chambers of* SIR WILFRID ROBARTS, *QC.*

The scene is SIR WILFRID's *private office. It is a narrow room with the door
Left and a window Right. The window has a deep built-in windowseat
and overlooks a tall plain brick wall. There is a fireplace Centre of the back
wall, flanked by bookcases filled with heavy legal volumes. There is a desk
Right Centre with a swivel chair Right of it and a leather-covered upright
chair Left of it. A second upright chair stands against the bookcases Left of
the fireplace. In the corner up Right is a tall reading desk, and in the corner
up Left are some coat-hooks attached to the wall. At night the room is lit by
electric candle-lamp wall-brackets Right and Left of the fireplace and an
angle-poise lamp on the desk. The light switch is below the door Left. There
is a bell-push Left of the fireplace. The desk has a telephone on it and is
littered with legal documents. There are the usual deed-boxes and there is a
litter of documents on the windowseat.*

*When Curtain rises, it is afternoon and there is sunshine streaming in through the
window Right. The office is empty.* GRETA, SIR WILFRID's *typist,
enters immediately. She is an adenoidal girl with a good opinion of herself.
She crosses to the fireplace, doing a 'square dance' step, and takes a paper
from a box-file on the mantelpiece.* CARTER, *the Chief Clerk, enters. He
carries some letters.* GRETA *turns, sees* CARTER, *crosses and quietly
exits.* CARTER *crosses to the desk and puts the letters on it. The telephone
rings.* CARTER *lifts the receiver.*

CARTER. (*Into the telephone*) Sir Wilfrid Robarts' Chambers ...
Oh, it's you, Charles ... No, Sir Wilfrid's in Court ...
Won't be back just yet ... Yes, Shuttleworth case ... What
– with Myers for the prosecution and Banter trying it? ...
He's been giving judgement for close on two hours already
... No, not an earthly this evening. We're full up. Can give

you an appointment tomorrow . . . No, couldn't possibly. I'm expecting Mayhew, of Mayhew and Brinskill, you know, any minute now . . . Well, so long. (*He replaces the receiver and sorts the documents on the desk.*)

GRETA. (*Enters. She is painting her nails*) Shall I make the tea, Mr Carter?

CARTER. (*Looking at his watch*) It's hardly time yet, Greta.

GRETA. It is by my watch.

CARTER. Then your watch is wrong.

GRETA. (*Crossing to Centre*) I put it right by the radio.

CARTER. Then the radio must be wrong.

GRETA. (*Shocked*) Oh, not the radio, Mr Carter. That *couldn't* be wrong.

CARTER. This watch was my father's. It never gains nor loses. They don't make watches like that nowadays. (*He shakes his head, then suddenly changes his manner and picks up one of the typewritten papers.*) Really, your typing. Always mistakes. (*He crosses to Right of* GRETA.) You've left out a word.

GRETA. Oh, well – just one word. Anyone might do that.

CARTER. The word you have left out is the word *not*. The omission of it entirely alters the sense.

GRETA. Oh, does it? That's rather funny when you come to think of it. (*She giggles.*)

CARTER. It is not in the least funny. (*He tears the letter in half and hands the piece to her.*) Do it again. You may remember I told you last week about the celebrated case of Bryant and Horsfall. Case of a will and a trust fund, and entirely owing to a piece of careless copying by a clerk . . .

GRETA. (*Interrupting*) The wrong wife got the money, I remember.

CARTER. A woman divorced fifteen years previously. Absolutely contrary to the intention of the testator, as his lordship himself admitted. But the wording had to stand. They couldn't do anything about it. (*He crosses above the desk to Right of it.*)

GRETA. I think *that's* rather funny, too. (*She giggles.*)

CARTER. Counsel's Chambers are no place to be funny in. The Law, Greta, is a serious business and should be treated accordingly.

GRETA. You wouldn't think so – to hear some of the jokes Judges make.

CARTER. That kind of joke is the prerogative of the Bench.

GRETA. And I'm always reading in the paper about 'laughter in Court'.

CARTER. If that's not caused by one of the Judge's remarks you'll find he'll soon threaten to have the Court cleared.

GRETA. (*Crossing to the door*) Mean old thing. (*She turns and crosses to Left of the desk.*) Do you know what I read the other day, Mr Carter. (*Sententiously*) 'The Law's an Ass.' I'm not being rude. It's a quotation.

CARTER. (*Coldly*) A quotation of a facetious nature. Not meant to be taken seriously. (*He looks at his watch.*) You can make the tea – (*He pauses, waiting for the exact second.*) – now, Greta.

GRETA. (*Gladly*) Oh, thank you, Mr Carter. (*She crosses quickly to the door.*)

CARTER. Mr Mayhew, of Mayhew and Brinskill, will be here shortly. A Mr Leonard Vole is also expected. They may come together or separately.

GRETA. (*Excitedly*) Leonard Vole? (*She crosses to the desk.*) Why, that's the name – it was in the paper . . .

CARTER. (*Repressively*) The tea, Greta.

GRETA. Asked to communicate with the police as he might be able to give them useful information.

CARTER. (*Raising his voice*) Tea!

GRETA. (*Crossing to the door and turning*) It was only last . . .

(CARTER *glowers at* GRETA.)

The tea, Mr Carter. (GRETA, *abashed but unsatisfied, exits.*)

CARTER. (*Continues his arrangement of the papers, muttering to himself*) These girls. Sensational – inaccurate – I don't know what the Temple's coming to. (*He examines a typewritten document, makes an angry sound, picks up a pen and makes a correction.*)

GRETA. (*Enters. Announcing*) Mr Mayhew.

(MR MAYHEW *and* LEONARD VOLE *enter.* MAYHEW *is a typical middle-aged solicitor, shrewd and rather dry and precise in manner.* LEONARD *is a likeable, friendly young man, about twenty-seven. He is looking faintly worried.* MAYHEW *carries a briefcase.*)

MAYHEW. (*Giving his hat to* GRETA) Sit down, Mr Vole. (*He crosses and stands above the desk.*) Good afternoon, Carter. (*He puts his briefcase on the desk.*)

(GRETA *takes* LEONARD's *hat and hangs both on the pegs above the door. She then exits, staring at* LEONARD *over her shoulder.*)

CARTER. Good afternoon, Mr Mayhew. Sir Wilfrid shouldn't be long, sir, although you never can tell with Mr Justice Banter. I'll go straight over to the Robing Room and tell him that you're here! (*He hesitates*) with . . . (*He crosses below the desk to Right of* LEONARD.)

MAYHEW. With Mr Leonard Vole. Thank you, Carter. I'm afraid our appointment was at rather short notice. But in this case time is – er – rather urgent.

(CARTER *crosses to the door.*)

How's the lumbago?

CARTER. (*Turning*) I only feel it when the wind is in the East. Thank you for remembering, Mr Mayhew. (CARTER *exits hurriedly.*)

(MAYHEW *sits Left of the desk.* LEONARD *prowls uneasily.*)

MAYHEW. Sit down, Mr Vole.

LEONARD. Thanks – I'd rather walk about. I – this sort of thing makes you feel a bit jumpy. (*He crosses down Left.*)

MAYHEW. Yes, yes, very probably . . .

GRETA. (*Enters. She speaks to* MAYHEW, *but stares with fascinated interest at* LEONARD.) Would you care for a cup of tea, Mr Mayhew? I've just made it.

LEONARD. (*Appreciatively*) Thanks, I don't mind if I . . .

MAYHEW. (*Interrupting; decisively*) No, thank you.

(GRETA *turns to exit.*)

LEONARD. (*To* GRETA) Sorry. (*He smiles at her.*)

(GRETA *smiles at* LEONARD *and exits. There is a pause.*)

(*He crosses up Right. Abruptly and with a rather likeable air of bewilderment.*) What I mean is, I can't believe it's *me* this is happening to. I keep thinking – perhaps it's all a dream and I'll wake up presently.

MAYHEW. Yes, I suppose one might feel like that.

LEONARD. (*Moving to Right of the desk*) What I mean is – well, it seems so silly.

MAYHEW. (*Sharply*) Silly, Mr Vole?

LEONARD. Well, yes. I mean I've always been a friendly sort of chap – get on with people and all that. I mean, I'm not the sort of fellow that does – well, anything violent. (*He pauses.*) But I suppose it will be – all right, won't it? I mean you don't get convicted for things you haven't done in this country, do you?

MAYHEW. Our English judicial system is, in my opinion, the finest in the world.

LEONARD. (*Is not much comforted. Crossing above the desk to Left*) Of course there was that case of – what was his name – Adolf Beck. I read about it only the other day. After he'd been in prison for years, they found out it was another chap called Smith. They gave him a free pardon then. That's a thing that seems odd to me – giving you a 'pardon' for something you haven't done.

MAYHEW. It is the necessary legal term.

LEONARD. (*Bringing the chair from Left of the fireplace and setting it Centre*) Well, it doesn't seem right to me.

MAYHEW. The important thing was that Beck was set at liberty.

LEONARD. Yes, it was all right for him. But if it had been murder now – (*He sits astride the chair Centre.*) if it had been murder it would have been too late. He would have been hanged.

MAYHEW. (*Dry but kindly*) Now, Mr Vole, there is really no need to take a – er – morbid point of view.

LEONARD. (*Rather pathetically*) I'm sorry, sir. But you see, in a way, I'm rather getting the wind up.

MAYHEW. Well, try and keep calm. Sir Wilfrid Robarts will be here presently and I want you to tell your story to him exactly as you told it to me.

LEONARD. Yes, sir.

MAYHEW. But meantime perhaps we might fill out a little more of the detail – er – background. You are at present, I understand, out of a job?

LEONARD. (*Embarrassed*) Yes, but I've got a few pounds put by. It's not much, but if you can see your way . . .

MAYHEW. (*Upset*) Oh, I'm not thinking of – er – legal fees. It's just the – er – picture I'm trying to get clear. Your surroundings and – er – circumstances. How long have you been unemployed?

LEONARD. (*Answers everything readily, with an engaging friendliness*) About a couple of months.

MAYHEW. What were you doing before that?

LEONARD. I was in a motor servicing firm – kind of mechanic, that's what I was.

MAYHEW. How long had you worked there?

LEONARD. Oh, about three months.

MAYHEW. (*Sharply*) Were you discharged?

LEONARD. No, I quit. Had words with the foreman. Proper old b – (*He breaks off.*) That is, he was a mean sort of chap, always picking on you.

MAYHEW. Hm! And before that?

LEONARD. I worked in a petrol station, but things got a bit awkward and I left.

MAYHEW. Awkward? In what way?

LEONARD. (*Embarrassed*) Well – the boss's daughter – she was only a kid, but she took a – well, a sort of fancy to me – and there was nothing there shouldn't have been between us, but the old man got a bit fed up and said I'd better go. He was quite nice about it and gave me a good chit. (*He rises and suddenly grins.*) Before *that*, I was selling egg beaters on commission. (*He replaces the chair Left of the fireplace*)

MAYHEW. Indeed.

LEONARD. (*Crossing and standing above the desk; boyishly*) And a rotten job they were, too. I could have invented a better egg beater myself. (*Catching* MAYHEW*'s mood*) You're thinking I'm a bit of a drifter, sir. It's true in a way – but I'm not really like that. Doing my Army service unsettled me a bit – that and being abroad. I was in Germany. It was fine there. That's where I met my wife. She's an actress. Since I've come back to this country I can't seem somehow to settle down properly. I don't know really just what I want to do – I like working on cars best and thinking out new gadgets for them. That's interesting, that is. And you see . . .

(SIR WILFRID ROBARTS, QC., *enters. He is followed on by* CARTER. SIR WILFRID *is wearing his QC's jacket and bands and carries his wig and gown.* CARTER *carries* SIR WILFRID's *ordinary jacket and bow tie.*)

SIR WILFRID. Hullo, John.

MAYHEW. (*Rising*) Ah, Wilfrid.

SIR WILFRID. (*Handing the wig and gown to* CARTER) Carter told you I was in Court? Banter really surpassed himself. (*He looks at* LEONARD.) And this is Mr – er – Vole? (*He crosses to Left of* LEONARD.)

MAYHEW. This is Leonard Vole.

LEONARD. How do you do, sir?

(MAYHEW *moves to the fireplace.*)

SIR WILFRID. How do you do, Vole? Won't you sit down?

(LEONARD *sits Left of the desk.*)

How's the family, John? (*He crosses to* CARTER.)

(CARTER *assists* SIR WILFRID *to change his jacket and remove his bands.*)

MAYHEW. Molly's got a touch of this twenty-four-hour flu.

SIR WILFRID. Too bad!

MAYHEW. Yes, damnable. Did you win your case, Wilfrid?

SIR WILFRID. Yes, I'm glad to say.

MAYHEW. It always gives you satisfaction to beat Myers, doesn't it?

SIR WILFRID. It gives me satisfaction to beat anyone.

MAYHEW. But especially Myers.

SIR WILFRID. (*Taking the bow tie from* CARTER) Especially Myers. (*He crosses to the mirror Right.*) He's an irritating – gentleman. (*He puts on his bow tie.*) He always seems to bring out the worst in me.

MAYHEW. That would appear to be mutual. You irritate him because you hardly ever let him finish a sentence.

(CARTER *exits, taking the wig, gown, jacket and bands with him.*)

SIR WILFRID. He irritates me because of that mannerism of his. (*He turns and stands Right of the desk.*) It's this – (*He clears his throat and adjusts an imaginary wig.*) that drives me to distraction, and he will call me Ro-barts – Ro-barts. But he's a very able advocate, if only he'd remember not to ask leading questions when he knows damn well he shouldn't. But let's get down to business.

MAYHEW. (*Moving above the desk*) Yes. I brought Vole here, because I am anxious for you to hear his story exactly as he told it to me. (*He takes some typewritten papers from his briefcase.*) There is some

urgency in the matter, it seems. (*He hands the papers to* SIR
WILFRID)

SIR WILFRRID. Oh?

LEONARD. My wife thinks I'm going to be arrested. (*He looks embarrassed.*) She's much cleverer than I am – so she may be right.

SIR WILFRID. Arrested for what?

LEONARD. (*Still more embarrassed*) Well – for murder.

(SIR WILFRID *perches himself on the down Right corner of the desk.*)

MAYHEW. (*Crossing to Centre*) It's the case of Miss Emily French.
You've probably seen the reports in the Press?

(SIR WILFRID *nods.*)

She was a maiden lady, living alone but for an elderly housekeeper, in a house at Hampstead. On the night of October the
fourteenth her housekeeper returned at eleven o'clock to find
that apparently the place had been broken into, and that her
mistress had been coshed on the back of the head and killed.
(*To* LEONARD) That is right?

LEONARD. That's right. It's quite an ordinary sort of thing to
happen nowadays. And then, the other day, the papers said
that the police were anxious to interview a Mr Leonard Vole,
who had visited Miss French earlier on the evening in question,
as they thought he might be able to give them useful information. So of course I went along to the police station and they
asked me a lot of questions.

SIR WILFRID. (*Sharply*) Did they caution you?

LEONARD. (*Vaguely*) I don't quite know. I mean they said would I
like to make a statement and they'd write it down, and it might
be used in Court. Is that cautioning me?

(SIR WILFRID *exchanges a glance with* MAYHEW, *and speaks more to him
than to* LEONARD)

SIR WILFRID. (*Rising*) Oh well, can't be helped now. (*He crosses
above the desk to Left.*)

LEONARD. Anyway, it sounded damned silly to me. I told them all I
could and they were very polite and seemed quite satisfied and
all that. When I got home and told Romaine about it – my
wife, that is – well, she got the wind up. She seemed to think

that they – well – that they'd got hold of the idea that I might have done it.

(SIR WILFRID *moves the chair from Left of the fireplace to Centre for* MAYHEW, *who sits.*)

So I thought perhaps I ought to get hold of a solicitor – (*To* MAYHEW) so I came along to you. I thought you'd be able to tell me what I ought to do about it. (*He looks anxiously from one to the other.*)

SIR WILFRID. (*Moving down Left*) You knew Miss French well?

(LEONARD *rises, but* SIR WILFRID *motions him to sit.*)

LEONARD. Oh yes, she'd been frightfully kind to me. (*He resumes his seat.*) Actually it was a bit of a bore sometimes – she positively fussed over me, but she meant it very well, and when I saw in the paper that she'd been killed I was awfully upset, because, you see, I'd really got fond of her.

MAYHEW. Tell Sir Wilfrid, just as you told me, how it was you came to make Miss French's acquaintance.

LEONARD. (*Turning obediently to* SIR WILFRID) Well, it was one day in Oxford Street. I saw an old lady crossing the road carrying a lot of parcels and in the middle of the street she dropped them, tried to get hold of them again and found a bus was almost on top of her.

(SIR WILFRID *crosses slowly below the others to Right of desk.*)

Just managed to get to the kerb safely. Well, I recovered her parcels from the street, wiped some of the mud off them as best I could, tied up one again that had burst open with string and generally soothed the old dear down. You know the sort of thing.

SIR WILFRID. And she was grateful?

LEONARD. Oh yes, she seemed very grateful. Thanked me a lot and all that. Anyone would think I'd saved her life instead of her parcels.

SIR WILFRID. There was actually no question of your having saved her life? (*He takes a packet of cigarettes from the desk drawer.*)

LEONARD. Oh, no. Nothing heroic. I never expected to see her again.

SIR WILFRID. Cigarette?

LEONARD. No, thanks, sir, never do. But by an extraordinary coincidence, two days later I happened to be sitting behind her in the theatre. She looked round and recognized me and we began to talk, and in the end she asked me to come and see her.

SIR WILFRID. And you went?

LEONARD. Yes. She'd urged me to name a day specially and it seemed rather churlish to refuse. So I said I'd go on the following Saturday.

SIR WILFRID. And you went to her house at . . . (*He looks at one of the papers.*)

MAYHEW. Hampstead.

LEONARD. Yes.

SIR WILFRID. What did you know about her when you first went to the house? (*He perches himself on the down Right corner of the desk.*)

LEONARD. Well, nothing really but what she'd told me, that she lived alone and hadn't very many friends. Something of that kind.

SIR WILFRID. She lived with only a housekeeper?

LEONARD. That's right. She had eight cats, though. Eight of them. The house was beautifully furnished and all that, but it smelt a bit of cat.

SIR WILFRID. (*Rising and moving above the desk*) Had you reason to believe she was well off?

LEONARD. Well, she talked as though she was.

SIR WILFRID. And you yourself? (*He crosses and stands up Left of* LEONARD.)

LEONARD (*Cheerfully*) Oh, I'm practically stony broke and have been for a long time.

SIR WILFRID. Unfortunate.

LEONARD. Yes, it is rather. Oh, you mean people will say I was sucking up to her for her money?

SIR WILFRID. (*Disarmed*) I shouldn't have put it quite like that, but in essence, yes, that is possibly what people might say.

LEONARD. It isn't really true, you know. As a matter of fact, I was sorry for her. I thought she was lonely. I was brought up by an old aunt, my Aunt Betsy, and I like old ladies.

SIR WILFRID. You say old ladies. Do you know what age Miss French was?

LEONARD. Well, I didn't know, but I read it in the paper after she was murdered. She was fifty-six.

SIR WILFRID. Fifty-six. You consider that old, Mr Vole, but I should doubt if Miss Emily French considered herself old.

LEONARD. But you can't call it a chicken, can you?

SIR WILFRID. (*Crossing above the desk and sitting Right of it*) Well, let us get on. You went to see Miss French fairly frequently?

LEONARD. Yes, I should say once, twice a week perhaps.

SIR WILFRID. Did you take your wife with you?

LEONARD. (*Slightly embarrassed*) No, no, I didn't.

SIR WILFRID. Why didn't you?

LEONARD. Well – well, frankly, I don't think it would have gone down very well if I had.

SIR WILFRID. Do you mean with your wife or with Miss French?

LEONARD. Oh, with Miss French. (*He hesitates.*)

MAYHEW. Go on, go on.

LEONARD. You see, she got rather fond of me.

SIR WILFRID. You mean, she fell in love with you?

LEONARD. (*Horrified*) Oh, good Lord, no, nothing of that kind. Just sort of pampered me and spoiled me, that sort of thing.

SIR WILFRID. (*After a short pause*) You see, Mr Vole, I have no doubt part of the police case against you – if there *is* a case against you, which as yet we have no definite reason to suppose – will be why did you, young, good-looking, married, devote so much of your time to an elderly woman with whom you could hardly have very much in common?

LEONARD. (*Gloomily*) Yes, I know they'll say I was after her for her money. And in a way perhaps that's true. But only in a way.

SIR WILFRID. (*Slightly disarmed*) Well, at least you're frank, Mr Vole. Can you explain a little more clearly?

LEONARD. (*Rising and moving to the fireplace*) Well, she made no secret of the fact that she was rolling in money. As I told you, Romaine and I – that's my wife – are pretty hard up. (*He moves and stands above his chair.*) I'll admit that I did hope that if I was really in a tight place she'd lend me some money. I'm being honest about it.

SIR WILFRID. Did you ask her for a loan?

LEONARD. No, I didn't. I mean, things weren't desperate. (*He becomes suddenly rather more serious, as though he realizes the gravity of that.*) Of course I can see – it does look rather bad for me. (*He resumes his seat.*)

SIR WILFRID. Miss French knew you were a married man?

LEONARD. Oh, yes.

SIR WILFRID. But she didn't suggest that you should bring your wife to see her?

LEONARD. (*Slightly embarrassed*) No. She – well, she seemed to take it for granted my wife and I didn't get on.

SIR WILFRID. Did you deliberately give her that impression?

LEONARD. No, I didn't. Indeed I didn't. But she seemed to – well, assume it, and I thought perhaps if I kept dragging Romaine into it she'd well, lose interest in me. I didn't want exactly to cadge money from her, but I'd invented a gadget for a car – a really good idea it is – and if I could have persuaded her to finance that, well, I mean it would have been *her* money, and it might have brought her in a lot. Oh, it's very difficult to explain – but I wasn't sponging on her. Sir Wilfrid, really I wasn't.

SIR WILFRID. What sums of money did you obtain at any time from Miss French?

LEONARD. None. None at all.

SIR WILFRID. Tell me something about the housekeeper.

LEONARD. Janet MacKenzie? She was a regular old tyrant, you know, Janet was. Fairly bullied poor Miss French. Looked after her very well and all that, but the poor old dear couldn't call her soul her own when Janet was about. (*Thoughtfully*) Janet didn't like me at all.

SIR WILFRID. Why didn't she like you?

LEONARD. Oh, jealous, I expect. I don't think she liked my helping Miss French with her business affairs.

SIR WILFRID. Oh, so you helped Miss French with her business affairs?

LEONARD. Yes. She was worried about some of her investments and things, and she found it a bit difficult to fill up forms and all that sort of thing. Yes, I helped her with a lot of things like that.

SIR WILFRID. Now, Mr Vole, I'm going to ask you a very serious question. And it's one to which it's vital I should have a truthful answer. You were in low water financially, you had the handling of this lady's affairs. Now did you at any time convert to your own use the securities that you handled?

(LEONARD *is about to repudiate this hotly.*)

Now, wait a minute, Mr Vole, before you answer. Because, you see, there are two points of view. Either we can make a feature of your probity and honesty or, if you swindled the woman in any way, then we must take the line that you had no motive for murder, since you had already a profitable source of income. You can see that there are advantages in either point of view. What I want is the truth. Take your time if you like before you reply.

LEONARD. I assure you, Sir Wilfrid, that I played dead straight and you won't find anything to the contrary. Dead straight.

SIR WILFRID. Thank you, Mr Vole. You relieve my mind very much. I pay you the compliment of believing that you are far too intelligent to lie over such a vital matter. And we now come to October the . . . (*He hesitates.*)

MAYHEW. The fourteenth.

SIR WILFRID. Fourteenth. (*He rises.*) Did Miss French ask you to go and see her that night?

LEONARD. No, she didn't, as a matter of fact. But I'd come across a new kind of gadget and I thought she'd like it. So I slipped up there that evening and got there about a quarter to eight. It was Janet MacKenzie's night out and I knew she'd be alone and might be rather lonely.

SIR WILFRID. It was Janet MacKenzie's night out and you knew that fact.

LEONARD. (*Cheerfully*) Oh yes, I knew Janet always went out on a Friday.

SIR WILFRID. That's not quite so good.

LEONARD. Why not? It seems very natural that I should choose that evening to go and see her.

SIR WILFRID. Please go on, Mr Vole.

LEONARD. Well, I got there at a quarter to eight. She'd finished her supper but I had a cup of coffee with her and we played a game of Double Demon. Then at nine o'clock I said good night to her and went home.

(SIR WILFRID *crosses below the* OTHERS *to Left.*)

MAYHEW. You told me the housekeeper said she came home that evening earlier than usual.

LEONARD. Yes, the police told me she came back for something she'd forgotten and she heard – or she says she heard – somebody talking with Miss French. Well, whoever it was, it wasn't me.

SIR WILFRID. Can you prove that, Mr Vole?

LEONARD. Yes, of course I can prove it. I was at home again with my wife by then. That's what the police kept asking me. Where I was at nine-thirty. Well, I mean some days one wouldn't know where one was. As it happens I can remember quite well that I'd gone straight home to Romaine and we hadn't gone out again.

SIR WILFRID. (*Crossing up Centre*) You live in a flat?

LEONARD. Yes. We've got a tiny maisonette over a shop behind Euston Station.

SIR WILFRID. (*Standing up Left of* LEONARD) Did anybody see you returning to the flat?

LEONARD. I don't suppose so. Why should they?

SIR WILFRID. It might be an advantage if they had.

LEONARD. But surely you don't think – I mean if she were really killed at half past nine my wife's evidence is all I need, isn't it?

(SIR WILFRID *and* MAYHEW *look at each other.* SIR WILFRID *crosses and stands Left.*)

MAYHEW. And your wife will say definitely that you were at home at that time?

LEONARD. Of course she will.

MAYHEW. (*Rising and moving to the fireplace*) You are very fond of your wife and your wife is very fond of you?

LEONARD. (*His face softening*) Romaine is absolutely devoted to me. She's the most devoted wife any man could have.

MAYHEW. I see. You are happily married.

LEONARD. Couldn't be happier. Romaine's wonderful, absolutely wonderful. I'd like you to know her, Mr Mayhew.

(*There is a knock at the door.*)

SIR WILFRID. (*Calling*) Come in.

GRETA. (*Enters. She carries an evening paper.*) The evening paper, Sir Wilfrid. (*She points to a paragraph as she hands the paper to him.*)

SIR WILFRID. Thank you, Greta.

GRETA. Would you like a cup of tea, sir?

SIR WILFRID. No, thank you. Oh, would you like a cup, Vole?

LEONARD. No thank you, sir.

SIR WILFRID. No, thank you, Greta. (*He crosses below the* OTHERS *to Right of the desk.*)

(GRETA *exits.*)

MAYHEW. I think it would be advisable for us to have a meeting with your wife.

LEONARD. You mean have a regular round-table conference?

(SIR WILFRID *sits Right of the desk.*)

MAYHEW. I wonder, Mr Vole, if you are taking this business quite seriously enough?

LEONARD. (*Nervously*) I am. I am, really, but it seems – well, I mean it seems so much like a bad dream. I mean that it should be happening to me. Murder. It's a thing you read about in books or newspapers, but you can't believe it's a thing that could ever happen to you, or touch you in any way. I suppose that's why I keep trying to make a joke of it, but it isn't a joke, really.

MAYHEW. No, I'm afraid it's not a joke.

LEONARD. But I mean it's all right, isn't it? Because I mean if they think Miss French was killed at half past nine and I was at home with Romaine . . .

MAYHEW. How did you go home? By bus or underground?

LEONARD. I walked. It took me about twenty-five minutes, but it was a fine night – a bit windy.

MAYHEW. Did you see anyone you knew on the way?

LEONARD. No, but does it matter? I mean Romaine . . .

SIR WILFRID. The evidence of a devoted wife unsupported by any other evidence may not be completely convincing, Mr Vole.

LEONARD. You mean, they'd think Romaine would tell a lie on my account?

SIR WILFRID. It has been known, Mr Vole.

LEONARD. Oh, I'm sure she would, too, only in this case I mean she won't be telling a lie. I mean it really is so. You do believe me, don't you?

SIR WILFRID. Yes, I believe you, Mr Vole, but it's not me you will have to convince. You are aware, are you not, that Miss French left a will leaving you all her money?

LEONARD. (*Absolutely flabbergasted*) Left all her money to me? You're joking!

(MAYHEW *resumes his seat Centre.*)

SIR WILFRID. I'm not joking. It's in tonight's evening paper. (*He hands the paper across the desk.*)

LEONARD. (*Reads the paragraph*) Well, I can hardly believe it.

SIR WILFRID. You knew nothing about it?

LEONARD. Absolutely nothing. She never said a word. (*He hands the paper to* MAYHEW.)

MAYHEW. You're quite sure of that, Mr Vole?

LEONARD. Absolutely sure. I'm very grateful to her – yet in a way I rather wish now that she hadn't. I mean it – it's a bit unfortunate as things are, isn't it, sir?

SIR WILFRID. It supplies you with a very adequate motive. That is, if you knew about it, which you say you didn't. Miss French never talked to you about making a will?

LEONARD. She said to Janet once, 'You're afraid I shall make my will again,' but that was nothing to do with me. I mean, it was just a bit of a dust-up between them. (*His manner changes.*) Do you really think they're going to arrest me?

SIR WILFRID. I think you must prepare yourself, Mr Vole, for that eventuality.

LEONARD. (*Rising*) You – you will do the best you can for me, won't you, sir?

SIR WILFRID. (*With friendliness*) You may rest assured, my dear Mr Vole, that I will do everything in my power to help you. Don't worry. Leave everything in my hands.

LEONARD. You'll look after Romaine, won't you? I mean, she'll be in an awful state – it will be terrible for her.

SIR WILFRID. Don't worry, my boy. Don't worry.

LEONARD. (*Resuming his seat; to* MAYHEW) Then the money side, too. That worries me. I've got a few quid, but it's not much. Perhaps I oughtn't to have asked you to do anything for me.

MAYHEW. I think we shall be able to put up adequate defence. The Court provides for these cases, you know.

LEONARD. (*Rising and moving above the desk*) I can't believe it. I can't believe that I, Leonard Vole, may be standing in a dock saying 'Not guilty'. People staring at me. (*He shakes himself as though it were a bad dream, then turns to* MAYHEW.) I can't see why they don't think it was a burglar. I mean, apparently the window was forced and smashed and a lot of things were strewn around, so the papers said. (*He resumes his seat.*) I mean, it seems much more probable.

MAYHEW. The police must have some good reason for not thinking that it was a burglary.

LEONARD. Well, it seems to me . . .

(CARTER *enters.*)

SIR WILFRID. Yes, Carter?

CARTER. (*Crossing above the desk*) Excuse me, sir, there are two gentlemen here asking to see Mr Vole.

SIR WILFRID. The police?

CARTER. Yes, sir.

(MAYHEW *rises.*)

SIR WILFRID. (*Rising and crossing to the door*) All right, John, I'll go and talk to them.

(SIR WILFRID *exits and* CARTER *follows him off.*)

LEONARD. My God! Is this – it?

MAYHEW. I'm afraid it may be, my boy. Now take it easy. Don't lose heart.

(*He pats* LEONARD *on the shoulder.*) Make no further statement – leave it all to us. (*He replaces his chair Left of the fireplace.*)

LEONARD. But how did they know I'm here?

MAYHEW. It seems probable that they have had a man watching you.

LEONARD. (*Still unable to believe it*) Then they really do suspect me.

(SIR WILFRID, DETECTIVE INSPECTOR HEARNE *and a plain-*

clothes DETECTIVE *enter. The* INSPECTOR *is a tall, good-looking officer.*)

INSPECTOR. (*As he enters; to* SIR WILFRID) I'm sorry to trouble you, sir.

SIR WILFRID. (*Standing up Left*) This is Mr Vole.

(LEONARD *rises.*)

INSPECTOR. (*Crossing to* LEONARD) Is your name Leonard Vole?

LEONARD. Yes.

INSPECTOR. I am Detective Inspector Hearne. I have here a warrant for your arrest on the charge of murdering Emily French on October fourteenth last. I must warn you that anything you say may be taken down and used in evidence.

LEONARD. OK. (*He looks nervously at* SIR WILFRID, *then crosses and takes his hat from the hooks up Left.*) I'm ready.

MAYHEW. (*Moving to Left of the* INSPECTOR) Good afternoon, Inspector Hearne. My name is Mayhew. I am representing Mr Vole.

INSPECTOR. Good afternoon, Mr Mayhew. That's quite all right. We'll take him along and charge him now.

(LEONARD *and the* DETECTIVE *exit.*)

(*He crosses to* SIR WILFRID. *To* MAYHEW) Very seasonable weather we're having just now. Quite a nip of frost last night. We'll be seeing you later, sir, I expect. (*He crosses to the door.*) Hope we haven't inconvenienced you, Sir Wilfrid.

SIR WILFRID. I am never inconvenienced.

(*The* INSPECTOR *laughs politely and exits.*)

(*He closes the door.*) I must say, John, that that young man is in a worse mess than he seems to think.

MAYHEW. He certainly is. How does he strike you?

SIR WILFRID. (*Crossing to Left of* MAYHEW) Extraordinarily naïve. Yet in some ways quite shrewd. Intelligent, I should say. But he certainly doesn't realize the danger of his position.

MAYHEW. Do you think he did it?

SIR WILFRID. I've no idea. On the whole, I should say *not.* (*Sharply*) You agree?

MAYHEW. (*Taking his pipe from his pocket*) I agree.

(SIR WILFRID *takes the tobacco jar from the mantelpiece and hands it to* MAYHEW, *who crosses, stands above the desk and fills his pipe.*)

SIR WILFRID. Oh well, he seems to have impressed both of us favourably. I can't think why. I never heard a weaker story. God knows what we're going to do with it. The only evidence in his favour seems to be his wife's – and who's going to believe a wife?

MAYHEW. (*With dry humour*) It has been known to happen.

SIR WILFRID. She's a foreigner, too. Nine out of the twelve in a jury box believe a foreigner is lying anyway. She'll be emotional and upset, and won't understand what the prosecuting counsel says to her. Still, we shall have to interview her. You'll see, she'll have hysterics all over my Chambers.

MAYHEW. Perhaps you'd prefer not to accept the brief.

SIR WILFRID. Who says I won't accept it? Just because I point out that the boy has an absolute tomfool story to tell.

MAYHEW. (*Crossing and handing the tobacco jar to* SIR WILFRID) But a true one.

SIR WILFRID. (*Replacing the jar on the mantelpiece*) It must be a true one. It couldn't be so idiotic if it wasn't true. Put all the facts down in black and white and the whole thing is utterly damning.

(MAYHEW *feels in his pockets for matches.*)

And yet, when you talk to the boy, and he blurts out these damning facts, you realize that the whole thing could happen just as he said. Damn it, I had the equivalent of an Aunt Betsy myself. I loved her dearly.

MAYHEW. He's got a good personality, I think. Sympathetic.

SIR WILFRID. (*Taking a matchbox from his pocket and handing it to* MAYHEW) Yes, he ought to go down well with the jury. That cuts no ice with the Judge, though. And he's the simple sort of chap who may get rattled easily in the box.

(MAYHEW *finds that the box is empty and throws it in the waste-paper basket.*)

A lot depends on this girl.

(*There is a knock at the door.*)

(*He calls.*) Come in.

(GRETA *enters. She is excited and a little scared. She closes the door.*)

Yes, Greta, what is it?

GRETA. (*In a whisper*) Mrs Leonard Vole is here.

MAYHEW. Mrs Vole.

SIR WILFRID. Come here. You saw that young man? He's been arrested for murder.

GRETA. (*Crossing to Left of* SIR WILFRID) I know. Isn't it exciting?

SIR WILFRID. Do you think he did it?

GRETA. Oh no, sir, I'm sure he didn't.

SIR WILFRID. Oh, why not?

GRETA. He's far too nice.

SIR WILFRID. (*To* MAYHEW) That makes three of us. (*To* GRETA) Bring Mrs Vole in.

(GRETA *crosses and exits.*)

And we're probably three credulous fools – (*He crosses to the chair Left of the desk*) taken in by a young man with a pleasing personality. (*He sets the chair in readiness for* ROMAINE.)

CARTER. (*Enters and stands to one side. Announcing*) Mrs Vole.

(ROMAINE *enters. She is a foreign woman of great personality, but very quiet. Her voice has a strangely ironic inflection.*)

MAYHEW. (*Crossing to Right of* ROMAINE) My dear Mrs Vole. (*He goes towards her with a great air of sympathy, but is slightly rebuffed by her personality.*)

(CARTER *exits, closing the door behind him.*)

ROMAINE. Ah! You are Mr Mayhew.

MAYHEW. Yes. This is Sir Wilfrid Robarts, who has agreed to handle your husband's case for him.

ROMAINE. (*Crossing to Centre*) How do you do, Sir Wilfrid?

SIR WILFRID. How do you do?

ROMAINE. I have just come from your office, Mr Mayhew. They told me you were here with my husband.

SIR WILFRID. Quite, quite.

ROMAINE. Just as I arrived I thought I saw Leonard getting into a car. There were two men with him.

SIR WILFRID. Now, my dear Mrs Vole, you must not upset yourself.

(ROMAINE *is not in the least upset.*)

(*He is slightly disconcerted.*) Won't you sit down, here?

ROMAINE. Thank you. (*She sits in the chair Left of the desk.*)

SIR WILFRID. (*Moving above the desk to Right of it*) There is nothing to be alarmed about as yet, and you must not give way. (*He moves below the desk.*)

ROMAINE. (*After a pause.*) Oh, no, I shall not give way.

SIR WILFRID. Then let me tell you that, as perhaps you already suspect, your husband has just been arrested.

ROMAINE. For the murder of Miss Emily French?

SIR WILFRID. I'm afraid so, yes. But please don't be upset.

ROMAINE. You keep saying that, Sir Wilfrid, but I am not upset.

SIR WILFRID. No. No, I see you have great fortitude.

ROMAINE. You can call it that if you like.

SIR WILFRID. The great thing is to be calm and to tackle all this sensibly.

ROMAINE. That suits me very well. But you must not hide anything from me, Sir Wilfrid. You must not try and spare me. I want to know everything. (*With a slightly different inflection*) I want to know – the worst.

SIR WILFRID. Splendid. Splendid. That's the right way to tackle things. (*He moves to Right of the desk.*) Now, dear lady, we're not going to give way to alarm or despondency, we're going to look at things in a sensible and straightforward manner. (*He sits Right of the desk.*) Your husband became friendly with Miss French about six weeks ago. You were – er – aware of that friendship?

ROMAINE. He told me that he had rescued an old lady and her parcels one day in the middle of a crowded street. He told me that she had asked him to go and see her.

SIR WILFRID. All very natural, I think. And your husband did go and see her.

ROMAINE. Yes.

SIR WILFRID. And they became great friends.

ROMAINE. Evidently.

SIR WILFRID. There was no question of your accompanying your husband on any occasion?

ROMAINE. Leonard thought it better not.

SIR WILFRID. (*Shooting a keen glance at her*) He thought it better not. Yes. Just between ourselves, why did he think it better not?

ROMAINE. He thought Miss French would prefer it that way.

SIR WILFRID. (*A little nervously and sliding off the subject*) Yes, yes, quite. Well, we can go into that some other time. Your husband, then, became friends with Miss French, he did her various little services, she was a lonely old woman with time on her hands and she found your husband's companionship congenial to her.

ROMAINE. Leonard can be very charming.

SIR WILFRID. Yes, I'm sure he can. He felt, no doubt, it was a kindly action on his part to go and cheer up the old lady.

ROMAINE. I daresay.

SIR WILFRID. You yourself did not object at all to your husband's friendship with this old lady?

ROMAINE. I do not think I objected, no.

SIR WILFRID. You have, of course, perfect trust in your husband, Mrs Vole. Knowing him as well as you do . . .

ROMAINE. Yes, I know Leonard very well.

SIR WILFRID. I can't tell you how much I admire your calm and your courage, Mrs Vole. Knowing as I do how devoted you are to him . . .

ROMAINE. So you know how devoted I am to him?

SIR WILFRID. Of course.

ROMAINE. But excuse me, I am a foreigner. I do not always know your English terms. But is there not a saying about knowing something of your own knowledge? You do not know that I am devoted to Leonard, of your own knowledge, do you, Sir Wilfrid? (*She smiles.*)

SIR WILFRID. (*Slightly disconcerted*) No, no, that is of course true. But your husband told me.

ROMAINE. Leonard told you how devoted I was to him?

SIR WILFRID. Indeed, he spoke of your devotion in the most moving terms.

ROMAINE. Men, I often think, are very stupid.

SIR WILFRID. I beg your pardon?

ROMAINE. It does not matter. Please go on.

SIR WILFRID. (*Rising and crossing above the desk to Centre*) This Miss French was a woman of some considerable wealth. She had no near relations. Like many eccentric elderly ladies she was fond of making wills. She had made several wills in her lifetime. Shortly after meeting your husband she made a fresh will. After some small bequests she left the whole of her fortune to your husband.

ROMAINE. Yes.

SIR WILFRID. You know that?

ROMAINE. I read it in the paper this evening.

SIR WILFRID. Quite, quite. Before reading it in the paper, you had no idea of the fact? Your husband had no idea of it?

ROMAINE. (*After a pause*) Is that what he told you?

SIR WILFRID. Yes. You don't suggest anything different?

ROMAINE. No, Oh, no. I do not suggest anything.

SIR WILFRID. (*Crossing above the desk to Right of it and sitting*) There seems to be no doubt that Miss French looked upon your husband rather in the light of a son, or perhaps a very favourite nephew.

ROMAINE. (*With distinct irony*) You think Miss French looked upon Leonard as a son?

SIR WILFRID. (*Flustered*) Yes, I think so. Definitely I think so. I think that could be regarded as quite natural, quite normal under the circumstances.

ROMAINE. What hypocrites you are in this country.

(MAYHEW *sits on the chair Left of the fireplace.*)

SIR WILFRID. My dear Mrs Vole!

ROMAINE. I shock you? I am so sorry.

SIR WILFRID. Of course, of course. You have a continental way of looking at these things. But I assure you, dear Mrs Vole, that is *not* the line to take. It would be most unwise to suggest in any way that Miss French had – er – any – er – feelings for Leonard Vole other than those of a – of a mother or – shall we say – an aunt.

ROMAINE. Oh, by all means let us say an aunt, if you think it best.

SIR WILFRID. One has to think of the effect on the jury of all these things, Mrs Vole.

ROMAINE. Yes. I also wish to do that. I have been thinking of that a good deal.

SIR WILFRID. Quite so. We must work together. Now we come to the evening of October fourteenth. That is just over a week ago. You remember that evening?

ROMAINE. I remember it very well.

SIR WILFRID. Leonard Vole called on Miss French that evening. The housekeeper, Janet MacKenzie, was out. Mr Vole played a game of Double Demon with Miss French and finally took leave of her about nine o'clock. He returned home on foot, he tells me, arriving at approximately twenty-five minutes past nine. (*He looks interrogatively at her.*)

(ROMAINE *rises and moves to the fireplace.* SIR WILFRID *and* MAYHEW *rise.*)

ROMAINE. (*Without expression; thoughtfully*) Twenty-five past nine.

SIR WILFRID. At half past nine the housekeeper returned to the house to get something she had forgotten. Passing the sitting-room door she heard Miss French's voice in conversation with a man. She assumed that the man with Miss French was Leonard Vole, and Inspector Hearne says that it is this statement of hers which has led to your husband's arrest. Mr Vole, however, tells me that he has an absolute alibi for that time, since he was at home with you at nine-thirty.

(*There is a pause.* ROMAINE *does not speak, although* SIR WILFRID *looks at her.*)

That is so, is it not? He was with you at nine-thirty?

(SIR WILFRID *and* MAYHEW *look at* ROMAINE.)

ROMAINE. That is what Leonard says? That he was home with me at nine-thirty?

SIR WILFRID. (*Sharply*) Isn't it true?

(*There is a long silence.*)

ROMAINE. (*Moving to the chair Left of the desk; presently*) But of course. (*She sits.*)

SIR WILFRID. (*Sighs with relief and resumes his seat Right of the desk*) Possibly the police have already questioned you on that point?

ROMAINE. Oh yes, they came to see me yesterday evening.

SIR WILFRID. And you said . . .?

ROMAINE. (*As though repeating something that she has learned by rote*) I said Leonard came in at nine-twenty-five that night and did not go out again.

MAYHEW. (*A little uneasily*) You said . . .? Oh! (*He sits on the chair Left of the fireplace.*)

ROMAINE. That was right, was it not?

SIR WILFRID. What do you mean by that, Mrs Vole?

ROMAINE. (*Sweetly*) That is what Leonard wants me to say, is it not?

SIR WILFRID. It's the truth. You said so just now.

ROMAINE. I have to understand – to be sure. If I say yes, it is so, Leonard was with me in the flat at nine-thirty – will they acquit him?

(SIR WILFRID *and* MAYHEW *are puzzled by* ROMAINE*'s manner.*)

Will they let him go?

MAYHEW. (*Rising and crossing to Left of her*) If you are both speaking the truth then they will – er – have to acquit him.

ROMAINE. But when I said – that – to the police, I do not think they believed me. (*She is not distressed; instead she seems faintly satisfied.*)

SIR WILFRID. What makes you think they did not believe you?

ROMAINE. (*With sudden malice*) Perhaps I did not say it very well?

(SIR WILFRID *and* MAYHEW *exchange glances.* MAYHEW *resumes his seat.* ROMAINE*'s cool, impudent glance meets* SIR WILFRID*'s. There is a definite antagonism between them.*)

SIR WILFRID. (*Changing his manner*) You know, Mrs Vole, I don't quite understand your attitude in all this.

ROMAINE. So you don't understand? Well, perhaps it is difficult.

SIR WILFRID. Perhaps your husband's position is not quite clear to you?

ROMAINE. I have already said that I want to understand fully just how black the case against – my husband is. I say to the police, Leonard was at home with me at nine-thirty – and they do not believe me. But perhaps there is someone who saw him leave Miss French's house, or who saw him in the street on his way home? (*She looks sharply and rather slyly from one to the other.*)

(SIR WILFRID *looks enquiringly at* MAYHEW.)

MAYHEW. (*Rising and moving Centre; reluctantly*) Your husband cannot think of, or remember, anything helpful of that kind.

ROMAINE. So it will be only his word – and mine. (*With intensity*) And mine. (*She rises abruptly.*) Thank you, that is what I wanted to know. (*She crosses to Left.*)

MAYHEW. But, Mrs Vole, please don't go. There is a lot more to be discussed.

ROMAINE. Not by me.

SIR WILFRID. Why not, Mrs Vole?

ROMAINE. I shall have to swear, shall I not, to speak the truth and all the truth and nothing but the truth? (*She seems amused.*)

SIR WILFRID. That is the oath you take.

ROMAINE. (*Crossing and standing above the chair Left of the desk; now openly mocking*) And suppose that then, when you ask me – (*She imitates a man's voice*) 'When did Leonard Vole come that night?' I should say . . .

SIR WILFRID. Well?

ROMAINE. There are so many things I could say.

SIR WILFRID. Mrs Vole, do you love your husband?

ROMAINE. (*Shifting her mocking glance to* MAYHEW) Leonard says I do.

MAYHEW. Leonard Vole believes so.

ROMAINE. But Leonard is not very clever.

SIR WILFRID. You are aware, Mrs Vole, that you cannot by law be called to give testimony damaging to your husband?

ROMAINE. How very convenient.

SIR WILFRID. And your husband can . . .

ROMAINE. (*Interrupting*) He is not my husband.

SIR WILFRID. What?

ROMAINE. Leonard Vole is not my husband. He went through a form of marriage with me in Berlin. He got me out of the

Russian zone and brought me to this country. I did not tell him, but I had a husband living at the time.

SIR WILFRID. He got you out of the Russian sector and safely to this country? You should be very grateful to him. (*Sharply*) Are you?

ROMAINE. One can get tired of gratitude.

SIR WILFRID. Has Leonard Vole ever injured you in any way?

ROMAINE. (*Scornfully*) Leonard? Injured me? He worships the ground I walk on.

SIR WILFRID. And you?

(*Again there is a duel of eyes between them, then she laughs and turns away.*)

ROMAINE. You want to know too much. (*She crosses to the door.*)

MAYHEW. I think we must be quite clear about this. Your statements have been somewhat ambiguous. What exactly happened on the evening of October fourteenth?

ROMAINE. (*In a monotonous voice*) Leonard came in at twenty-five minutes past nine and did not go out again. I have given him an alibi, have I not?

SIR WILFRID. (*Rising*) You have. (*He crosses to her.*) Mrs Vole . . . (*He catches her eye and pauses.*)

ROMAINE. Yes?

SIR WILFRID. You're a very remarkable woman, Mrs Vole.

ROMAINE. And you are satisfied, I hope? (ROMAINE *exits.*)

SIR WILFRID. I'm damned if I'm satisfied.

MAYHEW. Nor I.

SIR WILFRID. She's up to something, that woman – but what? I don't like it, John.

MAYHEW. She certainly hasn't had hysterics all over the place.

SIR WILFRID. Cool as a cucumber.

MAYHEW. (*Sitting on the chair Left of the desk*) What's going to happen if we put her into the witness box?

SIR WILFRID. (*Crossing to Centre*) God knows!

MAYHEW. The prosecution would break her down in no time, especially if it were Myers.

SIR WILFRID. If it's not the Attorney-General, it probably will be.

MAYHEW. Then what's your line of attack?

SIR WILFRID. The usual. Keep interrupting – as many objections as possible.

MAYHEW. What beats me is that young Vole is convinced of her devotion.

SIR WILFRID. Don't put your trust in that. Any woman can fool a man if she wants to and if he's in love with her.

MAYHEW. He's in love with her all right. And trusts her completely.

SIR WILFRID. More fool he. Never trust a woman.

CURTAIN

ACT TWO

SCENE: *The Central Criminal Court, London – better known as the Old Bailey. Six weeks later. Morning.*

The section of the Court Room seen has a tall rostrum, the bench, running from down Right to up Centre. On it are the armchairs and desks for the Judge, his Clerk and the Alderman. Access to the bench is by a door in the up Right corner and by steps up Right from the floor of the Court. On the wall over the Judge's chair are the Royal Arms and the Sword of Justice. Below the bench are small desks and chairs for the Clerk of the Court and the Court Stenographer. There is a small stool Right of the desks for the Usher. The witness box is immediately below the up Centre end of the bench. Up Centre is a door leading to the Barristers' robing room and up Left Centre are glass-panelled double doors leading to a corridor and other parts of the building. Up Left Centre, between the doors, are two pews for the Barristers. Below the pews is a table with three chairs and a stool. The dock is Left and is entered by a door in the Left wall and a gate in the up-stage rail. There are chairs in the dock for Leonard and the Warder. The jury box is down Right, only the back of the three end seats being visible to the audience.

When Curtain rises, the Court has opened. The Judge, MR JUSTICE WAIN-WRIGHT, is seated Right and the ALDERMAN is seated Left of the Judge. The CLERK OF THE COURT and the STENOGRAPHER are in their seats below the bench. MR MYERS, QC, for the Prosecution, is seated Right of the front row of Barristers with his ASSISTANT Left of him. SIR WILFRID, for the Defence, is seated Left of the front row of Barristers with his ASSISTANT Right of him. Four BARRISTERS, one a woman, are seated in the back row of the Barristers' seats. LEO-NARD is standing in the dock with the WARDER beside him. DR WYATT is seated on the stool Right of the table. The INSPECTOR is seated on the chair above the Right end of the table. MAYHEW is seated

Left of the table. A POLICEMAN *stands at the double doors. Three* MEMBERS *of the* JURY *are seen, the first a man, the* FOREMAN, *the second a* WOMAN *and the third a* MAN. *The* USHER *is administering the oath to the* WOMAN JUROR, *who is standing.*

WOMAN JUROR. (*Holding the Bible and oath card*) . . . lady the Queen and the prisoner at the Bar whom I shall have in charge, and a true verdict give according to the evidence. (*She hands the Bible and oath card to the* USHER, *then sits.*)

(*The* USHER *gives the Bible and oath card to the* FOREMAN.)

FOREMAN. (*Rising*) I swear by Almighty God that I will well and truly try and true deliverance make between our sovereign lady the Queen and the prisoner at the Bar whom I shall have in charge, and a true verdict give according to the evidence. (*He hands the Bible and oath card to the* USHER, *then sits.*)

(*The* USHER *puts the Bible and card on the ledge of the jury box, then sits on his stool down Right.*)

CLERK. (*Rising*) Leonard Vole, you are charged on indictment for that you on the fourteenth day of October in the County of London murdered Emily Jane French. How say you, Leonard Vole, are you guilty or not guilty?

LEONARD. Not guilty.

CLERK. Members of the Jury, the prisoner stands indicted for that he on the fourteenth day of October murdered Emily Jane French. To this indictment he has pleaded not guilty, and it is your charge to say, having heard the evidence, whether he be guilty or not. (*He motions to* LEONARD *to sit, then resumes his own seat.*)

(LEONARD *and the* WARDER *sit.* MYERS *rises.*)

JUDGE. One moment, Mr Myers.

(MYERS *bows to the* JUDGE *and resumes his seat.*)

(*He turns to the jury.*) Members of the Jury, the proper time for me to sum up the evidence to you, and instruct you as to the law, is after you have heard all the evidence. But because there has been a considerable amount of publicity about this case in the Press, I would just like to say this to you now. By the oath which each of you has just taken you swore to try this case on the evidence. That means on the evidence that you are now going to hear and see. It does not mean that you are to consider also anything you have heard or read before taking your oaths. You must shut out from your minds everything except what will take place in this Court. You must not let anything else influence your minds in favour of or against the prisoner. I am quite sure that you will do your duty conscientiously in the way that I have indicated. Yes, Mr Myers.

(MYERS *rises, clears his throat and adjusts his wig in the manner taken off by* SIR WILFRID *in the previous scene.*)

MYERS. May it please you, my lord. Members of the Jury, I appear in this case with my learned friend Mr Barton for the prosecution, and my learned friends Sir Wilfrid Robarts and Mr Brogan-Moore appear for the defence. This is a case of murder. The facts are simple and up to a certain point are not in dispute. You will hear how the prisoner, a young and, you may think, a not unattractive man, made the acquaintance of Miss Emily French, a woman of fifty-six. How he was treated by her with kindness and even with affection. The nature of that affection you will have to decide for yourselves. Dr Wyatt will tell you that in his opinion death occurred at some time between nine-thirty and ten on the night of the fourteenth of October last. You will hear the evidence of Janet MacKenzie, who was Miss French's faithful and devoted housekeeper. The fourteenth of October – it was a Friday – was Janet MacKenzie's night out, but on this occasion she happened to return for a few minutes at nine twenty-five. She let herself in with a key and upon going upstairs to her room she passed the door of the sitting-room. She will tell you that in the sitting-room she heard the voices of Miss French and of the prisoner, Leonard Vole.

LEONARD. (*Rising*) That's not true. It wasn't me.

(*The* WARDER *restrains* LEONARD *and makes him resume his seat.*)

MYERS. Janet MacKenzie was surprised, since as far as she knew,

Miss French had not expected Leonard Vole to call that evening. However, she went out again and when she returned finally at eleven she found Miss Emily French murdered, the room in disorder, a window smashed and the curtains blowing wildly. Horror-stricken, Janet MacKenzie immediately rang up the police. I should tell you that the prisoner was arrested on the twentieth of October. It is the case for the prosecution that Miss Emily Jane French was murdered between nine-thirty and ten P.M. on the evening of the fourteenth of October, by a blow from a cosh, and that the blow was struck by the prisoner. I will now call Inspector Hearne.

(*The* INSPECTOR *rises. He holds a file of papers which he refers to often during the scene. He hands a typewritten sheet to the* CLERK *and another to the* STENOGRAPHER. *He then enters the witness box. The* CLERK *hands the sheet to the* JUDGE. *The* USHER *rises, crosses and stands by the witness box. The* INSPECTOR *picks up the oath card and Bible from the ledge of the box.*)

INSPECTOR. I swear by Almighty God that the evidence that I shall give shall be the truth, the whole truth and nothing but the truth. Robert Hearne, Detective Inspector, Criminal Investigation Department, New Scotland Yard. (*He puts the Bible and oath card on the ledge of the box.*)

(*The* USHER *crosses and sits on his stool.*)

MYERS. Now, Inspector Hearne, on the evening of the fourteenth October last, were you on duty when you received an emergency call?

INSPECTOR. Yes, sir.

MYERS. What did you do?

INSPECTOR. With Sergeant Randell I proceeded to twenty-three Ashburn Grove. I was admitted to the house and established that the occupant, whom I later ascertained was Miss Emily French, was dead. She was lying on her face, and had received severe injuries to the back of her head. An attempt had been made to force one of the windows with some implement which might have been a chisel. The window had been broken near the catch. There was glass strewn about the floor, and I also later found fragments of glass on the ground outside the window.

MYERS. Is there any particular significance in finding glass both inside and outside the window?

INSPECTOR. The glass outside was not consistent with the window having been forced from outside.

MYERS. You mean that if it had been forced from the inside there had been an attempt to make it look as though it had been done from the outside?

SIR WILFRID. (*Rising*) I object. My learned friend is putting words into the witness's mouth. He really must observe the rules of evidence. (*He resumes his seat.*)

MYERS. (*To the* INSPECTOR) You have been engaged on several cases of burglary and housebreaking?

INSPECTOR. Yes, sir.

MYERS. And in your experience when a window is forced from the outside, where is the glass?

INSPECTOR. On the inside.

MYERS. In any other case where the windows have been forced from the outside, have you found glass on the outside of the window some distance below, on the ground?

INSPECTOR. No.

MYERS. No. Will you go on?

INSPECTOR. A search was made, photographs were taken, the place was fingerprinted.

MYERS. What fingerprints did you discover?

INSPECTOR. Those of Miss Emily French herself, those of Janet MacKenzie and some which proved later to be those of the prisoner, Leonard Vole.

MYERS. No others?

INSPECTOR. No others.

MYERS. Did you subsequently have an interview with Mr Leonard Vole?

INSPECTOR. Yes, sir. Janet MacKenzie was not able to give me his address, but as a result of a broadcast and a newspaper appeal, Mr Leonard Vole came and saw me.

MYERS. And on October the twentieth, when arrested, what did the prisoner say?

INSPECTOR. He replied, 'OK I'm ready.'

MYERS. Now, Inspector, you say the room had the appearance of a robbery having been committed?

SIR WILFRID. (*Rising*) That is just what the Inspector did not say. (*To the* JUDGE) If your lordship remembers, that was a suggestion made by my friend – and quite improperly made – to which I objected.

JUDGE. You are quite right, Sir Wilfrid.

(MYERS *sits.*)

At the same time, I'm not sure that the Inspector is not entitled to give evidence of any facts which might tend to prove that the disorder of the room was not the work of a person who broke in from outside for the purpose of robbery.

SIR WILFRID. My lord, may I respectfully agree with what your lordship has said. Facts, yes. But not the mere expression of opinion without even the facts on which it is based. (*He sits.*)

MYERS. (*Rising*) Perhaps, my lord, if I phrased my question in this way my friend would be satisfied. Inspector, could you say from what you saw whether there had or had not been a bona fide breaking in from outside the house?

SIR WILFRID. (*Rising*) My lord, I really must continue my objection. My learned friend is again seeking to obtain an opinion from this witness. (*He sits.*)

JUDGE. Yes. Mr Myers, I think you will have to do a little better than that.

MYERS. Inspector, did you find anything inconsistent with a breaking in from outside?

INSPECTOR. Only the glass, sir.

MYERS. Nothing else?

INSPECTOR. No, sir, there was nothing else.

JUDGE. We all seem to have drawn a blank there, Mr Myers.

MYERS. Was Miss French wearing jewellery of any value?

INSPECTOR. She was wearing a diamond brooch, two diamond rings, value of about nine hundred pounds.

MYERS. And these were left untouched?

INSPECTOR. Yes, sir.

MYERS. Was in fact anything taken?

INSPECTOR. According to Janet MacKenzie, nothing was missing.

MYERS. In your experience, when anyone breaks into a house do they leave without taking anything?

INSPECTOR. Not unless they're interrupted, sir.

MYERS. But in this case it does not seem as if the burglar *was* interrupted.

INSPECTOR. No, sir.

MYERS. Do you produce a jacket, Inspector?

INSPECTOR. Yes, sir.

(*The* USHER *rises, crosses to the table, picks up the jacket and hands it to the* INSPECTOR.)

MYERS. Is that it?

INSPECTOR. Yes, sir. (*He returns the jacket to the* USHER.)

(*The* USHER *replaces the jacket on the table.*)

MYERS. From where did you get it?

INSPECTOR. I found it at the prisoner's flat some time after he was arrested, and later handed it to Mr Clegg at the lab to test for possible bloodstains.

MYERS. Lastly, Inspector, do you produce the will of Miss French?

(*The* USHER *picks up the will from the table and hands it to the* INSPECTOR.)

INSPECTOR. I do, sir.

MYERS. Dated October the eighth?

INSPECTOR. Yes, sir. (*He returns the will to the* USHER.)

(*The* USHER *replaces the will on the table, crosses and resumes his seat.*)

MYERS. After certain bequests, the residue is left to the prisoner?

INSPECTOR. That's right, sir.

MYERS. And what is the net value of that estate?

INSPECTOR. It will be, as far as can be ascertained at the moment, about eighty-five thousand pounds.

(MYERS *resumes his seat.* SIR WILFRID *rises.*)

SIR WILFRID. You say that the only fingerprints you found in the room were those of Miss French herself, the prisoner Leonard Vole and Janet MacKenzie. In your experience, when a burglar breaks in does he usually leave fingerprints or does he wear gloves?

INSPECTOR. He wears gloves.

SIR WILFRID. Invariably?

INSPECTOR. Almost invariably.

SIR WILFRID. So the absence of fingerprints in a case of robbery would hardly surprise you?

INSPECTOR. No, sir.

SIR WILFRID. Now, these chisel marks on the window. Were they on the inside or the outside of the casement?

INSPECTOR. On the outside, sir.

SIR WILFRID. Isn't that consistent – and only consistent – with a breaking in from the outside?

INSPECTOR. He could have gone out of the house afterwards to have done that, sir, or he could have made those marks from the inside.

SIR WILFRID. From the inside, Inspector? Now how could he have possibly done that?

INSPECTOR. There are two windows together there. Both are casements, and with their catches adjacent. It would have been easy for anyone in the room to open one window, lean out, and force the catch of the other.

SIR WILFRID. Tell me, did you find any chisel near the premises, or at the prisoner's flat?

INSPECTOR. Yes, sir. At the prisoner's flat.

SIR WILFRID. Oh?

INSPECTOR. But it didn't fit the marks on the window.

SIR WILFRID. It was a windy night, was it not, on October fourteenth?

INSPECTOR. I really can't remember, sir. (*He refers to his notes.*)

SIR WILFRID. According to my learned friend, Janet MacKenzie said that the curtains were blowing. Perhaps you noticed that fact yourself?

INSPECTOR. Well, yes, sir, they did blow about.

SIR WILFRID. Indicating that it was a windy night. I suggest that if a burglar had forced the window from the outside and then swung it back, some of the loose glass might easily have fallen down *outside* the window, the window having been blown back violently by the wind. That is possible, is it not?

INSPECTOR. Yes, sir.

SIR WILFRID. Crimes of violence, as we all have been unhappily aware, have been much on the increase lately. You would agree to that, would you not?

INSPECTOR. It's been a little above normal, sir.

SIR WILFRID. Let us take the case that some young thugs had broken in, who meant to attack Miss French and steal; it is possible that if one of them coshed her and found that she was dead, they might give way to panic and leave without taking anything? Or they might even have been looking for money and would be afraid to touch anything in the nature of jewellery?

MYERS. (*Rising*) I submit that it is impossible for Inspector Hearne to guess at what went on in the minds of some *entirely* hypothetical young criminals who may not even exist. (*He sits.*)

SIR WILFRID. The prisoner came forward of his own accord and gave his statement quite willingly?

INSPECTOR. That is so.

SIR WILFRID. Is it the case that at all times the prisoner has protested his innocence?

INSPECTOR. Yes, sir.

SIR WILFRID. (*Indicating the knife on the table*) Inspector Hearne, will you kindly examine that knife?

(*The* USHER *rises, crosses, picks up the knife and hands it to the* INSPECTOR.)

You have seen that knife before?

INSPECTOR. I may have.

SIR WILFRID. This is the knife taken from the kitchen table in Leonard Vole's flat and which was brought to your attention by the prisoner's wife on the occasion of your first interview with her.

MYERS. (*Rising*) My lord, to save the time of the Court, may I say that we accept this knife as being a knife in the possession of Leonard Vole and shown to the Inspector by Mrs Vole. (*He sits.*)

SIR WILFRID. That is correct, Inspector?

INSPECTOR. Yes, sir.

SIR WILFRID. It is what is known, I believe, as a French vegetable knife?

INSPECTOR. I believe so, sir.

SIR WILFRID. Just test the edge of the knife with your finger – carefully.

(*The* INSPECTOR *tests the knife edge.*)

You agree that the cutting edge and the point are razor sharp?

INSPECTOR. Yes, sir.

SIR WILFRID. And if you were cutting – say, ham – carving it, that is, and your hand slipped with this knife, it would be capable of inflicting a very nasty cut, and one which would bleed profusely?

MYERS. (*Rising*) I object. That is a matter of opinion, and medical opinion at that. (*He sits.*)

(*The* USHER *takes the knife from the* INSPECTOR, *puts it on the table, crosses and resumes his seat.*)

SIR WILFRID. I withdraw the question. I will ask you instead, Inspector, if the prisoner, when questioned by you as to the stains on the sleeve of his jacket, drew your attention to a recently healed scar on his wrist, and stated that it had been caused by a household knife when he was slicing ham?

INSPECTOR. That is what he said.

SIR WILFRID. And you were told the same thing by the prisoner's wife?

INSPECTOR. The first time. Afterwards . . .

SIR WILFRID. (*Sharply*) A simple yes or no, please. Did the prisoner's wife show you this knife, and tell you that her husband had cut his wrist with it slicing ham?

INSPECTOR. Yes, she did.

(SIR WILFRID *resumes his seat.*)

MYERS. (*Rising*) What first drew your attention to that jacket, Inspector?

INSPECTOR. The sleeve appeared to have been recently washed.

MYERS. And you're told this story about an accident with a kitchen knife?

INSPECTOR. Yes, sir.

MYERS. And your attention was drawn to a scar on the prisoner's wrist?

INSPECTOR. Yes, sir.

MYERS. Granted that the scar was made by this particular knife, there was nothing to show whether it was an accident or done deliberately?

SIR WILFRID. (*Rising*) Really, my lord, if my learned friend is going to answer his own questions, the presence of the witness seems to be superfluous. (*He sits.*)

MYERS. (*Resignedly*) I withdraw the question. Thank you, Inspector.

(*The* INSPECTOR *stands down, crosses and exits up Left. The* POLICE-MAN *closes the door behind him.*)

Doctor Wyatt.

(DOCTOR WYATT *rises and enters the box. He carries some notes. The* USHER *rises, crosses, hands the Bible to him and holds up the oath card.*)

WYATT. I swear by Almighty God that the evidence that I shall give shall be the truth, the whole truth and nothing but the truth.

(*The* USHER *puts the Bible and oath card on the ledge of the witness box, crosses and resumes his seat.*)

MYERS. You are Doctor Wyatt?

WYATT. Yes.

MYERS. You are a police surgeon attached to the Hampstead Division?

WYATT. Yes.

MYERS. Doctor Wyatt, will you kindly tell the Jury what you know regarding the death of Miss Emily French?

WYATT. (*Reading from his notes*) At eleven P.M. on October fourteenth, I saw the dead body of the woman who subsequently proved to be Miss French. By examination of the body I was of the opinion that the death had resulted from a blow on the head, delivered from an object such as a cosh. Death would have been practically instantaneous. From the temperature of the body and other factors, I placed the time of death at not less than an hour previously and not more than, say, an hour and a half. That is to say between the hours of nine-thirty and ten P.M.

MYERS. Had Miss French struggled with her adversary at all?

WYATT. There was no evidence that she had done so. I should say, on the contrary, that she had been taken quite unprepared.

(MYERS *resumes his seat.*)

SIR WILFRID. (*Rising*) Doctor, where exactly on the head had this blow been struck? There was only one blow, was there not?

WYATT. Only one. On the left side at the asterion.

SIR WILFRID. I beg your pardon? Where?

WYATT. The asterion. The junction of the parietal, occipital and temple bones.

SIR WILFRID. Oh, yes. And in layman's language, where is that?

WYATT. Behind the left ear.

SIR WILFRID. Would that indicate that the blow had been struck by a left-handed person?

WYATT. It's difficult to say. The blow appeared to have been struck directly from behind, because the bruising ran perpendicularly. I should say it is really impossible to say whether it was delivered by a right- or left-handed man.

SIR WILFRID. We don't know yet that it was a *man*, Doctor. But will you agree, from the position of the blow, that if anything it is more likely to have been delivered by a left-handed person?

WYATT. That is possibly so. But I would prefer to say that it is uncertain.

SIR WILFRID. At the moment the blow was struck, would blood have been likely to have got on to the hand or arm that struck the blow?

WYATT. Yes, certainly.

SIR WILFRID. And only on that hand or arm?

WYATT. Probably only on that hand and arm, but it's difficult to be dogmatic.

SIR WILFRID. Quite so, Doctor Wyatt. Now, would great strength have been needed to strike such a blow.

WYATT. No. From the position of the wound no great strength would have been needed.

SIR WILFRID. It would not necessarily be a man who had struck the blow. A woman could have done so equally well?

WYATT. Certainly.

SIR WILFRID. Thank you. (*He sits.*)

MYERS. (*Rising*) Thank you, Doctor. (*To the* USHER) Call Janet MacKenzie.

(WYATT *stands down, crosses and exits up Left. The* POLICEMAN *opens the door. The* USHER *rises and crosses to Centre.*)

USHER. Janet MacKenzie.

POLICEMAN. (*Calling*) Janet MacKenzie.

(JANET MACKENZIE *enters up Left. She is a tall, dour-looking Scotswoman. Her face is set in a grim line. Whenever she looks at* LEONARD, *she does so with loathing. The* POLICEMAN *closes the door.* JANET *crosses and enters the witness box. The* USHER *moves and stands beside the witness box.* JANET *picks up the Bible in her left hand.*)

USHER. Other hand, please. (*He holds out the oath card.*)

JANET. (*Puts the Bible into her right hand*) I swear by Almighty God that the evidence that I shall give shall be the truth, the whole truth and nothing but the truth. (*She hands the Bible to the* USHER.)

(*The* USHER *puts the Bible and oath card on the ledge of the witness box, crosses and resumes his seat.*)

MYERS. Your name is Janet MacKenzie?

JANET. Aye – that's my name.

MYERS. You were companion housekeeper to the late Miss Emily French?

JANET. I was her housekeeper. I've no opinion of companions, poor feckless bodies, afraid to do a bit of honest domestic work.

MYERS. Quite so, quite so, I meant only that you were held in esteem and affection by Miss French, and were on friendly terms together. Not quite those of mistress and servant.

JANET. (*To the* JUDGE) Twenty years I've been with her and looked after her. She knew me and she trusted me, and many's the time I've prevented her doing a foolish action!

JUDGE. Miss MacKenzie, would you please address your remarks to the Jury.

MYERS. What sort of a person was Miss French?

JANET. She was a warm-hearted body – too warm-hearted at times, I'm thinking. A wee bit impulsive too. There were times when she'd have no sense at all. She was easily flattered, you see.

MYERS. When did you first see the prisoner, Leonard Vole?

JANET. He came to the house, I mind, at the end of August.

MYERS. How often did he come to the house?

JANET. To begin with once a week, but later it was oftener. Two and even three times he'd come. He'd sit there flattering her, telling her how young she looked and noticing any new clothes she was wearing.

MYERS. (*Rather hastily*) Quite, quite. Now will you tell the Jury in your own words, Miss MacKenzie, about the events of October the fourteenth.

JANET. It was a Friday and my night out. I was going round to see some friends of mine in Glenister Road, which is not above three minutes' walk. I left the house at half past seven. I'd promised to take my friend the pattern of a knitted cardigan that she'd admired. When I got there I found I'd left it behind, so after supper I said I'd slip back to the house at twenty-five past nine. I let myself in with my key and went upstairs to my room. As I passed the sitting-room door I heard the prisoner in there talking to Miss French.

MYERS. You were sure it was the prisoner you heard?

JANET. Aye, I know his voice well enough. With him calling so often. An agreeable voice it was, I'll not say it wasn't. Talking and laughing they were. But it was no business of mine so I went up and fetched the pattern, came down and let myself out and went back to my friend.

MYERS. Now I want these times very exact. You say that you re-entered the house at twenty-five past nine.

JANET. Aye. It was just after twenty past nine when I left Glenister Road.

MYERS. How do you know that, Miss MacKenzie?

JANET. By the clock on my friend's mantelpiece, and I compared it with my watch and the time was the same.

MYERS. You say it takes three or four minutes to walk to the house, so that you entered the house at twenty-five minutes past nine, and you were there . . .

JANET. I was there under ten minutes. It took me a few minutes to search for the pattern as I wasna' sure where I'd left it.

MYERS. And what did you do next?

JANET. I went back to my friend in Glenister Road. She was delighted with the pattern, simply delighted. I stayed there until twenty to eleven, then I said good night to them and came home. I went into the sitting-room then to see if the mistress wanted anything before she went to bed.

MYERS. What did you see?

JANET. She was there on the floor, poor body, her head beaten in. And all the drawers of the bureau out on the ground, everything tossed hither and thither, the broken vase on the floor and the curtains flying in the wind.

MYERS. What did you do?

JANET. I rang the police.

MYERS. Did you really think that a burglary had occurred?

SIR WILFRID. (*Jumping up*) Really, my lord, I must protest. (*He sits.*)

JUDGE. I will not allow that question to be answered, Mr Myers. It should not have been put to the witness.

MYERS. Then let me ask you this, Miss MacKenzie. What did you do after you had telephoned the police?

JANET. I searched the house.

MYERS. What for?

JANET. For an intruder.

MYERS. Did you find one?

JANET. I did not. Nor any signs of disturbance save in the sitting-room.

MYERS. How much did you know about the prisoner, Leonard Vole?

JANET. I knew that he needed money.

MYERS. Did he ask Miss French for money?

JANET. He was too clever for that.

MYERS. Did he help Miss French with her business affairs – with her income tax returns, for instance?

JANET. Aye – not that there was any need of it.

MYERS. What do you mean by not any need of it?

JANET. Miss French had a good, clear head for business.

MYERS. Were you aware of what arrangements Miss French had made for the disposal of her money in the event of her death?

JANET. She'd make a will as the fancy took her. She was a rich woman and she had a lot of money to leave and no near relatives. 'It must go where it can do the most good,' she would say. Once it was to orphans she left it, and once to an old people's home, and another time a dispensary for cats and dogs, but it always came to the same in the end. She'd quarrel with the people and then she'd come home and tear up the will and make a new one.

MYERS. Do you know when she made her last will?

JANET. She made it on October the eighth. I heard her speaking to
Mr Stokes, the lawyer. Saying he was to come tomorrow, she
was making a new will. He was there at the time – the prisoner,
I mean, kind of protesting, saying, 'No, no.'

(LEONARD *hastily scribbles a note*.)

And the mistress said, 'But I want to, my dear boy. I want to.
Remember that day I was nearly run over by a bus. It might
happen any time.'

(LEONARD *leans over the dock and hands the note to* MAYHEW, *who passes
it to* SIR WILFRID.)

MYERS. Do you know when your mistress made a will previous to
that one?

JANET. In the spring it was.

MYERS. Were you aware, Miss MacKenzie, that Leonard Vole was
a married man?

JANET. No, indeed. Neither was the mistress.

SIR WILFRID. (*Rising*) I object. What Miss French knew or did not
know is pure conjecture on Janet MacKenzie's part. (*He sits.*)

MYERS. Let us put it this way: You formed the opinion that Miss
French thought Leonard Vole a single man? Have you any
facts to support that opinion?

JANET. There was the books she ordered from the library. There
was the *Life of Baroness Burdett Coutts* and one about Disraeli and
his wife. Both of them about women who'd married men years
younger than themselves. I knew what she was thinking.

JUDGE. I'm afraid we cannot admit that.

JANET. Why?

JUDGE. Members of the Jury, it is possible for a woman to read the
life of Disraeli without contemplating marriage with a man
younger than herself.

MYERS. Did Mr Vole ever mention a wife?

JANET. Never.

MYERS. Thank you. (*He sits.*)

SIR WILFRID. (*Rises. Gently and kindly*) I think we all appreciate how
very devoted to your mistress you were.

JANET. Aye – I was.

SIR WILFRID. You had great influence over her?

JANET. Aye – maybe.

SIR WILFRID. In the last will Miss French made – that is to say, the one made last spring – Miss French left almost the whole of her fortune to you. Were you aware of that fact?

JANET. She told me so. 'All crooks, these charities,' she said. 'Expenses here and expenses there and the money not going to the object you give it for. I've left it to you, Janet, and you can do what you think's right and good with it.'

SIR WILFRID. That was an expression of great trust on her part. In her present will, I understand, she has merely left you an annuity. The principal beneficiary is the prisoner, Leonard Vole.

JANET. It will be wicked injustice if he ever touches a penny of that money.

SIR WILFRID. Miss French, you say, had not many friends and acquaintances. Now why was that?

JANET. She didn't go out much.

SIR WILFRID. When Miss French struck up this friendship with Leonard Vole it made you very sore and angry, didn't it?

JANET. I didn't like seeing my dear lady imposed upon.

SIR WILFRID. But you have admitted that Mr Vole did not impose upon her. Perhaps you mean that you didn't like to see someone else supplanting you as an influence on Miss French?

JANET. She leaned on him a good deal. Far more than was safe, I thought.

SIR WILFRID. Far more than you personally liked?

JANET. Of course. I've said so. But it was of her good I was thinking.

SIR WILFRID. So the prisoner had a great influence over Miss French, and she had a great affection for him?

JANET. That was what it had come to.

SIR WILFRID. So that if the prisoner had ever asked her for money, she would almost certainly have given him some, would she not?

JANET. I have not said that.

SIR WILFRID. But he never received any money from her?

JANET. That may not have been for want of trying.

SIR WILFRID. Returning to the night of October the fourteenth, you say you heard the prisoner and Miss French talking together. What did you hear him say?

JANET. I didn't hear what they actually said.

SIR WILFRID. You mean you only heard the voices – the murmur of voices?

JANET. They were laughing.

SIR WILFRID. You heard a man's voice and a woman's and they were laughing. Is that right?

JANET. Aye.

SIR WILFRID. I suggest that is exactly what you did hear. A man's voice and a woman's voice laughing. You didn't hear what was said. What makes you say that the man's voice was Leonard Vole's?

JANET. I know his voice well enough.

SIR WILFRID. The door was closed, was it not?

JANET. Aye. It was closed.

SIR WILFRID. You heard a murmur of voices through a closed door and you swear that one of the voices was that of Leonard Vole. I suggest that is mere prejudice on your part.

JANET. It was Leonard Vole.

SIR WILFRID. As I understand it you passed the door twice, once going to your room, and once going out?

JANET. That is so.

SIR WILFRID. You were no doubt in a hurry to get your pattern and return to your friend?

JANET. I was in no particular hurry. I had the whole evening.

SIR WILFRID. What I am suggesting is that on both occasions you walked quickly past that door.

JANET. I was there long enough to hear what I heard.

SIR WILFRID. Come, Miss MacKenzie, I'm sure you don't wish to suggest to the Jury that you were eavesdropping.

JANET. I was doing no such thing. I've better things to do with my time.

SIR WILFRID. Exactly. You are registered, of course, under the National Health Insurance?

JANET. That's so. Four and sixpence I have to pay out every week. It's a terrible lot of money for a working woman to pay.

SIR WILFRID. Yes, yes, many people feel that. I think, Miss MacKenzie, that you recently applied for a national hearing apparatus?

JANET. Six months ago I applied for it and not got it yet.

SIR WILFRID. So your hearing isn't very good, is that right? (*He lowers his voice.*) When I say to you, Miss MacKenzie, that you could not possibly recognize a voice through a closed door, what do you answer? (*He pauses.*) Can you tell me what I said?

JANET. I can no' hear anyone if they mumble.

SIR WILFRID. In fact you didn't hear what I said, although I am only a few feet from you in an open court. Yet you say that behind a closed door with two people talking in an ordinary conversational tone, you definitely recognized the voice of Leonard Vole as you swept past that door on two occasions.

JANET. It was him, I tell you. It was him.

SIR WILFRID. What you mean is you want it to be him. You have a preconceived notion.

JANET. Who else could it have been?

SIR WILFRID. Exactly. Who else could it have been? That was the way your mind worked. Now tell me, Miss MacKenzie, was Miss French sometimes lonely all by herself in the evening?

JANET. No, she was not lonely. She had books from the library.

SIR WILFRID. She listened to the wireless, perhaps?

JANET. Aye, she listened to the wireless.

SIR WILFRID. She was fond of a talk on it, perhaps, or of a good play?

JANET. Yes, she liked a good play.

SIR WILFRID. Wasn't it possible that on that evening when you returned home and passed the door, that what you really heard was the wireless switched on and a man and woman's voice, and laughter? There was a play called *Lover's Leap* on the wireless that night.

JANET. It was not the wireless.

SIR WILFRID. Oh, why not?

JANET. The wireless was away being repaired that week.

SIR WILFRID. (*Slightly taken aback*) It must have upset you very much, Miss MacKenzie, if you really thought Miss French intended to marry the prisoner.

JANET. Naturally it would upset me. It was a *daft* thing to do.

SIR WILFRID. For one thing, if Miss French had married the prisoner it's quite possible, isn't it, that he might have persuaded her to dismiss you.

JANET. She'd never have done that, after all these years.

SIR WILFRID. But you never know what anyone will do, do you? Not if they're strongly influenced by anyone.

JANET. He would have used his influence, oh yes, he would have done his best to make her get rid of me.

SIR WILFRID. I see. You felt the prisoner was a very real menace to your present way of life at the time.

JANET. He'd have changed everything.

SIR WILFRID. Yes, very upsetting. No wonder you feel so bitterly against the prisoner. (*He sits.*)

MYERS. (*Rising*) My learned friend has been at great pains to extract from you an admission of vindictiveness towards the prisoner . . .

SIR WILFRID. (*Without rising, and audibly for the benefit of the Jury*) A painless extraction – quite painless.

MYERS. (*Ignoring him*) Did you really believe your mistress might have married the prisoner?

JANET. Indeed I did. I've just said so.

MYERS. Yes, indeed you have. In your view had the prisoner such an influence over Miss French that he could have persuaded her to dismiss you?

JANET. I'd like to have seen him try. He'd not have succeeded.

MYERS. Had the prisoner ever shown any dislike of you in any way?

JANET. No, he had his manners.

MYERS. Just one more question. You say you recognized Leonard Vole's voice through that closed door. Will you tell the Jury how you knew it was his?

JANET. You know a person's voice without hearing exactly what they are saying.

MYERS. Thank you, Miss MacKenzie.

JANET. (*To the* JUDGE) Good morning. (*She stands down and crosses to the door up Left.*)

MYERS. Call Thomas Clegg.

(*The* POLICEMAN *opens the door.*)

USHER. (*Rising and crossing to Centre*) Thomas Clegg.

POLICEMAN. (*Calling*) Thomas Clegg.

(JANET *exits.* THOMAS CLEGG *enters up Left. He carries a notebook. The*

POLICEMAN closes the door. *The* USHER *moves to the witness box and picks up the Bible and oath card.* CLEGG *crosses and enters the witness box and takes the Bible from the* USHER.)

CLEGG. (*Saying the oath by heart*) I swear by Almighty God that the evidence that I shall give shall be the truth, the whole truth and nothing but the truth. (*He puts the Bible on the ledge of the witness box.*)

(*The* USHER *puts the oath card on the ledge of the witness box, crosses and resumes his seat.*)

MYERS. You are Thomas Clegg?

CLEGG. Yes, sir.

MYERS. You are an assistant in the forensic laboratory at New Scotland Yard?

CLEGG. I am.

MYERS. (*Indicating the jacket on the table*) Do you recognize that coat?

(*The* USHER *rises, crosses to the table and picks up the jacket.*)

CLEGG. Yes. It was given to me by Inspector Hearne and tested by me for traces of blood.

(*The* USHER *hands the coat up to* CLEGG, *who brushes it aside. The* USHER *replaces the jacket on the table, crosses and resumes his seat.*)

MYERS. Will you tell me your findings?

CLEGG. The coat sleeves had been washed, though not properly pressed afterwards, but by certain tests I am able to state that there are traces of blood on the cuffs.

MYERS. Is this blood of a special group or type?

CLEGG. Yes. (*He refers to his notebook.*) It is of the type O.

MYERS. Were you also given a sample of blood to test?

CLEGG. I was given a sample labelled 'Blood of Miss Emily French'. The blood group was of the same type – O.

(MYERS *resumes his seat.*)

SIR WILFRID. (*Rising*) You say there were traces of blood on both cuffs?

CLEGG. That is right.

SIR WILFRID. I suggest that there were traces of blood on only one cuff – the left one.

CLEGG. (*Looking at his notebook*) Yes. I am sorry, I made a mistake. It was only the left cuff.

SIR WILFRID. And it was only the left sleeve that had been washed?

CLEGG. Yes, that is so.

SIR WILFRID. Are you aware that the prisoner had told the police that he had cut his wrist, and that that blood was on the cuff of this coat?

CLEGG. So I understand.

(SIR WILFRID *takes a certificate from his* ASSISTANT.)

SIR WILFRID. I have here a certificate stating that Leonard Vole is a blood donor at the North London Hospital, and that his blood group is O. That is the same blood group, is it not?

CLEGG. Yes.

SIR WILFRID. So the blood might equally well have come from a cut on the prisoner's wrist?

CLEGG. That is so.

(SIR WILFRID *resumes his seat.*)

MYERS. (*Rising*) Blood group O is a very common one, is it not?

CLEGG. O? Oh, yes. At least forty-two per cent of people are in blood group O.

MYERS. Call Romaine Heilger.

(CLEGG *stands down and crosses to the door up Left.*)

USHER. (*Rising and crossing to Centre*) Romaine Heilger.

POLICEMAN. (*Opens the door. Calling*) Romaine Heilger.

(CLEGG *exits.* ROMAINE *enters up Left. There is a general buzz of conversation in the Court as she crosses to the witness box. The* POLICEMAN *closes the door. The* USHER *moves to the witness box and picks up the Bible and oath card.*)

USHER. Silence! (*He hands the Bible to* ROMAINE *and holds up the card.*)

ROMAINE. I swear by Almighty God that the evidence that I shall give shall be the truth, the whole truth and nothing but the truth.

(*The* USHER *replaces the Bible and oath card on the ledge of the witness box, crosses and resumes his seat.*)

MYERS. Your name is Romaine Heilger?

ROMAINE. Yes.

MYERS. You have been living as the wife of the prisoner, Leonard Vole?

ROMAINE. Yes.

MYERS. Are you actually his wife?

ROMAINE. I went through a form of marriage with him in Berlin. My former husband is still alive, so the marriage is not . . . (*She breaks off.*)

MYERS. Not valid.

SIR WILFRID. (*Rising*) My lord, I have the most serious objection to this witness giving evidence at all. We have the undeniable fact of marriage between this witness and the prisoner, and no proof whatsoever of this so-called previous marriage.

MYERS. If my friend had not abandoned his customary patience, and had waited for one more question, your lordship would have been spared this further interruption.

(SIR WILFRID *resumes his seat.*)

(*He picks up a document.*) Mrs Heilger, is this a certificate of a marriage between yourself and Otto Gerthe Heilger on the eighteenth of April, nineteen forty-six, in Leipzig?

(*The* USHER *rises, takes the certificate from* MYERS *and takes it to* ROMAINE.)

ROMAINE. It is.

JUDGE. I should like to see that certificate.

(*The* USHER *gives the certificate to the* CLERK, *who hands it to the* JUDGE.)

It will be exhibit number four, I think.

MYERS. I believe it will be, my lord.

JUDGE. (*After examining the document*) I think, Sir Wilfrid, this witness is competent to give evidence. (*He hands the certificate to the* CLERK.)

(*The* CLERK *gives the certificate to the* USHER, *who hands it to* MAYHEW. *The* USHER *then crosses and resumes his seat.* MAYHEW *shows the certificate to* SIR WILFRID.)

MYERS. In any event, Mrs Heilger, are you willing to give evidence against the man you have been calling your husband?

ROMAINE. I'm quite willing.

(LEONARD *rises, followed by the* WARDER.)

LEONARD. Romaine! What are you doing here? – What are you saying?

JUDGE. I must have silence. As your counsel will tell you, Vole, you will very shortly have an opportunity of speaking in your own defence.

(LEONARD *and the* WARDER *resume their seats.*)

MYERS. (*To* ROMAINE) Will you tell me in your own words what happened on the evening of October the fourteenth.

ROMAINE. I was at home all the evening.

MYERS. And Leonard Vole?

ROMAINE. Leonard went out at half past seven.

MYERS. When did he return?

ROMAINE. At ten minutes past ten.

(LEONARD *rises, followed by the* WARDER.)

LEONARD. That's not true. You know it's not true. It was about twenty-five past nine when I came home.

(MAYHEW *rises, turns to* LEONARD *and whispers to him to be quiet.*)

Who's been making you say this? I don't understand. (*He shrinks back and puts his hands to his face. Half whispering*) I – I don't understand. (*He resumes his seat.*)

(MAYHEW *and the* WARDER *sit.*)

MYERS. Leonard Vole returned, you say, at ten minutes past ten? And what happened next?

ROMAINE. He was breathing hard, very excited. He threw off his coat and examined the sleeves. Then he told me to wash the cuffs. They had blood on them.

MYERS. Did he speak about the blood?

ROMAINE. He said, 'Dammit, there's blood on them.'

MYERS. What did you say?

ROMAINE. I said, 'What have you done?'

MYERS. What did the prisoner say to that?

ROMAINE. He said, 'I've killed her.'

LEONARD. (*Rising, frenzied*) It's not true, I tell you. It's not true.

(*The* WARDER *rises and restrains* LEONARD.)

JUDGE. Please control yourself.

LEONARD. Not a word of this is true. (*He resumes his seat.*)

(*The* WARDER *remains standing.*)

JUDGE. (*To* ROMAINE) You know what you're saying, Mrs Heilger?

ROMAINE. I am to speak the truth, am I not?

MYERS. The prisoner said, 'I have killed her.' Did you know to whom he referred?

ROMAINE. Yes, I knew. It was the old woman he had been going to see so often.

MYERS. What happened next?

ROMAINE. He told me that I was to say he had been at home with me all that evening, especially he said I was to say he was at home at half past nine. I said to him, 'Do the police know you've killed her?' And he said, 'No, they will think it's a burglary. But anyway, remember I was at home with you at half past nine.'

MYERS. And you were subsequently interrogated by the police?

ROMAINE. Yes.

MYERS. Did they ask you if Leonard Vole was at home with you at half past nine?

ROMAINE. Yes.

MYERS. What did you answer to that?

ROMAINE. I said that he was.

MYERS. But you have changed your story now. Why?

ROMAINE. (*With sudden passion*) Because it is murder. I cannot go on lying to save him. I am grateful to him, yes. He married me and brought me to this country. What he has asked me to do always I have done it because I was grateful.

MYERS. Because you loved him?

ROMAINE. No, I never loved him.

LEONARD. Romaine!

ROMAINE. I never loved him.

MYERS. You were grateful to the prisoner. He brought you to this country. He asked you to give him an alibi and at first you consented, but later you felt that what he had asked you to do was wrong?

ROMAINE. Yes, that is it exactly.

MYERS. Why did you feel it was wrong?

ROMAINE. When it is murder. I cannot come into Court and lie and say that he was there with me at the time it was done. I cannot do it. I cannot *do* it.

MYERS. So what did you do?

ROMAINE. I did not know what to do. I do not know your country and I am afraid of the police. So I write a letter to my ambassador, and I say that I do not wish to tell any more lies. I wish to speak the truth.

MYERS. That *is* the truth – that Leonard Vole returned that night at ten minutes past ten. That he had blood on the sleeves of his coat, that he said to you, 'I have killed her.' That is the truth before God?

ROMAINE. That is the truth.

(MYERS *resumes his seat.*)

SIR WILFRID. (*Rising*) When the prisoner went through this form of marriage with you, was he aware that your first husband was still alive?

ROMAINE. No.

SIR WILFRID. He acted in good faith?

ROMAINE. Yes.

SIR WILFRID. And you were very grateful to him?

ROMAINE. I was grateful to him, yes.

SIR WILFRID. You've shown your gratitude by coming here and testifying against him.

ROMAINE. I have to speak the truth.

SIR WILFRID. (*Savagely*) Is it the truth?

ROMAINE. Yes.

SIR WILFRID. I suggest to you that on the night of October the fourteenth Leonard Vole was at home with you at nine-thirty, the time that the murder was committed. I suggest to you that this whole story of yours is a wicked fabrication, that you have for some reason a grudge against the prisoner, and that this is your way of expressing it.

ROMAINE. No.

SIR WILFRID. You realize that you are on oath?

ROMAINE. Yes.

SIR WILFRID. I warn you, Mrs Heilger, that if you care nothing for the prisoner, be careful on your own account. The penalty for perjury is heavy.

MYERS. (*Rising and interposing*) Really, my lord. I don't know whether these theatrical outbursts are for the benefit of the Jury, but I do most respectfully submit that there is nothing to suggest that this witness has spoken anything but the truth.

JUDGE. Mr Myers. This is a capital charge, and within the bounds of reason I would like the defence to have every latitude. Yes, Sir Wilfrid.

(MYERS *resumes his seat.*)

SIR WILFRID. Now then. You have said – that there was blood on both cuffs?

ROMAINE. Yes.

SIR WILFRID. *Both* cuffs?

ROMAINE. I have told you, that is what Leonard said.

SIR WILFRID. No, Mrs Heilger, you said, 'He told me to wash the cuffs. They had blood on them.'

JUDGE. That is precisely my note, Sir Wilfrid.

SIR WILFRID. Thank you, my lord. (*To* ROMAINE) What you were saying is that you had washed both cuffs.

MYERS. (*Rising*) It is my friend's turn to be inaccurate now, my lord. Nowhere has this witness said she washed both cuffs, or indeed that she washed even one. (*He sits.*)

SIR WILFRID. My friend is right. Well, Mrs Heilger, did you wash the sleeves?

ROMAINE. I remember now. It was only one sleeve that I washed.

SIR WILFRID. Thank you. Perhaps your memory as to other parts of your story is equally untrustworthy. I think your original story to the police was that the blood on the jacket came from a cut caused while carving ham?

ROMAINE. I said so, yes. But it was not true.

SIR WILFRID. Why did you lie?

ROMAINE. I said what Leonard told me to say.

SIR WILFRID. Even going so far as to produce the actual knife with which he was cutting the ham?

ROMAINE. When Leonard found he had blood on him, he cut himself to make it seem the blood was his.

LEONARD. (*Rising*) I never did.

SIR WILFRID. (*Silencing* LEONARD) Please, please.

(LEONARD *resumes his seat.*)

(*To* ROMAINE) So you admit that your original story to the police was all lies? You seem to be a very good liar.

ROMAINE. Leonard told me what to say.

SIR WILFRID. The question is whether you were lying then or whether you are lying *now*. If you were really appalled at murder having been committed, you could have told the truth to the police when they first questioned you.

ROMAINE. I was afraid of Leonard.

SIR WILFRID. (*Gesturing towards the woeful figure of* LEONARD) You were afraid of Leonard Vole – afraid of the man whose heart and spirit you've just broken. I think the Jury will know which of you to believe. (*He sits.*)

MYERS. (*Rising*) Romaine Heilger. I ask you once more, is the evidence you have given the truth, the whole truth and nothing but the truth?

ROMAINE. It is.

MYERS. My lord, that is the case for the prosecution. (*He sits.*)

(ROMAINE *stands down and crosses to the door up Left. The* POLICEMAN *opens the door.*)

LEONARD. (*As* ROMAINE *passes him*) Romaine!

USHER. (*Rising*) Silence!

(ROMAINE *exits up Left. The* POLICEMAN *closes the door. The* USHER *resumes his seat.*)

JUDGE. Sir Wilfrid.

SIR WILFRID. (*Rising*) My lord, members of the Jury, I will not submit to you, as I might, that there is no case for the prisoner to answer. There *is* a case. A case of very strong circumstantial evidence. You have heard the police and other expert witnesses. They have given fair, impartial evidence as is their duty. Against them I have nothing to say. On the other hand, you have heard Janet MacKenzie and the woman who calls herself Romaine Vole. Can you believe that their testimony is not warped? Janet MacKenzie – cut out of her rich mistress's will because her position was usurped, quite unwittingly, by this unfortunate boy. (*He pauses.*) Romaine Vole – Heilger – whatever she calls herself, who trapped him into marriage, whilst concealing from him the fact that she was married already. That woman owes him more than she can ever repay. She used him to save her from political persecution. But she admits no love for him. He has served his purpose. I will ask you to be very careful how you believe her testimony, the testimony of a woman who, for all we know, has been brought up to believe the pernicious doctrine that lying is a weapon to be used to serve one's own ends. Members of the Jury, I call the prisoner. Leonard Vole.

(*The* USHER *rises and crosses to the witness box.* LEONARD *rises, crosses and goes into the witness box. The* WARDER *follows* LEONARD *and stands behind him. The* USHER *picks up the Bible, hands it to* LEONARD *and holds up the oath card.*)

LEONARD. I swear by Almighty God that the evidence that I shall give shall be the truth, the whole truth and nothing but the truth. (*He puts the Bible on the ledge of the witness box.*)

(*The* USHER *replaces the oath card on the ledge of the witness box and sits Right of the table.*)

SIR WILFRID. Now, Mr Vole, we have heard of your friendship with Miss Emily French. Now I want you to tell us how often you visited her.

LEONARD. Frequently.

SIR WILFRID. Why was that?

LEONARD. Well, she was awfully nice to me and I got fond of her. She was like my Aunt Betsy.

SIR WILFRID. That was an aunt who brought you up?

LEONARD. Yes. She was a dear. Miss French reminded me of her.

SIR WILFRID. You've heard Janet MacKenzie say Miss French thought you were a single man, and that there was some question of marrying you. Is there any truth in this?

LEONARD. Of course not. It's an absurd idea.

SIR WILFRID. Miss French knew that you were married?

LEONARD. Yes.

SIR WILFRID. So there was no question of marriage between you?

LEONARD. Of course not. I've told you, she treated me as though she was an indulgent aunt. Almost like a mother.

SIR WILFRID. And in return you did everything for her that you could.

LEONARD. (*Simply*) I was very fond of her.

SIR WILFRID. Will you tell the Jury in your own words exactly what happened on the night of October the fourteenth?

LEONARD. Well, I'd come across a kind of a cat brush – a new thing in that line – and I thought it would please her. So I took it along that evening. I'd nothing else to do.

SIR WILFRID. What time was that?

LEONARD. Just before eight I got there. I gave her the cat brush. She was pleased. We tried it out on one of the cats and it was a success. Then we played a game of Double Demon – Miss French was very fond of Double Demon – and after that I left.

SIR WILFRID. Yes, but did you not . . .

JUDGE. Sir Wilfrid, I don't understand this piece of evidence at all. What is a cat brush?

LEONARD. It's a brush for brushing cats.

JUDGE. Oh!

LEONARD. A sort of brush and comb combined. Miss French kept cats – eight of them she had, and the house smelt a bit . . .

SIR WILFRID. Yes, yes.

LEONARD. I thought the brush might be useful.

SIR WILFRID. Did you see Janet MacKenzie?

LEONARD. No. Miss French let me in herself.

SIR WILFRID. Did you know Janet MacKenzie was out?

LEONARD. Well, I didn't think about it.

SIR WILFRID. At what time did you leave?

LEONARD. Just before nine. I walked home.

SIR WILFRID. How long did that take you?

LEONARD. Oh, I should say about twenty minutes to half an hour.

SIR WILFRID. So that you reached home . . .?

LEONARD. I reached home at twenty-five minutes past nine.

SIR WILFRID. And your wife – I will call her your wife – was at home then?

LEONARD. Yes, of course she was. I – I think she must have gone mad. I . . .

SIR WILFRID. Never mind that now. Just go on with your story. Did you wash your coat when you got in?

LEONARD. No, of course I didn't.

SIR WILFRID. Who did wash your coat?

LEONARD. Romaine did, the next morning. She said it had got blood on it from a cut on my wrist.

SIR WILFRID. A cut on your wrist?

LEONARD. Yes. Here. (*He holds out his arm and shows his wrist.*) You can still see the mark.

SIR WILFRID. When was the first you heard of the murder?

LEONARD. I read about it in the evening paper the next day.

SIR WILFRID. And what did you feel?

LEONARD. I was stunned. I could hardly believe it. I was very upset too. The papers said it was a burglary. I never dreamed of anything else.

SIR WILFRID. And what happened next?

LEONARD. I read that the police were anxious to interview me, so of course I went along to the police station.

SIR WILFRID. You went along to the police station and made a statement?

LEONARD. Yes.

SIR WILFRID. You were not nervous? Reluctant to do so?

LEONARD. No, of course not. I wanted to help in any way possible.

SIR WILFRID. Did you ever receive any money from Miss French?

LEONARD. No.

SIR WILFRID. Were you aware that she had made a will in your favour?

LEONARD. She said she was ringing up her lawyers and going to make a new will. I asked her if she often made new wills and she said, 'From time to time.'

SIR WILFRID. Did you know what the terms of this new will were to be?

LEONARD. I swear I didn't.

SIR WILFRID. Had she ever suggested to you that she might leave you anything at all in her will?

LEONARD. No.

SIR WILFRID. You have heard the evidence that your wife – or the woman whom you considered as your wife – has given in Court.

LEONARD. Yes – I heard. I can't understand – I . . .

SIR WILFRID. (*Checking him*) I realize, Mr Vole, that you are very upset, but I want to ask you to put aside all emotion and to answer the question plainly and simply. Was what that witness said true or untrue?

LEONARD. No, of course it wasn't true.

SIR WILFRID. You arrived home at nine-twenty-five that night, and had supper with your wife?

LEONARD. Yes.

SIR WILFRID. Did you go out again?

LEONARD. No.

SIR WILFRID. Are you right- or left-handed?

LEONARD. Right-handed.

SIR WILFRID. I'm going to ask you just one more question, Mr Vole. *Did you kill* Emily French?

LEONARD. No, I did not.

(SIR WILFRID *sits.*)

MYERS. (*Rising*) Have you ever tried to get money out of anybody?

LEONARD. No.

MYERS. How soon in your acquaintance with Miss French did you learn that she was a very wealthy woman?

LEONARD. Well, I didn't know she *was* rich when I first went to see her.

MYERS. But, having gained that knowledge, you decided to cultivate her acquaintance further?

LEONARD. I suppose that's what it looks like. But I really liked her, you know. Money had nothing to do with it.

MYERS. You would have continued to visit her, no matter how poor she'd been?

LEONARD. Yes, I would.

MYERS. You yourself are in poor circumstances?

LEONARD. You know I am.

MYERS. Kindly answer the question, yes or no.

JUDGE. You must answer the question, yes or no.

LEONARD. Yes.

MYERS. What salary do you earn?

LEONARD. Well, as a matter of fact I haven't got a job at the moment. Haven't had one for some time.

MYERS. You were recently discharged from your position?

LEONARD. No, I wasn't – I quit.

MYERS. At the time of your arrest how much money had you in the bank?

LEONARD. Well, actually only a few pounds. I was expecting some money in, in a week or two.

MYERS. How much?

LEONARD. Not very much.

MYERS. I put it to you, you were pretty desperate for money?

LEONARD. Not desperate. I – well, I felt a bit worried.

MYERS. You were worried about money, you met a wealthy woman and you courted her acquaintance assiduously.

LEONARD. You make it sound all twisted. I tell you I liked her.

MYERS. We have heard that Miss French used to consult you on her income tax returns.

LEONARD. Yes, she did. You know what those forms are. You can't make head or tail of them – or she couldn't.

MYERS. Janet MacKenzie has told us that Miss French was a very good businesswoman, well able to deal with her own affairs.

LEONARD. Well, that's not what she said to me. She said those forms worried her terribly.

MYERS. In filling up her income tax forms for her you no doubt learned the exact amount of her income?

LEONARD. No.

MYERS. No?

LEONARD. Well – I mean naturally, yes.

MYERS. Yes, very convenient. How was it, Mr Vole, that you never took your wife to see Miss French?

LEONARD. I don't know. It just didn't seem to crop up.

MYERS. You say Miss French knew you were married?

LEONARD. Yes.

MYERS. Yet she never asked you to bring your wife with you to the house?

LEONARD. No.

MYERS. Why not?

LEONARD. Oh, I don't know. She didn't like women, I don't think.

MYERS. She preferred, shall we say, personable young men? And you didn't insist on bringing your wife?

LEONARD. No, of course I didn't. You see, she knew my wife was a foreigner and she – oh, I don't know, she seemed to think we didn't get on.

MYERS. That was the impression you gave her?

LEONARD. No, I didn't. She – well, I think it was wishful thinking on her part.

MYERS. You mean she was infatuated with you?

LEONARD. No, she wasn't infatuated, but she – oh, it's like mothers are sometimes with a son.

MYERS. How?

LEONARD. They don't want him to like a girl or get engaged or anything of that kind.

MYERS. You hoped, didn't you, for some monetary advantage from your friendship with Miss French?

LEONARD. Not in the way you mean.

MYERS. Not in the way I mean? You seem to know what I mean better than I know myself. In what way, then, did you hope for monetary advantage? (*He pauses.*) I repeat, in what way did you hope for monetary advantage?

LEONARD. You see, there's a thing I've invented. A kind of windscreen wiper that works in snow. I was looking for someone to finance that and I thought perhaps Miss French would. But that wasn't the only reason I went to see her. I tell you I liked her.

MYERS. Yes, yes, we've heard that very often, haven't we – how much you liked her.

LEONARD. (*Sulkily*) Well, it's true.

MYERS. I believe, Mr Vole, that about a week before Miss French's death, you were making enquiries of a travel agency for particulars of foreign cruises.

LEONARD. Supposing I did – it isn't a crime, is it?

MYERS. Not at all. Many people go for cruises *when they can pay for it.* But you couldn't pay for it, could you, Mr Vole?

LEONARD. I was hard up. I told you so.

MYERS. And yet you came into this particular travel agency – with a blonde – a strawberry blonde – I understand – and . . .

JUDGE. A strawberry blonde, Mr Myers?

MYERS. A term for a lady with reddish fair hair, my lord.

JUDGE. I thought I knew all about blondes, but a strawberry blonde . . . Go on, Mr Myers.

MYERS. (*To* LEONARD) Well?

LEONARD. My wife isn't a blonde and it was only a bit of fun, anyway.

MYERS. You admit that you asked for particulars, not of cheap trips, but of the most expensive and luxurious cruises. How did you expect to pay for such a thing?

LEONARD. I didn't.

MYERS. I suggest that you knew that in a week's time you would have inherited a large sum of money from a trusting elderly lady.

LEONARD. I didn't know anything of the kind. I just was feeling fed up – and there were the posters in the window – palm trees and coconuts and blue seas, and I went in and asked. The clerk gave me a sort of supercilious look – I *was* a bit shabby – but it riled me. And so I put on a bit of an act – (*He suddenly grins as though enjoying remembrance of the scene.*) and began asking for the swankiest tours there were – all *de luxe* and a cabin on the boat deck.

MYERS. You really expect the Jury to believe that?

LEONARD. I don't expect anyone to believe anything. But that's the way it was. It was make-believe and childish if you like – but it was fun and I enjoyed it. (*He looks suddenly pathetic.*) I wasn't thinking of killing anybody or of inheriting money.

MYERS. So it was just a remarkable coincidence that Miss French should be killed, leaving you her heir, only a few days later.

LEONARD. I've told you – I didn't kill her.

MYERS. Your story is that on the night of the fourteenth, you left Miss French's house at four minutes to nine, that you walked home and you arrived there at twenty-five minutes past nine, and stayed there the rest of the evening.

LEONARD. Yes.

MYERS. You have heard the woman Romaine Heilger rebut that story in Court. You have heard her say that you came in not at *twenty-five minutes* past nine but at *ten minutes past ten.*

LEONARD. It's not true!

MYERS. That your clothes were bloodstained, that you definitely admitted to her that you had killed Miss French.

LEONARD. It's not true, I tell you. Not one word of it is true.

MYERS. Can you suggest any reason why this young woman, who has been passing as your wife, should deliberately give the evidence she has given if it were not true?

LEONARD. No, I can't. That's the awful thing. There's no reason at all. I think she must have gone mad.

MYERS. You think she must have gone mad? She seemed extremely sane, and self-possessed. But insanity is the only reason you can suggest.

LEONARD. I don't understand it. Ah, God, what's happened – what's changed her?

MYERS. Very effective, I'm sure. But in this Court we deal with facts. And the fact is, Mr Vole, that we have only your word for it that you left Emily French's house at the time you say you did, and that you arrived home at five and twenty minutes past nine, and that you did not go out again.

LEONARD. (*Wildly*) Someone must have seen me – in the street – or going into the house.

MYERS. One would certainly think so – but the only person who did see you come home that night says it was at ten minutes past ten. And that person says that you had blood on your clothes.

LEONARD. I cut my wrist.

MYERS. A very easy thing to do in case any questions should arise.

LEONARD. (*Breaking down*) You twist everything. You twist everything I say. You make me sound like a different kind of person from what I am.

MYERS. You cut your wrist deliberately.

LEONARD. No, I didn't. I didn't do anything, but you make it all sound as though I did. I can hear it myself.

MYERS. You came home at ten past ten.

LEONARD. No, I didn't. You've *got* to believe me. You've got to *believe* me.

MYERS. You killed Emily French.

LEONARD. I didn't do it.

(*The LIGHTS fade quickly, leaving two spots on* LEONARD *and* MYERS. *These fade too as he finishes speaking and the Curtain falls.*)

I didn't kill her. I've never killed anybody. Oh God! It's a nightmare. It's some awful, evil dream.

CURTAIN

ACT THREE

Scene I

SCENE: *The Chambers of Sir Wilfrid Robarts, QC. The same evening.*

When Curtain rises, the stage is empty and in darkness. The window curtains are open. GRETA *enters immediately and holds the door open.* MAYHEW *and* SIR WILFRID *enter.* MAYHEW *carries his briefcase.*

GRETA. Good evening, Sir Wilfrid. It's a nasty night, sir. (GRETA *exits, closing the door behind her.*)

SIR WILFRID. Damned fog! (*He switches on the wall-brackets by the switch below the door and crosses to the window.*)

MAYHEW. It's a beast of an evening. (*He removes his hat and overcoat and hangs them on the pegs up Left.*)

SIR WILFRID. (*Closing the window curtains*) Is there no justice? We come out of a stuffy Court Room gasping for fresh air, and what do we find? (*He switches on the desk lamp.*) Fog!

MAYHEW. It's not as thick as the fog we're in over Mrs Heilger's antics. (*He crosses to the desk and puts his case on the up Left corner.*)

SIR WILFRID. That damned woman. From the very first moment I clapped eyes on her, I scented trouble. I knew she was up to something. A thoroughly vindictive piece of goods and much too deep for that simple young fool in the dock. But what's *her* game, John? What's she up to? Tell me that. (*He crosses below the desk to Left.*)

MAYHEW. Presumably, it would seem, to get young Leonard Vole convicted of murder.

SIR WILFRID. (*Crossing down Right*) But why? Look what he's done for her.

MAYHEW. He's probably done too much for her.

SIR WILFRID. (*Moving up Right of the desk*) And she despises him for it. That's likely enough. Ungrateful beasts, women. But why be vindictive? After all, if she was bored with him, all she had to do was walk out. (*He crosses above the desk to Left.*) There doesn't seem to be any financial reason for her to remain with him.

GRETA. (*Enters and crosses to the desk. She carries a tray with two cups of tea*) I've brought you your tea, Sir Wilfrid, and a cup for Mr Mayhew, too. (*She puts one cup on each side of the desk.*)

SIR WILFRID. (*Sitting Left of the fireplace*) Tea? Strong drink is what we need.

GRETA. Oh, you know you like your tea really, sir. How did it go today?

SIR WILFRID. Badly.

(MAYHEW *sits Left of the desk.*)

GRETA. (*Crossing to* SIR WILFRID) Oh, no, sir. Oh, I do hope not. Because he didn't do it. I'm sure he didn't do it. (*She crosses to the door.*)

SIR WILFRID. You're still sure he didn't do it. (*He looks thoughtfully at her.*) Now why's that?

GRETA. (*Confidently*) Because he's not the sort. He's *nice*, if you know what I mean – ever so nice. He'd never go coshing an old lady on the head. But you'll get him off, won't you, sir?

SIR WILFRID. I'll – get – him – off.

(GRETA *exits.*)

(*He rises. Almost to himself.*) God knows how. Only one woman on the jury – pity – evidently the women like him – can't think why – he's not particularly – (*He crosses to Right of the desk.*) good-looking. Perhaps he's got something that arouses the maternal instinct. Women want to mother him.

MAYHEW. Whereas Mrs Heilger – is *not* the maternal type.

SIR WILFRID. (*Picking up his tea and crossing with it to Left*) No, she's the passionate sort. Hot-blooded behind that cool self-control. The kind that would knife a man if he double-crossed her. God, how I'd like to break her down. Show up her lies. Show *her* for what she is.

MAYHEW. (*Rising and taking his pipe from his pocket*) Forgive me, Wilfrid, but aren't you letting this case become a personal duel between you and her? (*He moves to the fireplace, takes a pipe cleaner from the jar on the mantelpiece and cleans his pipe.*)

SIR WILFRID. Am I? Perhaps I am. But she's an evil woman, John. I'm convinced of that. And a young man's life depends on the outcome of that duel.

MAYHEW. (*Thoughtfully*) I don't think the Jury liked her.

SIR WILFRID. No, you're right there, John. I don't think they did. To begin with, she's a foreigner, and they distrust foreigners. Then she's not married to the fellow – she's more or less admitting to committing bigamy.

(MAYHEW *tosses the pipe cleaner into the fireplace, then crosses to Left of the desk.*)

None of that goes down well. And at the end of it all, she's not sticking to her man when he's down. We don't like that in this country.

MAYHEW. That's all to the good.

SIR WILFRID. (*Crossing above the desk to Right of it*) Yes, but it isn't enough. There's no corroboration of his statements whatsoever. (*He puts his tea on the desk.*)

(MAYHEW *crosses to Left.*)

He admits being with Miss French that evening, his fingerprints are all over the place, we haven't managed to find anybody who saw him on the way home, and there's the altogether damning matter of the will. (*He stands above the desk.*) That travel-agency business doesn't help. The woman makes a will in his favour and immediately he goes enquiring about luxury cruises. Couldn't be more unfortunate.

MAYHEW. (*Moving to the fireplace*) I agree. And his explanation was hardly convincing.

SIR WILFRID. (*With a sudden complete change of manner and becoming very human*) And yet, you know, John, my wife does it.

MAYHEW. Does what?

SIR WILFRID. (*Smiling indulgently*) Gets travel agencies to make out itineraries for extensive foreign tours. For both of us. (*He takes the tobacco jar from the mantelpiece and puts it on the desk.*)

MAYHEW. Thank you, Wilfrid. (*He sits Left of the desk and fills his pipe.*)

SIR WILFRID. She'll work it all out to the last detail and bemoan the fact that the boat misses a connection at Bermuda. (*He moves to Right of the desk.*) She'll say to me that we could save time by flying but that we wouldn't see anything of the country, and (*He sits Right of the desk.*) what do I think? And I say: 'It's all the same to me, my dear. Arrange it as you like.' We both know that it's a kind of game, and we'll end up with the same old thing – staying at home.

MAYHEW. Ah, now with *my* wife, it's houses.

SIR WILFRID. Houses?

MAYHEW. Orders to view. Sometimes I think that there's hardly a house in England that's ever been up for sale that my wife hasn't been over. She plans how to apportion the rooms, and works out any structural alterations that will be necessary. She even plans the curtains and the covers and the general colour scheme. (*He rises, puts the tobacco jar on the mantelpiece and feels in his pocket for matches.*)

(SIR WILFRID *and* MAYHEW *look at each other and smile indulgently.*)

SIR WILFRID. H'm – well . . . (*He becomes the QC again.*) The fantasies of our wives aren't evidence, worse luck. But it helps one to understand why young Vole went asking for cruise literature.

MAYHEW. Pipe dreams.

SIR WILFRID. (*Taking a matchbox from the desk drawer*) There you are, John. (*He puts the box on the desk.*)

MAYHEW. (*Crossing to Left of the desk and picking up the matchbox*) Thank you, Wilfrid.

SIR WILFRID. I think we've had a certain amount of luck with Janet MacKenzie.

MAYHEW. Bias, you mean?

SIR WILFRID. That's right. Overdoing her prejudice.

MAYHEW. (*Sitting Left of the desk*) That was a very telling point of yours about her deafness.

SIR WILFRID. Yes, yes, we got her there. But she got her own back over the wireless.

(MAYHEW *finds that the matchbox is empty, throws it in the waste-paper basket and puts his pipe in his pocket.*)

Not smoking, John?

MAYHEW. No, not just now.

SIR WILFRID. John, what really happened that night? Was it robbery with violence after all? The police have to admit that it might have been.

MAYHEW. But they don't really think so and they don't often make a mistake. That inspector is quite convinced that it *was* an inside job – that that window was tampered with from the inside.

SIR WILFRID. (*Rising and crossing below the desk to Left*) Well, he may be wrong.

MAYHEW. I wonder.

SIR WILFRID. But if so, who was the man Janet MacKenzie heard talking to Miss French at nine-thirty? Seems to me there are two answers to that.

MAYHEW. The answers being . . .?

SIR WILFRID. First that she made the whole thing up, when she saw that the police weren't satisfied about its being a burglary.

MAYHEW. (*Shocked*) Surely she wouldn't do a thing like that?

SIR WILFRID. (*Crossing to Centre*) Well, what did she hear, then? Don't tell me it was a burglar chatting amicably with Miss French – (*He takes his handkerchief from his pocket.*) before he coshed her on the head, you old clown. (*He coshes* MAYHEW *with the handkerchief.*)

MAYHEW. That certainly seems unlikely.

SIR WILFRID. I don't think that that rather grim old woman would stick at making up a thing like that. I don't think she'd stick at anything, you know. No – (*Significantly.*) I don't think – she'd stick – at – *anything*.

MAYHEW. (*Horrified*) Good Lord! Do you mean . . .?

CARTER. (*Enters and closes the door behind him.*) Excuse me, Sir Wilfrid. A young woman is asking to see you. She says it has to do with the case of Leonard Vole.

SIR WILFRID. (*Unimpressed.*) Mental?

CARTER. Oh, no, Sir Wilfrid. I can always recognize that type.

SIR WILFRID. (*Moving above the desk and picking up the tea-cups*) What sort of a young woman? (*He crosses to Centre.*)

CARTER. (*Taking the cups from* SIR WILFRID) Rather a common young woman, sir, with a free way of talking.

SIR WILFRID. And what does she want?

CARTER. (*Quoting somewhat distastefully*) She says she 'knows something that might do the prisoner a bit of good'.

SIR WILFRID. (*With a sigh*) Highly unlikely. Bring her in.

(CARTER *exits, taking the cups with him.*)

What do you think, John?

MAYHEW. Oh well, we can't afford to leave any stone unturned.

(CARTER *enters and ushers in a* WOMAN. *She appears to be aged almost thirty-five and is flamboyantly but cheaply dressed. Blonde hair falls over one side of her face. She is violently and crudely made up. She carries a shabby handbag.* MAYHEW *rises.*)

CARTER. The young lady. (CARTER *exits.*)

WOMAN. (*Looking sharply from* SIR WILFRID *to* MAYHEW) Here, what's this? Two o'yer? I'm not talking to two of yer. (*She turns to go.*)

SIR WILFRID. This is Mr Mayhew. He is Leonard Vole's solicitor. I am Sir Wilfrid Robarts, Counsel for the Defence.

WOMAN. (*Peering at* SIR WILFRID) So you are, dear. Didn't recognize you without your wig. Lovely you all look in them wigs.

(MAYHEW *gives* SIR WILFRID *a nudge, then stands above the desk.*)

Havin' a bit of a confab, are you? Well, maybe I can help you if you make it worth my while.

SIR WILFRID. You know, Miss – er . . .

WOMAN. (*Crossing and sitting Left of the desk*) No need for names. If I did give you a name, it mightn't be the right one, might it?

SIR WILFRID. (*Standing Centre*) As you please. You realize you are in duty bound to come forward to give any evidence that may be in your possession.

WOMAN. Aw, come off it! I didn't say I knew anything, did I? I've *got* something. That's more to the point.

MAYHEW. What is it you have got, madam?

WOMAN. Aye-aye! I was in Court today. I watched the – that trollop give her evidence. So high and mighty about it too. She's a wicked one. A Jezebel, that's what she is.

SIR WILFRID. Quite so. But as to this special information you have . . .

WOMAN. (*Cunningly*) Ah, but what's in it for me? It's valuable, what I've got. A hundred quid, that's what I want.

MAYHEW. I'm afraid we could not countenance anything of that character, but perhaps if you tell us a little more about what you have to offer . . .

WOMAN. You don't buy unless you get a butcher's, is that it?

SIR WILFRID. A butcher's?

WOMAN. A butcher's 'ook – look.

SIR WILFRID. Oh, yes – yes.

WOMAN. I've got the goods on her all right. (*She opens her handbag.*) It's letters, that's what it is. Letters.

SIR WILFRID. Letters written by Romaine Vole to the prisoner?

WOMAN. (*Laughing coarsely*) To the prisoner? Don't make me laugh. Poor ruddy prisoner, he's been took in by her all right. (*She winks.*) I've got something to *sell*, dear, and don't you forget it.

MAYHEW. (*Smoothly*) If you will let us see these letters, we shall be able to advise you as to how pertinent they are.

WOMAN. Putting it in your own language, aren't you? Well, as I say, I don't expect you to buy without seeing. But fair's fair. If those letters will do the trick, if they'll get the boy off, and put that foreign bitch where she belongs, well, it's a hundred quid for me. Right?

MAYHEW. (*Taking his wallet from his pocket and extracting ten pounds*) If these letters contain information that is useful to the defence – to help your expenses in coming here – I am prepared to offer you ten pounds.

WOMAN. (*Almost screaming*) Ten bloody quid for letters like these. Think again.

SIR WILFRID. (*Crossing to* MAYHEW *and taking the wallet from him*) If you have a letter there that will help to prove my client's innocence, twenty pounds would, I think, not be an unreasonable sum for your expenses. (*He crosses to Right of the desk, takes ten pounds from the wallet, returns the empty wallet to* MAYHEW, *and takes the first ten pounds from him.*)

WOMAN. Fifty quid and it's a bargain. That's if you're satisfied with the letters.

SIR WILFRID. Twenty pounds. (*He puts the notes on the desk.*)

(*The* WOMAN *watches him and wets her lips. It is too much for her.*)

WOMAN. All right, blast you, 'Ere, take 'em. Quite a packet of 'em. (*She takes the letters from her handbag.*) The top one's the one will do the trick. (*She puts the letters on the desk, then goes to pick up the money.*)

(SIR WILFRID *is too quick for the* WOMAN *and picks up the money. The* WOMAN *quickly retrieves the letters.*)

SIR WILFRID. Just a moment. I suppose this is her handwriting?

WOMAN. It's her handwriting all right. She wrote 'em. It's all fair and square.

SIR WILFRID. We have only your word for that.

MAYHEW. Just a moment. I have a letter from Mrs Vole – not here, but at my office.

SIR WILFRID. Well, madam, it looks as though we'll have to trust you – (*He hands her the notes.*) for the moment. (*He takes the letters from her, smooths them out and begins to read.*)

(*The* WOMAN *slowly counts the notes, carefully watching the* OTHERS *meanwhile.* MAYHEW *moves to* SIR WILFRID *and peers at the letters. The* WOMAN *rises and crosses towards the door.*)

(*To* MAYHEW) It's incredible. Quite incredible.

MAYHEW. (*Reading over his shoulder*) The cold-blooded vindictiveness.

SIR WILFRID. (*Crossing to the* WOMAN) How did you get hold of these?

WOMAN. That'd be telling.

SIR WILFRID. What have you got against Romaine Vole?

(*The* WOMAN *crosses to the desk, suddenly and dramatically turns her head, swings the desk lamp so that it flows on to her face on the side that has been turned away from the audience, pushing her hair back as she does so, revealing that her cheek is all slashed, scarred and disfigured.* SIR WILFRID *starts back with an ejaculation.*)

WOMAN. See that?

SIR WILFRID. Did *she* do that to you?

WOMAN. (*Crossing to Centre*) Not her. The chap I was going with. Going with him steady, I was too. He was a bit younger than me, but he was fond of me and I loved him. Then she came along. She took a fancy to him and she got him away from me. She started to see him on the sly and then one day he cleared out. I knew where he'd gone. I went after him and I found

them together. (*She sits Left of the desk.*) I told 'er what I thought
of 'er and 'e set on me. In with one of the razor gangs, he was.
He cut my face up proper. 'There,' he says, 'no man'll ever
look at you now.'

SIR WILFRID. Did you go to the police about it?

WOMAN. Me? Not likely. 'Sides, it wasn't 'is fault. Not really. It was
hers, all hers. Getting him away from me, turning 'im against
me. But I waited my time. I followed 'er about and watched
'er. I know some of the things she's bin up to. I know where the
bloke lives who she goes to see on the sly sometimes. That's
how I got hold of them letters. So now you know the whole
story, Mister. (*She rises, thrusts her face forward and pushes her hair
aside.*) Want to kiss me?

(SIR WILFRID *shrinks back.*)

I don't blame yer. (*She crosses to Left.*)

SIR WILFRID. I'm deeply sorry, deeply sorry. Got a fiver, John?

(MAYHEW *shows his empty wallet.*)

(*He takes his wallet from his pocket and extracts a five-pound note.*)

Er – we'll make it another five pounds.

WOMAN. (*Grabbing the note*) 'Oldin' out on me, were yer? Willin' to
go up another five quid. (*She advances on* SIR WILFRID.)

(SIR WILFRID *backs towards* MAYHEW.)

Ah, I knew I was being too soft with you. Those letters are the
goods, aren't they?

SIR WILFRID. They will, I think, be very useful. (*He turns to*
MAYHEW *and holds out a letter.*) Here, John, have a butcher's
at this one.

(*The* WOMAN *slips quickly out of the door.*)

MAYHEW. We'll have a handwriting expert on these for safety's
sake, and he can give evidence if necessary.

SIR WILFRID. We shall require this man's surname and his address.

MAYHEW. (*Looking around*) Hullo, where has she gone? She mustn't
leave without giving us further particulars. (*He crosses to Centre.*)

SIR WILFRID. (*Crosses and exits hurriedly. Off, calling*) Carter! Carter!

CARTER. (*Off*) Yes, Sir Wilfrid?

SIR WILFRID. (*Off*) Carter, where did that young woman go?

CARTER. (*Off*) She went straight out, sir.

SIR WILFRID. (*Off*) Well, you shouldn't have let her go. Send
Greta after her.

CARTER. (*Off*) Very good, Sir Wilfrid.

(SIR WILFRID *enters and crosses to Left of* MAYHEW.)

MAYHEW. She's gone?

SIR WILFRID. Yes, I've sent Greta after her, but there's not a hope
in this fog. Damn! We must have this man's surname and
address.

MAYHEW. We won't get it. She thought things out too carefully.
Wouldn't give us her name, and slipped out like an eel as soon
as she saw us busy with the letters. She daren't risk having to
appear in the witness box. Look what the man did to her last
time.

SIR WILFRID. (*Without conviction*) She'd have protection.

MAYHEW. Would she? For how long? He'd get her in the end, or
his pals would. She's already risked something coming here.
She doesn't want to bring the man into it. It's Romaine Heilger
she's after.

SIR WILFRID. And what a beauty our Romaine is. But we've got
something to go on at last. Now as to procedure . . .

CURTAIN

Scene II

SCENE: *The Old Bailey. The next morning.*

When Curtain rises, the Court is awaiting the entry of the JUDGE. LEONARD
and the WARDER *are seated in the dock. Two* BARRISTERS *are seated
at the Left end of the back row of* BARRISTERS´ *seats.* SIR WILFRID
and his ASSISTANT *are in their places.* MAYHEW *is standing Left of*

the table talking to SIR WILFRID. *The* CLERK OF THE COURT,
the JUDGE's *clerk and the* STENOGRAPHER *are in their places.
The three visible* MEMBERS OF THE JURY *are seated. The*
POLICEMAN *is at the doors up Left. The* USHER *is standing at the
top of the steps up Right Centre.* MYERS, *his* ASSISTANT *and two*
BARRISTERS *enter up Centre.* MYERS *crosses to* SIR WILFRID
and starts talking angrily. The ASSISTANT *and the* BARRISTERS
take their seats. There are three knocks on the JUDGE's *door. The*
USHER *comes down the steps to Right Centre.*

USHER. Stand up.

(ALL *stand. The* JUDGE *and* ALDERMAN *enter by the* JUDGE's *door
and take their seats.*)

All persons who have anything further to do before my lady the
Queen's justices of Oyer and Terminer and general gaol delivery for the jurisdiction of the Central Criminal Court draw
near and give your attendance. God Save the Queen.

(*The* JUDGE *bows to the Court and* ALL *take their seats. The* USHER *sits
on the stool down Right.*)

SIR WILFRID. (*Rising*) My lord, since this was adjourned, certain
evidence of a rather startling character has come into my
hands. This evidence is such that I am taking it upon myself
to ask your lordship's permission to have the last witness for the
prosecution, Romaine Heilger, recalled.

(*The* CLERK *rises and whispers to the* JUDGE.)

JUDGE. When exactly, Sir Wilfrid, did this evidence come to your
knowledge?

(*The* CLERK *sits.*)

SIR WILFRID. It was brought to me after the Court was adjourned
last night.

MYERS. (*Rising*) My lord, I must object to my learned friend's
request. The case for the prosecution is closed and . . .

(SIR WILFRID *sits.*)

JUDGE. Mr Myers, I had not intended to rule on this question without first observing the customary formality of inviting your observations on the matter. Yes, Sir Wilfrid?

(MYERS *sits.*)

SIR WILFRID. (*Rising*) My lord, in a case where evidence vital to the prisoner comes into possession of his legal advisers at any time before the jury have returned their verdict, I contend that such evidence is not only admissible, but desirable. Happily there is clear authority to support my proposition, to be found in the case of the King against Stillman, reported in nineteen twenty-six *Appeal Cases* at page four-six-three. (*He opens a law volume in front of him.*)

JUDGE. You needn't trouble to cite the authority, Sir Wilfrid, I am quite familiar with it. I should like to hear the prosecution. Now, Mr Myers.

(SIR WILFRID *sits.*)

MYERS. (*Rising*) In my respectful submission, my lord, the course my friend proposes is, save in exceptional circumstances, quite unprecedented. And what, may I ask, is this startling new evidence of which Sir Wilfrid speaks?

SIR WILFRID. (*Rising*) Letters, my lord. Letters from Romaine Heilger.

JUDGE. I should like to see these letters to which you refer, Sir Wilfrid.

(SIR WILFRID *and* MYERS *sit. The* USHER *rises, crosses to* SIR WILFRID, *collects the letters, passes them to the* CLERK, *who hands them to the* JUDGE. *The* JUDGE *studies the letters. The* USHER *resumes his seat.*)

MYERS. (*Rising*) My friend was good enough to tell me only as we came into Court that he intended to make this submission, so that I have had no opportunity to examine the authorities. But I seem to remember a case in, I think, nineteen thirty, the King against Porter, I believe . . .

JUDGE. No, Mr Myers, the King against Potter, and it was reported in nineteen thirty-one. I appeared for the prosecution.

MYERS. And if my memory serves me well, your lordship's similar objection was sustained.

JUDGE. Your memory for once serves you ill, Mr Myers. My objection then was overruled by Mr Justice Swindon – as yours is now, by me.

(MYERS *sits*.)

SIR WILFRID. (*Rising*) Call Romaine Heilger.

USHER. (*Rises and moves down Centre*) Romaine Heilger.

POLICEMAN. (*Opens the door. Calling*) Romaine Heilger.

JUDGE. If these letters are authentic, it raises very serious issues. (*He hands the letters to the* CLERK.)

(*The* CLERK *hands the letters to the* USHER, *who returns them to* SIR WILFRID. *During the slight wait that ensues,* LEONARD *is very agitated. He speaks to the* WARDER, *then puts his hands to his face. The* USHER *sits on the stool Right of the table.* MAYHEW *rises, speaks to* LEONARD *and calms him down.* LEONARD *shakes his head and looks upset and worried.* ROMAINE *enters up Left, crosses and enters the witness box. The* POLICEMAN *closes the door.*)

SIR WILFRID. Mrs Heilger, you appreciate that you are still on your oath?

ROMAINE. Yes.

JUDGE. Romaine Heilger, you are recalled to this box so that Sir Wilfrid may ask you further questions.

SIR WILFRID. Mrs Heilger, do you know a certain man whose Christian name is Max?

ROMAINE. (*Starts violently at the mention of the name*) I don't know what you mean.

SIR WILFRID (*Pleasantly*) And yet it's a very simple question. Do you or do you not know a man called Max?

ROMAINE. Certainly not.

SIR WILFRID. You're quite sure of that?

ROMAINE. I've never known anyone called Max. Never.

SIR WILFRID. And yet I believe it's a fairly common Christian name, or contraction of a name, in your country. You mean that you have never known anyone of that name.?

ROMAINE. (*Doubtfully*) Oh, in Germany – yes – perhaps, I do not remember. It is a long time ago.

SIR WILFRID. I shall not ask you to throw your mind back such a long way as that. A few weeks will suffice. Let us say – (*He picks*

up one of the letters and unfolds it, making rather a parade of it.) the
seventeenth of October last.

ROMAINE. (*Startled*) What have you got there?

SIR WILFRID. A letter

ROMAINE. I don't know what you're talking about.

SIR WILFRID. I'm talking about a letter. A letter written on the
seventeenth of October. You remember that date, perhaps.

ROMAINE. Not particularly, why?

SIR WILFRID. I suggest that on that day, you wrote a certain letter
– a letter addressed to a man called Max.

ROMAINE. I did nothing of the kind. These are lies that you are
telling. I don't know what you mean.

SIR WILFRID. That letter was one of a series written to the same
man over a considerable period of time.

ROMAINE. (*Agitated*) Lies – all lies!

SIR WILFRID. You would seem to have been on – (*Significantly*)
intimate terms with this man.

LEONARD. (*Rising*) How dare you say a thing like that?

(*The* WARDER *rises and attempts to restrain* LEONARD).

(*He waves the* WARDER *aside.*) It isn't true!

JUDGE. The prisoner, in his own interest, will remain silent.

(LEONARD *and the* WARDER *resume their seats.*)

SIR WILFRID. I am not concerned with the general trend of this
correspondence. I am only interested in one particular letter.
(*He reads.*) 'My beloved Max. An extraordinary thing has
happened. I believe all our difficulties may be ended . . .'

ROMAINE. (*Interrupting in a frenzy*) It's a lie – I never wrote it. How
did you get hold of that letter? Who gave it to you?

SIR WILFRID. How the letter came into my possession is irrelevant.

ROMAINE. You stole it. You are a thief as well as a liar. Or did
some woman give it to you? Yes, I am right, am I not?

JUDGE. Kindly confine yourself to answering Counsel's questions.

ROMAINE. But I will not listen.

JUDGE. Proceed, Sir Wilfrid.

SIR WILFRID. So far you have only heard the opening phrases
of the letter. Am I to understand that you definitely deny
writing it?

ROMAINE. Of course I never wrote it. It is a forgery. It is an outrage that I should be forced to listen to a pack of lies – lies made up by a jealous woman.

SIR WILFRID. I suggest it is *you* who have lied. You have lied flagrantly and persistently in this Court and upon oath. And the reason *why* you have lied is made clear by – (*He taps the letter.*) this letter – written down by you in black and white.

ROMAINE. You are crazy. Why should I write down a lot of nonsense?

SIR WILFRID. Because a way had opened before you to freedom – and in planning to take that way, the fact that an innocent man would be sent to his death meant nothing to you. You have even included that final deadly touch of how you yourself managed accidentally to wound Leonard Vole with a ham knife.

ROMAINE. (*Carried away with fury*) I never wrote that. I wrote that he did it himself cutting the ham . . . (*Her voice dies away.*)

(*All eyes in Court turn on her.*)

SIR WILFRID. (*Triumphantly*) So you know what is in the letter – before I have read it.

ROMAINE. (*Casting aside all restraint*) Damn you! Damn you! Damn you!

LEONARD. (*Shouting*) Leave her alone. Don't bully her.

ROMAINE. (*Looking wildly around*) Let me get out of here – let me go (*She comes out of the witness box.*)

(*The* USHER *rises and restrains* ROMAINE).

JUDGE. Usher, give the witness a chair.

(ROMAINE *sinks on the stool Right of the table, sobs hysterically and buries her face in her hands. The* USHER *crosses and sits on the stool down Right.*)

Sir Wilfrid, will you now read the letter aloud so that the Jury can hear it.

SIR WILFRID. (*Reading*) 'My beloved Max. An extraordinary thing has happened. I believe all our difficulties may be ended. I can come to you without any fear of endangering the valuable work you are doing in this country. The old lady I told you about has been murdered and I think Leonard is suspected. He was there earlier that night and his fingerprints will be all over the place. Nine-thirty seems to be the time. Leonard was home by then, but his alibi depends on me – on *me*. Supposing I say he came home much later and that he had blood on his clothes -- he did have blood on his sleeve, because he cut his wrist at supper, so you see it would all fit in. I can even say he told me he killed her. Oh, Max, beloved! Tell me I can go ahead – it would be so wonderful to be free from playing the part of a loving, grateful wife. I know the Cause and the Party comes first, but if Leonard was convicted of murder, I could come to you safely and we could be together for always. Your adoring Romaine.'

JUDGE. Romaine Heilger, will you go back into the witness box?

(ROMAINE *rises and enters the witness box*).

You have heard that letter read. What have you to say?

ROMAINE. (*Frozen in defeat*) Nothing.

LEONARD. Romaine, tell him you didn't write it. I know you didn't write it.

ROMAINE. (*Turning and fairly spitting out the words*) Of course I wrote it.

SIR WILFRID. That, my lord, concludes the case for the defence.

JUDGE. Sir Wilfrid, have you any evidence as to whom these letters were addressed?

SIR WILFRID. My lord, they came into my possession anonymously, and there has been as yet no time to ascertain any further facts. It would seem likely that he came to this country illegally and is engaged on some subversive operations here . . .

ROMAINE. You will never find out who he is – never. I don't care what you do to me. You shall never know.

JUDGE. Do you wish to re-examine, Mr Myers?

(SIR WILFRID *sits*.)

MYERS. (*Rising rather unhappily*) Really, my lord, I find it somewhat difficult in view of these startling developments. (*To* RO- MAINE) Mrs Heilger, you are, I think, of a highly nervous temperament. Being a foreigner, you may not quite realize the responsibilities that lie upon you when you take the oath in an English Court of law. If you have been intimidated into admitting something that is not true, if you wrote a letter under stress or in some spirit of make-believe, do not hesitate to say so now.

ROMAINE. Must you go on and on torturing me? I wrote the letter. Now let me go.

MYERS. My lord, I submit that this witness is in such a state of agitation that she hardly knows what she is saying or admitting.

JUDGE. You may remember, Mr Myers, that Sir Wilfrid cautioned the witness at the time of her previous statement and impressed upon her the sacred nature of the oath she had taken.

(MYERS *sits*.)

Mrs Heilger, I wish to warn you that this is not the end of the matter. In this country you cannot commit perjury without being brought to account for it, and I may tell you that I have no doubt proceedings for perjury will shortly be taken against you. The sentence for perjury can be severe. You may stand down.

(ROMAINE *stands down. The* POLICEMAN *opens the door.* ROMAINE *crosses and exits. The* POLICEMAN *closes the door.*)

Sir Wilfrid, will you now address the Jury on behalf of the defence?

SIR WILFRID. (*Rising*) Members of the Jury, when truth is clearly evident it speaks for itself. No words of mine, I'm sure, can add to the impression made upon you by the straightforward story which the prisoner has told, and by the very wicked attempt to incriminate him, evidence of which you have just witnessed . . .

(*As* SIR WILFRID *speaks the LIGHTS dim to black-out. After a few seconds the LIGHTS come up. The* JURY *are out but are just re-entering the box.*)

CLERK. (*Rising*) Vole, stand up.

(LEONARD *rises.*)

Members of the Jury, are you all agreed upon your verdict?

FOREMAN. (*Standing*) We are.

CLERK. Do you find the prisoner, Leonard Vole, guilty or not guilty?

FOREMAN. Not guilty, my lord.

(*A buzz of approbation goes round the Court.*)

USHER. (*Rising and moving down Centre*) Silence!

JUDGE. Leonard Vole, you have been found not guilty of the murder of Emily French on October fourteenth. You are hereby discharged and are free to leave the Court. (*He rises.*)

(ALL *rise. The* JUDGE *bows to the Court and exits up Right, followed by the* ALDERMAN *and the* JUDGE'S CLERK.)

USHER. All persons who have anything further to do before my lady the Queen's justices of Oyer and Terminer and general gaol delivery for the jurisdiction of the Central Criminal Court may depart hence and give your attendance here again tomorrow morning at ten-thirty o'clock. God Save The Queen.

(*The* USHER, *the* JURY *and the* STENOGRAPHER *exit down Right. The* BARRISTERS, ASSISTANTS *and the* CLERK OF THE COURT *exit up Centre. The* WARDER *and the* POLICEMAN *exit up Left.* LEONARD *leaves the dock and crosses to* MAYHEW.)

MAYHEW. Congratulations, my boy!

LEONARD. I can't thank you enough.

MAYHEW. (*Tactfully indicating* SIR WILFRID) This is the man you've got to thank.

(LEONARD *crosses to Centre to meet* SIR WILFRID, *but comes face to face with* MYERS, *who glares at him, and exits up Centre.* SIR WILFRID *crosses to Right of* LEONARD.)

LEONARD. (*Turning to* SIR WILFRID) Thank you, sir (*His tone is less spontaneous than it was to* MAYHEW. *He dislikes* SIR WILFRID, *it seems.*) You – you've got me out of a very nasty mess.

SIR WILFRID. Nasty mess! Do you hear that, John? Your troubles are over now, my boy.

MAYHEW. (*Moving to Left of* LEONARD) But it was a near thing, you know.

LEONARD. (*Unwillingly*) Yes, I suppose it was.

SIR WILFRID. If we hadn't been able to break that woman down . . .

LEONARD. Did you have to go for her the way you did? It was

terrible the way she went to pieces. I can't believe . . .

SIR WILFRID. (*With all the force of his personality*) Look here, Vole, you're not the first young man I've known who's been so crazy over a woman that he's been blinded to what she's really like. That woman did her level best to put a rope round your neck.

MAYHEW. And don't you forget it.

LEONARD. Yes, but why? I can't see why. She's always seemed so devoted. I could have sworn she loved me – and yet all the time she was going with this other fellow. (*He shakes his head.*) It's unbelievable – there's something there I don't understand.

WARDER. (*Enters up Left and moves to Left of the table*) Just two or three minutes more, sir. We'll slip you out to a car by the side entrance.

LEONARD. Is there still a crowd?

(ROMAINE, *escorted by the* POLICEMAN, *enters up Left.*)

POLICEMAN. (*In the doorway.*) Better wait in here, ma'am. The crowd's in a nasty mood. I'd let them disperse before you try to leave.

ROMAINE. (*Moving down Left of the table*) Thank you.

(*The* POLICEMAN *and the* WARDER *exit up Left.* ROMAINE *crosses towards* LEONARD.)

SIR WILFRID. (*Intercepting* ROMAINE) No, you don't.

ROMAINE. (*Amused*) Are you protecting Leonard from me? Really, there's no need.

SIR WILFRID. You've done enough harm.

ROMAINE. Mayn't I even congratulate Leonard on being free?

SIR WILFRID. No thanks to you.

ROMAINE. And rich.

LEONARD. (*Uncertainly*) Rich?

MAYHEW. Yes, I think, Mr Vole, that you will certainly inherit a great deal of money.

LEONARD. (*Boyishly*) Money doesn't seem to mean so much after what I've been through. Romaine, I can't understand . . .

ROMAINE. (*Smoothly*) Leonard, I can explain.

SIR WILFRID. No!

(SIR WILFRID *and* ROMAINE *look at each other like antagonists.*)

ROMAINE. Tell me, do those words the Judge said mean that I shall – go to prison?

SIR WILFRID. You will quite certainly be charged with perjury and tried for it. You will probably go to prison.

LEONARD. (*Awkwardly*) I'm sure that – that everything will come right. Romaine, don't worry.

MAYHEW. Will you never see sense, Vole? Now we must consider practicalities – this matter of probate.

(MAYHEW *draws* LEONARD *down Right, where they murmur together.* SIR WILFRID *and* ROMAINE *remain, measuring each other.*)

SIR WILFRID. It may interest you to know that I took your measure the first time we met. I made up my mind then to beat you at your little game, and by God I've done it. I've got him off – in spite of you.

ROMAINE. In *spite* – of me.

SIR WILFRID. You don't deny, do you, that you did your best to hang him?

ROMAINE. Would they have believed me if I had said that he was at home with me that night, and did not go out? Would they?

SIR WILFRID. (*Slightly uncomfortable*) Why not?

ROMAINE. Because they would have said to themselves: this woman loves this man – she would say or do anything for him. They would have had sympathy with me, yes. But they would not have *believed* me.

SIR WILFRID. If you'd been speaking the truth they would.

ROMAINE. I wonder. (*She pauses.*) I did not want their sympathy – I wanted them to dislike me, to mistrust me, to be convinced that I was a liar. And then, when my lies were broken down – then they believed . . . (*In the Cockney accent of the* WOMAN *who visited* SIR WILFRID *at his office*) So now you know the whole story, Mister – like to kiss me?

SIR WILFRID. (*Thunderstruck*) My God!

ROMAINE. (*As herself*) Yes, the woman with the letters. I wrote those letters. I brought them to you. I was that woman. It wasn't *you* who won freedom for Leonard. It was *I*. And because of it I shall go to prison. (*Her eyes close.*) But at the end of it Leonard and I will be together again. Happy – loving each other.

SIR WILFRID. (*Moved*) My dear . . . But couldn't you trust me? We believe, you know, that our British system of justice upholds the truth. We'd have got him off.

ROMAINE. I couldn't risk it. (*Slowly*) You see, you *thought* he was innocent . . .

SIR WILFRID. (*With quick appreciation*) And you *knew* he was innocent. I understand.

ROMAINE. But you do not understand at all. *I* knew he was *guilty*.

SIR WILFRID. (*Thunderstruck*) But aren't you afraid?

ROMAINE. Afraid?

SIR WILFRID. Of linking your life with a murderer's.

ROMAINE. You don't understand – we love each other.

SIR WILFRID. The first time I met you I said you were a very remarkable woman – I see no reason to change my opinion. (*Crosses and exits up Centre.*)

WARDER. (*Off up Left*) It's no good going in there, Miss. It's all over.

(*There is a* COMMOTION *off up Left and then a* GIRL *comes running on up Left. She is a very young strawberry blonde with a crude, obvious appeal. She rushes to* LEONARD *through the QC's bench and meets him down Right Centre.*)

GIRL. Len, darling, you're free. (*She embraces him.*) Isn't it wonderful? They're trying to keep me out. Darling, it's been awful. I've been nearly crazy.

ROMAINE. (*With sudden violent harshness*) Leonard – who – is – this girl!

GIRL. (*To* ROMAINE, *defiantly*) I'm Len's girl. I know all about you. You're not his wife. Never have been. (*She crosses to Right of* ROMAINE.) You're years older than him, and you just got hold of him – and you've done your best to hang him. But that's all over now. (*She turns to* LEONARD.) We'll go abroad like you said on one of your cruises – to all those grand places. We'll have a wonderful time.

ROMAINE. Is – this – true? Is she your girl, Leonard?

LEONARD. (*Hesitates, then decides that the situation must be accepted*) Yes, she is.

(*The* GIRL *crosses above* LEONARD *to Right of him.*)

ROMAINE. After all I've done for you . . . What can *she* do for you that can compare with that?

LEONARD. (*Flinging off all disguise of manner, and showing coarse brutality*) She's fifteen years younger than you are. (*He laughs.*)

(ROMAINE *flinches as though struck.*)

(*He crosses to Right of* ROMAINE. *Menacingly*) I've got the money. I've been acquitted, and I can't be tried again, so don't go shooting off your mouth, or you'll just get *yourself* hanged as an accessory after the fact. (*He turns to the* GIRL *and embraces her.*)

ROMAINE. (*Picks up the knife from the table. Throwing her head back in sudden dignity*) No, that will not happen. I shall not be tried as an accessory after the fact. I shall not be tried for perjury. I shall be tried for murder – (*She stabs* LEONARD *in the back.*) the murder of the only man I ever loved.

(LEONARD *drops. The* GIRL *screams.* MAYHEW *bends over* LEONARD, *feels his pulse and shakes his head.*)

(*She looks up at the* JUDGE's *seat.*) Guilty, my lord.

CURTAIN

TOWARDS ZERO

Presented by Peter Saunders at the St James's Theatre, London, on 4th September 1956, with the following cast of characters:

(in the order of their appearance)

THOMAS ROYDE	*Cyril Raymond*
KAY STRANGE	*Mary Law*
MARY ALDIN	*Gillian Lind*
MATHEW TREVES	*Frederick Leister*
NEVILE STRANGE	*George Baker*
LADY TRESSILIAN	*Janet Barrow*
AUDREY STRANGE	*Gwen Cherrell*
TED LATIMER	*Michael Scott*
SUPERINTENDENT BATTLE, CID, *Scotland Yard*	*William Kendall*
INSPECTOR LEACH, *local* CID	*Max Brimmell*
PC BENSON	*Michael Nightingale*

The play directed by Murray MacDonald

Décor by Michael Weight

SYNOPSIS OF SCENES

The action of the play passes in the drawing-room at Gull's Point,
Lady Tressilian's house at Saltcreek, Cornwall

ACT I

SCENE 1   A morning in September
SCENE 2   After dinner, four days later

ACT II

SCENE 1   Early the following morning
SCENE 2   Two hours later

ACT III

SCENE 1   The next morning
SCENE 2   The same evening

Time: the present

ACT ONE

Scene I

SCENE: *The drawing-room at Gull's Point,* LADY TRESSILIAN's *house at Saltcreek, Cornwall. A morning in September. It is a large, very beautiful room, obviously belonging to somebody with exquisite taste. It has been furnished to combine elegance with comfort. There is a deep, arched alcove up Right with French windows opening on to a terrace overlooking the garden and tennis court. A large curved-bay window up Left, with a built-in windowseat, shows a view across the river to East-erhead Bay, with a large hotel on the cliff opposite. This window is slightly raised above the rest of the stage on a platform or rostrum. A door down Left leads to the other parts of the house. There is a chaise-longue Right Centre; easy chairs down Right and down Left and armchairs Left Centre and Right. In the alcove Right there is a bureau-bookcase with a carver chair, a small table and an upright chair. A waste-paper basket stands Left of the bureau. Down Right there is a small table, and on it a framed photograph of* AUDREY. *A standing work-basket is Right of the armchair Left Centre. On the rostrum in the bay window is a low butler's tray with a variety of drinks and glasses. A large circular coffee table stands Centre. A low bookcase, with a table-lamp on it, is Left of the window, and there is a corner table Right of the window. On the windowseat, at the Left end, is a portable record player with some loose records. At night the room is lit by electric-candle wall-brackets down Left and above and below the alcove Right. The switches are below the door down Left.*

When Curtain rises, the room is empty. An incongruous carpet sweeper stands negligently against the easy chair down Left. THOMAS ROYDE *enters immediately by the French windows. He is a bronzed middle-aged man, good-looking in a rugged way. He carries a suitcase and a set of golf clubs. As he reaches the up-stage end of the chaise, the door down Left is banged by someone as though rushing out of the room.* ROYDE *shrugs, moves to the window bay, puts his case and clubs at the Left end of it, opens the Centre sash of the window, then takes his pipe and pouch from his pocket and stands gazing out of the window and filling his pipe.* KAY STRANGE *rushes in Right. She is dressed in tennis kit and carries a towel. Clearly upset about something, she does not see* ROYDE, *tosses the towel on the chaise, goes to the table down Right and takes a cigarette from the box on it. As she does so, she sees the photograph of* AUDREY, *drops the cigarette, picks up the photograph, rips it from the frame, tears it in half and throws it angrily into the waste-paper basket.* ROYDE *turns sharply.* KAY *pauses a moment, then looks round and sees* ROYDE. *She looks at once like a guilty child and is for a moment too startled to say anything.*

KAY. Oh! Who are you?

ROYDE. (*Moving to Right of the rostrum*) I've just walked up from the bus stop. I'm . . .

KAY. (*Interrupting*) I know who you are. You're the man from Malaya.

ROYDE. (*Gravely*) Yes, I'm the man from Malaya.

KAY. (*Moving to the coffee table Centre*) I just – came in, to get a cigarette. (*She takes a cigarette from the box on the coffee table, crosses to the French windows and turns.*) Oh, hell, what's the good of explaining? What do I care what *you* think, anyway? (KAY *rushes out Right.* ROYDE *stares thoughtfully after her.* MARY ALDIN *enters Left. She is a dark-haired woman of about thirty-six, pleasant and noncommittal in manner and entirely competent. Nevertheless there is something faintly intriguing about her reserve.* ROYDE *turns to* MARY.)

MARY. (*Moving Left Centre*) Mr Royde? (ROYDE *moves to Right of* MARY *and shakes hands with her.*) Lady Tressilian is not down yet. I am Mary Aldin – Lady Tressilian's dogsbody.

ROYDE. Dogsbody?

MARY. The official term is secretary – but as I don't know shorthand and such talents I have are purely domestic, 'dogsbody' is a much better word.

ROYDE. I know all about you. Lady Tressilian told me in her Christmas letter what a wonderful difference you had made to her.

MARY. I've become very fond of her. She has a lot of personality.

ROYDE. (*Moving to Left of the chaise*) That's quite an understatement. (*He turns to* MARY.) How's her arthritis?

MARY. It makes her rather helpless, poor dear.

ROYDE. I'm sorry about that.

MARY. (*Moving on to the rostrum*) Can I offer you a drink?

ROYDE. No, thank you. (*He moves on to the Right end of the rostrum and looks out of the window.*) What's that great caravanserai over there?

MARY. That's the new *Easterhead Bay Hotel.* It was only finished last year – isn't it a horror? (*She closes the window.*) Lady Tressilian doesn't like this window opened, she's always afraid that someone might fall out. Yes, Easterhead Bay is a terrific resort, you know, nowadays. (*She crosses to the chaise, picks up* KAY*'s towel and tidies the cushions.*) I suppose when you came here as a boy there was nothing the other side of the estuary except a few fishermen's cottages. (*She pauses.*) You did come here for your school holidays, didn't you? (*She puts the towel tidily on the end of the chaise.*)

ROYDE. Yes, old Sir Mortimer used to take me out sailing – he was mad keen on sailing.

MARY. Yes. He was drowned out there.

ROYDE. Lady Tressilian saw it happen, I wonder she can go on living here.

MARY. I think she preferred to remain with her memories. But she won't have any boat kept here – she even had the boathouse pulled down.

ROYDE. So if I want to sail or go for a row, I've got to go to the ferry.

MARY. (*Crossing to the butler's tray*) Or cross to the Easterhead side. That's where all the boats are nowadays.

ROYDE. (*Moving above the chaise*) I hate changes. Always have. (*Rather self-consciously*) May I ask who else is staying here?

MARY. Old Mr Treves – you know him? (ROYDE *nods.*) And the Stranges.

ROYDE. (*Moving to Right of her*) The Stranges? You mean – Audrey Strange, Nevile's first wife?

MARY. Audrey, yes. But Nevile Strange and his – new wife are here, too.

ROYDE. Isn't that a bit odd?

MARY. Lady Tressilian thinks it very odd indeed.

ROYDE. Bit awkward – what? (MATHEW TREVES *enters by the French windows Right, fanning himself with an old-fashioned Panama hat. He is an elderly and distinguished lawyer of ripe experience and great shrewdness. He retired from his London firm some years ago and is now a keen observer of human nature. His voice is dry and precise.*)

TREVES. (*As he enters*) Rather too much glare on the terrace today . . . (*He sees* ROYDE.) Ah, Thomas. Nice to see you after all these years. (*He stands up Left of the chaise.*)

ROYDE. (*Moving to* TREVES) I'm very glad to be here. (*He shakes hands with* TREVES.)

MARY. (*Moving to* ROYDE*'s suitcase*) Shall I take your things up to your room?

ROYDE. (*Crossing quickly to* MARY) No, no, I can't let you do that. (*He picks up his suitcase and golf clubs.* MARY *leads the way to the door Left, sees the sweeper and picks it up.*)

MARY. (*With a vexed exclamation*) Really! Mrs Barrett . . . these daily women are impossible. It makes Lady Tressilian very angry when things are left all over the place.

ROYDE. (*Following* MARY *to the door Left*) I think my sudden arrival on the terrace frightened the poor woman. (*He looks towards* TREVES. TREVES *smiles.*)

MARY. Oh, I see. (MARY *and* ROYDE *exit Left.* TREVES *turns to the bureau, sees the torn photograph in the waste-paper basket, stoops with a little difficulty and picks up the pieces. His eyebrows rise and he makes a little sound like 'Tut, tut'.*)

KAY. (*Off Left; calling*) Where are you going to, Nevile?

NEVILE. (*Off Left*) Only into the house for a moment. (TREVES *puts the pieces of the photograph into the waste-paper basket.* NEVILE STRANGE *enters by the French windows Left. He wears tennis kit and carries the remains of a glass of lemonade. He crosses to the coffee table and puts the glass on it.*) Isn't Audrey here?

TREVES. No.

NEVILE. Where is she? Do you know?

TREVES. I have no idea.

KAY. (*Off, calling*) Nevile – Nevile. (TREVES *moves down Right of the chaise.*)

NEVILE. (*Frowning*) Oh, damn!

KAY. (*Off, nearer*) Nevile.

NEVILE. (*Crossing to the French windows and calling*) Coming – coming. (ROYDE *enters Left.*)

ROYDE. (*Moving to Left of the coffee table*) Nevile.

NEVILE. (*Moving to Right of the coffee table*) Hullo, Thomas. (*They shake hands above the coffee table.*) What time did you get here?

ROYDE. Just now.

NEVILE. Must be quite a long time since I saw you last. When was it you were home, three years ago?

ROYDE. Seven.

NEVILE. Good Lord, is it, really? How time flies.

KAY. (*Off*) Nevile!

NEVILE. (*Moving above the chaise*) All right, Kay. (KAY *enters by the French windows Right.*)

KAY. (*Moving to Right of* NEVILE) Why can't you come? Ted and I are waiting.

NEVILE. I just came to see if Audrey . . .

KAY. (*Turning away*) Oh, bother Audrey – we can get on quite well . . . (KAY *and* NEVILE *exit by the French windows Right. Their voices die away.*)

ROYDE. And who is Kay?

TREVES. (*Moving below the chaise to Right of the coffee table*) The present Mrs Nevile Strange. (LADY TRESSILIAN *enters Left.* MARY *assists her on.* LADY TRESSILIAN *uses a walking stick. She is a white-haired, aristocratic-looking woman, a little younger than* TREVES. MARY *carries* LADY TRESSILIAN'S *sewing.*) Good morning, Camilla.

LADY TRESSILIAN. Good morning, Mathew. (*She greets* ROYDE *affectionately.*) Well, Thomas, so here you are. I'm very glad to see you.

ROYDE. (*Rather shyly*) Very glad to be here. (MARY *puts the sewing in the work-box and arranges the cushion in the armchair Left Centre.*)

LADY TRESSILIAN. Tell me all about yourself.

ROYDE. (*Mumbling*) Nothing to tell.

LADY TRESSILIAN. (*Studying him*) You look exactly the same as you did at fourteen. That same boiled owl look. And no more conversation now than you had then. (TREVES *moves up Centre.* MARY *moves to the butler's tray.*)

ROYDE. Never had the gift of the gab.

LADY TRESSILIAN. Then it's time you learnt. Have some sherry? Mathew? Thomas?

ROYDE. Thank you. (MARY *pours two glasses of sherry.*)

LADY TRESSILIAN. (*Indicating the sofa*) Then go and sit down. Somebody's got to amuse me by bringing me all the gossip. (*She sits in the armchair Left Centre.*) Why can't you be more like Adrian? I wish you'd known his brother, Mary, a really brilliant young man, witty, amusing – (ROYDE *sits on the chaise.*) all the things that Thomas isn't. And don't go grinning at me, Thomas Royde, as though I were praising you. I'm scolding you.

ROYDE. Adrian was certainly the showman of our family.

MARY. (*Handing a glass of sherry to* TREVES) Did he – was he – killed in the war?

ROYDE. No, he was killed in a motor accident two years ago.

MARY. How dreadful! (*She hands a glass of sherry to* ROYDE.)

TREVES. The impossible way young people drive cars nowadays . . . (LADY TRESSILIAN *picks up her sewing.*)

ROYDE. In his case it was some fault in the steering. (*He takes his pipe from his pocket and looks at* LADY TRESSILIAN.) I'm so sorry, may I? (MARY *pours another glass of sherry.*)

LADY TRESSILIAN. I wouldn't know you without your pipe. But don't think you can just sit back and puff contentedly while you're here. You've got to exert yourself and *help*.

ROYDE. (*Surprised*) Help? (TREVES *perches himself on the up-stage end of the chaise.*)

LADY TRESSILIAN. We've got a difficult situation on our hands. Have you been told who's here? (MARY *takes the glass of sherry to* LADY TRESSILIAN. *To* MARY) No, no, much too early, pour it back into the decanter. (MARY *resignedly pours the glass of sherry into the decanter.*)

ROYDE. Yes, I've just heard.

LADY TRESSILIAN. Well, don't you think it's disgraceful?

ROYDE. Well . . .

TREVES. You'll have to be a little more explicit, Camilla.

LADY TRESSILIAN. I intend to be. When I was a girl such things did not happen. Men had their affairs, naturally, but they did *not* allow them to break up their married life.

TREVES. Regrettable though the modern point of view may be, one has to accept it, Camilla. (MARY *moves to the easy chair down Left and sits on the up-stage arm of it.*)

LADY TRESSILIAN. That's not the point. We were all delighted when Nevile married Audrey. Such a sweet gentle girl. (*To* ROYDE.) You were all in love with her – you, Adrian and Nevile. Nevile won.

ROYDE. Naturally. He always wins.

LADY TRESSILIAN. Of all the defeatist . . .

ROYDE. I don't blame her, Nevile had everything – good looks, first-class athlete – even had a shot at swimming the Channel.

TREVES. And all the kudos of that early Everest attempt – never stuck up about it.

ROYDE. *Mens sana in corpore sano.*

LADY TRESSILIAN. Sometimes I think that's the only bit of Latin you men ever learn in your expensive education.

TREVES. My dear Camilla, you must allow for its being invariably quoted by one's housemaster whenever he is slightly embarrassed.

LADY TRESSILIAN. Mary, I wish you wouldn't sit on the arms of chairs – you know how much I dislike it.

MARY. (*Rising*) Sorry, Camilla. (*She sits in the easy chair down Left.* TREVES *rises guiltily and quickly, then sits above* ROYDE *on the chaise.*)

LADY TRESSILIAN. Now where was I?

MARY. You were saying that Audrey married Nevile.

LADY TRESSILIAN. Oh, yes. Well, Audrey married Nevile and we were all delighted. Mortimer was particularly pleased, wasn't he, Mathew?

TREVES. Yes, yes.

LADY TRESSILIAN. And they were very happy together until this creature Kay came along; how Nevile could leave Audrey for a girl like Kay I simply cannot imagine.

TREVES. I can – I've seen it happen so often.

LADY TRESSILIAN. Kay is quite the wrong wife for Nevile, no background.

TREVES. But a singularly attractive young woman.

LADY TRESSILIAN. Bad stock, her mother was notorious all over the Riviera.

ROYDE. What for?

LADY TRESSILIAN. Never you mind. What an upbringing for a girl. Kay made a dead set at Nevile from the moment they met, and never rested until she got him to leave Audrey and go off with her. I blame Kay entirely for the whole thing.

TREVES. (*Rising and moving above the coffee table; fairly amused*) I'm sure you do. You're very fond of Nevile.

LADY TRESSILIAN. Nevile's a fool. Breaking up his marriage for a silly infatuation. It nearly broke poor Audrey's heart. (*To* ROYDE) She went to your mother at the Vicarage and practically had a nervous breakdown.

ROYDE. Er – yes – I know.

TREVES. When the divorce went through, Nevile married Kay.

LADY TRESSILIAN. If I had been true to my principles I should have refused to receive them here.

TREVES. If one sticks too rigidly to one's principles one would hardly see anybody.

LADY TRESSILIAN. You're very cynical, Mathew – but it's quite true. I've accepted Kay as Nevile's wife – though I shall never really like her. But I must say I was dumbfounded and very much upset, wasn't I, Mary?

MARY. Yes, you were, Camilla.

LADY TRESSILIAN. When Nevile wrote asking if he could come home with Kay, under the pretext, if you please, that it would be nice if Audrey and Kay could be friends – (*Scornfully*) friends – I said I couldn't entertain such a suggestion for a moment and that it would be very painful for Audrey.

TREVES. (*Putting his glass on the coffee table*) And what did he say to that?

LADY TRESSILIAN. He replied that he had already consulted Audrey and she thought it a good idea.

TREVES. And did Audrey think it a good idea?

LADY TRESSILIAN. Apparently, yes. (*She tosses a knot of silk to* MARY.) Unravel that.

MARY. Well, she said she did, quite firmly.

LADY TRESSILIAN. But Audrey is obviously embarrassed and unhappy. If you ask me, it's just Nevile being like Henry the Eighth.

ROYDE. (*Puzzled*) Henry the Eighth?

LADY TRESSILIAN. Conscience. Nevile feels guilty about Audrey and is trying to justify himself. (MARY *rises, moves above the armchair Left Centre and puts the silks in the work-basket.*) Oh! I don't understand *any* of this modern nonsense. (*To* MARY) Do you? (ROYDE *puts his glass on the coffee table.*)

MARY. In a way.

LADY TRESSILIAN. And you, Thomas?

ROYDE. Understand Audrey – but I don't understand Nevile. It's not like Nevile.

TREVES. I agree. Not like Nevile at all, to go looking for trouble. (MARY *transfers* ROYDE's *and* TREVES's *glasses to the butler's tray.*)

MARY. Perhaps it was Audrey's suggestion.

LADY TRESSILIAN. Oh, no. Nevile says it was entirely his idea.

MARY. Perhaps he thinks it was. (TREVES *looks sharply at* MARY.)

LADY TRESSILIAN. What a fool the boy is, bringing two women together who are both in love with him. (ROYDE *looks sharply at* LADY TRESSILIAN.) Audrey has behaved perfectly, but Nevile himself has paid far too much attention to her, and as a result Kay has become jealous, and as she has no kind of self-control, it is all most embarrassing – (*To* TREVES) isn't it? (TREVES, *gazing towards the French windows, does not hear.*) Mathew?

TREVES. There is undeniably a certain tension . . .

LADY TRESSILIAN. I'm glad you admit it. (*There is a knock on the door Left.*) Who's that?

MARY. (*Moving to the door Left*) Mrs Barrett, I expect, wanting to know something.

LADY TRESSILIAN. (*Irritably*) I wish you could teach these women that they only knock on *bedroom* doors. (*Mary exits Left.*) The last so-called butler we had actually whistled *Come into the garden, Maud,* as he served at table. (MARY *enters Left.*)

MARY. It's only about the lunch, Camilla. I'll see to it. (MARY *exits Left.*)

LADY TRESSILIAN. I don't know what I should do without Mary. She's so self-effacing that I sometimes wonder whether she *has* a self of her own.

TREVES. I know. She's been with you nearly two years now, but what's her background?

LADY TRESSILIAN. Her father was a professor of some kind, I

believe. He was an invalid and she nursed him for years. Poor Mary, she's never had any life of her own. And now, perhaps, it's too late. (*She rises and puts her sewing in the work-box.*)

TREVES. I wonder. (*He strolls to the French windows.*) They're still playing tennis. (ROYDE *rises, moves and stands behind* TREVES, *gazing off Right.*)

LADY TRESSILIAN. Nevile and Kay?

TREVES. No, Kay and that friend of hers from the *Easterhead Bay Hotel* – young Latimer.

LADY TRESSILIAN. That theatrical-looking young man. (*She moves to Left of the coffee table.*) Just the sort of friend she would have.

TREVES. One wonders what he does for a living.

LADY TRESSILIAN. Lives by his wits, I imagine.

TREVES. (*Moving slowly down Right*) Or by his looks. A decorative young man. (*Dreamily*) Interesting-shaped head. The last man I saw with a head shaped like that was at the Central Criminal Court – a case of brutal assault on an elderly jeweller.

LADY TRESSILIAN. Mathew! Do you mean to tell me . . .?

TREVES. (*Perturbed*) No, no, no, you misunderstand me. I am making no suggestion of any kind. I was only commenting on a matter of anatomical structure.

LADY TRESSILIAN. Oh, I thought . . .

TREVES. What reminded me of that was that I met a very old friend of mine this morning, Superintendent Battle of Scotland Yard. He's staying down here on holiday with his nephew, who's in the local police.

LADY TRESSILIAN. You and your interest in criminology. The truth is I am thoroughly jumpy – I feel the whole time as though something was going to happen. (*She moves on to the rostrum.*)

TREVES. (*Crossing and standing down Right of* LADY TRESSILIAN) Yes, there is a suggestion of gunpowder in the air. One little spark might set off an explosion.

LADY TRESSILIAN. Must you talk as though you were Guy Fawkes? Say something cheerful.

TREVES. (*Turning and smiling at her*) What can I say? 'Men have died from time to time, and worms have eaten them – but not for love.'

LADY TRESSILIAN. And he calls that cheerful. I shall go out on the terrace for a little. (TREVES *crosses to the French windows and looks off. She moves up Left of the chaise. To* ROYDE; *confidentially*) Don't make a fool of yourself a second time.

ROYDE. What do you mean?

LADY TRESSILIAN. You know quite well what I mean. Last time, you let Nevile walk off with Audrey under your nose.

ROYDE. (*Moving above the chaise*) Is it likely she'd have preferred me to Nevile?

LADY TRESSILIAN. (*Moving above the chaise*) She might have – if you'd asked her. (ROYDE *moves to Left of* LADY TRESSILIAN.) Are you going to ask her this time?

ROYDE. (*With sudden force*) You bet your life I am. (AUDREY *enters by the French windows. She is very fair and has an Undine-like look. There is something strange about her air of repressed emotion. With* ROYDE *she is natural and happy.*)

LADY TRESSILIAN. (*As* AUDREY *enters*) Thank God for that. (AUDREY, *with hands outstretched, crosses below* TREVES *and* LADY TRESSILIAN *to Right of* ROYDE.)

AUDREY. Thomas – dear Thomas. (ROYDE *takes* AUDREY's *hands.* LADY TRESSILIAN *looks for a moment at* ROYDE *and* AUDREY.)

LADY TRESSILIAN. Mathew, your arm. (TREVES *assists* LADY TRESSILIAN, *and exits with her by the French windows.*)

AUDREY. (*After a pause*) It's lovely to see you.

ROYDE. (*Shyly*) Good to see you.

AUDREY. (*Crossing below* ROYDE *to Left*) It's years since you've been home. Don't they give you any leave on rubber plantations?

ROYDE. I *was* coming home two years ago . . . (*He breaks off awkwardly.*)

AUDREY. Two years ago! And then you didn't.

ROYDE. My dear, you know – there were reasons.

AUDREY. (*Sitting in the armchair Left Centre, with affection*) Oh, Thomas – you look just the same as when we last met – pipe and all.

ROYDE. (*Moving to Left of the coffee table, after a pause*) Do I?

AUDREY. Oh, Thomas – I am so glad you've come back. Now at last I can talk to someone. Thomas – there's something wrong.

ROYDE. Wrong?

AUDREY. Something's changed about this place. Ever since I arrived I've felt there was something not quite right. Don't you feel there's something different? No – how can you, you've only just come. The only person who doesn't seem to feel it is Nevile.

ROYDE. Damn Nevile!

AUDREY. You don't like him?

ROYDE. (*With intensity*) I hate his guts – always have. (*He quickly recovers himself.*) Sorry.

AUDREY. I – didn't know . . .

ROYDE. Lots of things one – doesn't know – about people.

AUDREY. (*Thoughtfully*) Yes – lots of things.

ROYDE. Gather there's a spot of bother. What made you come here at the same time as Nevile and his new wife? Did you have to agree?

AUDREY. (*Rising and standing Left of the armchair Left Centre.*) Yes, Oh, I know you can't understand . . .

ROYDE. (*Moving to Right of the armchair Left Centre*) But I do understand. I know all about it. (AUDREY *looks doubtfully at* ROYDE.) I know exactly what you've been through – (*With meaning*) But it's all *past*, Audrey, it's *over*. You must forget the past and think of the future. (NEVILE *enters by the French windows and moves up Right of the chaise.*)

NEVILE. Hullo, Audrey, where have you been all the morning? (AUDREY *moves to Right of the easy chair down Left.* ROYDE *moves above the coffee table.*)

AUDREY. I haven't been anywhere particular.

NEVILE. I couldn't find you anywhere. What about coming down to the beach for a swim before lunch?

AUDREY. (*Crossing to the coffee table*) No, I don't think so. (*She looks among the magazines on the table.* ROYDE *moves on to the rostrum.*) Have you seen this week's *London Illustrated News*?

NEVILE. (*Moving to Right of* AUDREY) No. Come on – the water will be really warm today.

AUDREY. Actually, I told Mary I'd go into Saltington with her to shop.

NEVILE. Mary won't mind. (AUDREY *picks up a magazine. He takes her hand.*) Come on, Audrey.

AUDREY. No, really . . . (KAY *enters by the French windows.*)

NEVILE. (*As he sees* KAY) I'm trying to persuade Audrey to come bathing.

KAY. (*Moving to Right of the chaise*) Oh? And what does Audrey say?

AUDREY. Audrey says 'no'. (AUDREY *withdraws her hand from* NEVILE*'s and exits Left.*)

ROYDE. If you'll excuse me, I'll go and unpack. (ROYDE *pauses a moment by the bookshelves up Left, selects a book, then exits Left.*)

KAY. So that's that. Coming, Nevile?

NEVILE. Well, I'm not sure. (*He takes a magazine from the coffee table, sits on the chaise, leans back and puts his feet up.*)

KAY. (*Impatiently*) Well, make up your mind.

NEVILE. I'm not sure I won't just have a shower and laze in the garden.

KAY. It's a perfect day for bathing. Come on.

NEVILE. What have you done with the boyfriend?

KAY. Ted? I left him on the beach and came up to find you. You can laze on the beach. (*She touches his hair.*)

NEVILE. (*Moving her hand from his hair*) With Latimer, I suppose? (*He shakes his head.*) Doesn't appeal to me a lot.

KAY. You don't like Ted, do you?

NEVILE. Not madly. But if it amuses you to pull him around on a string . . .

KAY. (*Tweaking his ear*) I believe you're jealous.

NEVILE. (*Pushing her hand from his ear*) Of Latimer? Nonsense, Kay.

KAY. Ted's very attractive.

NEVILE. I'm sure he is. He has that lithe South American charm.

KAY. You needn't sneer. He's very popular with women.

NEVILE. Especially with the ones over fifty.

KAY. (*Pleased*) You are jealous.

NEVILE. My dear – I couldn't care less – he just doesn't count.

KAY. I think you're very rude about my friends. I have to put up with yours.

NEVILE. What do you mean by that?

KAY. (*Moving above the chaise to Right of the coffee table*) Dreary old Lady Tressilian and stuffy old Mr Treves and all the rest of them. (*She sits on the coffee table, facing* NEVILE.) Do you think I find them amusing? (*Suddenly*) Nevile, do we *have* to stay on here? Can't we go away – tomorrow? It's so boring . . .

NEVILE. We've only just come.

KAY. We've been here four days – four whole long days. *Do* let's go, Nevile, please.

NEVILE. Why?

KAY. I want to go. We could easily find some excuse. Please, darling.

NEVILE. Darling, it's out of the question. We came for a fortnight and we're going to stay a fortnight. You don't seem to understand. Sir Mortimer Tressilian was my guardian. I came here for holidays as a boy. Gull's Point was practically my home. Camilla would be terribly hurt. (*He smiles.*)

KAY. (*Rising and moving to the window up Left, impatiently*) Oh, all right, all right. I suppose we have to suck up to old Camilla, because of getting all that money when she dies.

NEVILE. (*Rising and moving on to the rostrum; angrily*) It's not a question of sucking up. I wish you wouldn't look at it like that. She's no control over the money. Old Mortimer left it in trust to come to me and my wife at her death. Don't you realize it's a question of *affection*?

KAY. Not with me, it isn't. She hates me.

NEVILE. Don't be stupid.

KAY. (*Moving to Left of the armchair Left Centre*) Yes, she does. She looks down that bony nose of hers at me, and Mary Aldin talks to me as though I were someone she'd just met on a train. They only have me here on sufferance. You don't seem to know what goes on.

NEVILE. They always seem to me to be very nice to you. (*He moves to the coffee table and throws the magazine on it.*) You imagine things.

KAY. Of course they're polite. But they know how to get under my skin all right. I'm an interloper. That's what they feel.

NEVILE. Well – I suppose that's only natural . . .

KAY. Oh, yes, I daresay it's quite natural. They're devoted to Audrey, aren't they? (*She turns and looks towards the door Left.*) Dear, well-bred, cool, colourless Audrey. Camilla has never forgiven me for taking Audrey's place. (*She turns, moves above the armchair Left Centre and leans on the back of it.*) I'll tell you something – Audrey gives me the creeps. You never know what she's thinking.

NEVILE. (*Sitting on the chaise*) Oh, nonsense, Kay, don't be absurd.

KAY. Audrey's never forgiven you for marrying me. Once or twice I've seen her looking at you – and the way she looked at you frightened me.

NEVILE. You're prejudiced, Kay. Audrey's been charming. No one could have been nicer.

KAY. It seems like that, but it isn't true. There's something behind it all. (*She runs above the chaise to Right of* NEVILE *and kneels beside him.*) Let's go away – at once – before it's too late.

NEVILE. Don't be melodramatic. I'm not going to upset old Camilla just because you work yourself up into a state about nothing at all.

KAY. It isn't nothing at all. I don't think you know the first thing about your precious Audrey. (LADY TRESSILIAN *and* TREVES *enter by the French windows.*)

NEVILE. (*Furiously*) She isn't my – precious Audrey. (LADY TRESSILIAN *moves above the chaise.*) ·

KAY. Isn't she? Anyone would think so, the way you follow her about. (*She sees* LADY TRESSILIAN.)

LADY TRESSILIAN. Are you going down to bathe, Kay?

KAY. (*Rising, nervously*) Yes – yes, I was.

LADY TRESSILIAN. Almost high tide. It ought to be very pleasant. (*She knocks her stick against the leg of the chaise.*) What about you, Nevile?

NEVILE. (*Sulkily*) I don't want to bathe.

LADY TRESSILIAN. (*To* KAY) Your friend, I think, is down there waiting for you. (KAY *hesitates a moment, then crosses and exits by the French window.* TREVES *moves down Right.*) Nevile, you're behaving very badly. You really must stand up when I come into the room. What's the matter with you – forgetting your manners?

NEVILE. (*Rising quickly*) I'm sorry.

LADY TRESSILIAN. (*Crossing to the armchair Left Centre*) You're making us all very uncomfortable. I don't wonder your wife is annoyed.

NEVILE. My wife? Audrey?

LADY TRESSILIAN. Kay is your wife now.

NEVILE. With your High Church principles I wonder you admit the fact.

LADY TRESSILIAN. (*Sitting in the armchair Left Centre*) Nevile, you are exceedingly rude. (NEVILE *crosses to Right of* LADY TRESSILIAN, *takes her hand and kisses her on the cheek.*)

NEVILE. (*With sudden disarming charm*) I'm very sorry, Camilla. Please forgive me. I'm so worried I don't know what I'm saying. (TREVES *sits in the easy chair down Right.*)

LADY TRESSILIAN. (*With affection*) My dear boy, what else could you expect with this stupid idea of being all friends together?

NEVILE. (*Wistfully*) It still seems to me the sensible way to look at things.

LADY TRESSILIAN. Not with two women like Audrey and Kay.

NEVILE. Audrey doesn't seem to care.

TREVES. How did the matter first come up, Nevile? (NEVILE *withdraws his hand from* LADY TRESSILIAN's *and moves down Left of the chaise.*)

NEVILE. (*Eagerly*) Well, I happened to run across Audrey in London, quite by chance, and she was awfully nice about things – didn't seem to bear any malice or anything like that. While I was talking to her the idea came to me how sensible it would be if – if she and Kay could be friends – if we could all get together. And it seemed to me that this was the place where it could happen quite naturally.

TREVES. You thought of that – all by yourself?

NEVILE. Oh, yes, it was all my idea. And Audrey seemed quite pleased and ready to try.

TREVES. Was Kay equally pleased?

NEVILE. Well – no – I had a spot of bother with Kay. I can't think why. I mean if anyone was going to object, you'd think it would be Audrey.

LADY TRESSILIAN. (*Rising*) Well, I'm an old woman. (TREVES *rises.*) Nothing people do nowadays seems to make any sense. (*She moves to the door Left.*)

TREVES. (*Crossing to the door Left*) One has to go with the times, Camilla. (*He opens the door.*)

LADY TRESSILIAN. I feel very tired. I shall rest before lunch. (*She turns to* NEVILE.) But you must behave yourself, Nevile. With or without reason, Kay is jealous. (*She emphasizes her following words by banging her stick on the carpet.*) I will not have these discordant scenes in my house. (*She speaks off Left.*) Ah, Mary – I shall lie down on the library sofa. (LADY TRESSILIAN *exits Left.* TREVES *closes the door.*)

NEVILE. (*Sitting on the chaise*) She speaks to me as though I were six.

TREVES. (*Moving up Right Centre and standing with his back to the audience*) At her age, she doubtless feels you *are* six.

NEVILE. (*Recovering his temper with an effort*) Yes, I suppose so. It must be ghastly to be old.

TREVES. (*After a slight pause; turning*) It has its compensations, I assure you. (*Drily*) There is no longer any question of emotional involvements.

NEVILE. (*Grinning*) That's certainly something. (*He rises and moves above the chaise to the French windows.*) I suppose I'd better go and make my peace with Kay. I really can't see, though, why she has to fly off the handle like this. Audrey might very well be jealous of *her*, but I can't see why she should be jealous of Audrey. Can you? (NEVILE *grins and exits by the French windows.* TREVES *thoughtfully strokes his chin for a moment or two, then goes to the waste-paper basket, takes out the pieces of the torn photograph and turns to the bureau to put the pieces into a pigeonhole.* AUDREY *enters Left, looking round rather cautiously for* NEVILE. *She carries a magazine.*)

AUDREY. (*Crossing to the coffee table; surprised*) What are you doing with my photograph? (*She puts the magazine on the table.*)

TREVES. (*Turning and holding out the pieces of the photograph*) It seems to have been torn.

AUDREY. Who tore it?

TREVES. Mrs Barrett, I suppose – that *is* the name of the woman in the cloth cap who cleans this room? I thought I would put it in here until it can be mended. (TREVES*'s eyes meet* AUDREY*'s for a moment, then he puts the pieces of the photograph in the bureau.*)

AUDREY. It wasn't Mrs Barrett, was it?

TREVES. I have no information – but I should think probably not.

AUDREY. Was it Kay?

TREVES. I told you – I have no information. (*There is a pause, during which* AUDREY *crosses to Right of the armchair Right.*)

AUDREY. Oh, dear, this is all very uncomfortable.

TREVES. Why did you come here, my dear?

AUDREY. I suppose because I always come here at this time. (*She crosses and stands below the armchair Left Centre.*)

TREVES. But with Nevile coming here, wouldn't it have been better to have postponed your visit?

AUDREY. I couldn't do that. I have a job, you know. I have to earn my living. I have two weeks' holiday and once that is arranged I can't alter it.

TREVES. An interesting job?

AUDREY. Not particularly, but it pays quite well.

TREVES. (*Moving to Right of the coffee table*) But, my dear Audrey, Nevile is a very well-to-do man. Under the terms of your divorce he has to make suitable provision for you.

AUDREY. I have never taken a penny from Nevile. I never shall.

TREVES. Quite so. Quite so. Several of my clients have taken that point of view. It has been my duty to dissuade them. In the end, you know, one must be guided by common sense. You have hardly any money of your own, I know. It is only just and right that you should be provided for suitably by Nevile, who can well afford it. Who were your solicitors, because I could . . .

AUDREY. (*Sitting in the armchair Left Centre*) It's nothing to do with solicitors. I won't take anything from Nevile – anything at all.

TREVES. (*Eyeing her thoughtfully*) I see – you feel strongly – very strongly.

AUDREY. If you like to put it that way, yes.

TREVES. Was it really Nevile's idea to come here all together?

AUDREY. (*Sharply*) Of course it was.

TREVES. But you agreed?

AUDREY. I agreed. Why not?

TREVES. It hasn't turned out very well, has it?

AUDREY. That's not my fault.

TREVES. No, it isn't your fault – ostensibly.

AUDREY. (*Rising*) What do you mean?

TREVES. I was wondering . . .

AUDREY. You know, Mr Treves, sometimes I think I'm just a little frightened of you.

TREVES. Why should you be?

AUDREY. I don't know. You're a very shrewd observer. I sometimes . . . (MARY *enters Left.*)

MARY. Audrey, will you go to Lady Tressilian? She's in the library.

AUDREY. Yes. (AUDREY *crosses and exits Left.* TREVES *sits on the chaise.* MARY *goes to the butler's tray and collects the dirty sherry glasses.*)

TREVES. Miss Aldin, who do you think is behind this plan of meeting here?

MARY. (*Moving to Right of the butler's tray*) Audrey.

TREVES. But why?

MARY. (*Moving to Left of* TREVES) I suppose – he still cares for him.

TREVES. You think it's that?

MARY. What else can it be? He's not really in love with Kay, you know.

TREVES. (*Primly*) These sudden passionate infatuations are very often not of long duration.

MARY. You'd think Audrey would have more pride.

TREVES. In my experience, pride is a word often on women's lips – but they display little sign of it where love affairs are concerned.

MARY. (*With bitterness*) Perhaps. I wouldn't know. (*She looks towards the French windows.*) Excuse me. (MARY *exits Left.* ROYDE *enters by the French windows. He carries a book.*)

TREVES. Ah, Thomas, have you been down to the ferry?

ROYDE. (*Crossing to Centre*) No, I've been reading a detective story. Not very good. (*He looks down at the book.*) Always seems to me these yarns begin in the wrong place. Begin with the murder. But the murder's not really the beginning.

TREVES. Indeed? Where would you begin?

ROYDE. As I see it, the murder is the end of the story. (*He sits in the armchair Left Centre.*) I mean, the real story begins long before – years before, sometimes. Must do. All the causes and events that bring the people concerned to a certain place on a certain day at a certain time. And then, over the top – zero hour.

TREVES. (*Rising*) That is an interesting point of view.

ROYDE. (*Apologetically*) Not very good at explaining myself, I'm afraid.

TREVES. (*Moving above the coffee table*) I think you've put it very clearly, Thomas. (*He uses the coffee table as a globe.*) All sorts of people converging towards a given spot and hour – all going towards zero. (*He pauses briefly.*) Towards Zero. (TREVES *looks at* ROYDE, *and the LIGHTS fade to black-out, as – the Curtain falls.*)

CURTAIN

Scene II

SCENE: *The same. After dinner, four days later. When Curtain rises, the lights are on. The curtains of the bay window are half closed. The French windows are open, the curtains undrawn. The night is very warm, sultry and cloudy.* KAY *is seated on the chaise, smoking a cigarette. She is in evening dress and looks rather sulky and bored.* TED LATIMER *is standing on the rostrum, gazing out of the window. He is a very dark, good-looking man of about twenty-six. His dinner suit fits him a shade too well.*

KAY. (*After a pause*) This is what I call a wildly hilarious evening, Ted.

LATIMER. (*Turning*) You should have come over to the hotel as I suggested. (*He moves to the down-stage edge of the rostrum.*) They've got a dance on. The band's not so hot, but it's fun.

KAY. I wanted to, but Nevile wasn't keen.

LATIMER. So you behaved like a dutiful wife.

KAY. Yes – and I've been rewarded by being bored to death.

LATIMER. The fate of most dutiful wives. (*He moves to the record player on the windowseat.*) Aren't there any dance records? We could at least dance.

KAY. There's nothing like that *here*. Only Mozart and Bach – all classical stuff.

LATIMER. (*Moving to the coffee table*) Oh, well – at least we've been spared the old battleaxe tonight. (*He takes a cigarette from the box.*) Doesn't she ever appear at dinner, or did she just shirk it because I was there? (*He lights his cigarette.*)

KAY. Camilla always goes to bed at seven. She's got a groggy heart or something. She has her dinner sent up on a tray.

LATIMER. Not what you'd call a gay life.

KAY. (*Rising abruptly*) I hate this place. (*She moves below the chaise, then up Right of it.*) I wish to God we'd never come here.

LATIMER. (*Moving to Left of her*) Steady, honey. What's the matter?

KAY. I don't know. (*She crosses and stands below the armchair Left Centre.*) It's just – sometimes I get – scared.

LATIMER. (*Moving to Right of the coffee table*) That doesn't sound like you, Kay.

KAY. (*Recovering*) It doesn't, does it? But there's something queer going on. I don't know what, but I'll swear that Audrey's behind it all.

LATIMER. It was a damn silly idea of Nevile's – coming here with you at the same time as his ex-wife.

KAY. (*Sitting in the armchair Left Centre*) I don't think it *was* his idea. I'm convinced *she* put him up to it.

LATIMER. Why?

KAY. I don't know – to cause trouble probably.

LATIMER. (*Moving to* KAY *and touching her arm*) What *you* want is a drink, my girl.

KAY. (*Moving his hand from her arm; irritably*) I don't want a drink and I'm not your girl.

LATIMER. You would have been if Nevile hadn't come along. (*He moves to the butler's tray and pours two glasses of whisky and soda.*) Where *is* Nevile, by the way?

KAY. I've no idea.

LATIMER. They're not a very sociable crowd, are they? Audrey's out on the terrace talking to old Treves, and that fellow Royde's strolling about the garden all by himself, puffing at that eternal pipe of his. Nice, cheery lot.

KAY. (*Crossly*) I wouldn't care a damn if they were all at the bottom of the sea – except Nevile.

LATIMER. I should have felt much happier, darling, if you'd included Nevile. (*He picks up the drinks and takes one to* KAY.) You drink that, my sweet. You'll feel much better. (KAY *takes her drink and sips it.*)

KAY. God, it's strong.

LATIMER. More soda?

KAY. No, thanks. I wish you wouldn't make it so clear you don't like Nevile.

LATIMER. Why should I like him? He's not my sort. (*Bitterly*) The ideal Englishman – good at sport, modest, good-looking, always the little pukka sahib. Getting everything he wants all along the line – even pinched my girl.

KAY. I wasn't your girl.

LATIMER. (*Moving above the coffee table*) Yes, you were. If I'd been as well off as Nevile . . .

KAY. I didn't marry Nevile for his money.

LATIMER. Oh, I know, and I understand – Mediterranean nights and dewy-eyed romance . . .

KAY. I married Nevile because I fell in love with him.

LATIMER. I'm not saying you didn't, my sweet, but his money helped you to fall.

KAY. Do you *really* think that?

LATIMER. (*Moving up Centre*) I try to – it helps soothe my injured vanity.

KAY. (*Rising and moving to Left of him*) You're rather a dear, Ted – I don't know what I should do without you, sometimes.

LATIMER. Why try? I'm always around. You should know that by this time. The faithful swain – or should it be swine? Probably depends which you happen to be – the wife or the husband. (*He kisses* KAY*'s shoulder.* MARY *enters Left. She wears a plain dinner frock.* KAY *moves hastily on to the rostrum up Left.*)

MARY. (*Pointedly*) Have either of you seen Mr Treves? Lady Tressilian wants him.

LATIMER. He's out on the terrace, Miss Aldin.

MARY. Thank you, Mr Latimer. (*She closes the door.*) Isn't it stifling? I'm sure there's going to be a storm. (*She crosses to the French windows.*)

LATIMER. I hope it holds off until I get back to the hotel. (*He moves to Left of* MARY *and glances off.*) I didn't bring a coat. I'll get soaked to the skin going over in the ferry if it rains.

MARY. I daresay we could find you an umbrella if necessary, or Nevile could lend you his raincoat. (MARY *exits by the French windows.*)

LATIMER. (*Moving up Centre*) Interesting woman, that – bit of a dark horse.

KAY. I feel rather sorry for her. (*She moves to the armchair Left Centre, sits and sips her drink.*) Slaving for that unpleasant old woman – and she won't get anything for it, either. All the money comes to me and Nevile.

LATIMER. (*Moving to Right of* KAY) Perhaps she doesn't know that.

KAY. That would be rather funny. (*They laugh.* AUDREY *and* TREVES *enter by the French windows.* TREVES *is wearing an old-fashioned dinner suit.* AUDREY *is in evening dress. She notices* LATIMER *and* KAY *together, then moves below the chaise.* TREVES *stops in the doorway and speaks over his shoulder.*)

TREVES. I shall *enjoy* a little gossip with Lady Tressilian, Miss Aldin. With, perhaps, the remembering of a few old scandals. A touch of malice, you know, adds a certain savour to conversation. (*He crosses to the door Left.*) Doesn't it, Audrey?

AUDREY. She chooses the person she wants and summons them by a kind of Royal Command.

TREVES. Very aptly put, Audrey. I am always sensible of the royal touch in Lady Tressilian's manner. (TREVES *exits Left.*)

AUDREY. (*Listlessly*) It's terribly hot, isn't it? (*She sits on the chaise.*)

LATIMER. (*With a step towards the butler's tray*) Would you – like a drink?

AUDREY. (*Shaking her head*) No, thank you. I think I shall go to bed very soon. (*There is a short silence.* NEVILE *enters Left. He is wearing a dinner suit and is carrying a magazine.*)

KAY. What *have* you been doing all this time, Nevile?

NEVILE. I had a couple of letters to write – thought I might as well get 'em off my chest.

KAY. (*Rising*) You might have chosen some other time. (*She moves to the butler's tray and puts her glass on it.*)

NEVILE. (*Crossing and standing above the coffee table*) Better the hour, better the deed. By the way, here's the *Illustrated News*. Somebody wanted it.

KAY. (*Holding out her hand*) Thank you, Nevile.

AUDREY. (*At almost the same moment*) Oh! Thank you, Nevile. (*She holds out her hand.* NEVILE *hesitates between them, smiling.*)

KAY. (*With a slight note of hysteria*) I want it. Give it to me.

AUDREY. (*Withdrawing her hand; slightly confused*) Oh, sorry. I thought you were speaking to me, Nevile. (NEVILE *hesitates for a moment, then holds out the magazine to* AUDREY.)

NEVILE. (*Quietly*) Here you are, Audrey.

AUDREY. Oh, but I . . .

KAY. (*In suppressed fury, and almost crying*) It is stifling in here. (*She moves quickly to the coffee table, picks up her evening bag and rushes below the chaise to the French windows.*) Let's go out in the air, Ted. I can't stand being cooped up in this lousy hole any longer. (KAY *almost stumbles as she exits by the French windows.* LATIMER, *with an angry look at* NEVILE, *follows* KAY *off.* NEVILE *tosses the magazine on to the coffee table.*)

AUDREY. (*Rising; reproachfully*) You shouldn't have done that, Nevile.

NEVILE. Why not?

AUDREY. (*Crossing below the coffee table and standing down Left*) It was stupid. You'd better go after Kay and apologize.

NEVILE. I don't see why I should apologize.

AUDREY. I think you'd better. You were very rude to your wife. (MARY *enters by the French windows and stands above the chaise.*)

NEVILE. (*In a low voice*) You're my wife, Audrey. You always will be. (*He sees* MARY.) Ah – Miss Aldin – are you going up to Lady Tressilian? (AUDREY *moves on to the Left end of the rostrum.*)

MARY. (*Crossing to Left Centre*) Yes – when Mr Treves comes down. (ROYDE *enters by the French windows and stands Right of the chaise.* NEVILE *stares for a moment at* ROYDE, *then exits by the French windows. Wearily*) Oh, dear! I don't think I've ever felt so tired in my life. If Lady Tressilian's bell rings tonight, I'm quite certain I shall never hear it. (*She sits in the armchair Left Centre.*)

AUDREY. (*Turning and moving to the down-stage edge of the rostrum*) What bell?

MARY. It rings in my room – in case Lady Tressilian should want anything in the night. It's one of those old-fashioned bells – on a spring and worked with a wire. It makes a ghastly jangle, but Lady Tressilian insists that it's more reliable than electricity. (*She yawns.*) Excuse me – it's this dreadful sultry weather, I think.

AUDREY. You ought to go to bed, Mary. You look worn out.

MARY. I shall – as soon as Mr Treves has finished talking to Lady Tressilian. Then I shall tuck her up for the night and go to bed myself. Oh, dear. It's been a very trying day. (LATIMER *enters by the French windows and moves down Right.*)

ROYDE. It certainly has.

AUDREY. (*After a look at* LATIMER) Thomas! Let's go on to the terrace. (*She crosses to the French windows.*)

ROYDE. (*Moving to* AUDREY) Yes – I want to tell you about a detective story I've been reading . . . (AUDREY *and* ROYDE *exit by the French windows. There is a pause, as* LATIMER *looks after* ROYDE *and* AUDREY *for a moment.*)

LATIMER. You and I, Miss Aldin, seem to be the odd men out. We must console each other. (*He moves to the butler's tray.*) Can I get you a drink?

MARY. No, thank you.

LATIMER. (*Pouring a drink for himself*) One conjugal reconciliation in the rose garden, one faithful swain nerving himself to pop the question. Where do we come in? Nowhere. We're the outsiders. (*He moves to the down-stage edge of the rostrum and raises his glass.*) Here's to the outsiders – and to hell with all those inside the ringed fence. (*He drinks.*)

MARY. How bitter you are.

LATIMER. So are you.

MARY. (*After a pause*) Not really.

LATIMER. (*Moving below the coffee table to Right of it*) What's it like, fetching and carrying, running up and down stairs, endlessly waiting on an old woman?

MARY. There are worse things.

LATIMER. I wonder. (*He turns and looks towards the terrace.*)

MARY. (*After a pause*) You're very unhappy.

LATIMER. Who isn't?

MARY. Have – (*She pauses.*) you always been in love with Kay?

LATIMER. More or less.

MARY. And she?

LATIMER. (*Moving up Right Centre*) I thought so – until Nevile came along. Nevile with his money and his sporting record. (*He moves to Left of the chaise.*) I could go climbing in the Himalayas if I'd ever had the cash.

MARY. You wouldn't want to.

LATIMER. Perhaps not. (*Sharply*) What do you want out of life?

MARY. (*Rising; after a pause*) It's almost too late.

LATIMER. But not quite.

MARY. No – not quite. (*She moves on to the rostrum.*) All I want is a little money – not very much – just enough.

LATIMER. Enough for what?

MARY. Enough to have some sort of life of my own before it's too late. I've never had anything.

LATIMER. (*Moving to Right of* MARY) Do you hate them, too, those inside the fence?

MARY. (*Violently*) Hate them – I . . . (*She yawns.*) No – no – I'm too tired to hate anybody. (TREVES *enters Left.*)

TREVES. Ah, Miss Aldin, Lady Tressilian would like you to go to her now if you will be so kind. I think she's feeling sleepy.

MARY. That's a blessing. Thank you, Mr Treves. I'll go up at once. (*She crosses to the door Left.*) I shan't come down again, so I'll say good night now. Good night, Mr Latimer. Good night, Mr Treves.

LATIMER. Good night. (MARY *exits Left.* TREVES *moves on to the left end of the rostrum.*) I must be running along myself. With luck I shall get across the ferry and back to the hotel before the storm breaks. (*He moves above the chaise.* ROYDE *enters by the French windows.*)

ROYDE. Are you going, Latimer? Would you like a raincoat?

LATIMER. No, thanks, I'll chance it.

ROYDE. (*Moving on to the rostrum*) Hell of a storm coming.

TREVES. Is Audrey on the terrace?

ROYDE. I haven't the faintest idea. (*He crosses to the door Left.*) I'm for bed. Good night. (ROYDE *exits Left. There is a flash of LIGHT-NING, and a low rumble of THUNDER is heard off.*)

LATIMER. (*With malice*) It would seem that the course of true love has not run smoothly. Was that thunder? Some way away still – (*He moves to the French windows.*) but I think I'll make it.

TREVES. I'll come with you and bolt the garden gate. (*He crosses to the French windows.* LATIMER *and* TREVES *exit by the French windows.*)

AUDREY. (*Off; to* LATIMER) Good night. (AUDREY *enters rather quickly by the French windows. There is a flash of LIGHTNING and a rumble of THUNDER.* AUDREY *stands for a moment looking around the room, then moves slowly on to the rostrum, sits on the window-seat and looks out at the night.* NEVILE *enters by the French windows and moves above the chaise.*)

NEVILE. Audrey.

AUDREY. (*Rising quickly and moving to the Left end of the rostrum.*) I'm going to bed, Nevile. Good night.

NEVILE. (*Moving on to the rostrum*) Don't go yet. I want to talk to you.

AUDREY. (*Nervously*) I think you'd better not.

NEVILE. (*Moving to Right of her*) I must. I've got to. Please listen to me, Audrey.

AUDREY. (*Backing to the Left wall of the window bay*) I'd rather you didn't.

NEVILE. That means you know what I'm going to say. (AUDREY *does not reply.*) Audrey, can't we go back to where we were? Forget everything that has happened?

AUDREY. (*Turning a little*) Including – Kay?

NEVILE. Kay will be sensible.

AUDREY. What do you mean by – sensible?

NEVILE. (*Eagerly*) I shall tell her the truth – that you are the only woman I've ever loved. That *is* the truth, Audrey. You've got to believe that.

AUDREY. (*Desperately*) You loved Kay when you married her.

NEVILE. My marriage to Kay was the biggest mistake I ever made. I realize now what a damned fool I've been. I . . . (KAY *enters by the French windows.*)

KAY. (*Moving to Right Centre*) Sorry to interrupt this touching scene, but I think it's about time I did.

NEVILE. (*Moving to Centre of the rostrum.*) Kay, listen . . .

KAY. (*Furiously*) Listen! I've heard all I want to hear – too much.

AUDREY. (*With relief*) I'm going to bed. (*She moves to the door Left*) Good night.

KAY. (*Crossing to Right of* AUDREY) That's right. Go to bed! You've done all the mischief you wanted to do, haven't you? But you're not going to get out of it as easily as all that. I'll deal with you after I've had it out with Nevile.

AUDREY. (*Coldly*) It's no concern of mine. Good night. (AUDREY *exits Left. There is a flash of LIGHTNING and a peal of THUNDER off.*)

KAY. (*Looking after* AUDREY) Of all the damned, cool . . .

NEVILE. (*Moving to Right of the coffee table.*) Look here, Kay, Audrey had absolutely nothing to do with this. It's not her fault. Blame me if you like . . .

KAY. (*Working herself up*) And I do like. What sort of man do you think you are? (*She turns to* NEVILE. *Her voice rises.*) You leave your wife, come bald-headed after me, get your wife to divorce you. Crazy about me one minute, tired of me the next. Now I suppose you want to go back to that – (*She looks towards the door Left.*) whey-faced, mewling, double-crossing little cat . . .

NEVILE. (*Angrily*) Stop that, Kay.

KAY. (*Moving on to the rostrum*) That's what she is. A crafty, cunning, scheming little . . .

NEVILE. (*Moving to* KAY *and gripping her arms*) Stop it!

KAY. (*Releasing herself*) Leave me alone! (*She moves slowly to Left of the chaise.*) What the hell *do* you want?

NEVILE. (*Turning and facing up stage*) I can't go on. I'm every kind of worm you like to call me. But it's no good, Kay. I can't go on. (KAY *sits on the chaise. He turns.*) I think – really – I must have loved Audrey all the time. I've only just realized it. My love for you was – was a kind of madness. But it's no good – you and I don't *belong*. It's better to cut our losses. (*He moves above the chaise to Right of it.*)

KAY. (*In a deceptively quiet voice*) What exactly are you suggesting, Nevile?

NEVILE. We can get a divorce. You can divorce me for desertion.

KAY. You'd have to wait three years for it.

NEVILE. I'll wait.

KAY. And then, I suppose, you'll ask dear, sweet, darling Audrey to marry you all over again? Is *that* the idea?

NEVILE. If she'll have me.

KAY. She'll have you all right. And where do I come in?

NEVILE. Naturally, I'll see you're well provided for.

KAY. (*Losing control of herself*) Cut out the bribes. (*She rises and moves to* NEVILE.) Listen to me, Nevile. I'll *not* divorce you. (*She beats her hands against his chest.*) You fell in love with me and you married me and I'm not going to let you go back to the sly little bitch who's got her hooks into you again.

NEVILE. (*Throwing* KAY *on to the chaise*) Shut up, Kay. For God's sake. You can't make this kind of scene here.

KAY. She meant this to happen. It's what she's been playing for. She's probably gloating over her success now. But she's not going to bring it off. You'll see what I can do. (*She flings herself on the chaise in a paroxysm of hysterical sobbing.* NEVILE *gives a despairing gesture.* TREVES *enters by the French windows and stands watching. At the same moment there is a brilliant flash of LIGHTNING, a rolling peal of THUNDER, and the storm bursts as – the Curtain falls.*)

CURTAIN

ACT TWO

Scene I

SCENE: *The same. Early the following morning.*

When Curtain rises, it is a fine morning with the sun streaming in through the bay window. The French windows are open. The butler's tray has been removed. The room is empty. ROYDE *enters by the French windows. He is sucking at his pipe, which appears to have become stopped up. He looks around for an ashtray, sees one on the coffee table, moves to it and knocks out the ashes from his pipe. Finding it is still stopped up, he takes a penknife from his pocket and gently probes the bowl.* TREVES *enters down Left.*

TREVES. Good morning, Thomas.

ROYDE. (*Moving above the coffee table*) 'Morning. Going to be another lovely day by the look of it.

TREVES. Yes. (*He goes on to the Left end of the rostrum and looks out of the window.*) I thought possibly the storm might have broken up the spell of fine weather, but it has only removed that oppressive heat – which is all to the good. (*He moves to the Right end of the rostrum.*) You've been up for hours as usual, I presume?

ROYDE. Since just after six. Been for a walk along the cliffs. Only just got back, as a matter of fact.

TREVES. Nobody else appears to be about yet. Not even Miss Aldin.

ROYDE. Um.

TREVES. Possibly she is fully occupied attending to Lady Tressilian. I should imagine she may be rather upset after that unfortunate incident last night. (*He moves to Left of the chaise.*)

ROYDE. (*Blowing down his pipe*) Bit of a rumpus, wasn't there?

TREVES. (*Moving down Right*) You have a positive genius for understatement, Thomas. That unpleasant scene between Nevile
and Kay . . .

ROYDE. (*Surprised*) Nevile and *Kay*? The row *I* heard was between
Nevile and Lady Tressilian.

TREVES. (*Moving Right of the chaise.*) When was this?

ROYDE. Must have been about twenty past ten. They were going at
it hammer and tongs. Couldn't help hearing. My room's practically opposite hers, you know.

TREVES. (*Moving above the chaise; troubled*) Dear, dear, this is news to
me.

ROYDE. Thought that was what you meant.

TREVES. (*Moving to Right of* ROYDE) No, no, I was referring to a
most distressing scene that took place in here earlier, to part of
which I was a reluctant witness. That unfortunate young woman – er – Kay had a fit of violent hysterics.

ROYDE. What was the row about?

TREVES. I'm afraid it was Nevile's fault.

ROYDE. That doesn't surprise me. He's been behaving like a damn
fool. (*He moves on to the rostrum.*)

TREVES. I entirely agree. His conduct has been most reprehensible.
(*He sighs and sits on the chaise.*)

ROYDE. Was – Audrey mixed up in the row?

TREVES. She was the cause of it. (KAY *enters quickly Left. She looks
subdued and tired. She carries her handbag.*)

KAY. Oh! Good – good morning.

TREVES. (*Rising*) Good morning, Kay.

ROYDE. Good morning.

KAY. (*Moving Left Centre; nervous and ill at ease*) We're – we're the only
ones up, aren't we?

TREVES. I think so. I haven't seen anyone else. I breakfasted in – er
– solitary state.

ROYDE. Haven't had mine yet. Think I'll go and hunt some up. (*To
KAY*) Have you had breakfast?

KAY. No. I've only just come down. I – I don't want any breakfast. I
feel like hell.

ROYDE. Um – could eat a house, myself. (*He crosses below* KAY *to the
door Left.*) See you later. (ROYDE *exits Left.*)

KAY. (*With a step or two towards* TREVES, *after a slight pause*) Mr

Treves – I – I'm afraid I behaved – rather badly last night.

TREVES. It was very natural that you should be upset.

KAY. I lost my temper and I said a lot of – of foolish things.

TREVES. We are all apt to do that at times. You had every provocation. Nevile was, in my opinion, very much to blame.

KAY. He was led into it. Audrey's been determined to cause trouble between Nevile and me ever since we came here.

TREVES. (*Moving above the coffee table*) I don't think you're being quite fair to her.

KAY. She planned this, I tell you. She knows that Nevile's always – always felt guilty at the way he treated her.

TREVES. (*Moving to Right of* KAY) No, no, I'm sure you're wrong.

KAY. No, no, I'm not wrong. You see, Mr Treves, I went over it all in the night, and Audrey thought that if she could get us all here together and – (*She crosses to Right of the coffee table.*) and pretend to be friendly and forgiving, that she could get him back. She's worked on his conscience. Pale and aloof – creeping about like a – like a grey ghost. She knew what effect *that* would have on Nevile. He's always reproached himself because he thought he'd treated her badly. (*She sits on the chaise.*) Right from the beginning – or nearly the beginning – Audrey's shadow has been between us. Nevile couldn't quite forget about her – she was always there at the back of his mind.

TREVES. You can hardly blame her for that.

KAY. Oh, don't you *see*? She *knew* how Nevile felt. She *knew* what the result would be if they were thrown together again.

TREVES. I think you are giving her credit for more cunning than she possesses.

KAY. You're all on her side – all of you.

TREVES. My dear Kay!

KAY. (*Rising*) You'd *like* to see Nevile go back to Audrey. I'm the interloper – I don't *belong* – Nevile said so last night and he was right. Camilla's always disliked me – she's put up with me for Nevile's sake. I'm supposed to see everyone's point of view but my own. What I feel or think doesn't matter. If *my* life is all smashed up it's just too bad, but it doesn't matter. It's only *Audrey* who matters.

TREVES. No, no, no.

KAY. (*Her voice rising*) Well, she's not going to smash up my life. I don't care what I do to stop it, but I will. I'll make it impossible for Nevile to go back to her. (NEVILE *enters Left.*)

NEVILE. (*Taking in the situation*) What's the matter *now*? More trouble?

KAY. What do you expect after the way you behaved last night? (*She sits on the chaise and takes a handkerchief from her bag.* TREVES *moves on to the Right end of the rostrum.*)

NEVILE. (*Crossing slowly and standing up Left of* KAY) It was you who made all the fuss, Kay. I was prepared to talk the matter over calmly.

KAY. Calmly! Did you imagine that I was going to accept your suggestion that I should divorce you, and leave the way clear for Audrey, as if – as if you were inviting me to – to go to a dance? (TREVES *crosses to the Left of the rostrum.*)

NEVILE. No, but at least you needn't behave in this hysterical fashion when you're staying in other people's houses. For goodness' sake control yourself and try to behave properly.

KAY. Like *she* does, I suppose?

NEVILE. At any rate, Audrey doesn't make an exhibition of herself.

KAY. She's turning you against me – just as she intended.

NEVILE. Look here, Kay, this isn't Audrey's fault. I told you that last night. I explained the situation. I was quite open and honest about it.

KAY. (*Scornfully*) Open and honest!

NEVILE. Yes. I can't help feeling the way I do.

KAY. How do you suppose I feel? You don't care about that, do you?

TREVES. (*Moving down Centre and interposing*) I really think, Nevile, that you should very seriously consider your attitude in this – er – matter. Kay is your wife. She has certain rights of which you cannot deprive her in this – this cavalier manner.

NEVILE. I admit that, but – I'm willing to do the – the right thing.

KAY. The *right* thing!

TREVES. Furthermore, it is hardly the – er – proper procedure to discuss this under Lady Tressilian's roof. It is bound to upset her very seriously. (*He crosses below* NEVILE *to Left of* KAY.) My sympathies are entirely with Kay, but I think you *both* have a duty to your hostess and to your fellow guests. I suggest that you postpone any further discussion of the matter until your visit here has terminated.

NEVILE. (*A little shamefacedly*) I suppose you're right, Mr Treves – yes, of course, you're right. I'm willing. What do you say, Kay?

KAY. As long as Audrey doesn't try and . . .

NEVILE. (*Sharply*) Audrey hasn't tried anything.

TREVES. (*To* KAY) Ssh! I think, my dear, you would be well advised to agree to my suggestion. It is only a question of a few more days.

KAY. (*Rising, ungraciously*) Oh, very well then. (*She moves to the French windows.*)

NEVILE. (*Relieved*) Well, that's that. I'm going to get some breakfast. (*He moves to the door Left.*) We might all go sailing later on. (*He goes on to the Left end of the rostrum and glances out of the window.*) There's quite a good breeze. (*He looks at* TREVES.) Would you like to come?

TREVES. I'm afraid I'm a little too old for that sort of thing. (*He crosses towards the door Left.*)

NEVILE. What about you, Kay?

KAY. (*Moving Right Centre*) What about Ted? We promised him we'd go over this morning.

NEVILE. There's no reason why he shouldn't come, too. I'll get hold of Royde and Audrey and see what they think of the idea. It should be lovely out in the bay. (AUDREY *enters Left. She looks worried.*)

AUDREY. (*Anxiously*) Mr Treves – what do you think we ought to do? We can't wake Mary. (KAY *moves down Right of the chaise.*)

NEVILE. Can't *wake* her? (*He moves off the rostrum to Centre.*) What do you mean?

AUDREY. Just that. When Mrs Barrett came, she took up Mary's morning tea as usual (*She moves slowly Left Centre.*) Mary was fast asleep. Mrs Barrett drew the curtains and called to her, but Mary didn't wake up, so she left the tea on the bedside table. She didn't bother much when Mary didn't come down, but when Mary didn't come down to fetch Camilla's tea, Mrs Barrett went up again. Mary's tea was stone cold and she was still asleep.

TREVES. (*Moving down Left of the armchair Left Centre.*) She was very tired last night, Audrey.

AUDREY. But this isn't a *natural* sleep, Mr Treves. It *can't* be. Mrs Barrett shook her – hard – and she didn't wake. I went in to Mary and I tried to wake her, too. There's definitely something wrong with her.

NEVILE. Do you mean she's unconscious?

AUDREY. I don't know. She looks very pale and she just lies there – like a log.

KAY. Perhaps she took some sleeping pills.

AUDREY. (*Moving Centre*) That's what I thought, but it's so unlike Mary. (*She turns to* TREVES.) What shall we do?

TREVES. I think you should get a doctor. She may be ill.

NEVILE. (*Crossing to the door Left*) I'll go and phone Lazenby and get him to come at once. (NEVILE *exits quickly Left.*)

TREVES. (*Moving Left Centre*) Have you told Lady Tressilian, Audrey?

AUDREY. (*Moving Right Centre.*; *shaking her head*) No, not yet. I didn't want to disturb her. They're making her some fresh tea in the kitchen. I'm going to take it up. I'll tell her then.

TREVES. I sincerely hope it's nothing serious.

KAY. She's probably taken an overdose of sleeping stuff. (*She sits in the easy chair down Right.*)

TREVES. That *could* be extremely serious.

AUDREY. I can't imagine Mary doing such a thing. (ROYDE *enters Left.*)

ROYDE. (*Moving between* TREVES *and* AUDREY.) I heard Strange telephoning Doctor Lazenby. What's the matter?

AUDREY. It's Mary. She's still asleep and we can't get her to wake up. Kay thinks she may have taken an overdose of some drug.

KAY. Something like that must have happened or you'd be able to wake her.

ROYDE. Sleeping stuff, do you mean? Shouldn't think she'd have needed anything like that last night. She was dog tired.

TREVES. I'm sure she wouldn't take any sort of drug, you know – in case the bell rang.

KAY. Bell?

ROYDE. There's a bell in her room. Lady Tressilian always rings it if she wants anything in the night. (*To* AUDREY) Remember she was telling us about it last night?

AUDREY. Mary wouldn't take anything that would stop her hearing the bell, in case it was urgent. (NEVILE *enters quickly Left*.)

NEVILE. Lazenby's coming round right away.

AUDREY. (*Crossing to the door Left*) Oh, good. Before he gets here I'd better go and see about Camilla's tea. She'll be wondering what's happened.

NEVILE. Can I help?

AUDREY. No, thank you. I can manage. (AUDREY *exits Left*. KAY *rises and moves up Right of the chaise*.)

ROYDE. (*Moving to the chaise*) I wonder if it could be some kind of heart attack. (*He sits on the chaise*. TREVES *sits in the armchair Left Centre*.)

NEVILE. (*Crossing and standing on the Right end of the rostrum*) It's not much use conjecturing, is it? Lazenby'll be able to tell us. Poor old Mary. I don't know what will happen if she's really ill.

TREVES. It would be disastrous. Lady Tressilian relies on Mary for everything.

KAY. (*Moving to Right of* NEVILE; *hopefully*) I suppose we should all have to pack up and go?

NEVILE. (*Smiling at* KAY) Perhaps it isn't anything serious after all. (KAY *moves down Right*.)

ROYDE. Must be something pretty bad if she can't be wakened.

TREVES. It can't take Doctor Lazenby very long to get here, and then we shall know. He lives a very short distance away.

NEVILE. He ought to be here in about ten minutes, I should think.

TREVES. Possibly he will be able to relieve all our minds. I trust so.

NEVILE. (*With a determinedly cheerful air*) No good looking on the black side of things, anyway.

KAY. (*Moving to Right of the chaise*) Always the perfect optimist, aren't you, Nevile?

NEVILE. Well, things usually work out all right.

ROYDE. They certainly do for you.

NEVILE. (*Moving to Left of* ROYDE) I don't quite know what you mean by that, Thomas.

ROYDE. (*Rising*) I should have thought it was obvious.

NEVILE. What are you insinuating?

ROYDE. I'm not insinuating anything. I'm stating facts.

TREVES. (*Rising*) Ssh! (*He moves Centre and hastily changes the subject*.) Do you think – er – we ought to see if there is anything we could do to – er – help? Lady Tressilian might wish . . . (ROYDE *crosses above the others and stands on the Left end of the rostrum.*)

NEVILE. If Camilla wants us to do anything she'll soon say so. I wouldn't interfere unless she does, if I were you. (AUDREY *is heard to scream off Left.* ROYDE *exits hurriedly. There is a short pause.* AUDREY, *supported by* ROYDE, *enters Left. She looks almost dazed.*)

AUDREY. Camilla – Camilla . . .

TREVES. (*Concerned*) My dear! What's the matter?

AUDREY. (*In a husky whisper*) It's – Camilla.

NEVILE. (*Surprised*) Camilla? What's wrong with her?

AUDREY. She's – she's dead.

KAY. (*Sitting on the chaise*) Oh, no, no.

NEVILE. It must have been her heart.

AUDREY. No – it – it wasn't her heart. (*She presses her hands to her eyes. They all stare at her. She shouts*) There's blood – all over her head. (*She suddenly screams out hysterically.*) She's been murdered. Don't you understand? She's been murdered. (AUDREY *sinks into the easy chair down Left and the LIGHTS fade to black-out, as – the Curtain falls.*)

CURTAIN

Scene II

SCENE: *The same. Two hours later. The furniture has been moved to make the room more suitable for the police interrogations. The coffee table has been moved into the alcove Right, and the chaise on to the rostrum. A card table has been placed Right Centre with the upright chair from the alcove Left of it. The armchair Left Centre is now above the card table and the easy chair down Left is now Left Centre. On the card table is a small tray with a jug of water and two glasses. Also on the card table are a box of cigarettes, an ashtray and a box of matches. A copy of 'The Times' lies half open on the windowseat.*

When Curtain rises, TREVES *is standing Left of the card table, looking around the room. After a moment he moves up Centre on the rostrum.* SUPER-INTENDENT BATTLE *enters Left. He is a big man, aged about fifty, and is quietly dressed. His face is heavy but intelligent.*

TREVES. Ah. Battle.

BATTLE. That's fixed up, sir.

TREVES. It was all right, was it, Battle?

BATTLE. (*Crossing to Centre*) Yes, sir. The Chief Constable got through to the Yard. As I happened to be on the spot they've agreed to let me handle the case. (*He moves down Right, turns and looks around the room.*)

TREVES. (*Moving down Centre*) I'm very glad. It's going to make it easier having you instead of a stranger. Pity to have spoilt your holiday, though.

BATTLE. Oh, I don't mind that, sir. I'll be able to give my nephew a hand. It'll be his first murder case, you see.

TREVES. (*Moving to the bureau chair*) Yes, yes – I've no doubt he will find your experience of great help. (*He moves the chair to Right of the card table.*)

BATTLE. (*Crossing to Right Centre*) It's a nasty business.

TREVES. Shocking, shocking. (*He crosses and stands below the easy chair Left Centre.*)

BATTLE. I've seen the doctor. Two blows were struck. The first was sufficient to cause death. The murderer must have struck again to make sure, or in a blind rage.

TREVES. Horrible. (*He sits in the easy chair Left Centre*) I can't believe it could have been anyone in the house.

BATTLE. Afraid it was, sir. We've been into all that. No entry was forced. (*He moves in the direction of the French windows.*) All the doors and windows were fastened this morning as usual. And then there's the drugging of Miss Aldin – that must have been an inside job.

TREVES. How is she?

BATTLE. Still sleeping it off, but she was given a pretty heavy dose. It looks like careful planning on somebody's part. (*He crosses to Centre.*) Lady Tressilian might have pulled that bell which rings in Miss Aldin's room, if she'd been alarmed. That had to be taken care of – so Miss Aldin was doped.

TREVES. (*Troubled*) It still seems to me quite incredible.

BATTLE. We'll get to the bottom of it, sir, in the end. (*He moves to Left of the card table*). Death occurred, according to the doctor, between ten-thirty and midnight. Not earlier than ten-thirty, not later than midnight. That should be a help. (*He sits on the chair Left of the card table.*)

TREVES. Yes, yes. And the weapon used was a niblick?

BATTLE. Yes, sir. Thrown down by the bed, bloodstained and with white hairs sticking to it. (TREVES *makes a gesture of repulsion.*) I shouldn't have deduced a niblick from the appearance of the wound, but apparently the sharp edge of the club didn't touch the head. The doctor says it was the rounded part of the club hit her.

TREVES. The – er – murderer was incredibly stupid, don't you think, to leave the weapon behind?

BATTLE. Probably lost his head. It happens.

TREVES. Possibly – yes, possibly. I suppose there are no finger-prints?

BATTLE. (*Rising and moving up Right Centre*) Sergeant Pengelly is attending to that now, sir. I doubt if it's going to be as easy as that. (INSPECTOR LEACH *enters Left. He is a youngish man, about thirty-eight to forty, thin and dark. He speaks with a slight Cornish accent. He carries a niblick golf club.*)

LEACH. (*Crossing above the easy chair Left Centre to Left of* BATTLE) See here, Uncle. Pengelly has brought up a beautiful set of dabs on this – clear as day.

BATTLE. (*Warningly*) Be careful how you go handling that, my boy.

LEACH. It's all right, we've got photographs. Got specimens of the blood and hair, too. (*He shows the club to* BATTLE.) What do you think of these dabs? Clear as clear, aren't they? (BATTLE *inspects the fingerprints on the shaft of the club, then crosses to Right of* TREVES.)

BATTLE. They're clear enough. What a fool! (*He shows the club to* TREVES.)

LEACH. That's so to be sure.

BATTLE. All we've got to do now, my lad, is ask everyone nicely and politely if we may take their fingerprints – no compulsion, of course. Everyone will say 'yes' – and one of two things will happen. Either none of the prints will agree, or else . . .

LEACH. It'll be in the bag, eh? (*He crosses to the door Left.* BATTLE *nods.*)

TREVES. Doesn't it strike you as extremely odd, Battle, that the – er – murderer should have been so foolish as to leave such a damning piece of evidence behind – actually on the scene of the crime?

BATTLE. I've known 'em do things equally foolish, sir. (*He puts the club on the chaise.*) Well, let's get on with it. Where's everybody?

LEACH. (*Moving up Left*) In the library. Pollock is going through all their rooms. Except Miss Aldin's, of course. She's still sleeping off the effects of that dope.

BATTLE. We'll have 'em in here one at a time. (*To* TREVES) Which Mrs Strange was it who discovered the murder?

TREVES. Mrs Audrey Strange.

BATTLE. Oh, yes. Difficult when there are two Mrs Stranges. Mrs Audrey Strange is the divorced wife, isn't she?

TREVES. Yes. I explained to you the – er – situation.

BATTLE. Yes, sir. Funny idea of Mr Strange's. I should have thought that most men . . . (KAY *enters quickly Left. She is very upset and slightly hysterical.*)

KAY. (*Crossing towards the French windows; to* BATTLE) I'm not going to stay cooped up in that damned library any longer. I want some air and I'm going out. You can do what the hell you like about it. (LEACH *moves down Left.*)

BATTLE. Just a minute, Mrs Strange. (KAY *stops and turns by the French windows.*) There's no reason why you shouldn't go out if you wish, but it'll have to be later.

KAY. I want to go *now*.

BATTLE. I'm afraid that's impossible.

KAY. (*Moving slowly down Right*) You've no right to keep me here. I haven't done anything.

BATTLE. (*Soothingly*) No, no, of course you haven't. But you see, there'll be one or two questions we'll have to ask you.

KAY. What sort of questions? I can't help you. I don't know anything about it.

BATTLE. (*Moving down Centre; to* LEACH) Get Benson, will you, Jim? (LEACH *nods and exits Left.*) Now you just sit down here, Mrs Strange – (*He indicates the chair Left of the card table*) and relax.

KAY. (*Moving and sitting Left of the card table*) I've told you I don't know anything. Why do I have to answer a lot of questions when I don't know anything?

BATTLE. (*Moving above the card table and standing down Right of it, apologetically*) We've got to interview everybody, you see. It's just part of the routine. Not very pleasant for you, or for us, but there you are.

KAY. Oh, well – all right. (POLICE CONSTABLE BENSON *enters Left.* LEACH *follows him on.* BENSON *is a youngish man, fairish and very quiet. He moves to Left of the chaise and takes out a notebook and pencil.*)

BATTLE. (*Sitting Right of the card table*) Now, just tell us about last night, Mrs Strange.

KAY. What about last night?

BATTLE. What did you do – say from after dinner, onwards?

KAY. I had a headache. I – I went to bed quite early.

BATTLE. How early?

KAY. I don't know exactly. It was about a quarter to ten, I think.

TREVES. (*Interposing gently*) Ten minutes to ten.

KAY. Was it? I wouldn't know to the minute.

BATTLE. We'll take it it was ten minutes to ten. (*He makes a sign to* BENSON. BENSON *makes a note in his book.*) Did your husband accompany you?

KAY. No.

BATTLE. (*After a pause*) What time did *he* come to bed?

KAY. I've no idea. You'd better ask *him* that.

LEACH. (*Crossing to Left of* KAY) The door between your room and your husband's is locked. Was it locked when you went to bed?

KAY. Yes.

LEACH. Who locked it?

KAY. I did.

BATTLE. Was it usual for you to lock it?

KAY. No.

BATTLE. (*Rising*) Why did you do so last night, Mrs Strange? (KAY *does not reply.* LEACH *moves up Right Centre.*)

TREVES. (*After a pause*) I should tell them, Kay.

KAY. I suppose if I don't, you will. Oh, well, then. You can have it. Nevile and I had a row – a flaming row. (LEACH *looks at* BENSON, *who makes a note.*) I was furious with him. I went to bed and locked the door because I was still in a flaming rage with him.

BATTLE. I see – what was the trouble about?

KAY. Does it matter? I don't see how it concerns . . .

BATTLE. You're not compelled to answer, if you'd rather not.

KAY. Oh, I don't mind. My husband has been behaving like a perfect fool. It's all that woman's fault, though.

BATTLE. What woman?

KAY. Audrey – his first wife. It was she who got him to come here in the first place.

BATTLE. I understood that it was *Mr* Strange's idea.

KAY. Well, it wasn't. It was hers.

BATTLE. But why should Mrs Audrey Strange have suggested it? (*During the following speech,* LEACH *crosses slowly to the door Left.*)

KAY. To cause trouble, I suppose. Nevile thinks it was his own idea – poor innocent. But he never thought of such a thing until he met Audrey in the Park one day in London, and she put the idea into his head and made him believe he'd thought of it himself. I've seen her scheming mind behind it from the first. She's never taken *me* in.

BATTLE. Why should she be so anxious for you all to come here together?

KAY. (*Quickly and breathlessly*) Because she wanted to get hold of Nevile again. That's why. She's never forgiven him for going off with me. This is her revenge. She got him to fix it so that we'd be here together and then she got to work on him. She's been doing it ever since we arrived. (BATTLE *crosses above the card table to Centre.*) She's clever, damned clever. She knows just how to look pathetic and elusive. Poor sweet, injured little kitten – with all her blasted claws out.

TREVES. Kay – Kay . . .

BATTLE. I see. Surely, if you felt so strongly, you could have objected to this arrangement of coming here?

KAY. Do you think I didn't try? Nevile was set on it. He insisted.

BATTLE. But you're quite sure it wasn't his idea?

KAY. I'm positive. That white-faced little cat planned it all.

TREVES. You have no actual evidence on which to base such an assertion, Kay.

KAY. (*Rising and crossing to Right of* TREVES) I know, I tell you, and you know it, too, though you won't admit it. Audrey's been . . .

BATTLE. Come and sit down, Mrs Strange. (KAY *crosses reluctantly to*

Left of the card table and sits.) Did Lady Tressilian approve of the arrangement?

KAY. She didn't approve of anything in connection with me. Audrey was her pet. She disliked me for taking Audrey's place with Nevile.

BATTLE. Did you – quarrel with Lady Tressilian?

KAY. No.

BATTLE. After you'd gone to bed, Mrs Strange, did you hear anything? Any unusual sounds in the house?

KAY. I didn't hear anything. I was so upset I took some sleeping stuff. I fell asleep almost at once.

BATTLE. (*Crossing to Right of the card table*) What kind of sleeping stuff?

KAY. They're little blue capsules. I don't know what's in them. (BATTLE *looks at* BENSON, *who makes a note.*)

BATTLE. (*Moving to the chaise*) You didn't see your husband after you went up to bed?

KAY. No, no, no. I've already told you that I locked the door.

BATTLE. (*Picking up the niblick and bringing it to Left of* KAY) Have you ever seen this before, Mrs Strange?

KAY. (*Shrinking away*) How – how horrible. Is that what – what it was done with?

BATTLE. We believe so. Have you any idea to whom it belongs?

KAY. (*Shaking her head*) There are packets of golf clubs in the house. Mr Royde's – Nevile's – mine . . .

BATTLE. This is a man's club. It wouldn't be one of yours.

KAY. Then it must be . . . I don't know.

BATTLE. I see. (*He moves to the chaise and replaces the niblick on it.*) Thank you, Mrs Strange, that's all for the present. (KAY *rises and moves down Right.*)

LEACH. There's just one other thing. (KAY *turns. He crosses to Left of* KAY.) Would you object to letting Detective Sergeant Pengelly take your fingerprints?

KAY. My – fingerprints?

BATTLE. (*Smoothly*) It's just a matter of routine, Mrs Strange. We're asking everybody.

KAY. I don't mind anything – so long as I don't have to go back to that menagerie in the library.

LEACH. I'll arrange for Sergeant Pengelly to take your fingerprints in the breakfast room. (KAY *crosses below* LEACH *to Left Centre, looks closely at* TREVES *for a moment, then exits Left.* LEACH *crosses and exits Left.* BENSON *closes his notebook and waits stolidly.*)

BATTLE. Benson. Go and ask Pollock if he saw some small blue capsules in Mrs Strange's room – Mrs *Kay* Strange. I want a specimen of them.

BENSON. Yes, sir. (*He moves to the door Left.*)

BATTLE. (*Moving Centre*) Come back here when you've done that.

BENSON. Yes, sir. (BENSON *exits Left.*)

TREVES. (*Rising*) Do you think the same drug was used to – er – dope Miss Aldin?

BATTLE. (*Moving on to the Right end of the rostrum*) It's worth checking up on. Would you mind telling me, sir, who stands to gain by Lady Tressilian's death?

TREVES. Lady Tressilian had very little money of her own. The late Sir Mortimer Tressilian's estate was left in trust for her during her lifetime. On her death it is to be equally divided between Nevile and his wife.

BATTLE. Which wife?

TREVES. His first wife.

BATTLE. *Audrey* Strange?

TREVES. Yes. The bequest is quite clearly worded, 'Nevile Henry Strange, and his wife, Audrey Elizabeth Strange, née Standish'. The subsequent divorce makes no difference whatever to that bequest.

BATTLE. (*Moving down Right*) Mrs Audrey Strange is, of course, fully aware of that?

TREVES. Certainly.

BATTLE. And the present Mrs Strange – does she know that she gets nothing?

TREVES. Really I cannot say. (*His voice is doubtful.*) Presumably her husband has made it clear to her. (*He moves to Left of the card table.*)

BATTLE. If he hadn't she might be under the impression that she was the one who benefited?

TREVES. It's possible – yes. (*He sits Left of the card table.*)

BATTLE. Is the amount involved a large one, sir?

TREVES. Quite considerable. Approaching one hundred thousand pounds.

BATTLE. Whew! That's quite something, even in these days. (LEACH *enters Left. He is carrying a crumpled dinner jacket.*)

LEACH. (*Moving Left Centre*) I say, take a look at this. Pollock has just found it bundled down in the bottom of Nevile Strange's wardrobe. (BATTLE *crosses to Right of* LEACH. *He points to the sleeve.*) Look at these stains. That's blood, or I'm Marilyn Monroe.

BATTLE. (*Taking the jacket from* LEACH) You're certainly not Marilyn Monroe, Jim. It's spattered all up the sleeve as well. Any other suits in the room?

LEACH. Dark grey pinstripe hanging over a chair. And there's a lot of water round the wash basin on the floor – quite a pool of it. Looks as if it had slopped over.

BATTLE. Such as might have been made if he'd washed the blood off his hands in the devil of a hurry, eh?

LEACH. Yes. (*He takes some small tweezers from his pocket and picks some hairs off the inside of the collar.*)

BATTLE. Hairs! A woman's fair hairs on the inside of the collar.

LEACH. Some on the sleeve, too.

BATTLE. Red ones, these. Mr Strange seems to have had his arm around one wife and the other one's head on his shoulder.

LEACH. Quite a Mormon. Looks bad for him, don't it?

BATTLE. We'll have to have the blood on this tested later to see if it's the same group as Lady Tressilian's.

LEACH. I'll try and arrange it, Uncle.

TREVES. (*Rising and moving down Right, very perturbed*) I can't *believe*, I really can't believe that Nevile, whom I've known all his life, is capable of such a terrible act. There *must* be a mistake.

BATTLE. (*Moving and putting the jacket on the chaise*) I hope so, I'm sure, sir. (*To* LEACH) We'll have Mr Royde in next. (LEACH *nods and exits Left.*)

TREVES. I'm quite sure there must be some innocent explanation, Battle, for that stained dinner jacket. Quite apart from lack of motive, Nevile is . . .

BATTLE. Fifty thousand pounds is a pretty good motive, sir, to my mind.

TREVES. But Nevile is well off. He's not in need of money.

BATTLE. There may be something we know nothing about, sir.

(BENSON *enters Left and crosses to Left of* BATTLE. *He carries a small round box.*)

BENSON. Pollock found the pills, sir. (*He hands the box to* BATTLE.) Here you are.

BATTLE. (*Looking into the box*) These are the things. I'll get the doctor to tell us whether they contain the same stuff that was given to Miss Aldin. (*He moves up Right.* ROYDE *enters Left.*)

ROYDE. (*Moving Left Centre*) You want to see me?

BATTLE. (*Moving down Right Centre*) Yes, Mr Royde. (*He indicates the chair Left of the card table.*) Will you sit down, sir?

ROYDE. Rather stand.

BATTLE. Just as you like. (BENSON *takes out his notebook and pencil.* TREVES *sits in the easy chair down Right.*) I'd like you to answer one or two questions, if you've no objection.

ROYDE. No objection at all. Nothing to hide.

BATTLE. (*Moving below the card table*) I understand that you have only just returned from Malaya, Mr Royde.

ROYDE. That's right. First time I've been home for seven years.

BATTLE. You've known Lady Tressilian for a long time?

ROYDE. Ever since I was a boy.

BATTLE. Can you suggest a reason why anyone should want to kill her?

ROYDE. No.

BATTLE. (*Moving up Right of the card table*) How long have you known Mr Nevile Strange?

ROYDE. Practically all my life.

BATTLE. (*Moving up Right Centre*) Do you know him sufficiently well to be aware if he was worried over money?

ROYDE. No, but I shouldn't think so. Always seems to have plenty.

BATTLE. If there was any trouble like that, he wouldn't be likely to confide in you?

ROYDE. Very unlikely.

BATTLE. (*Moving down Left of the card table*) What time did you go to bed last night, Mr Royde?

ROYDE. Round about half past nine, I should think.

BATTLE. That seems to be very early.

ROYDE. Always go to bed early. Like to get up early.

BATTLE. I see. Your room is practically opposite Lady Tressilian's, isn't it?

ROYDE. Practically.

BATTLE. Did you go to sleep immediately you went to bed?

ROYDE. No. Finished a detective story I was reading. Not very good – it seems to me they always . . .

BATTLE. Yes, yes. Were you still awake at half past ten?

ROYDE. Yes.

BATTLE. (*Sitting Left of the card table*) Did you – this is very important, Mr Royde – did you hear any unusual sounds round about that time? (ROYDE *does not reply*.) I'll repeat that question. Did you . . .?

ROYDE. There's no need. I heard you.

BATTLE. (*After a pause*) Well, Mr Royde?

ROYDE. Heard a noise in the attic over my head, rats, I expect. Anyway, that was later.

BATTLE. I don't mean that.

ROYDE. (*Looking at* TREVES; *reluctantly*) There was a bit of a rumpus.

BATTLE. What sort of rumpus?

ROYDE. Well – an argument.

BATTLE. An argument? Who was the argument between?

ROYDE. Lady Tressilian and Strange.

BATTLE. Lady Tressilian and Mr Strange were quarrelling?

ROYDE. Well, yes. I suppose you'd call it that.

BATTLE. (*Rising and moving to Right of* ROYDE) It's not what *I* would call it, Mr Royde. Do you call it that?

ROYDE. Yes.

BATTLE. Thank you. What was this quarrel about?

ROYDE. Didn't listen. Not my business.

BATTLE. But you are quite sure they *were* quarrelling?

ROYDE. Sounded like it. Their voices were raised pretty high.

BATTLE. Can you place the time exactly?

ROYDE. About twenty past ten I should think.

BATTLE. Twenty past ten. You didn't hear anything else?

ROYDE. Strange slammed the door when he left.

BATTLE. You heard nothing more after that?

ROYDE. (*Crossing below* BATTLE *to the card table*) Only rats. (*He knocks out his pipe in the ashtray*.)

BATTLE. (*Moving to the chaise*) Never mind the rats. (*He picks up the niblick.* ROYDE *fills and lights his pipe. He moves to Left of* ROYDE.)

Does this belong to you, Mr Royde? (ROYDE, *engrossed with his pipe, does not reply.*) Mr Royde!

ROYDE. (*Looking at the niblick*) No. All my clubs have got T.R. scratched on the shaft.

BATTLE. Do you know to whom it does belong?

ROYDE. No idea. (*He moves up Right.*)

BATTLE. (*Replacing the niblick on the chaise*) We shall want to take your fingerprints, Mr Royde. Have you any objection to that?

ROYDE. Not much use objecting, is it? Your man's already done it. (BENSON *laughs quietly.*)

BATTLE. Thank you, then, Mr Royde. That's all for the present.

ROYDE. Do you mind if I go out for a bit? Feel like some fresh air. Only out on the terrace, if you want me.

BATTLE. That'll be quite all right, sir.

ROYDE. Thanks. (ROYDE *exits by the French windows.* BENSON *sits on the windowseat.*)

BATTLE. (*Moving Centre*) The evidence seems to be piling up against Mr Strange, sir.

TREVES. (*Rising and moving to Right of the card table*) It's incredible – incredible. (LEACH *enters Left and crosses to Left Centre.*)

LEACH. (*Jubilantly*) The fingerprints are Nevile Strange's all right.

BATTLE. That would seem to clinch it, Jim. He leaves his weapon – he leaves his fingerprints; I wonder he didn't leave his visiting card.

LEACH. Been easy, hasn't it?

TREVES. It *can't* have been Nevile. There must be a mistake. (*He pours himself a glass of water.*)

BATTLE. It all adds up. We'll see what Mr Strange has to say, anyhow. Bring him in, Jim. (LEACH *exits Left.*)

TREVES. I don't understand it. I'm sure there's something wrong. (BATTLE *moves down Left Centre.*) Nevile's not a complete and utter fool. Even if he were capable of committing such a brutal act – which I refuse to believe – would he have left all this damning evidence strewn about so carelessly? (*He moves up Right.*)

BATTLE. Well, sir, apparently he did. (*He moves to Right of the easy chair Left Centre.*) You can't get away from facts. (NEVILE *and* LEACH *enter Left.* NEVILE *looks worried and a little nervous. He stands a moment in the doorway. He indicates the chair Left of the card table.*) Come and sit down, Mr Strange.

NEVILE. (*Crossing to the chair Left of the card table*) Thank you. (*He sits. TREVES crosses slowly above the others and stands down Left.*)

BATTLE. We should like you to answer certain questions, but it's my duty to caution you that you are not bound to answer these questions unless you wish.

NEVILE. Go ahead. Ask me anything you wish.

BATTLE. (*Moving Centre*) You realize that anything you say will be taken down in writing and may subsequently be used in evidence in a court of law?

NEVILE. Are you threatening me?

BATTLE. No, no, Mr Strange. Warning you.

TREVES. (*Moving below the easy chair Left Centre*) Superintendent Battle is obliged to conform to the regulations, Nevile. You need say nothing unless you wish to.

NEVILE. Why shouldn't I wish to?

TREVES. It might be wiser not to.

NEVILE. Nonsense! Go ahead, Superintendent. Ask me anything you like. (TREVES *makes a despairing gesture and sits in the easy chair Left Centre.* BENSON *rises.*)

BATTLE. (*Crossing below* NEVILE *and standing down Right*) Are you prepared to make a statement?

NEVILE. If that's what you call it. I'm afraid, though, I can't help you very much.

BATTLE. Will you begin by telling us exactly what you did last night? From dinner onwards? (*He sits Right of the card table.*)

NEVILE. Let me see. Immediately after dinner I went up to my room and wrote a couple of letters – I'd been putting them off for a long time and I thought I might as well get them done. When I'd finished I came down here.

BATTLE. What time would that be?

NEVILE. I suppose it was about a quarter past nine. That's as near as dammit, anyhow. (BATTLE *helps himself to a cigarette.*)

BATTLE. (*Offering the cigarettes to* NEVILE) I'm so sorry.

NEVILE. No, thank you.

BATTLE. What did you do after that? (*He lights his cigarette.*)

NEVILE. I talked to – to Kay, my wife, and Ted Latimer.

BATTLE. Latimer – who's he?

NEVILE. A friend of ours who's staying at the *Easterhead Bay Hotel*. He'd come over for dinner. He left soon after and everybody else went off to bed.

BATTLE. Including your wife?

NEVILE. Yes, she was feeling a bit off colour.

BATTLE. (*Rising*) I understand there was some sort of – unpleasantness?

NEVILE. Oh – (*He looks at* TREVES.) you've heard about that, have you? It was purely a domestic quarrel. Can't have anything to do with this horrible business.

BATTLE. I see. (*He crosses below the table and moves up Centre. After a pause*) After everybody else had gone to bed, what did you do then?

NEVILE. I was a bit bored. It was still fairly early and I decided to go across to the *Easterhead Bay Hotel*.

BATTLE. In the storm? It had broken by this time, surely?

NEVILE. Yes, it had. But it didn't worry me. I went upstairs to change . . .

BATTLE. (*Moving quickly to* NEVILE, *breaking in quickly*) Change into what, Mr Strange?

NEVILE. I was wearing a dinner jacket. As I proposed to take the ferry across the river and it was raining pretty heavily, I changed. Into a grey pinstripe – (*He pauses.*) if it interests you.

BATTLE. (*After a pause*) Go on, Mr Strange.

NEVILE. (*Showing signs of increasing nervousness*) I went up to change, as I said. I was passing Lady Tressilian's door, which was ajar, when she called, 'Is that you, Nevile?' and asked me to come in. I went in and – and we chatted for a bit.

BATTLE. How long were you with her?

NEVILE. About twenty minutes, I suppose. When I left her I went to my room, changed, and hurried off. I took the latchkey with me because I expected to be late.

BATTLE. What time was it then?

NEVILE. (*Reflectively*) About half past ten, I should think, I just caught the ten-thirty-five ferry and went across to the Easterhead side of the river. I had a drink or two with Latimer at the hotel and watched the dancing. Then we had a game of billards. In the end I found I'd missed the last ferry back. It goes at one-thirty. Latimer very decently got out his car and drove me home. It's fifteen miles round by road, you know. (*He pauses.*) We left the hotel at two o'clock and reached here at half past. Latimer wouldn't come in for a drink, so I let myself in and went straight up to bed. (BATTLE *and* TREVES *exchange looks.*)

BATTLE. (*Crossing below* NEVILE *to Right of the card table*) During your conversation with Lady Tressilian – was she quite normal in her manner? (*He stubs out his cigarette in the ashtray on the card table.*)

NEVILE. Oh, yes, quite.

BATTLE. (*Moving above the card table*) What did you talk about?

NEVILE. This and that.

BATTLE. (*Moving behind* NEVILE) Amiably?

NEVILE. Of course.

BATTLE. (*Moving down Left Centre; smoothly*) You didn't have a violent quarrel?

NEVILE. (*Rising; angrily*) What the devil do you mean?

BATTLE. You'd better tell the truth, Mr Strange. I'll warn you – you were overheard.

NEVILE. (*Crossing slowly below the card table to Right of it*) Well, we *did* have a difference of opinion. She – she disapproved of my behaviour over – over Kay and – and my first wife. I may have got a bit heated, but we parted on perfectly friendly terms. (*He bangs his fist on the table. With a sudden burst of temper*) I didn't bash her over the head because I lost my temper – if that's what you think. (BATTLE *moves to the chaise, picks up the niblick, then moves to Left of the card table.*)

BATTLE. Is this your property, Mr Strange?

NEVILE. (*Looking at the niblick*) Yes. It's one of Walter Hudson's niblicks from *St Egbert's*.

BATTLE. This is the weapon we think was used to kill Lady Tressilian. Have you any explanation for your fingerprints being on the grip?

NEVILE. But – of course they would be – it's my club. I've often handled it.

BATTLE. Any explanation, I mean, for the fact that your fingerprints show that you were the *last* person to have handled it?

NEVILE. That's not true. It *can't* be. Somebody could have handled it after me – someone wearing gloves.

BATTLE. Nobody could have handled it in the sense you mean – by raising it to strike – without blurring your own marks.

NEVILE. (*Staring at the niblick in sudden realization*) It can't be! (*He sits Right of the card table and covers his face with his hands.*) Oh, God! (*After a pause he takes his hands away and looks up.*) It isn't that! It simply isn't true. You think I killed her, but I didn't. I swear I didn't. There's some horrible mistake. (BATTLE *replaces the niblick on the chaise.*)

TREVES. (*Rising and crossing to Left of the card table*) Can't you think of any explanation to account for those fingerprints, Nevile? (BATTLE *picks up the dinner jacket.*)

NEVILE. No – no – I can't think – of anything. (TREVES *moves above the card table.*)

BATTLE. (*Moving to Left of the card table*) Can you explain why the cuffs and sleeve of this dinner jacket – *your* dinner jacket – are stained with blood?

NEVILE. (*In a horror-stricken whisper*) Blood? It couldn't be.

TREVES. You didn't, for instance, cut yourself?

NEVILE. (*Rising and pushing his chair violently backwards*) No – no, of course I didn't. It's fantastic – simply fantastic. It's none of it true.

BATTLE. The facts are true enough, Mr Strange.

NEVILE. But why should I do such a dreadful thing? It's unthinkable – unbelievable. I've known Lady Tressilian all my life. (*He moves to Right of* TREVES.) Mr Treves – you don't believe it, do you? You don't believe that I would do a thing like this? (BATTLE *replaces the jacket on the chaise.*)

TREVES. No, Nevile, I can't believe it.

NEVILE. I didn't. I swear I didn't. What reason could I have . . .?

BATTLE. (*Turning and standing on the rostrum*) I believe that you inherit a great deal of money on Lady Tressilian's death, Mr Strange.

NEVILE. (*Moving down Right*) You mean – You think that . . .? It's ridiculous! I don't need money. I'm quite well off. You've only to enquire at my bank . . . (TREVES *sits Right of the card table.*)

BATTLE. We shall check up on that. But there may be some reason why you suddenly require a large sum of money – some reason unknown to anyone except yourself.

NEVILE. There's nothing of the sort.

BATTLE. As to that – we shall see.

NEVILE. (*Crossing slowly below the card table to Right of* BATTLE.) Are you going to arrest me?

BATTLE. Not yet – we propose to give you the benefit of the doubt.

NEVILE. (*Bitterly*) You mean that you've made up your mind I did it, but you want to be sure of my motive so as to clinch the case against me. (*He moves above the armchair Right Centre.*) That's it, isn't it? (*He grips the back of the armchair.*) My God! It's like some awful dream. Like being caught in a trap and you can't get out. (*He pauses.*) Do you want me any more now? I'd like to – to get out – by myself – and think over all this. It's been rather a shock.

BATTLE. We've finished with you for the present, sir.

NEVILE. Thank you.

BATTLE. (*Moving down Left Centre*) Don't go *too* far away, though, will you, sir?

NEVILE. (*Moving to the French windows*) You needn't worry. I shan't try and run away – if *that's* what you mean. (*He glances off Right.*) I see you've taken your precautions, anyway. (NEVILE *exits by the French windows.* BENSON *sits on the windowseat.*)

LEACH. (*Moving to Left of* BATTLE) He did it all right.

BATTLE. (*Moving Centre*) I don't know, Jim. If you want the truth, I don't like it. I don't like *any* of it. There's *too much* evidence against him. Besides, it doesn't quite fit. Lady Tressilian calls him into the room, and he goes happening to have a niblick in his hand. Why?

LEACH. So as to bash her over the head.

BATTLE. Meaning it's premeditated? All right, he's drugged Miss Aldin. But he can't count on her being asleep so soon. He couldn't count on *anybody* being asleep so soon.

LEACH. Well then, say he's cleaning his clubs. Lady T calls him. They have a row – he loses his temper and bashes her with the club he just *happens* to be holding.

BATTLE. That doesn't account for the drugging of Mary Aldin. And she *was* drugged – the doctor says so. Of course – (*Meditatively*) she could have drugged herself.

LEACH. Why?

BATTLE. (*Moving to Left of the card table; to* TREVES) Is there any possible motive in Miss Aldin's case?

TREVES. Lady Tressilian left her a legacy – not a very large one – a few hundreds a year. As I told you, Lady Tressilian had very little personal fortune.

BATTLE. A few hundreds a year. (*He sits Left of the card table.*)

TREVES. (*Rising and moving down Right*) I agree. An inadequate motive.

BATTLE. (*Sighing*) Well, let's see the first wife. Jim, get Mrs Audrey Strange. (LEACH *exits Left.*) There's something peculiar about this business, sir. A mixture of cold premeditation and unpremeditated violence, and the two don't mix.

TREVES. Exactly, Battle. The drugging of Miss Aldin suggests premeditation . . .

BATTLE. And the way the murder was carried out looks as though it was done in a fit of blind rage. Yes, sir. It's all *wrong*.

TREVES. Did you notice what he said – about a trap?

BATTLE. (*Thoughtfully*) 'A trap.' (LEACH *enters Left and holds the door open.* AUDREY *enters Left. She is very pale but completely composed.* BENSON *rises.* TREVES *moves up Right.* LEACH *exits Left and closes the door.*)

AUDREY. (*Crossing to Centre*) You wish to see me?

BATTLE. (*Rising*) Yes. (*He indicates the chair Left of the card table.*) Please sit down, Mrs Strange. (AUDREY *crosses quickly to the chair Left of the card table and sits.*) You've already told me how you came to make the discovery, so we needn't go into that again.

AUDREY. Thank you.

BATTLE. (*Moving down Right*) I'm afraid, however, that I shall have to ask you several questions that you may find embarrassing. You are not compelled to answer them unless you like.

AUDREY. I don't mind. I only wish to help. (TREVES *moves slowly down Left.*)

BATTLE. First of all, then, will you tell us what you did after dinner last night?

AUDREY. I was on the terrace for some time talking to Mr Treves. Then Miss Aldin came out to say that Lady Tressilian would like to see him in her room, and I came in here. I talked to Kay and Mr Latimer and, later, to Mr Royde and Nevile. Then I went up to bed.

BATTLE. What time did you go to bed?

AUDREY. I think it was about half past nine. I'm not sure of the time exactly. It may have been a little later.

BATTLE. There was some sort of trouble between Mr Strange and his wife, I believe. Were you mixed up in that?

AUDREY. Nevile behaved very stupidly. I think he was rather excited and overwrought. I left them together and went to bed. I don't know what happened after that, naturally. (TREVES *sits in the easy chair Left Centre.*)

BATTLE. Did you go to sleep at once?

AUDREY. No. I was reading for some little while.

BATTLE. (*Moving on to the rostrum*) And you heard nothing unusual during the night?

AUDREY. No, nothing. My room is on the floor above Cam – Lady Tressilian's. I wouldn't have heard anything.

BATTLE. (*Picking up the niblick*) I'm sorry, Mrs Strange – (*He moves to Left of* AUDREY *and shows her the niblick.*) we believe this was used to kill Lady Tressilian. It has been identified by Mr Strange as his property. It also bears his fingerprints.

AUDREY. (*Drawing in her breath sharply*) Oh, you – you're not suggesting that it was – *Nevile* . . .

BATTLE. Would it surprise you?

AUDREY. Very much. I'm sure you're quite wrong, if you think so. Nevile would never do a thing like that. Besides, he had no reason.

BATTLE. Not if he wanted money very urgently?

AUDREY. He wouldn't. He's not an extravagant person – he never has been. You're quite, quite wrong if you think it was Nevile.

BATTLE. You don't think he would be capable of violence in a fit of temper?

AUDREY. Nevile? Oh, no!

BATTLE. (*Moving and replacing the niblick on the chaise*) I don't want to pry into your private affairs, Mrs Strange, but will you explain why you are here? (*He moves to Left of* AUDREY.)

AUDREY. (*Surprised*) Why? I always come here at this time.

BATTLE. But not at the same time as your ex-husband.

AUDREY. He did ask me if I'd mind.

BATTLE. It was his suggestion?

AUDREY. Oh, yes.

BATTLE. Not yours?

AUDREY. No.

BATTLE. But you agreed?

AUDREY. Yes, I agreed – I didn't feel that I could very well refuse.

BATTLE. Why not? You must have realized that it might be embarrassing?

AUDREY. Yes – I did realize that.

BATTLE. You were the injured party?

AUDREY. I beg your pardon?

BATTLE. It was you who divorced your husband?

AUDREY. Oh, I see – yes.

BATTLE. Do you feel any animosity towards him, Mrs Strange?

AUDREY. No – none at all.

BATTLE. You have a very forgiving nature. (AUDREY *does not reply. He crosses and stands down Right.*) Are you on friendly terms with the present Mrs Strange?

AUDREY. I don't think she likes me very much.

BATTLE. Do *you* like her?

AUDREY. I really don't know her.

BATTLE. (*Moving to Right of the card table*) You are quite sure it was not your idea – this meeting?

AUDREY. Quite sure.

BATTLE. I think that's all, Mrs Strange, thank you.

AUDREY. (*Rising; quietly*) Thank you. (*She crosses to the door Left then hesitates, turns and moves Left Centre.* TREVES *rises. Nervously and quickly*) I would just like to say – you think Nevile did this – that he killed her because of the money? I'm quite sure that isn't so. Nevile never cared much about money. I do know that. I was married to him for several years, you see. It – it – isn't *Nevile.* I know my saying this isn't of any value as evidence – but I do wish you would believe it. (AUDREY *turns quickly and exits Left.* BENSON *sits on the windowseat*).

BATTLE. (*Moving Right Centre*) It's difficult to know what to make of *her*, sir. I've never seen anyone so devoid of emotion.

TREVES. (*Moving Left Centre*) H'm. She didn't show any, Battle, but it's there – some very strong emotion. I thought – but I may have been wrong . . . (MARY, *assisted by* LEACH, *enters Left.* MARY *is wearing a dressing-gown. She sways a little. He moves to* MARY.) Mary! (*He leads her to the easy chair Left Centre.* MARY *sits in the easy chair Left Centre.*)

BATTLE. Miss Aldin! You shouldn't . . .

LEACH. She insisted on seeing you, Uncle. (*He stands above the door Left.*)

MARY. (*Faintly*) I'm all right. I just feel – a little dizzy still. (TREVES *crosses to the card table and pours a glass of water.*) I had to come. They told me something about your suspecting Nevile. Is that true? Do you suspect Nevile? (TREVES *crosses with the glass of water to Right of* MARY.)

BATTLE. (*Moving down Right Centre*) Who told you so?

MARY. The cook. She brought me up some tea. She heard them talking in his room. And then – I came down – and I saw Audrey – and she said it *was* so. (*She looks from one to the other.*)

BATTLE. (*Moving down Right; evasively*) We are not contemplating an arrest – at this moment.

MARY. But it *can't* have been Nevile. I had to come and tell you. Whoever did it, it wasn't Nevile. That I *know*.

BATTLE. (*Crossing to Centre*) How do you know?

MARY. Because I saw her – Lady Tressilian – alive after Nevile had left the house.

BATTLE. What?

MARY. My bell rang, you see. I was terribly sleepy. I could only just get up. It was a minute or two before half past ten. As I came out of my room Nevile was in the hall below. I looked over the banisters and saw him. He went out of the front door and slammed it behind him. Then I went in to Lady Tressilian.

BATTLE. And she was alive and well?

MARY. Yes, of course. She seemed a little upset and said Nevile had shouted at her.

BATTLE. (*To* LEACH) Get Mr Strange. (LEACH *crosses and exits by the French windows.* MARY *takes the glass from* TREVES *and sips the water. He sits on the chair Left of the card table.*) What did Lady Tressilian say exactly?

MARY. She said – (*She thinks.*) Oh, dear, what did she say? She said, 'Did I ring for you? I can't remember doing so. Nevile has behaved very badly – losing his temper – shouting at me. I feel most upset.' I gave her some aspirin and some hot milk from the Thermos and she settled down. Then I went back to bed. I was desperately sleepy. Doctor Lazenby asked me if I'd taken any sleeping pills . . .

BATTLE. Yes, we know . . . (NEVILE *and* LEACH *enter by the French windows.* KAY *follows them on and stands down Right of the card table.* LEACH *stands up Right. He rises and moves Left Centre.*) You are a very lucky man, Mr Strange.

NEVILE. (*Moving above the card table*) Lucky? Why?

BATTLE. Miss Aldin saw Lady Tressilian alive *after* you left the house, and we've already established you were on the ten-thirty-five ferry.

NEVILE. (*Bewildered*) Then – that lets me out? But the bloodstained jacket – (*He moves to Right of the chaise.*) The niblick with my fingerprints on it . . .? (KAY *sits in the easy chair down Right.*)

BATTLE. (*Moving to Left of the chaise*) Planted. Very ingeniously planted. Blood and hair smeared on the niblick head. *Someone* put on your jacket to commit the crime and then stuffed it away in your wardrobe to incriminate you.

NEVILE. (*Moving behind the chair Left of the card table*) But why? I can't believe it.

BATTLE. (*Impressively*) Who hates you, Mr Strange? Hates you so much that they wanted you to be hanged for a murder you didn't commit?

NEVILE. (*After a pause; shaken*) Nobody – nobody . . . (ROYDE *enters by the French windows and moves slowly towards the card table as* – *the Curtain falls.*)

CURTAIN

ACT THREE

Scene I

SCENE: *The same. The next morning.*

Most of the furniture has been replaced in its original position, but the coffee table is now on the rostrum up Centre and the work-basket has been removed.

When Curtain rises it is about eleven o'clock. The sun is shining brightly and the bay and French windows are open. ROYDE *is standing on the rostrum, gazing out of the window.* MARY *enters by the French windows. She looks a little pale and worried. She moves above the chaise and sees* ROYDE.

MARY. Oh, dear!

ROYDE. (*Closing the window and turning*) Anything the matter?

MARY. (*Laughing with a slight note of hysteria*) Nobody but you could say a thing like that, Thomas. A murder in the house and you just say 'Is anything the matter?' (*She sits on the chaise, at the up-stage end.*)

ROYDE. I meant anything fresh.

MARY. Oh, I know what you meant. It's really a wonderful relief to find anyone so gloriously just-the-same-as-usual as you are.

ROYDE. Not much good, is it, getting all het up over things?

MARY. No, you're very sensible, of course. It's how you manage to do it, beats me.

ROYDE. (*Moving down Left Centre*) I'm not so – close to things as you are.

MARY. That's true. I don't know what we should have done without you. You've been a tower of strength.

ROYDE. The human buffer, eh?

MARY. The house is still full of policemen.

ROYDE. Yes, I know. Found one in the bathroom this morning. I had to turf him out before I could shave. (*He sits in the armchair Left Centre.*)

MARY. I know – you come across them in the most unexpected places. (*She rises.*) They're looking for something. (*She shivers and moves up Right.*) It was a very near thing for poor Nevile, wasn't it?

ROYDE. Yes, very near. (*Grimly*) I can't help feeling pleased he's had a bit of a kick in the pants. He's always so damned complacent.

MARY. It's just his manner.

ROYDE. He's had the devil's own luck. If it had been some other poor chap with all that evidence piled against him, he wouldn't have had a hope.

MARY. It *must* have been someone from outside.

ROYDE. It wasn't. They've proved *that*. Everything was fastened up and bolted in the morning. (MARY *moves to the Centre bay window and examines the catch.*) Besides, what about your dope? That must have been someone in the house.

MARY. (*Shaking her head*) I just can't believe it could have been one of – us. (*She moves to the Right end of the rostrum.* LATIMER *enters by the French windows. He carries his jacket.*)

LATIMER. (*Moving to Right of the chaise*) Hullo, Royde. Good morning, Miss Aldin. I'm looking for Kay. Do you know where she is?

MARY. I think she's up in her room, Mr Latimer.

LATIMER. (*Putting his jacket over the up-stage end of the chaise*) I thought she might like to come and have lunch at the hotel. Not very cheerful for her here, in the circumstances.

MARY. You can hardly expect us to be very cheerful after what's happened, can you?

LATIMER. (*Moving down Right*) That's what I meant. It's different for Kay, though, you know. The old girl didn't mean so much to her.

MARY. Naturally. She hasn't known Lady Tressilian as long as we have.

LATIMER. Nasty business. I've had the police over at the hotel this morning.

MARY. What did they want?

LATIMER. Checking up on Strange, I suppose. They asked me all sorts of questions. I told them he was with me from after eleven until half past two, and they seemed satisfied. Lucky thing for him that he decided to follow me over to the hotel that night, wasn't it?

ROYDE. (*Rising*) Very lucky. (*He moves to the door Left.*) I'm going upstairs, Latimer. I'll tell Kay you're here, if I can find her.

LATIMER. Thanks. (ROYDE *exits Left. He looks toward the door Left for a moment, then goes to his jacket and takes his cigarettes from the pocket.*) A queer chap. Always seems to be keeping himself bottled up and afraid the cork might come out. Is Audrey going to reward at long last the dog-like devotion of a lifetime? (*He lights a cigarette for himself.*)

MARY. (*Crossing to the door Left; annoyed*) I don't know, and it's no business of ours. (*She hesitates and turns.*) When you saw the police, did they say anything – I mean – did you get any idea as to who they suspect now? (*She moves to Left of the armchair Left Centre.*)

LATIMER. They weren't making any confidences.

MARY. I didn't suppose they were, but I thought, perhaps from the questions they asked . . . (KAY *enters Left.*)

KAY. (*Crossing to* LATIMER) Hullo, Ted. It was sweet of you to come over.

LATIMER. I thought you could probably do with a bit of cheering up, Kay.

KAY. My God, how right you were. It was bad enough before in this house, but *now* . . .

LATIMER. What about a run in the car and lunch at the hotel – or anywhere else you like? (MARY *moves down Left.*)

KAY. I don't know what Nevile's doing . . .

LATIMER. I'm not asking Nevile – I'm asking *you*.

KAY. I couldn't come without Nevile, Ted. I'm sure it would do him good to get away from here for a bit.

LATIMER. (*Shrugging his shoulders*) All right – bring him along if you want to, Kay. I'm easy.

KAY. Where *is* Nevile, Mary?

MARY. I don't know. I think he's in the garden somewhere.

KAY. (*Crossing to the French windows*) I'll see if I can find him. I won't be long, Ted. (KAY *exits by the French windows.*)

LATIMER. (*Moving up Right; angrily*) What she sees in him I can't think. He's treated her like dirt.

MARY. (*Moving up Left of the armchair Left Centre*) I think she'll forgive him.

LATIMER. She shouldn't – now she's got her share of the old girl's money – she can go where she pleases, do what she likes. She's got a chance now of having a life of her own.

MARY. (*Sitting in the armchair Left Centre; with obscure feeling*) Can one ever really have a life of one's own? Isn't that just the illusion that lures us on – thinking – planning – for a future that will never really exist?

LATIMER. That wasn't what you were saying the other night.

MARY. I know. But that seems a long time ago. So much has happened since then.

LATIMER. Specifically, one murder.

MARY. You wouldn't talk so flippantly about murder if . . .

LATIMER. If what, Miss Aldin? (*He moves to Right of* MARY.)

MARY. If you had been as close to murder as I have.

LATIMER. This time it is better to be an outsider. (KAY *and* NEVILE *enter by the French windows.* KAY *looks a little annoyed.*)

KAY. (*As she enters*) It's no good, Ted. (*She goes on to the Right end of the rostrum.*) Nevile won't come so we can't go.

NEVILE. (*Moving down Right*) I don't see very well how we can. It's awfully nice of you, Latimer, but it would hardly be the thing, would it, after what's happened?

LATIMER. (*Moving above the chaise*) I don't see what harm it would do to go out to lunch – you've got to eat.

NEVILE. We can eat here. (*He crosses to Right of* KAY.) Hang it all, Kay, we can't go joy-riding about the country. The inquest hasn't been held yet.

LATIMER. If you feel like that about it, Strange, I suppose we'd better call it off. (*He picks up his jacket and moves to the French windows.*)

MARY. (*Rising*) Perhaps you would care to stay and lunch with *us*, Mr Latimer?

LATIMER. Well, that's very nice of you, Miss Aldin . . .

NEVILE. (*Moving above the chaise*) Yes, do, Latimer.

KAY. (*Moving to Left of the rostrum*) Will you, Ted?

LATIMER. (*Moving to Right of the chaise*) Thanks, I'd like to.

MARY. You'll have to take pot luck. I'm afraid the domestic arrangements are just a little disorganized with the police popping in and out of the kitchen every two minutes.

LATIMER. If it's going to be any trouble . . .

MARY. (*Moving to the door Left*) Oh, no – it'll be no trouble at all. (AUDREY *enters Left*. KAY *looks at the magazines on the coffee table.*)

AUDREY. Has anyone seen Mr Treves this morning?

NEVILE. I haven't seen him since breakfast. (LATIMER *moves down Right.*)

MARY. He was talking to the Inspector in the garden about half an hour ago. Do you want him particularly?

AUDREY. (*Crossing to Left Centre*) Oh, no – I just wondered where he was.

NEVILE. (*Looking off Right*) They're coming now. Not Mr Treves. Superintendent Battle and Inspector Leach.

MARY. (*Nervously*) What do you think they want now? (*They all wait nervously.* BATTLE *and* LEACH *enter by the French windows.* LEACH *carries a long brown-paper parcel. He stands Right of the chaise.*)

BATTLE. (*Crossing to Right Centre*) Hope we're not disturbing you all. There are one or two things we'd like to know about.

NEVILE. I should have thought you'd exhausted everything by now, Superintendent.

BATTLE. Not quite, Mr Strange. (*He takes a small chamois leather glove from his pocket.*) There's this glove, for instance – who does it belong to? (*They all stare at the glove without answering. To* AUDREY) Is it yours, Mrs Strange?

AUDREY. (*Shaking her head*) No, no, it isn't mine. (*She sits in the armchair Left Centre.*)

BATTLE. (*Holding the glove out towards* MARY) Miss Aldin?

MARY. I don't think so. I have none of that colour. (*She sits in the easy chair down Left.*)

BATTLE. (*To* KAY) What about you?

KAY. No. I'm sure it doesn't belong to *me*.

BATTLE. (*Moving to* KAY) Perhaps you'd just slip it on? It's the left-hand glove. (KAY *tries on the glove, but it is too small. He crosses to* MARY.) Will you try, Miss Aldin? (MARY *tries on the glove, but it is too small. He moves to Left of* AUDREY.) I think you'll find it fits *you* all right. Your hand is smaller than the other two ladies'. (AUDREY *reluctantly takes the glove.*)

NEVILE. (*Moving Right Centre; sharply*) She's already told you that it isn't her glove.

BATTLE. (*Blandly*) Perhaps she made a mistake – or forgot.

AUDREY. It may be mine – gloves are so alike, aren't they?

BATTLE. Try it on, Mrs Strange. (AUDREY *slips the glove on her left hand. It fits perfectly.*) It seems as if it is yours – at any rate it was found outside your window, pushed down into the ivy – with the other one that goes with it.

AUDREY. (*With difficulty*) I – I don't know – anything about it. (*She hastily removes the glove and gives it to* BATTLE.)

NEVILE. Look here, Superintendent, what are you driving at?

BATTLE. (*Crossing to Left of* NEVILE) Perhaps I might have a word with you *privately*, Mr Strange?

LATIMER. (*Moving to the French windows*) Come on, Kay, let's go out in the garden. (KAY *and* LATIMER *exit by the French windows.*)

BATTLE. There's no need to disturb everybody. (*To* NEVILE) Isn't there somewhere else we could . . .?

MARY. (*Rising quickly*) I was just going, in any case. (*To* AUDREY) You coming with me, Audrey?

AUDREY. (*Almost in a dream*) Yes – yes. (*She nods in a dazed, frightened manner, and rises slowly.* MARY *puts her arm around* AUDREY, *and they exit Left.*)

NEVILE. (*Sitting on the chaise*) Now, Superintendent. What's this absurd story about gloves outside Audrey's window?

BATTLE. It's not absurd, sir. We've found some very curious things in this house.

NEVILE. Curious? What do you mean by *curious*?

BATTLE. Give us the exhibit, Jim. (LEACH *moves to Right of* BATTLE, *extracts a heavy, steel-headed poker from his parcel, hands it to* BATTLE, *then moves down Left Centre. He shows the poker to* NEVILE.) Old-fashioned Victorian fire-iron.

NEVILE. You think that this –

BATTLE. – was what was really used? Yes, Mr Strange, I do.

NEVILE. But why? There's no sign . . .

BATTLE. Oh, it's been cleaned, and put back in the grate of the room where it belonged. But you can't remove bloodstains as easily as all that. We found traces all right. (*He moves up Centre and puts the poker on the windowseat.*)

NEVILE. (*Hoarsely*) Whose room was it in?

BATTLE. (*With a quick glance at* NEVILE) We'll come to that presently. I've got another question to ask you. That dinner jacket you wore last night, it's got fair hairs on the inside of the collar and on the shoulders. Do you know how they got there? (*He moves to the Left end of the rostrum.*)

NEVILE. No.

BATTLE. (*Crossing and standing up Right*) They're a lady's hairs, sir. Fair hairs. There were several red hairs, as well, on the sleeves.

NEVILE. These would be my wife's – Kay's. You are suggesting that the others are Audrey's? .

BATTLE. Oh, they are, sir. Unquestionably. We've had them compared with hairs from her brush.

NEVILE. Very likely they are. What about it? I remember I caught my cuff button in her hair the other night on the terrace.

LEACH. In that case the hairs would be on the cuff, sir. Not on the inside of the collar.

NEVILE. (*Rising*) What are you insinuating?

BATTLE. There are traces of powder, too, inside the jacket collar. Primavera Naturelle, a very pleasant-scented powder, and expensive. It's no good telling me that *you* use it, Mr Strange, because I shan't believe you. And Mrs Kay Strange uses Orchid Sun Kiss. Mrs Audrey Strange uses Primavera Naturelle.

NEVILE. Supposing she does?

BATTLE. It seems obvious that on some occasion Mrs Audrey Strange actually *wore* your dinner jacket. It's the only reasonable way the hairs and the powder could have got *inside* the collar. You've seen the glove that was found in the ivy outside her window. It's hers all right. It was the left-hand glove. Here's the right-hand one. (*He takes the glove from his pocket and holds it up. It is crumpled and stained with dried blood.*)

NEVILE. (*Huskily*) What – what's that on it?

BATTLE. Blood, Mr Strange. (*He holds the glove out to* LEACH. LEACH *moves on to the rostrum and takes the glove from* BATTLE.) Blood of the same group as Lady Tressilian's. An unusual blood group.

NEVILE. (*Moving slowly down Right*) Good God! Are you suggesting that Audrey – *Audrey* – would make all these elaborate preparations to kill an old lady she had known for years so that she could get hold of that money? (*His voice rises.*) Audrey? (ROYDE *enters quickly Left.*)

ROYDE. (*Crossing to Left of the chaise*) Sorry to interrupt, but I'd like to be in on this.

NEVILE. (*Annoyed*) Do you mind, Thomas? This is all rather private.

ROYDE. I'm afraid I don't care about that. You see, I heard Audrey's name mentioned . . .

NEVILE. (*Moving to Right of the chaise, angrily*) What the hell has Audrey's name got to do with you?

ROYDE. What has it to do with you, if it comes to that? I came here meaning to ask her to marry me, and I think she knows it. What's more, I mean to marry her.

NEVILE. I think you've got a damn nerve . . .

ROYDE. You can think what you like. I'm stopping here. (BATTLE *coughs.*)

NEVILE. Oh, all right! Sorry, Superintendent, for the interruption. (*To* ROYDE) The Superintendent is suggesting that Audrey – *Audrey* committed a brutal assault on Camilla and killed her. Motive – money.

BATTLE. (*Moving down Left Centre*) I didn't say the motive was money. I don't think it was, though fifty thousand pounds is a very sizeable motive. No, I think that this crime was directed against *you*, Mr Strange.

NEVILE. (*Startled*) Me?

BATTLE. I asked you – yesterday – who hated you. The answer, I think, is Audrey Strange.

NEVILE. Impossible. Why should she? I don't understand.

BATTLE. Ever since you left her for another woman, Audrey Strange has been brooding over her hatred of you. In my opinion – and strictly off the record – I think she's become mentally unbalanced. I daresay we'll have these high-class doctors saying so with a lot of long words. Killing you wasn't enough to satisfy her hate. She decided to get you hanged for murder. (ROYDE *moves up to Right.*)

NEVILE. (*Shaken*) I'll never believe that. (*He perches on the back of the chaise.*)

BATTLE. She wore your dinner jacket, she planted your niblick, smearing it with Lady Tressilian's blood and hair. The only thing that saved you was something she couldn't foresee.

Lady Tressilian rang her bell for Miss Aldin after you'd left . . .

NEVILE. It isn't true – it can't be true. You've got the whole thing wrong. Audrey's never borne a grudge against me. She's always been gentle – forgiving.

BATTLE. It's not my business to argue with you, Mr Strange. I asked for a word in private because I wanted to prepare you for what's about to happen. I'm afraid I shall have to caution Mrs Audrey Strange and ask her to accompany me . . .

NEVILE. (*Rising*) You mean – you're going to *arrest* her?

BATTLE. Yes, sir.

NEVILE. (*Crossing below the chaise to Right of* BATTLE) You can't – you can't – it's preposterous. (ROYDE *moves to Left of* NEVILE.)

ROYDE. (*Pushing* NEVILE *down on to the chaise*) Pull yourself together, Strange. Don't you see that the only thing that can help Audrey now is for you to forget all your ideas of chivalry and come out with the truth?

NEVILE. The truth? You mean . . .?

ROYDE. I mean the truth about Audrey and Adrian. (*He turns to* BATTLE.) I'm sorry, Superintendent, but you've got your *facts* wrong. Strange didn't leave Audrey for another woman. *She* left *him*. She ran away with my brother Adrian. Then Adrian was killed in a car accident on his way to meet her. Strange behaved very decently to Audrey. He arranged for her to divorce *him* and agreed to take the blame.

NEVILE. I didn't want her name dragged through the mud. I didn't know anyone knew.

ROYDE. Adrian wrote to me and told me all about it just before he was killed. (*To* BATTLE) You see, that knocks your motive out, doesn't it? (*He moves up Right Centre*) Audrey has no *cause* to hate Strange. On the contrary, she has every reason to be grateful to him.

NEVILE. (*Rising, eagerly*) Royde's right. He's right. That cuts out the motive. Audrey can't have done it. (KAY *enters quickly by the French windows*. LATIMER *slowly follows* KAY *on and stands down Right*.)

KAY. She did. She did. Of course she did.

NEVILE. (*Angrily*) Have you been listening?

KAY. Of course I have. And Audrey did it, I tell you. I've known she did it all the time. (*To* NEVILE) Don't you understand? She tried to get you hanged.

NEVILE. (*Crossing to Right of* BATTLE) You won't go through with it – not now?

BATTLE. (*Slowly*) I seem to have been wrong – about the motive. But there's still the money.

KAY. (*Moving below the chaise*) What money?

BATTLE. (*Crossing below* NEVILE *to Left of* KAY) Fifty thousand pounds comes to Mrs Audrey Strange at Lady Tressilian's death.

KAY. (*Dumbfounded*) To *Audrey*? To *me*. The money comes to Nevile and his wife. I'm his wife. Half the money comes to me. (NEVILE *moves slowly down Left*.)

BATTLE. I am informed – definitely – that the money was left in trust for Nevile Strange and 'his wife Audrey Strange'. She gets it, not you. (*He makes a sign to* LEACH. LEACH *exits quickly Left.* ROYDE *crosses slowly and stands up Left*.)

KAY. (*With a step towards* NEVILE) But you told me – you let me think . . .

NEVILE. (*Mechanically*) I thought you knew. We – I get fifty thousand. Isn't that enough? (*He moves to Left of the chaise*.)

BATTLE. Apart from all questions of motive, facts are facts. The facts point to her being guilty. (KAY *sits on the chaise*.)

NEVILE. All the facts showed that *I* was guilty yesterday.

BATTLE. (*Slightly taken aback*) That's true. (*He moves a little up Centre*.) But are you seriously asking me to believe that there's someone who hates *both* of you? Someone who, if the plan failed against you, laid a second trail to Audrey Strange? Can you think of anyone who hates both you *and* your former wife sufficiently for that?

NEVILE. (*Crushed*) No – no.

KAY. Of course Audrey did it. She planned it . . . (AUDREY *enters Left. She moves like a sleepwalker.* LEACH *follows her on.*)

AUDREY. (*Moving up Left Centre*) You wanted me, Superintendent? (ROYDE *moves quietly behind* AUDREY. NEVILE *faces* AUDREY, *his back to the audience*.)

BATTLE. (*Becoming very official*) Audrey Strange, I arrest you on the charge of murdering Camilla Tressilian on Thursday last, September the twenty-first. I must caution you that anything you say will be written down and may be used in evidence at your trial. (KAY *rises and moves to* LATIMER. LEACH *takes a notebook and pencil from his pocket, and stands waiting.* AUDREY *stares straight at* NEVILE *as though hypnotized.*)

AUDREY. So – it's come at last – it's come.

NEVILE. (*Turning away*) Where's Treves? Don't say anything. I'm going to find Treves. (NEVILE *exits by the French windows. Off. Calling*) Mr Treves. (AUDREY *sways and* ROYDE *holds her.*)

AUDREY. Oh – there's no escape – no escape. (*To* ROYDE) Dear Thomas, I'm so glad – it's all over – all over. (*She looks at* BATTLE.) I'm quite ready. (LEACH *writes down* AUDREY'*s words.* BATTLE *is impassive. The others stare at* AUDREY, *stupefied.* BATTLE *makes a sign to* LEACH, *who opens the door Left.* AUDREY *turns and exits slowly Left, followed by* BATTLE *and the others. The LIGHTS fade to black-out as – the Curtain falls.*)

CURTAIN

Scene II

SCENE: *The same. The same evening.*

When Curtain rises the windows and curtains are closed and the room is in darkness. NEVILE *is standing down Left. He crosses to the French windows, draws the curtains, opens the windows to get some air, then moves above the chaise. The door Left opens and a shaft of light illuminates* NEVILE. TREVES *enters down Left.*

TREVES. Ah, Nevile. (*He switches on the lights, closes the door and moves Left Centre.*)

NEVILE. (*Quickly and eagerly*) Did you see Audrey?

TREVES. Yes, I've just left her.

NEVILE. How is she? Has she got everything she wants? I tried to see her this afternoon, but they wouldn't let me.

TREVES. (*Sitting in the armchair Left Centre*) She doesn't wish to see anybody at present.

NEVILE. Poor darling. She must be feeling awful. We've got to get her out of it.

TREVES. I am doing everything that's possible, Nevile.

NEVILE. (*Moving down Right*) The whole thing's an appalling mistake. Nobody in their right senses would ever believe that *Audrey* would be capable – (*He moves Right of the chaise, then stands up Right Centre.*) of killing anyone – like *that*.

TREVES. (*Warningly*) The evidence is very strong against her.

NEVILE. I don't care a damn for the evidence.

TREVES. I'm afraid the police are more practical.

NEVILE. *You* don't believe it, do you? You don't believe . . .

TREVES. I don't know *what* to believe. Audrey has always been – an enigma.

NEVILE. (*Sitting on the chaise*) Oh, nonsense! She's always been sweet and *gentle*.

TREVES. She has always appeared so, certainly.

NEVILE. Appeared so? She *is*. Audrey and – and violence of any sort just don't go together. Only a muddle-headed fool like Battle would believe otherwise.

TREVES. Battle is far from being a muddle-headed fool, Nevile. I have always found him particularly shrewd.

NEVILE. Well, he hasn't proved himself very shrewd over this. (*He rises and moves up Right.*) Good God, you don't *agree* with him, do you? You can't believe this utterly stupid and fantastic story – that Audrey planned all this to – to get back on me for marrying Kay. It's too absurd.

TREVES. Is it? Love turns to hate very easily, you know, Nevile.

NEVILE. But she had no *reason* to hate me. (*He moves Right Centre.*) That motive was exploded when I told them about – about Adrian.

TREVES. I must confess that *that* was a surprise to me. I was always under the impression that *you* left *Audrey*.

NEVILE. I let everybody think so, of course. What else could I do? It's always so much worse for the woman – she'd have had to face the whole wretched business alone – with all the gossip and – and mud-slinging. I couldn't let her do that.

TREVES. It was very – generous of you, Nevile.

NEVILE. (*Sitting on the chaise*) Anybody would have done the same. Besides, in a way, it was my fault.

TREVES. Why?

NEVILE. Well – I'd met Kay, you see – while we were at Cannes – and I – I admit I was attracted. I flirted with her – in a harmless sort of way, and Audrey got annoyed.

TREVES. You mean she was jealous?

NEVILE. Well – yes, I think so.

TREVES. (*Rising*) If that was the case she couldn't have been – really – in love with Adrian.

NEVILE. I don't think she was.

TREVES. Then she left you for Adrian in a fit of pique – because she resented your – er – attentions to Kay?

NEVILE. Something like that.

TREVES. (*Moving to Left of* NEVILE) If that was the case, the original motive *still* holds good.

NEVILE. What do you mean?

TREVES. If Audrey was in love with you – if she only ran away with Adrian in a fit of pique – then she might still have *hated* you for marrying Kay.

NEVILE. (*Sharply*) No! She never hated me. She was very understanding about the whole thing.

TREVES. Outwardly – perhaps. What was she like *underneath*?

NEVILE. (*Rising; almost in a whisper*) You believe she did it, don't you? You believe she killed Camilla – in that horrible way? (*He pauses and crosses to the armchair Left Centre.*) It wasn't Audrey. I'll swear it wasn't Audrey. I know her, I tell you. I lived with her for four years – you can't do that and be mistaken in a person. But if *you* think she's guilty, what hope is there?

TREVES. I'll give you my candid opinion, Nevile. I don't think there is *any* hope. I shall brief the best possible counsel, of course, but there's very little case for the defence. Except insanity. I doubt if we'll get very far with that. (NEVILE *drops into the armchair Left Centre and covers his face with his hands.*)

NEVILE. (*Almost inaudibly*) Oh, God! (MARY *enters Left. She is very quiet and clearly under strain.*)

MARY. (*Not realizing that* NEVILE *is there*) Mr Treves! (*She sees* NEVILE.) Er – there are sandwiches in the dining-room when anyone wants them. (*She moves to Left of* NEVILE.)

NEVILE. (*Turning away*) Sandwiches!

TREVES. (*Moving up Right Centre; mildly*) Life has to go on, Nevile.

NEVILE. (*To* MARY) Do *you* think she did it, Mary?

MARY. (*After a definite pause*) No. (*She takes* NEVILE*'s hand.*)

NEVILE. Thank God somebody besides me believes in her. (KAY *enters by the French windows.*)

KAY. (*Moving to Right of the chaise*) Ted's just coming. He's running the car round into the drive. I came up through the garden.

NEVILE. (*Rising and moving above the chaise*) What's Latimer coming here for? Can't he keep away for five minutes?

TREVES. I sent for him, Nevile. Kay very kindly took the message. I also asked Battle to come. I would prefer not to explain in detail. Let us say, Nevile, that I am trying out a last forlorn hope.

NEVILE. To save Audrey?

TREVES. Yes.

KAY. (*To* NEVILE.) Can't you think of anything else but Audrey?

NEVILE. No, I can't. (KAY *moves to the easy chair down Right.* LATIMER *enters by the French windows and crosses to Right of* TREVES.)

LATIMER. I came as quickly as I could, Mr Treves. Kay didn't say what you wanted me for, only that it was urgent.

KAY. (*Sitting in the easy chair down Right.*) I said what I was told to say. I haven't the faintest idea what it's all about.

MARY. (*Crossing to the chaise and sitting*) We're all in the dark, Kay. As you heard, Mr Treves is trying to help Audrey.

KAY. Audrey, Audrey, Audrey. It's *always* Audrey. I suppose she'll haunt us for the rest of our lives.

NEVILE. (*Moving down Right of the chaise*) That's a beastly thing to say, Kay.

LATIMER. (*Angrily*) Can't you see that her nerves are all in shreds?

NEVILE. So are everybody's. (LATIMER *moves and stands above* KAY. ROYDE *enters Left.*)

ROYDE. Superintendent Battle is here. (*To* TREVES) He says he's expected.

TREVES. Bring him in. (ROYDE *turns and beckons off.* BATTLE *enters Left.*)

BATTLE. Good evening. (*He looks enquiringly at* TREVES.)

TREVES. (*Moving down Centre*) Thank you for coming, Superintendent. It is good of you to spare the time.

NEVILE. (*Bitterly*) Especially when you've got your victim.

TREVES. I don't think that kind of remark is going to get us any-where, Nevile. Battle has only done his duty as a police officer.

NEVILE. (*Moving up Right*) I'm – I'm sorry, Battle.

BATTLE. That's all right, sir.

TREVES. (*Indicating the easy chair Left Centre*) Sit down, Battle.

BATTLE. (*Sitting in the easy chair Left Centre*) Thank you, sir.

TREVES. Mr Royde said something to me the other day, Battle, that I've thought about a great deal since.

ROYDE. (*Surprised*) I did?

TREVES. Yes, Thomas. You were talking about a detective story you were reading. You said that they all begin in the *wrong* place. The murder should not be the *beginning* of the story but the end. And, of course, you were right. A murder *is* the culmination of a lot of different circumstances, all converging at a given moment at a given point. Rather fancifully, you called it *Zero Hour*.

ROYDE. I remember.

NEVILE. (*Impatiently*) What's this got to do with Audrey?

TREVES. A great deal – *it's Zero Hour now.* (*There is a rather uncomfortable pause.*)

MARY. But Lady Tressilian was murdered three days ago.

TREVES. It is not exactly Lady Tressilian's murder that I am talking about now. There are different kinds of murder. Superinten-dent Battle, when I put it to you, will you allow that all the evidence against Audrey Strange *could* have been faked? The weapon taken from her fender. *Her* gloves, stained with blood, and hidden in the ivy outside her window. *Her* face powder, dusted on the inside of Nevile's dinner jacket. Hairs from *her* brush placed there as well?

BATTLE. (*Stirring uncomfortably*) I suppose it *could* have been done, but . . .

KAY. But she admitted she was guilty – herself – when you arrested her.

ROYDE. (*Moving down Left*) No, she didn't.

KAY. She said that she couldn't escape.

MARY. She said that she was glad it was all over.

KAY. What more do you want? (TREVES *holds up a hand. They subside.* NEVILE *crosses slowly and stands on the Left end of the rostrum.*)

TREVES. (*Moving to Centre of the rostrum.*) Do you remember, Thomas, that when the Superintendent here was questioning you as to what you had heard on the night of the murder, you mentioned rats? Rats in the attic – over your head?

ROYDE. (*Sitting in the easy chair down Left*) Yes.

TREVES. That remark of yours interested me. I went up to the attic floor – I will admit, with no very clear idea in my head. The attic directly over your bedroom, Thomas, is used as a lumber room. It is full of what may be termed junk. Unwanted junk. There was heavy dust over everything except one thing. (*He crosses to the bureau.*) But there was one thing that was *not* covered with dust. (*He takes out a long coil of thin rope which has been concealed in the corner Right of the bureau.*) This. (*He crosses to Right of* BATTLE. BATTLE *takes the rope. His eyebrows rise in surprise.*)

BATTLE. It's damp.

TREVES. Yes, it's still damp. No dust on it – and damp. Thrown into the lumber room where someone thought it would never be noticed.

BATTLE. Are you going to tell us, sir, what it means? (*He returns the rope to* TREVES.)

TREVES. (*Moving on to the rostrum*) It means that during the storm on the night of the murder, that rope was hanging from one of the windows of this house. Hanging from a window down to the water below. (*He tosses the rope on to the coffee table.*) You said, Superintendent, that no one could have entered this house to commit murder from outside that night. That isn't quite true. Someone could have entered from outside – (LATIMER *moves very slowly above the chaise.*) if this rope was hanging ready for them to climb up from the estuary.

BATTLE. You mean someone came from the other side? The Easterhead side?

TREVES. Yes. (*He turns to* NEVILE.) You went over on the ten-thirty-five ferry. You must have got to the *Easterhead Bay Hotel* at about a quarter to eleven – but you weren't able to find Mr Latimer for some time, were you? (LATIMER *makes a move as though to speak, then stops himself.*)

NEVILE. No, that's true. I looked all around, too. He wasn't in his room – they telephoned up.

LATIMER. Actually, I was sitting out on the glass-enclosed terrace with a fat, talkative body from Lancashire. (*Easily*) She wanted to dance – but I stalled her off. Too painful on the feet.

TREVES. (*Moving Centre*) Strange wasn't able to find you until half past eleven. Three-quarters of an hour. Plenty of time . . .

LATIMER. Look here, what do you mean?

NEVILE. Do you mean that he . . .? (KAY *shows every sign of violent agitation, rises and moves to* LATIMER.)

TREVES. Plenty of time to strip, swim across the estuary – it's narrow just here – swarm up the rope – do what you had to do – swim back, get into your clothes and meet Nevile in the lounge of the hotel.

LATIMER. Leaving the rope hanging from the window? You're crazy – the whole thing's crazy.

TREVES. (*With a slight glance towards* KAY) The same person who arranged the rope for you could have drawn it up again and put it in the attic.

LATIMER. (*Frenzied*) You can't do this to me. You can't frame me – and don't you try. I couldn't climb up a rope all that way – and anyway, I can't swim. I tell you, I can't swim.

KAY. No, Ted can't swim. It's true, I tell you, he can't swim.

TREVES. (*Gently*) No, you can't swim. I have ascertained that fact. (*He moves on to the rostrum.* KAY *moves down. To* NEVILE) But you're a very fine swimmer, aren't you, Nevile? And you're an expert climber. It would be child's play to you to swim across, climb up the rope you'd left ready – (LATIMER *moves Right of the chaise.*) go along to Lady Tressilian's room, kill her, and go back the way you came. Plenty of time to dispose of the rope when you got back at two-thirty. You didn't see Latimer at the hotel between ten-forty-five and eleven-thirty – *but* he didn't see you either. It cuts both ways. (BATTLE *rises and stands in front of the door Left.*)

NEVILE. I never heard such rubbish! Swim across – kill Camilla. Why ever should I do such a fantastic thing?

TREVES. Because you wanted to hang the woman who had left you for another man. (KAY *collapses in the easy chair down Right.* MARY *rises, moves to* KAY *and comforts her.* ROYDE *rises and moves to Left of the armchair Left Centre.*) She had to be punished – your ego has been swelling for a long time – nobody must dare to oppose you.

NEVILE. It is likely I'd fake all those clues against *myself?*

TREVES. (*Crossing to Left of* NEVILE) It's exactly what you did do – and took the precaution of ringing Lady Tressilian's bell by pulling the old-fashioned bell wire outside her room, to make sure that Mary would see you leaving the house. Lady Tressilian didn't remember ringing that bell. *You* rang it.

NEVILE. (*Moving to the French windows*) What an absurd pack of lies. (LEACH *appears at the French windows.*)

TREVES. *You* murdered Lady Tressilian – but the real murder, the murder that you gloated over secretly, was the murder of Audrey Strange. You wanted her not only to die – but to suffer. You wanted her to be afraid – she was afraid – of you. You enjoyed the idea of her suffering, didn't you?

NEVILE. (*Sitting on the chaise; thickly*) All – a tissue of lies.

BATTLE. (*Crossing to Left of* NEVILE) Is it? I've met people like you before – people with a mental kink. Your vanity was hurt when Audrey Strange left you, wasn't it? You loved her and she had the colossal impertinence to prefer another man. (NEVILE's *face shows momentary agreement. He watches* NEVILE *narrowly.*) You wanted to think of something special – something clever, something quite out of the way. The fact that it entailed the killing of a woman who had been almost a mother to you didn't worry you.

NEVILE. (*With resentment*) She shouldn't have ticked me off like a child. But it's lies – all lies. And I haven't got a mental kink.

BATTLE. (*Watching* NEVILE). Oh, yes, you have. Your wife flicked you on the raw, didn't she, when she left you? You – the wonderful Nevile Strange. You saved your pride by pretending that *you'd* left *her* – and you married another girl just to bolster up that story.

KAY. Oh. (*She turns to* MARY. MARY *puts her arm around* KAY).

BATTLE. But all the time you were planning what you'd do to Audrey. Pity you didn't have the brains to carry it out better.

NEVILE. (*Almost whimpering*) It's not true.

BATTLE. (*Inexorably breaking him down*) Audrey's been laughing at you – while you've been preening yourself and thinking how clever you were. (*He raises his voice and calls*). Come in, Mrs Strange. (AUDREY *enters* NEVILE *gives a strangled cry and rises.* ROYDE *moves to* AUDREY *and puts an arm around her.*) She's never been really under arrest, you know. We just wanted to keep her out of your crazy reach. There was no knowing what you might do if you thought your silly childish plan was going wrong. (BENSON *appears at the French windows.* LEACH *moves above the chaise.*)

NEVILE. (*Breaking down and screaming with rage*) It wasn't silly. It was clever – it *was* clever. I thought out every detail. How was *I* to know that Royde knew the truth about Audrey and Adrian? Audrey and Adrian . . . (*He suddenly loses control and screams at* AUDREY). How dare you prefer Adrian to me? God damn and blast your soul, you *shall*, hang. They've *got* to hang you. They've got to. (*He makes a dash towards* AUDREY. BATTLE *makes a sign to* LEACH *and* BENSON, *who move one each side of* NEVILE. AUDREY *clings to* ROYDE. *Half sobbing*) Leave me alone. I want her to die *afraid* – to die afraid. I hate her. (AUDREY *and* ROYDE *turn away from* NEVILE *and move up Left*)

MARY. (*Moving to the chaise and sitting; almost inaudibly*) Oh, God!

BATTLE. Take him away, Jim. (LEACH *and* BENSON *close in on* NEVILE).

NEVILE. (*Suddenly quite calm*) You're making a great mistake, you know. I can . . . (LEACH *and* BENSON *lead* NEVILE *to the door Left.* NEVILE *suddenly kicks* BENSON *on the shin, pushes him into* LEACH, *and dashes off Left.* LEACH *and* BENSON *dash off after* NEVILE).

BATTLE. (*In alarm*) Look out! Stop him. (BATTLE *dashes off Left. Off; shouting*) After him – don't let him get away. (TREVES *and* ROYDE *run out Left.* AUDREY *moves slowly to Centre of rostrum.*)

ROYDE. (*Off; shouting*) He's locked himself in the dining-room.

BATTLE. (*Off; shouting*) Break the door open. (*The sound of heavy blows on wood is heard off.* KAY *rises*).

KAY. (*Burying her face in* LATIMER*'s shoulder*) Ted – oh, Ted . . . (*She sobs. There is a crash of breaking glass off, followed by the sound of the door breaking open*).

BATTLE. (*Off; shouting*) Jim – you go down by the road. I'll take the cliff path. (BATTLE *enters quickly Left, and crosses quickly to the French windows. He looks worried. Breathlessly*) He flung himself through the dining-room window. It's a sheer drop to the rocks below. I shouldn't think there was a chance. (BATTLE *exits by the French windows.* BENSON *enters Left, crosses, exits by the French windows, and is heard to give three shrill blasts on his whistle.*)

KAY. (*Hysterically*) I want to get away. I can't . . .

MARY. (*Rising and moving Centre*) Why don't you take her back to the hotel with you, Mr Latimer?

KAY. (*Eagerly*) Yes. Ted, please – anything to get away from here.

MARY. Take her. I'll have her things packed and sent over.

LATIMER. (*Gently*) Come along. (KAY *exits with* LATIMER *by the French windows.* MARY *nods and exits Left.* AUDREY *moves to the chaise, sits on it, with her back to the bay window, and sobs. There is a slight pause, then the curtains of the bay window are parted a little.* NEVILE *enters quietly over the sill of the bay window. His hair is dishevelled and there are streaks of dirt on his face and hands. There is a cruel and devilish smile on his face as he looks at* AUDREY. *He moves silently towards her.*)

NEVILE. Audrey! (AUDREY *turns quickly and sees* NEVILE. *In a low, tense voice*) You didn't think I'd come back, did you? I was too clever for them, Audrey. While they were breaking open the door I flung a stool through the window and climbed out on to the stone ledge. Only a man who is used to mountain climbing could have done it – a man with strong fingers – like mine. (*He moves slowly nearer and nearer to* AUDREY). Strong fingers, Audrey – and a soft throat. They wouldn't hang you as I wanted them to, would they? But you're going to die just the same. (*His fingers close on her throat.*) You'll never belong to anyone but me. (LEACH *dashes in Left.* BENSON *dashes in by the French windows.* LEACH *and* BENSON *drag* NEVILE *from* AUDREY *and exit with him by the French windows.* AUDREY *is left gasping for breath on the chaise.* ROYDE *enters Left. He stares in a puzzled way towards the French windows and crosses towards them. He has almost passed the up-stage end of the chaise when he realizes* AUDREY *is there.*)

ROYDE. (*Stopping and turning to* AUDREY) I say, are you all right?

AUDREY. Am I all right? Oh, Thomas! (*She laughs.* ROYDE, *with his arms outstretched, moves towards* AUDREY *as — the Curtain falls.*

CURTAIN

VERDICT

Presented by Peter Saunders at the Strand Theatre, London, on 22nd May 1958, with the following cast of characters:

(*in the order of their appearance*)

LESTER COLE	*George Roubicek*
MRS ROPER	*Gretchen Franklin*
LISA KOLETZKY	*Patricia Jessel*
PROFESSOR KARL HENDRYK	*Gerard Heinz*
DR STONER	*Derek Oldham*
ANYA HENDRYK	*Viola Keats*
HELEN ROLLANDER	*Moira Redmond*
SIR WILLIAM ROLLANDER	*Norman Claridge*
DETECTIVE INSPECTOR OGDEN	*Michael Golden*
POLICE SERGEANT PEARCE	*Gerald Sim*

The play directed by Charles Hickman

Décor by Joan Jefferson Farjeon

SYNOPSIS OF SCENES

The action of the play passes in the living-room of
Professor Hendryk's flat in Bloomsbury

ACT I

SCENE 1   An afternoon in early spring
SCENE 2   A fortnight later. Afternoon

ACT II

SCENE 1   Four days later. About midday
SCENE 2   Six hours later. Evening
SCENE 3   Two months later. Late afternoon

Time: the present

ACT ONE

Scene I

SCENE: *The living-room of* PROFESSOR HENDRYK'*s flat in Blooms-*
bury. An afternoon in early spring.

The flat is the upper floor of one of the old houses in Bloomsbury. It is a well-
proportioned room with comfortable, old-fashioned furniture. The main
feature that strikes the eye is books; books everywhere, in shelves against
the wall, lying on tables, on chairs, on the sofa and piled up in heaps on
the floor. Double doors up Centre lead to an entrance door in Right and a
passage leads off Left to the kitchen. In the room the door to ANYA'*s*
bedroom is down Right and there is a sash window Left leading on to a
small balcony with ivy-covered railings, overlooking the street below and a
row of houses opposite. KARL'*s desk is in front of the window with a*
chair in front of it. The desk is filled with books as well as the telephone,
blotter, calendar, etc. Below the desk is a record cabinet, filled with
records, more books and odd lecture papers. There is a record player
on top. Built into the walls either side of the double doors are book-
cases. Below the left one is ANYA'*s small work-table. Between the doors*
and the bookcase Left of it there is a three-tiered, round table with books
in each tier and a plant on the top one. Against the wall below the door
Right is a small console table with a plant on top and books piled below.
Hanging on the wall above the door down Right is a small set of shelves
with more books and ANYA'*s medicine in one corner. Under the shelves*
is a small cupboard with further books. More cupboards underneath. In
front of these shelves, there is a library ladder. A sofa is Right Centre
with a circular table behind it. Chairs stand above and Left of the table.
All three pieces of furniture have books on them. A large red armchair is
Left Centre, with still more books on it. At night the room is lit by a
wall-bracket each side of the window and table-lamps on the desk, on
the table Right Centre and on the cupboard Right. There are switches

Left of the double doors. In the hall there is a chair Right of the bedroom door.

When Curtain rises, the double doors are open. The stage is in darkness. When the LIGHTS come up LESTER COLE *is precariously balanced on the library ladder. He is a clumsy but likeable young man of about twenty-four, with a tousled head of hair. He is shabbily dressed. There is a pile of books on the top of the ladder.* LESTER *reaches up to the top shelf, selects a book now and again, pauses to read a passage and either adds it to the pile on the ladder or replaces it on the shelf.*

MRS ROPER. (*Off Left in the hall*) All right, Miss Koletzky, I'll see to it before I go home.

(MRS ROPER *enters the hall from Left. She is a rather shifty and unpleasant cleaning woman. She is carrying her outdoor clothes and a shopping bag. She crosses to Right of the hall then returns with great stealth, entering the room with her back against the right-hand door. She obviously does not see* LESTER, *who is engrossed in a book. She creeps towards the down-stage end of the desk, where there is a packet of cigarettes. She is just about to pocket them when* LESTER *shuts his book with a bang.* MRS ROPER, *startled out of her wits, spins round.*)

Oh, Mr Cole – I didn't know you were still here.

(LESTER *goes to return the book to the top shelf and nearly overbalances.*)

Do be careful. (*She crosses above the armchair Left Centre to Right of it and puts her bag on the floor.*) That thing's not safe, really it isn't. (*She puts on her hat.*) Come to pieces any minute, it might, and where would you be then, I'd like to know? (*She puts on her coat.*)
LESTER. Where indeed?

(*The LIGHTS begin to fade slowly for sunset.*)

MRS ROPER. Only yesterday I read in the papers of a gentleman as fell off a pair of steps in his library. Thought nothing of it at the time – but later he was took bad and they rushed him to hospital. (*She puts her scarf around her neck.*) Broken rib what had penetrated the lung. (*With satisfaction*) And the next day he was – (*She gives her scarf a final pull round her throat*) dead.

LESTER. What jolly papers you read, Mrs Roper. (*He becomes engrossed in a book and ignores* MRS ROPER.)

MRS ROPER. And the same will happen to you if you go stretching over like that. (*She glances at the desk where the cigarettes are, then back at* LESTER *again. Seeing that he is taking no notice of her, she starts to sidle over to the desk, humming quietly to herself and keeping an eye on* LESTER. *She empties the cigarettes from the packet into her pocket, then moves Centre holding the empty packet*) Oh, look! The professor's run out of cigarettes again.

(*A clock strikes five somewhere outside the window.*)

I'd better slip out and get him another twenty before they shut. Tell Miss Koletzky I won't be long fetching back that washing. (*She picks up her bag, goes into the hall and calls*) Bye!

(MRS ROPER *exits in the hall to Right. The front door is heard opening and closing.*)

LESTER. (*Without taking his nose out of the book*) I'll tell her.

(*A door is heard to slam off Left in the hall.* LESTER *jumps, knocking the pile of books off the top of the steps.* LISA KOLETZKY *enters up Centre from Left. She is a tall, handsome, dark woman of thirty-five, with a strong and rather enigmatic personality. She is carrying a hot-water bottle.*)

Sorry, Miss Koletzky, I'll pick 'em up. (*He comes down the ladder and picks up the books.*)

LISA. (*Moving Centre*) It does not matter. A few more books here and there are of no consequence.

LESTER. (*Placing the books on the table Right Centre*) You startled me, you see. How is Mrs Hendryk?

LISA. (*Tightening the stopper on the bottle*) The same as usual. She feels the cold. I have a fresh bottle here for her.

LESTER. (*Moving to Right of the sofa*) Has she been ill for a very long time?

LISA. (*Sitting on the Left arm of the sofa*) Five years.

LESTER. Will she ever get any better?

LISA. She has her bad and her good days.

LESTER. Oh, yes, but I mean really better.

(LISA *shakes her head.*)

I say, that's tough going, isn't it?

LISA. (*Rather foreign*) As you say, it is 'tough going'.

LESTER. (*Climbing up the ladder and falling up before reaching the top*) Can't the doctors do anything?

LISA. No. She has one of these diseases for which at present there is no known cure. Some day perhaps they will discover one. In the meantime – (*She shrugs her shoulders*) she can never get any better. Every month, every year, she gets a little weaker. She may go on like that for many, many years.

LESTER. Yes, that is tough. It's tough on him. (*He comes down the ladder.*)

LISA. As you say, it is tough on him.

LESTER. (*Moving to Right of the sofa*) He's awfully good to her, isn't he?

LISA. He cares for her very much.

LESTER. (*Sitting on the Right arm of the sofa*) What was she like when she was young?

LISA. She was very pretty. Yes, a very pretty girl, fair-haired and blue-eyed and always laughing.

LESTER. (*Bewildered by life*) You know, it gets me. I mean, time – what it does to you. How people change. I mean, it's hard to know what's real and what isn't – or if anything is real.

LISA. (*Rising and crossing to the door down Right*) This bottle seems to be real.

(LISA *exits down Right, leaving the door open.* LESTER *rises, collects his satchel from the table Right Centre, crosses to the armchair Left Centre and puts some books from the chair into the satchel.* LISA *can be heard talking to* ANYA, *but the words are indistinguishable.* LISA *re-enters down Right.*)

LESTER. (*Guiltily*) The professor said it would be all right to take anything I wanted.

LISA. (*Moving to Right of the table Right Centre and glancing at the books*) Of course, if he said so.

LESTER. He's rather wonderful, isn't he?

LISA. (*Absorbed in a book*) Hmm?

LESTER. The Prof., he's wonderful. We all think so, you know. Everybody's terrifically keen. The way he puts things. All the past seems to come alive. (*He pauses.*) I mean, when he talks

about it you see what everything means. He's pretty unusual,
isn't he?

LISA. He has a very fine brain.

LESTER. (*Sitting on the Right arm of the armchair*) Bit of luck for us that
he had to leave his own country and came here. But it isn't only
his brain, you know, it's something else.

(LISA *selects a 'Walter Savage Landor', moves and sits on the sofa at the Left
end.*)

LISA. I know what you mean. (*She reads.*)

LESTER. You just feel that he knows all about you. I mean, that he
knows just how difficult everything is. Because you can't get
away from it – life is difficult, isn't it?

LISA. (*Still reading*) I do not see why it should be so.

LESTER. (*Startled*) I beg your pardon?

LISA. I don't see why you say – and so many people say – that life is
difficult. I think life is very simple.

LESTER. Oh, come now – hardly simple.

LISA. But, yes. It has a pattern, the sharp edges, very easy to see.

LESTER. Well, I think it's just one unholy mess. (*Doubtfully, but hoping
he is right*) Perhaps you're a kind of Christian Scientist?

LISA. (*Laughing*) No, I'm not a Christian Scientist.

LESTER. But you really think life's easy and happy?

LISA. I did not say it was easy or happy. I said it was simple.

LESTER. (*Rising and crossing to Left of the sofa*) I know you're awfully
good – (*Embarrassed*) I mean, the way you look after
Mrs Hendryk and everything.

LISA. I look after her because I want to do so, not because it is
good.

LESTER. I mean, you could get a well-paid job if you tried.

LISA. Oh, yes, I could get a job quite easily. I am a trained physicist.

LESTER. (*Impressed*) I'd no idea of that. But then, surely you ought
to get a job, oughtn't you?

LISA. How do you mean – ought?

LESTER. Well, I mean it's rather a waste, isn't it, if you don't? Of
your ability, I mean.

LISA. A waste of my training, perhaps, yes. But ability – I think
what I am doing now I do well, and I like doing it.

LESTER. Yes, but . . .

(*The front door is heard opening and closing.* KARL HENDRYK *enters up Centre from Right. He is a virile and good-looking man of forty-five. He is carrying a briefcase and a small bunch of spring flowers. He switches on the wall-brackets, the table-lamp Right and the table-lamp Right Centre by the switches Left of the door. He smiles at* LISA, *who rises as he moves Centre, and his face lights up with pleasure to see* LESTER.)

KARL. Hullo, Lisa.

LISA. Hullo, Karl.

KARL. Look – spring. (*He hands her the flowers.*)

LISA. How lovely. (*She moves round below the sofa, puts the flowers on the table Right Centre, then continues round the table and takes* KARL's *coat and hat.*)

(LISA *exits off Centre to Left with the hat and coat.*)

KARL. So you have come for more books? Good. Let me see what you are taking.

(*They look over the books together.*)

Yes, Loshen is good – very sound. And the Verthmer. Salzen – I warn you – he is very unsound.

LESTER. Then, perhaps, sir, I'd better not . . .

KARL. No. No, take it. Read it. I warn you out of my own experience, but you must make your own judgements.

LESTER. Thank you, sir. I'll remember what you say. (*He crosses above* KARL *to the table Right Centre and picks up a book.*) I brought the Loftus back. It is just as you said – he really makes one think. (*He replaces the book on the table.*)

(KARL *crosses above the armchair to the desk, takes some books from his briefcase and puts them on the desk.*)

KARL. Why not stay and have some supper with us? (*He switches on the desk lamp.*)

LESTER. (*Putting books in his satchel*) Thank you so much, sir, but I've got a date.

KARL. I see. Well, goodbye till Monday, then. Take care of the books.

(LISA *enters up Centre from Left and crosses to Right of the table Right Centre.*)

LESTER. (*Flushing guiltily*) Oh, I will, sir. I'm awfully sorry — more sorry than I can tell you — about losing that other one.

KARL. (*Sitting at the desk*) Think no more about it. I have lost books myself in my time. It happens to all of us.

LESTER. (*Moving to the doors up Centre*) You've been awfully good about it. Awfully good. Some people wouldn't have lent me any more books.

KARL. Tcha! That would have been foolish. Go on, my boy.

(LESTER *exits rather unwillingly by the hall to Right.*)

(*To* LISA) How is Anya?

LISA. She has been very depressed and fretful this afternoon, but she settled down for a little sleep. I hope she is asleep, now.

KARL. I won't wake her if she is asleep. My poor darling, she needs all the sleep she can get.

LISA. I'll get some water for the flowers.

(LISA *takes a vase from the shelf Right, picks up the flowers and exits in the hall to Left.* LESTER *appears in the hall from Right and comes back into the room. He glances quickly round, makes sure he is alone with* KARL *and moves to Right of the armchair.*)

LESTER. (*With a rush*) I've got to tell you, sir, I must. I – I didn't lose that book.

(LISA *enters from up Centre and Left with the flowers in the vase, crosses very quietly to Left of the table and Right Centre and puts the vase on it.*)

I – I sold it.

KARL. (*Not turning and not really surprised, but kindly nodding his head*) I see. You sold it.

LESTER. I never meant to tell you. I don't know why I have. But I just felt you'd got to know. I don't know what you'll think of me.

KARL. (*Turning round, thoughtfully*) You sold it. For how much?

LESTER. (*Slightly pleased with himself*) I got two pounds for it. Two pounds.

KARL. You wanted the money?

LESTER. Yes, I did. I wanted it badly.

KARL. (*Rising*) What did you want the money for?

LESTER. (*Giving* KARL *a rather shifty glance*) Well, you see, my mother's been ill lately and . . . (*He breaks off and moves away from* KARL *down Centre.*) No, I won't tell you any more lies. I wanted it – you see, there was a girl. I wanted to take her out, and . . .

(KARL *suddenly smiles at* LESTER *and crosses below the armchair to Left of him.*)

KARL. Ah! You wanted it to spend on a girl. I see. Good. Very good – very good, indeed.

LESTER. Good? But . . .

KARL. So natural. Oh, yes, it was very wrong of you to steal my book and to sell it and to lie to me about it. But if you have to do bad things I am glad that you do them for a good motive. And at your age there is no better motive than that – to go out with a girl and enjoy yourself. (*He pats* LESTER *on the shoulder.*) She is pretty, your girl?

LESTER. (*Self-consciously*) Well, naturally, I think so. (*He gains confidence.*) Actually, she's pretty marvellous.

KARL. (*With a knowing chuckle*) And you had a good time on the two pounds?

LESTER. In a way. Well, I mean, I began by enjoying it awfully. But – but I did feel rather uncomfortable.

KARL. (*Sitting on the Right arm of the armchair*) You felt uncomfortable – yes, that's interesting.

LESTER. Do believe me, sir, I am terribly sorry and ashamed, and it won't happen again. And I'll tell you this, too, I'm going to save up and buy that book back and bring it back to you.

KARL. (*Gravely*) Then you shall do so if you can. Now, cheer up – that's all over and forgotten.

(LESTER *throws* KARL *a grateful glance and exits by the hall to Right.* LISA *comes slowly forward towards* KARL.)

(*He nods his head.*) I'm glad he came and told me about it himself. I hoped he would, but of course I wasn't at all sure.

LISA. (*Moving Right Centre*) You knew, then, that he'd stolen it?

KARL. Of course I knew.

LISA. (*Puzzled*) But you didn't let him know that you knew.

KARL. No.

LISA. Why?

KARL. Because, as I say, I hoped he would tell me about it himself.

LISA. (*After a pause*) Was it a valuable book?

KARL. (*Rising and moving to the desk*) Actually, it's quite irreplaceable.

LISA. (*Turning away*) Oh, Karl.

KARL. Poor devil – so pleased to have got two pounds for it. The dealer who bought it off him will probably have sold it for forty or fifty pounds by now.

LISA. So he won't be able to buy it back?

KARL. (*Sitting at the desk*) No.

LISA. (*Crossing to Right of the armchair*) I don't understand you, Karl. (*She begins to lose her temper.*) It seems to me sometimes you go out of your way to let yourself be played upon – you allow yourself to have things stolen from you, to be deceived . . .

KARL. (*Gently but amused*) But, Lisa, I wasn't deceived.

LISA. Well, that makes it worse. Stealing is stealing. The way you go on positively encourages people to steal.

KARL. (*Becoming thoughtful*) Does it? I wonder. I wonder.

(LISA *is very angry now and starts pacing below the sofa and back up Centre.*)

LISA. How angry you make me.

KARL. I know. I always make you angry.

LISA. (*Moving up Right*) That miserable boy . . .

KARL. (*Rising and standing up Left Centre*) That miserable boy has the makings of a very fine scholar – a really fine scholar. That's rare, you know, Lisa. That's very rare. There are so many of these boys and girls, earnest, wanting to learn, but not the real thing.

(LISA *sits on Left arm of the sofa.*)

(*He moves to Left of* LISA) But Lester Cole is the real stuff of which scholars are made.

(LISA *has calmed down by now and she puts her arm affectionately on* KARL's *arm.*)

(*He smiles ruefully. After a pause*) You've no idea of the difference one Lester Cole makes to a weary professor's life.

LISA. I can understand that. There is so much mediocrity.

KARL. Mediocrity and worse. (*He gives* LISA *a cigarette, lights it, then sits Centre of the sofa.*) I'm willing to spend time on the conscientious plodder, even if he isn't very bright, but the people who want to acquire learning as a form of intellectual snobbery, to try it on as you try on a piece of jewellery, who want just a smattering and only a smattering, and who ask for their food to be pre-digested, that I won't stand for. I turned one of them down today.

LISA. Who was that?

KARL. A very spoiled young girl. Naturally she's at liberty to attend classes and waste her time, but she wants private tuition – special lessons.

LISA. Is she prepared to pay for them?

KARL. That is her idea. Her father, I gather, has immense wealth and has always bought his daughter everything she wanted. Well, he won't buy her private tuition from me.

LISA. We could do with the money.

KARL. I know. I know, but it's not a question of money – it's the time, you see, Lisa. I really haven't got the time. There are two boys, Sydney Abrahamson – you know him – and another boy. A coal miner's son. They're both keen, desperately keen, and I think they've got the stuff in them. But they're handicapped by a bad superficial education. I've got to give them private time if they're to have a chance.

(LISA *rises, crosses above the armchair and flicks her cigarette ash into the ashtray on the desk.*)

And they're worth it, Lisa, they're worth it. Do you understand?

LISA. I understand that one cannot possibly change you, Karl. You stand by and smile when a student helps himself to a valuable book, you refuse a rich pupil in favour of a penniless one. (*She crosses to Centre.*) I'm sure it is very noble, but nobility doesn't pay the baker and the butcher and the grocer.

KARL. But surely, Lisa, we are really not so hard up.

LISA. No, we are not really so hard up, but we could always do with some more money. Just think what we could do with this room.

(*The thumping of a stick is heard off Right.*)

Ah! Anya is awake.

KARL. (*Rising*) I'll go to her.

(KARL *exits down Right.* LISA *smiles, sighs and shakes her head, then collects the books from the armchair and puts them on the table Right Centre. The music of a barrel organ is heard off.* LISA *picks up the 'Walter Savage Landor' from the table Right Centre, sits on the Left arm of the sofa and reads.* MRS ROPER *enters the hall from Right. She carries a large parcel of washing. She exits in the hall to Left, deposits the parcel, then re-enters and comes into the room with her shopping bag.*)

MRS ROPER. I got the washing. (*She goes to the desk.*) And I got a few more fags for the professor – he was right out again. (*She takes a packet of cigarettes from her shopping bag and puts them on the desk.*) Oh! Don't they carry on when they run out of fags? You should have heard Mr Freemantel at my last place. (*She puts her bag on the floor Right of the armchair.*) Screamed blue murder he did if he hadn't got a fag. Always sarcastic to his wife, he was. They were incompatible – you know, he had a secretary. Saucy cat! When the divorce came up, I could have told them a thing or two, from what I saw. I would have done, too, but for Mr Roper. I thought it was only right, but he said, 'No, Ivy, never spit against the wind'.

(*The front-door bell rings.*)

Shall I see who it is?
LISA. (*Rising*) If you please, Mrs Roper.

(MRS ROPER *exits by the hall to Right.*)

DOCTOR. (*Off*) Good evening, Mrs Roper.

(MRS ROPER *re-enters.* DOCTOR STONER *follows her on. He is a typical family doctor of the old school, aged about sixty. He is affectionately at home.*)

MRS ROPER. (*As she enters*) It's the doctor.
DOCTOR. Good evening, Lisa, my dear. (*He stands up Right and looks around the room at the masses of books everywhere.*)
LISA. (*Moving to Right of the table Right Centre*) Hullo, Doctor Stoner.
MRS ROPER. (*Picking up her bag*) Well, I must be off. Oh, Miss Koletzky, I'll bring in another quarter of tea in the morning, we're right out again. 'Bye!

(MRS ROPER *exits up Centre, closing the doors behind her. The* DOCTOR *crosses below the sofa to Right of it.*)

DOCTOR. Well, Lisa, and how goes it?

(LISA *moves about the table Right Centre and marks her place in the book, with a piece of flower wrapping paper.*)

Has Karl been buying books again, or is it only my fancy that there are more than usual? (*He busies himself clearing the books from the sofa and putting them on the table Right Centre.*)

(LISA *picks up the remainder of the wrapping paper, crosses to the waste-paper basket above the desk and drops the paper in it.*)

LISA. (*Moving to Left of the sofa*) I have forbidden him to buy more, Doctor. Already there is practically nowhere to sit down.

DOCTOR. You are quite right to read him the riot act, Lisa, but you won't succeed. Karl would rather have a book for dinner than a piece of roast beef. How is Anya?

LISA. She has been very depressed and in bad spirits today. Yesterday she seemed a little better and more cheerful.

DOCTOR. (*Sitting on the sofa at the Right end*) Yes, yes, that's the way it goes. (*He sighs.*) Is Karl with her now?

LISA. Yes.

DOCTOR. He never fails her.

(*The barrel-organ music ceases.*)

You realize, my dear, don't you, that Karl is a very remarkable man? People feel it, you know, they're influenced by him.

LISA. He makes his effect, yes.

DOCTOR. (*Sharply*) Now, what do you mean by that, young woman?

LISA. (*Taking the book from under her arm*) 'There are no fields of amaranth this side of the grave.'

(*The* DOCTOR *takes the book from* LISA *and looks at the title.*)

DOCTOR. H'm. Walter Savage Landor. What's your exact meaning, Lisa, in quoting him?

LISA. Just that you know and I know that there are no fields of amaranth this side of the grave. But Karl doesn't know. For

him the fields of amaranth are here and now, and that can be
dangerous.

DOCTOR. Dangerous – to him?

LISA. Not only to him. Dangerous to others, to those who care for
him, who depend on him. Men like Karl . . . (*She breaks off.*)

DOCTOR. (*After a pause*) Yes?

(*Voices are heard off down Right, and as* LISA *hears them she moves to the
work-table up Left and sets it Right of the armchair.* KARL *enters down
Right, pushing* ANYA HENDRYK *in a wheelchair.* ANYA *is a
woman of about thirty-eight, fretful and faded with a trace of former
prettiness. On occasions her manner shows she has at one time been a
coquettish and pretty young girl. Mostly she is a querulous and whining
invalid.*)

KARL. (*As he enters*) I thought I heard your voice, Doctor.

DOCTOR. (*Rising*) Good evening, Anya, you look very well this
evening.

(KARL *pushes the wheelchair to Centre and sets it Right of the work-table.*)

ANYA. I may look well, Doctor, but I don't feel it. How can I feel
well cooped up here all day?

DOCTOR. (*Cheerfully*) But you have that nice balcony outside your
bedroom window. (*He sits on the sofa.*) You can sit out there and
get the air and the sunshine and see what's going on all around
you.

ANYA. As if there's anything worth looking at going on round me.
All these drab houses and all the drab people who live in them.
Ah, when I think of our lovely little house and the garden and
all our nice furniture – everything gone. It's too much, Doctor,
it's too much to lose everything you have.

KARL. Come, Anya, you still have a fine upstanding husband.

(LISA *brings the flowers from the table Right Centre and puts them on the work-
table.*)

ANYA. Not such an upstanding husband as he was – (*To* LISA) is
he?

(LISA *laughs at* ANYA's *little joke and exits up Centre.*)

You stoop, Karl, and your hair is grey.

KARL. (*Sitting on the Left arm of the sofa*) That is a pity, but you must put up with me as I am.

ANYA. (*Miserably*) I feel worse every day, Doctor. My back aches and I've got a twitching in this left arm. I don't think that last medicine suits me.

DOCTOR. Then we must try something else.

ANYA. The drops are all right, the ones for my heart, but Lisa only gives me four at a time. She says that you said I mustn't take more. But I think I've got used to them and it would be better if I took six or eight.

DOCTOR. Lisa is carrying out my orders. That is why I have told her not to leave them near you in case you should take too many. They are dangerous, you know.

ANYA. It's just as well you don't leave them near me. I'm sure if you did, one day I should take the whole bottle and finish it all.

DOCTOR. No, no, my dear. You wouldn't do that.

ANYA. What good am I to anyone, just lying there, ill and a nuisance to everyone? Oh, I know they're kind enough, but they must feel me a terrible burden.

KARL. (*Rising and affectionately patting* ANYA's *shoulder*) You are not a burden to me, Anya.

ANYA. That's what you say, but I must be.

KARL. No, you're not.

ANYA. I know I am. It's not as though I am gay and amusing like I used to be. I'm just an invalid now, fretful and cross with nothing amusing to say or do.

KARL. No, no, my dear.

ANYA. If I were only dead and out of the way, Karl could marry – a young handsome wife who would help him in his career.

KARL. You would be surprised if you knew how many men's careers have been ruined by marrying young handsome wives when they themselves are middle-aged.

ANYA. You know what I mean. I'm just a burden on you.

(KARL *shakes his head at* ANYA, *gently smiling.*)

DOCTOR. (*Writing a prescription on his pad*) We'll try a tonic. A new tonic.

(LISA *enters up Centre. She carries a tray of coffee for four, which she puts on the table Right Centre.*)

LISA. Have you seen your flowers, Anya? Karl brought them for you. (*She pours the coffee.*)

(KARL *moves above the work-table and picks up the vase for* ANYA *to see.*)

ANYA. I don't want to be reminded of spring. Spring in this horrible city. You remember the woods and how we went and picked the little wild daffodils? Ah, life was so happy then, so easy. We didn't know what was coming. Now, the world is hateful, horrible, all drab grey, and our friends are scattered, and most of them are dead, and we have to live in a foreign country.

(LISA *hands a cup of coffee to the* DOCTOR.)

DOCTOR. Thank you, Lisa.

KARL. There are worse things.

ANYA. I know you think I complain all the time, but – if I were well I should be brave and bear it all.

(ANYA *puts her hand out and* KARL *kisses it.* LISA *hands a cup of coffee to* ANYA.)

KARL. I know, my dear, I know. You have a lot to bear.

ANYA. You don't know anything about it.

(*The front-door bell rings.* LISA *exits in the hall to Right.*)

You're well and strong and so is Lisa. What have I ever done that this should happen to me?

KARL. (*Taking her hand in his*) Dearest – dearest – I understand.

LISA. (*Off*) Good afternoon.

HELEN. (*Off*) Could I see Professor Hendryk, please?

LISA. (*Off*) Would you come this way, please.

(LISA *enters up Centre from Right.* HELEN ROLLANDER *follows her on.* HELEN *is a beautiful and self-assured girl of about twenty-three.* KARL *moves above the armchair.*)

(*She stands Left of the doors.*) Miss Rollander to see you, Karl.

(HELEN *goes straight towards* KARL. *Her manner is assured and charming.* LISA *watches her sharply. The* DOCTOR, *rising, is intrigued and interested.*)

HELEN. I do hope you don't mind my butting in like this. I got your private address from Lester Cole.

(LISA *crosses to the table Right Centre and pours more coffee.*)

KARL. (*Moving up Left of* ANYA) Of course I do not mind. May I introduce you to my wife – Miss Rollander.

(HELEN *stands Right of* ANYA. LISA *gives* KARL *a cup of coffee.*)

HELEN. (*With great charm*) How do you do, Mrs Hendryk?

ANYA. How do you do? I am, you see, an invalid. I cannot get up.

HELEN. Of course not. I'm so sorry. I hope you don't mind my coming, but I'm a pupil of your husband's. I wanted to consult him about something.

KARL. (*Indicating them in turn*) This is Miss Koletzky and Doctor Stoner.

HELEN. (*To* LISA) How do you do? (*She crosses to the* DOCTOR *and shakes hands.*) How do you do? (*She moves up Centre.*)

DOCTOR. How do you do?

HELEN. (*Looking round the room*) So this is where you live. Books, books, and books. (*She moves down to the sofa, then sits on it.*)

DOCTOR. Yes, Miss Rollander, you are very fortunate in being able to sit down. I cleared that sofa only five minutes ago.

HELEN. Oh, I'm always lucky.

KARL. Would you like some coffee?

HELEN. No, thank you. Professor Hendryk, I wonder if I could speak to you for a moment alone?

(LISA *looks up sharply from her coffee at* KARL.)

KARL. (*Rather coldly*) I'm afraid our accommodation is rather limited. This is the only sitting-room.

HELEN. Oh, well, I expect you know what I'm going to say. You told me today that your time was so taken up that you couldn't accept any more private pupils. I've come to ask you to change your mind, to make an exception in my favour.

(KARL *crosses above* ANYA *to Left of* HELEN, *looks at* LISA *as he passes and hands her his cup and saucer.*)

KARL. I'm very sorry, Miss Rollander, but my time is absolutely booked up.

(HELEN *speaks with great pace and assurance, almost gabbling.*)

HELEN. You can't put me off like that. I happen to know that after you refused me you agreed to take Sydney Abrahamson privately, so you see you had got time. You preferred him to me. Why?

KARL. If you want an honest answer . . .

HELEN. I do. I hate beating about the bush.

KARL. I think Sydney is more likely to profit than you are.

HELEN. Do you mean you think he's got a better brain than I have?

KARL. No, I would not say that, but he has, shall I say, a greater desire for learning.

HELEN. Oh, I see. You think I'm not serious?

(KARL *does not answer.*)

But I am serious. The truth is you're prejudiced. You think that because I'm rich, because I've been a deb, and done all the silly things that debs do – you think I'm not in earnest.

ANYA. (*Finding* HELEN's *chatter is too much; interrupting*) Karl.

HELEN. But, believe me, I am.

ANYA. Oh, dear – I wonder – Karl!

KARL. (*Moving to Right of* ANYA) Yes, my darling?

ANYA. My head – I don't feel terribly well.

(HELEN *is put out by* ANYA's *interruption, and takes some cigarettes and a lighter from her handbag.*)

I'm sorry – er – Miss Rollander, but if you'll excuse me I think I'll go back to my own room.

HELEN. (*Rather bored*) Of course, I quite understand.

(KARL *pushes the chair towards the door down Right. The* DOCTOR *moves to the door, opens it and takes charge of the chair.* KARL *stands Right of the sofa.*)

ANYA. My heart feels – very odd tonight. Doctor, don't you think you could . . .?

DOCTOR. Yes, yes, I think we can find something that will help you. Karl, will you bring my bag?

(*The* DOCTOR *wheels* ANYA *off down Right.* KARL *picks up the* DOCTOR'S *bag.*)

KARL. (*To* HELEN) Excuse me please.

(KARL *exits down Right.*)

HELEN. Poor Mrs Hendryk, has she been an invalid long? (*She lights her cigarette.*)

LISA. (*Drinking her coffee and watching* HELEN) Five years.

HELEN. Five years! Poor man.

LISA. Poor man?

HELEN. I was thinking of him dancing attendance on her all the time. She likes him to dance attendance, doesn't she?

LISA. He's her husband.

HELEN. (*Rising, crossing below the armchair and standing down Left*) He's a very kind man, isn't he? But one can be too kind. Pity is weakening, don't you think? I'm afraid I'm not in the least kind. I never pity anybody. I can't help it, I'm made that way. (*She sits on the Left arm of the armchair.*)

(LISA *moves to the work-table and takes* ANYA'S *cup and saucer to the tray.*)

Do you live here, too?

LISA. I look after Mrs Hendryk and the flat.

HELEN. Oh, you poor dear, how awful for you.

LISA. Not at all. I like it.

HELEN. (*Vaguely*) Don't they have household helps or something who go around and do that sort of thing for invalids? (*She rises and moves above the armchair.*) I should have thought it would be much more fun for you to train for something and take a job.

LISA. There is no need for me to train. I am already a trained physicist.

HELEN. Oh, but then you could get a job quite easily. (*She stubs out her cigarette in the ashtray on the desk.*)

LISA. I already have a job – here.

(KARL *enters down Right, collects the bottle of medicine and glass from the shelves by the door, then moves to the bookshelves up Right.* LISA *picks up the coffee and tray and exits with it up Centre.*)

HELEN. (*Crossing below the armchair to Centre*) Well, Professor Hendryk, can I come?

KARL. I'm afraid the answer is no. (*He pours some water from the jug on the bookcase shelf into the medicine glass, then moves to the door down Right*)

HELEN. (*Crossing to* KARL) You don't understand. I want to come. I want to be taught. Oh, please, you can't refuse me. (*She comes close to him and puts a hand on his arm.*)

KARL. (*Drawing back a little*) But I can refuse you, you know. (*He smiles at her quite gently and kindly.*)

HELEN. But why, why? Daddy'll pay you heaps if you let me come. Double the ordinary fee. I know he will.

KARL. I'm sure your father would do anything you ask him, but it's not a question of money.

(HELEN *turns to Centre.* LISA *enters up Centre and stands above the table Right Centre.*)

(*He turns to* LISA.) Lisa, give Miss Rollander a glass of sherry, will you. I must go back to Anya. (*He turns to go.*)

HELEN. Professor Hendryk!

KARL. My wife is having one of her bad days. I know you'll excuse me if I go back to her now.

(KARL *smiles very charmingly at* HELEN, *then exits down Right.* HELEN *looks after him.* LISA *takes a bottle of sherry from the bookcase, cupboard Right.* HELEN, *after a slight pause, makes a decision and collects her handbag and gloves from the sofa.*)

HELEN. No, thanks, I don't want any sherry. I'll be going now. (*She moves towards the double doors, then pauses and looks back.*)

(*The* DOCTOR *enters down Right and stands by the door.*)

I shall get my own way, you know. I always do.

(HELEN *sweeps out up Centre.*)

LISA. (*Taking some glasses from the cupboard*) You will have a glass of sherry, Doctor?

DOCTOR. Thank you. (*He crosses to Left Centre and puts his bag down.*) That's a very determined young woman.

LISA. (*Pouring two glasses of sherry*) Yes. She has fallen in love with Karl, of course.

DOCTOR. I suppose that happens fairly often?

LISA. Oh, yes. I remember being frightfully in love myself with my professor of mathematics. He never even noticed me. (*She crosses to the* DOCTOR, *hands him a glass of sherry, then sits on the Left arm of the sofa.*)

DOCTOR. But you were probably younger than that girl.

LISA. Yes, I was younger.

DOCTOR. (*Sitting in the armchair*) You don't think that Karl may respond?

LISA. One never knows. I don't think so.

DOCTOR. He's used to it, you mean?

LISA. He's not used to it from quite that type of girl. Most of the students are rather an unattractive lot, but this girl has beauty and glamour and money – and she wants him very badly.

DOCTOR. So you are afraid.

LISA. No, I'm not afraid, not for Karl. I know what Karl is. I know what Anya means to him and always will. If I am afraid . . . (*She hesitates.*)

DOCTOR. Yes?

LISA. Oh, what does it matter? (*She takes refuge in her sherry.*)

(KARL *enters down Right.*)

KARL. (*Crossing to Right Centre*) So my importunate young lady has gone.

(LISA *rises and pours a glass of sherry for* KARL.)

DOCTOR. A very beautiful girl. Are many of your students like that, Karl?

KARL. Fortunately, no, or we should have more complications than we have already. (*He sits on the sofa at the Left end.*)

DOCTOR. (*Rising*) You must be careful, my boy. (*He sets down his glass and picks up his bag, then moves up Centre.*)

KARL. (*Amused*) Oh, I am careful. I have to be.

(LISA *moves up Right Centre.*)

DOCTOR. And if you do give her private lessons, have Lisa there as chaperon. Good night, Lisa.

LISA. Good night, Doctor.

(*The* DOCTOR *exits up Centre, closing the doors behind him.* LISA *moves to Left of* KARL *and hands him the glass of sherry. There is a pause.*)

(*She moves to the door down Right.*) I'd better go to Anya.

KARL. No. She said she wanted to be left to rest a little. (*He pauses.*) I'm afraid it upset her, that girl coming.

LISA. Yes, I know.

KARL. It's the contrast between her life and – the other. And she says she gets jealous, too. Anya's always convinced I'm going to fall in love with one of my students.

LISA. (*Sitting beside* KARL *on the sofa*) Perhaps you will.

KARL. (*Sharply and significantly*) Can you say that?

LISA. (*Turning away and shrugging her shoulders*) It might happen.

KARL. Never. And you know it.

(*There is a rather constrained pause. They both stare into their glasses.*)

Why do you stay with us?

(LISA *does not answer.*)

(*After a pause.*) Why do you stay with us?

LISA. You know perfectly why I stay.

KARL. I think it's wrong for you. I think perhaps you should go back.

LISA. Go back? Go back where?

KARL. There's nothing against you and never was. You could go back and take up your old post. They'd leap at the chance of having you.

LISA. Perhaps, but I don't want to go.

KARL. But perhaps you should go.

LISA. Should go? Should go? What do you mean?

KARL. This is no life for you.

LISA. It's the life I choose.

KARL. It's wrong for you. Go back. Go away. Have a life of your own.

LISA. I have a life of my own.

KARL. You know what I mean. Marry. Have children.

LISA. I do not think I shall marry.

KARL. Not if you stay here, but if you go away . . .

LISA. Do you want me to go? (*She pauses.*) Answer me, do you want me to go?

KARL. (*With difficulty*) No, I don't want you to go.

LISA. Then don't let's talk about it. (*She rises, takes* KARL's *glass and puts it with her own on the bookcase shelf.*)

KARL. Do you remember the concert in the Kursaal that day? It was August and very hot. An immensely fat soprano sang the

Liebestod. She did not sing it well, either. We were not impressed, either of us. You had a green coat and skirt and a funny little velvet hat. Odd, isn't it, how there are some things that one never forgets, that one never will forget? I don't know what happened the day before that, or what happened the day after it, but I remember that afternoon very well. The gold chairs and the platform, the orchestra wiping their foreheads and the fat soprano bowing and kissing her hand. And then they played the Rachmaninov piano concerto. Do you remember, Lisa?

LISA. (*Calmly*) Of course.

(KARL *hums the tune of the 'Rachmaninov piano concerto'.*)

KARL. I can hear it now. (*He hums.*)

(*The front-door bell rings.*)

Now, who's that?

(LISA *turns abruptly and exits up Centre to Right.*)

ROLLANDER. (*Off*) Good evening. Is Professor Hendryk in?

(KARL *picks up a book and glances through it.*)

LISA. (*Off*) Yes. Will you come in, please?

(SIR WILLIAM ROLLANDER *enters up Centre from Right. He is a tall, grey-haired man of forceful personality.* LISA *follows him on, closes the doors and stands behind the armchair.*)

ROLLANDER. (*Moving down Centre*) Professor Hendryk? My name is Rollander. (*He holds out his hand.*)

(KARL *rises, puts the book on the table Right Centre and shakes ROL-LANDER's hand.*)

KARL. How do you do? This is Miss Koletzky.

ROLLANDER. How do you do?

LISA. How do you do?

ROLLANDER. I have a daughter who studies under you, Professor Hendryk.

KARL. Yes, that is so.

ROLLANDER. She feels that the attending of lectures in a class is not sufficient for her. She would like you to give her extra private tuition.

KARL. I'm afraid that is not possible. (*He moves away below the Right end of the sofa.*)

ROLLANDER. Yes, I know that she has already approached you on the matter and that you have refused. But I should like to reopen the subject if I may.

(LISA *sits in the desk chair.*)

KARL. (*Calmly*) Certainly, Sir William, but I do not think that you will alter my decision.

ROLLANDER. I should like to understand first your reasons for refusing. They are not quite clear to me.

KARL. They are quite simple. Please do sit down. (*He indicates the sofa.*) Your daughter is charming and intelligent, but she is not in my opinion the stuff of which true scholars are made.

ROLLANDER. (*Sitting on the sofa at the Left end*) Isn't that rather an arbitrary decision?

KARL. (*Smiling*) I think you have the popular belief that learning is a thing that can be stuffed into people as you put stuffing into a goose. (*He sits on the Right arm of the sofa.*) Perhaps it would be easier for you to understand if it was a question of music. If your daughter had a pretty and tuneful voice and you brought her to a singing teacher and wanted her trained for opera, a conscientious and honest teacher would tell you frankly that her voice was not suitable for opera. Would never be suitable with all the training in the world.

ROLLANDER. Well, you're the expert. I must, I suppose, bow to your ruling on that.

KARL. Do you, yourself, really believe that your daughter wants to take up an academic career?

ROLLANDER. No, quite frankly, I do not think so. But she thinks so, Professor Hendryk. Shall we put it as simply as this, that I want my daughter to have what she wants.

KARL. A common parental weakness.

ROLLANDER. As you say, a common parental weakness. My position, however, is more uncommon than that of some parents. I am, as you may or may not know, a rich man – to put it simply.

KARL. I am aware of that, Sir William. I read the newspapers. I think it was only a few days ago that I read the description of the exotically fitted luxury car which you were having specially built as a present for your daughter.

ROLLANDER. Oh, that! Probably seems to you foolish and ostentatious. The reasons behind it, let me tell you, are mainly business ones. Helen's not even particularly interested in the car. Her mind at the moment is set on serious subjects. That, I may say, is something of a change, for which I am thankful. She's run around for a couple of years now with a set of people whom I don't much care for. People without a thing in their heads except pleasure. Now she seems to want to go in for serious study and I am behind her one hundred per cent.

KARL. I can quite understand your point of view, but . . .

ROLLANDER. I'll tell you a little more, Professor Hendryk. Helen is all that I have. Her mother died when she was seven years old. I loved my wife and I've never married again. All that I have left of her is Helen. I've always given Helen every single mortal thing she wanted.

KARL. That was natural, I'm sure, but has it been wise?

ROLLANDER. Probably not, but it's become a habit of life, now. And Helen's a fine girl, Professor Hendryk. I dare say she's made her mistakes, she's been foolish, but the only way you can learn about life is by experience. The Spanish have a proverb, '"Take what you want and pay for it", says God.' That's sound, Professor Hendryk, very sound.

KARL. (*Rising and crossing to Right of the work-table*) The payment may be high.

ROLLANDER. Helen wants private tuition from you. I want to give it to her. I'm prepared to pay your price.

KARL. (*Coldly*) It's not a question of price, Sir William. I'm not in the market for the highest fees I can get. I have a responsibility to my profession. My time and energy are limited. I have two good scholars, poor men, but they rate with me in priority above your daughter. You will forgive me for speaking frankly.

ROLLANDER. I appreciate your point of view, but I am not so insensitive as you may think. I quite realize it isn't just a question of money. But in my belief, Professor Hendryk – and I'm a businessman – every man has his price.

(KARL *shrugs his shoulders and sits in the armchair.*)

KARL. You are entitled to your opinion.

ROLLANDER. Your wife is, I believe, suffering from disseminated sclerosis.

KARL. (*Surprised*) That is quite true. But how – did you . . .?

ROLLANDER. (*Interrupting*) When I approach a proposition I find out all about it beforehand. That disease, Professor Hendryk, is one about which very little is known. It responds to palliatives, but there is no known cure, and although the subject of it may live for many years, complete recovery is unknown. That, I think, speaking in non-medical terms, is fairly correct?

KARL. Yes, that is correct.

ROLLANDER. But you may have heard or read of a sensational new treatment started in America, of which there are great hopes. I don't pretend to speak with any kind of medical knowledge or accuracy, but I believe that a new expensively produced antibiotic has been discovered which has an appreciable effect upon the course of the disease. It is at present unprocurable in England, but a small quantity of the drug – or whatever you call it – has been sent to this country and will be used on a few specially selected cases. I have influence in that direction, Professor Hendryk. The Franklin Institute, where this work is going on, will accept your wife as a patient if I exert my influence there.

(LISA *rises and moves to Left of* KARL.)

KARL. (*Quietly*) Bribery and corruption.

ROLLANDER. (*Unoffended*) Oh, yes, just as you say. Bribery and corruption. Not personal bribery, it wouldn't work in your case. You would turn down any financial offer I made you. But can you afford to turn down a chance of your wife's recovering her health?

(*There is a pause, then* KARL *rises and goes to the double doors up Centre. He stands there for quite a while, then turns and comes down Centre.*)

KARL. You are quite right, Sir William. I will accept your daughter as a pupil. I will give her private tuition and as much care and attention as I would my best pupil. Does that satisfy you?

ROLLANDER. It will satisfy her. She is the kind of girl who doesn't take no for an answer. (*He rises and faces* KARL *Centre.*) Well, you have my word for it that when they are ready at the Franklin Institute, your wife will be accepted as a patient. (*He shakes hands with* KARL.) That will probably be in about two months' time.

(LISA *moves to the doors Centre, opens them, then stands to one side.*)

It only remains for me to hope the treatment will be as successful as these cases in the United States seem to have been, and that I may congratulate you in a year's time on your wife's being restored to health and strength. Good night, Professor Hendryk. (*He starts to go, then stops and turns.*) By the way my daughter is waiting in the car downstairs to hear the result of my embassy. Do you mind if she comes up for a moment or two? I know she'd like to thank you.

KARL. Certainly, Sir William.

(ROLLANDER *exits up Centre to Right.* LISA *follows him off.* KARL *moves to the desk chair and leans on the back of it.*)

ROLLANDER. (*Off*) Good night.
LISA. (*Off*) Good night, Sir William.

(LISA *re-enters, leaving the doors open. She stands up Left Centre.*)

So the girl wins.
KARL. Do you think I should have refused?
LISA. No.
KARL. I have made Anya suffer so much already. For sticking to my principles I was turned out of the university at home. Anya has never really understood why. She never saw my point of view. It seemed to her that I behaved foolishly and quixotically. She suffered through it far more than I did. (*He pauses.*) So now there is a chance of recovery and she must have it. (*He sits at the desk.*)
LISA. What about those two students? Won't one of them have to go to the wall?
KARL. Of course not. I shall make the time. I can sit up late at night to do my own work.

LISA. You're not so young as you were, Karl. You're already overworking yourself.

KARL. Those two boys mustn't suffer.

LISA. If you have a breakdown, everybody will suffer.

KARL. Then I mustn't have a breakdown. It's fortunate that no principle is involved here.

LISA. Very fortunate – (*She looks towards the door down Right*) for Anya.

KARL. What do you mean by that, Lisa?

LISA. Nothing, really.

KARL. I don't understand. I'm a very simple man.

LISA. Yes. That's what's so frightening about you.

(*The thump of* ANYA's *stick is heard off Right.*)

KARL. (*Rising*) Anya is awake. (*He moves towards the door down Right.*)

LISA. (*Moving down Centre*) No, I'll go. Your new pupil will want to see you. (*She goes towards the door down Right.*)

KARL. (*As she passes him*) You do believe that I have done right? (*He moves and stands below the armchair.*)

(HELEN *enters up Centre from Right.*)

LISA. (*Pausing at the doorway and turning to* KARL) What is right? How do we ever know till we see the result?

(LISA *exits down Right.*)

HELEN. (*In the doorway*) The door was open, so I came straight in. Is that all right?

KARL. (*Rather far away and staring after* LISA) Of course.

HELEN. (*Moving to Right of the armchair*) I do hope you're not angry. I dare say you feel I'm not much good as a scholar. But you see, I've never had any proper training. Only a silly sort of fashionable education. But I will work hard, I will, really.

KARL. (*Coming back to earth*) Good. (*He goes to the desk and makes some notes on a sheet of paper.*) We will commence a serious life of study. I can lend you some books. You shall take them away and read them, then you will come at an hour that we fix and I shall ask you certain questions as to the conclusions you draw from them. (*He turns to* HELEN.) You understand?

HELEN. (*Moving up Centre*) Yes. May I take the books now? Daddy's waiting for me in the car.

KARL. Yes. That is a good idea. You'll need to buy these. (*He gives her the list he has written.*) Now, let me see. (*He goes to the bookcase Right of the double doors and picks out two large volumes, murmuring under his breath as he does so.*)

(HELEN *watches* KARL.)

KARL. (*Almost to himself as he picks the volumes*) You must have Lecomte, yes, and possibly Wertfor. (*To* HELEN) Do you read German? (*He moves to Left of the table Right Centre*)

HELEN. (*Moving to Left of* KARL) I know a little hotel German.

KARL. (*Sternly*) You must study German. It is impossible to get anywhere without knowing French and German thoroughly. You should study German grammar and composition three days a week.

(HELEN *makes a slight grimace.*)

(*He looks sharply at* HELEN *and hands her the two books.*) The books are rather heavy, I'm afraid.

HELEN. (*Taking the books and nearly dropping them*) Ooh – I should say they are. (*She sits on the Left arm of the sofa and glances through the books.*) It looks rather difficult. (*She leans on* KARL*'s shoulder slightly as she looks at the books.*) You want me to read all of it?

KARL. I should like you to read it through with especial attention to chapter four and chapter eight.

HELEN. (*Leaning almost against him*) I see.

KARL. (*Crossing to the desk*) Shall we say next Wednesday afternoon at four o'clock?

HELEN. (*Rising*) Here? (*She puts the books on the sofa.*)

KARL. No. At my room in the university.

HELEN. (*Rather pleased*) Oh, thank you, Professor Hendryk. (*She crosses above the armchair to Right of* KARL.) I really am grateful. I am indeed, and I shall try very hard. Please don't be against me.

KARL. I'm not against you.

HELEN. Yes, you are. You feel you've been bullied into this by me and my father. But I'll do you credit. I will, really.

KARL. (*Smiling*) Then that is understood. There is no more to be said.

HELEN. It's sweet of you. Very sweet of you. I am grateful. (*She gives* KARL *a sudden quick kiss on the cheek, then turns away, gathers up the books, moves up Centre and stands in the doorway, smiling at* KARL. *Coyly*) Wednesday. At four?

(HELEN *exits up Centre to Right leaving the doors open.* KARL *looks after her with some surprise. His hand goes to his cheek and he finds lipstick on it. He wipes his cheek with his handkerchief, smiles, then shakes his head a little doubtfully. He goes to the record player, puts on the record of the 'Rachmaninov Piano Concerto', switches on, then goes to the desk and sits. He starts to do a little work, but pauses to listen to the music.* LISA *enters down Right. She stands there a moment, listening and watching* KARL, *but he is not aware that she is there. Her hands go up slowly to her face as she tries to retain composure, then suddenly she breaks down, rushes to the sofa and slumps on to the Right end of it.*)

LISA. Don't. Don't. Take it off.

(KARL, *startled, swings round.*)

KARL. (*Puzzled*) It's the Rachmaninov, Lisa. You and I have always loved it.

LISA. I know. That's why I can't bear it just now. Take it off.

(KARL *rises and stops the music.*)

KARL. (*Crossing to Left of the sofa*) You know, Lisa. You've always known.

LISA. Don't. We've never said anything.

KARL. But we've known, haven't we?

LISA. (*In a different, matter-of-fact voice*) Anya is asking for you.

KARL. (*Coming out of a kind of dream*) Yes. Yes, of course. I'll go to her.

(KARL *crosses and exits down Right.* LISA *stares after him in an attitude of despair.*)

LISA. Karl. (*She beats her hands on the sofa.*) Karl. Oh, Karl.

(LISA *collapses miserably, her head in her hands, over the Right arm of the sofa as the LIGHTS black-out and the Curtain falls.*)

CURTAIN

Scene II

SCENE: *The same. A fortnight later. Afternoon.*

When Curtain rises, the LIGHTS come up. The right half of the double doors is open. ANYA *is in her wheelchair Centre, with her work-table Left of her. She is knitting.* KARL *is seated at the desk, making notes from various books.* MRS ROPER *is dusting the shelves of the bookcase Right. Her vacuum cleaner is below the sofa.* LISA *enters from her bedroom, comes into the room and picks up her handbag from the armchair. She is dressed ready for going out.*

ANYA. (*Vexedly; half crying*) I've dropped another stitch. Two stitches. Oh, dear!

(LISA *replaces her handbag on the armchair, leans over the work-table and takes the knitting.*)

LISA. I'll pick them up for you.

ANYA. It's no good my trying to knit. Look at my hands. They won't keep still. It's all hopeless.

(MRS ROPER *moves to Right of the table Right Centre and dusts the books on it.*)

MRS ROPER. Our life's a vale of tears, they do say. Did you see that piece in the paper this morning? Two little girls drowned in a canal. Lovely children, they were. (*She leaves the duster on the table Right Centre, moves below the sofa, picks up the vacuum cleaner and moves towards the door down Right.*) By the way, Miss Koletzky, we're out of tea again.

(MRS ROPER *exits down Right.* LISA *has sorted out the knitting and returns it to* ANYA.)

LISA. There. That's all right now.

ANYA. Shall I ever get well again?

(MRS ROPER *re-enters down Right, collects her duster on the table Right Centre.*)

(*Wistfully and rather sweetly*) I want so much to get well.

MRS ROPER. 'Course you will, dearie, of course you will. Never say die. (*She dusts the chair Left of the table Right Centre.*) My Joyce's eldest, he has fits something shocking. Doctor says he'll grow out of it, but I don't know myself. (*She crosses above the table Right Centre to the door down Right, giving an odd flick with the duster here and there.*) I'll do the bedroom now, shall I? So that it'll be ready for you when the doctor comes.

LISA. If you please, Mrs Roper.

(MRS ROPER *exits down Right, leaving the door open.*)

ANYA. You'd better go, Lisa, you'll be late.

LISA. (*Hesitating*) If you would like me to stay . . .

ANYA. No, of course I don't want you to stay. Your friends are only here for one day. Of course you must see them. It's bad enough to be a helpless invalid without feeling that you're spoiling everybody else's pleasure.

(MRS ROPER, *off, interrupts the calm with the sound of the vacuum cleaner and by singing an old music-hall song in a raucous voice.*)

KARL. Oh, please!

LISA. (*Crossing to the door down Right and calling*) Mrs Roper. Mrs Roper.

(*The vacuum and the singing stop.*)

Do you mind? The Professor is trying to work.

MRS ROPER. (*Off*) Sorry, Miss.

(LISA *crosses above* ANYA *to the armchair and picks up her handbag. She is rather amused at the incident, and* KARL *and* ANYA *join in.* KARL *fills his briefcase with papers and books.*)

ANYA. Do you remember our little Mitzi?

LISA. Ah, yes, Mitzi.

ANYA. Such a nice, willing little maid. Always laughing and such pretty manners. She made good pastry, too.

LISA. She did.

KARL. (*Rising and picking up his briefcase*) There now, I am all ready for my lecture.

LISA. (*Moving to the doors up Centre*) I'll be back as soon as I can, Anya. Goodbye, Anya.

ANYA. Enjoy yourself.

LISA. Goodbye, Karl.

KARL. Goodbye, Lisa.

(LISA *exits up Centre to Right.*)

(*He moves below the armchair.*) Someday, sweetheart, you will be well and strong. (*He sits in the armchair and fastens his briefcase.*)

ANYA. No, I shan't. You talk to me as though I were a child or an imbecile. I'm ill. I'm very ill and I get worse and worse. You all pretend to be so bright and cheerful about it. You don't know how irritating it is.

KARL. (*Gently*) I am sorry. Yes, I can see it must be very irritating sometimes.

ANYA. And I irritate and weary you.

KARL. Of course you don't.

ANYA. Oh, yes, I do. You're so patient and so good, but really you must long for me to die and set you free.

KARL. Anya, Anya, don't say these things. You know they are not true.

ANYA. Nobody ever thinks of me. Nobody ever considers me. It was the same when you lost your Chair at the university. Why did you have to take the Schultzes in?

KARL. They were our friends, Anya.

ANYA. You never really liked Schultz or agreed with his views. When he got into trouble with the police we should have avoided them altogether. It was the only safe thing to do.

KARL. It was no fault of his wife and children, and they were left destitute. Somebody had to help them.

ANYA. It need not have been us.

KARL. But they were our friends, Anya. You can't desert your friends when they are in trouble.

ANYA. You can't, I know that. But you didn't think of me. The result of it was you were told to resign and we had to leave our home and our friends and come away to this cold, grey, horrible country.

KARL. (*Rising, crossing and putting his briefcase on the Left arm of the sofa*) Come now, Anya, it's not so bad.

ANYA. Not for you, I daresay. They've given you a post at the university in London and it's all the same to you, as long as you have books and your studies. But I'm ill.

KARL. (*Crossing to Right of* ANYA) I know, dearest.

ANYA. And I have no friends here. I lie alone day after day with no one to speak to, nothing interesting to hear, no gossip. I knit and I drop the stitches.

KARL. There now . . .

ANYA. You don't understand. You don't understand anything. You can't really care for me, or you would understand.

KARL. Anya, Anya. (*He kneels beside her.*)

ANYA. You're selfish, really, selfish and hard. You don't care for anyone but yourself.

KARL. My poor Anya.

ANYA. It's all very well to say 'poor Anya'. Nobody really cares about me or thinks about me.

KARL. (*Gently*) I think about you. I remember when I saw you first. In your little jacket all gaily embroidered in wool. We went for a picnic up the mountain. Narcissus were out. You took off your shoes and walked through the long grass. Do you remember? Such pretty little shoes and such pretty little feet.

ANYA. (*With a sudden pleased smile*) I always had small feet.

KARL. The prettiest feet in the world. The prettiest girl. (*He gently strokes her hair.*)

ANYA. Now I'm faded and old and sick. No use to anybody.

KARL. To me you are the same Anya. Always the same.

(*The front-door bell rings.*)

(*He rises.*) That's Doctor Stoner, I expect. (*He goes behind the wheelchair and straightens the cushions.*)

(MRS ROPER *enters down Right.*)

MRS ROPER. Shall I see who it is?

(MRS ROPER *exits-up Centre to Right.* KARL *goes to the desk, picks up a couple of pencils and puts them in his pocket. There is a sound of the front door opening and closing and voices off.* MRS ROPER *enters up Centre from Right.* HELEN *follows her on. She is carrying the two books which she borrowed.*)

It's a young lady to see you, sir. (*She moves slowly down Right.*)

(KARL *moves up Left Centre.*)

HELEN. (*Moving to Right of* KARL) I've brought some of your books back. I thought you might be wanting them. (*She stops on seeing* ANYA *and her face drops.*)

(MRS ROPER *exits down Right.*)

KARL. (*Taking the books from* HELEN *and moving to Left of* ANYA) Dearest, you remember Miss Rollander?

HELEN. (*Moving up Right of* ANYA) How are you, Mrs Hendryk? I do hope you are feeling better.

ANYA. I never feel better.

HELEN. (*Devoid of feeling*) I am sorry. (*She goes above the table Right Centre.*)

(*The front-door bell rings.* KARL *goes to the desk, puts the books down, then moves up Centre.*)

KARL. That'll be Doctor Stoner now.

(KARL *exits up Centre to Right.* MRS ROPER *enters down Right, carrying a waste-paper basket. She goes to the shelf below the bookcase Right and empties an ashtray into the basket.* HELEN *glances idly through a book on the table Right Centre.*)

MRS ROPER. I'll finish the bedroom later. I'd better slip out for the tea before he shuts.

KARL. (*Off*) Hullo, Doctor. Come in.

DOCTOR. (*Off*) Well, Karl, it's a lovely day.

(KARL *enters up Centre from Right and stands Left of the doorway. The* DOCTOR *follows him on.*)

KARL. I'd like a word with you alone, Doctor.

(MRS ROPER *exits up Centre to Left, leaving the door open.*)

DOCTOR. Yes, of course. (*He moves to Left of* ANYA.) Well, Anya, it's a lovely spring day.

ANYA. Is it?

KARL. (*Moving down Centre*) Will you excuse us a moment? (*He crosses below the sofa to the door down Right.*)

HELEN. (*Moving to Right of the table Right Centre*) Yes, of course.

DOCTOR. Good afternoon, Miss Rollander.

HELEN. Good afternoon, Doctor.

(*The* DOCTOR *crosses below* KARL *and exits down Right.* KARL *follows him off, closing the door behind him.* MRS ROPER *comes into the hall from Left. She carries her coat and shopping bag. She leaves the bag in the hall, comes into the room and puts on her coat.*)

MRS ROPER. It's too hot for the time of the year –

(HELEN *moves around Right of the sofa and sits on it at the Right end, takes a cigarette case from her handbag and lights a cigarette.*)

– gets me in the joints it does when it's like that. So stiff I was this morning I could hardly get out of bed. I'll be right back with the tea, Mrs Hendryk. Oh, and about the tea, I'll get half a pound, shall I?

ANYA. If you like, if you like.

MRS ROPER. Ta-ta, so long.

(MRS ROPER *goes into the hall, collects her shopping bag and exits to Right.*)

ANYA. It is she who drinks the tea. She always says we need more tea, but we use hardly any. We drink coffee.

HELEN. I suppose these women always pinch things, don't they?

ANYA. And they think we are foreigners and we shall not know.

(*There is a pause.* ANYA *knits.*)

I'm afraid it is very dull for you, Miss Rollander, with only me to talk to. Invalids are not very amusing company.

(HELEN *rises, moves up Right and looks at the books in the bookcase.*)

HELEN. I really only came to bring back those books.

ANYA. Karl has too many books. Look at this room – look at the books everywhere. Students come and borrow the books and read them and leave them about, and then take them away and lose them. It is maddening – quite maddening.

HELEN. Can't be much fun for you.

ANYA. I wish I were dead.

HELEN. (*Turning sharply to look at* ANYA) Oh, you mustn't say that.

ANYA. But it's true. I'm a nuisance and a bore to everybody. To my cousin, Lisa, and to my husband. Do you think it is nice to know one is a burden on people?

HELEN. Do you? (*She turns away to the bookcase.*)

ANYA. I'd be better dead, much better dead. Sometimes I think I will end it all. It will be quite easy. Just a little overdose of my heart medicine and then everybody will be happy and free and I'd be at peace. Why should I go on suffering?

(HELEN *crosses above the armchair to the desk and looks out of the window.*)

HELEN. (*Bored and unsympathetic; with a sigh*) Must be awful for you.

ANYA. You don't know, you can't possibly understand. You're young and good-looking and rich and have everything you want. And here am I, miserable, helpless, always suffering, and nobody cares. Nobody really cares.

(*The* DOCTOR *enters down Right and crosses to Right of* ANYA. KARL *follows him on and stands below the sofa.* HELEN *turns.*)

DOCTOR. Well, Anya, Karl tells me you're going into the clinic in about two weeks' time.

ANYA. It won't do any good. I'm sure of it.

DOCTOR. Come, come, you mustn't say that. I was reading a most interesting article in *The Lancet* the other day, which dealt with the matter. Only an outline, but it was interesting. Of course we're very cautious in this country about the prospect of this new treatment. Afraid to commit ourselves. Our American cousins rush ahead, but there certainly seems to be a good chance of success with it.

ANYA. I don't really believe in it, it won't do any good.

DOCTOR. Now, Anya, don't be a little misery. (*He pushes the wheelchair towards the door down Right.*)

(KARL *moves to the door down Right and holds it open.*)

We'll have your weekly overhaul now and I'll see whether you're doing me credit as a patient or not.

ANYA. I can't knit any more, my hands shake so, I drop the stitches.

(KARL *takes the chair from the* DOCTOR *and pushes* ANYA *off down Right.*)

KARL. There's nothing in that, is there, Doctor?

DOCTOR. No, no, nothing at all.

(KARL *exits with* ANYA *down Right. The* DOCTOR *follows them off.* KARL *re-enters and closes the door. He rather ignores* HELEN, *who stubs out her cigarette in the ashtray on the desk and crosses to Left Centre.*)

KARL. (*Collecting his briefcase*) I'm afraid I have to go out, I have a lecture at half past four.

HELEN. Are you angry with me for coming?

KARL. (*Formally*) Of course not. It is very kind of you to return the books.

HELEN. (*Moving to Left of* KARL) You are angry with me. You've been so brusque – so abrupt, lately. What have I done to make you angry? You were really cross yesterday.

KARL. (*Crossing above* HELEN *to the desk*) Of course I was cross. (*He takes a book from the desk and crosses below* HELEN *to Left of the sofa.*) You say that you want to learn, that you want to study and take your diploma, and then you do not work.

HELEN. Well, I've been rather busy lately – there's been a lot on . . .

KARL. You're not stupid, you've got plenty of intelligence and brains, but you don't take any trouble. How are you getting on with your German lessons?

HELEN. (*Very off-handedly*) I haven't arranged about them yet.

KARL. But you must, you must. It's essential that you should be able to read German. (*He crosses above the table Right Centre to the bookcase Right and takes a book.*) The books I give you to read, you do not read properly. I ask you questions and your answers are superficial. (*He puts the books in his briefcase.*)

(HELEN *moves below the sofa.*)

HELEN. (*Kneeling on the sofa in rather a languid pose*) It's such a bore, working.

KARL. But you were eager to study, to take your diploma.

HELEN. The diploma can go to hell for all I care.

KARL. (*Dumping his briefcase on the Left arm of the sofa in amazement*) Then I don't understand. You force me to teach you, you made your father come to me.

HELEN. I wanted to see you, to be near you. Are you quite blind, Karl? I'm in love with you.

KARL. (*Turning and taking a pace to Centre; amazed*) What? But, my dear child . . .

HELEN. Don't you like me even a little bit?

KARL. (*Crossing and standing down Right*) You're a very desirable young woman, but you must forget this nonsense.

HELEN. (*Rising and standing behind* KARL) It's not nonsense, I tell you I love you. Why can't we be simple and natural about it all? I want you and you want me. You know you do – you're the kind of man I want to marry. Well, why not? Your wife's no good to you.

KARL. How little you understand. You talk like a child. I love my wife.

(*He crosses to Centre.*)

HELEN. (*Sitting on the sofa*) Oh, I know. You're a terribly kind person. You look after her and bring her cups of Bengers and all that, no doubt. But that isn't love.

KARL. (*Crossing below the sofa to Right; rather at a loss what to say*) Isn't it? I think it is. (*He sits on the Right arm of the sofa.*)

HELEN. Of course you must see that she's properly looked after, but it needn't interfere with your life as a man. If we have an affair together your wife needn't know about it.

KARL. (*Firmly*) My dear child, we're not going to have an affair.

HELEN. I had no idea you were so straight-laced. (*She is struck by an idea.*) I'm not a virgin, you know, if that's what's worrying you. I've had lots of experience.

KARL. Helen, don't delude yourself. I am not in love with you.

HELEN. You may go on saying that till you're blue in the face, but I don't believe you.

KARL. Because you don't want to believe me. But it is true. (*He rises and moves down Right.*) I love my wife. She is dearer to me than anyone in the world.

HELEN. (*Like a bewildered child*) Why? Why? I mean, what can she possibly give you? I could give you everything. Money for research or for whatever you wanted.

KARL. But you would still not be Anya. (*He sits on the Right arm of the sofa.*) Listen . . .

HELEN. I daresay she was pretty and attractive once, but she's not like that now.

KARL. She is. We don't change. There is the same Anya there still. Life does things to us. Ill health, disappointment, exile, all these things form a crust covering over the real self. But the real self is still there.

HELEN. (*Rising, impatiently, moving down Left Centre and turning to face* KARL) I think you're talking nonsense. If it were a real marriage – but it isn't. It can't be, in the circumstances.

KARL. It is a real marriage.

HELEN. Oh, you're impossible! (*She moves down Left.*)

KARL. (*Rising*) You see, you are only a child, you don't understand.

(HELEN *crosses above the armchair to Left of* KARL. *She is losing her temper.*)

HELEN. You are the child, wrapped up in a cloud of sentimentality, and pretence. You even humbug yourself. If you had courage – now, I've got courage and I'm a realist. I'm not afraid to look at things and see them as they are.

KARL. You are a child that hasn't grown up.

HELEN. (*Exasperated*) Oh! (*She crosses above the armchair to the desk and stares rather furiously out of the window.*)

(*The* DOCTOR *pushes* ANYA *in down Right.*)

DOCTOR. (*As they enter; cheerfully*) All very satisfactory.

(KARL *takes over from the* DOCTOR *and pushes* ANYA *to her usual place Centre. The* DOCTOR *goes up Centre.*)

ANYA. (*As she is going across*) That's what he says. All doctors are liars.

(KARL *collects his briefcase.*)

DOCTOR. Well, I must be off. I have a consultation at half past four. Good-bye, Anya. Good afternoon, Miss Rollander. I'm going up Gower Street, Karl, I can give you a lift if you like.

KARL. Thank you, Doctor.

DOCTOR. I'll wait downstairs in the car.

(*The* DOCTOR *exits up Centre, closing the door behind him.* KARL *closes his briefcase and moves to Right of* ANYA.)

ANYA. Karl, forgive me, Karl.

KARL. Forgive you, sweetheart? What is there to forgive?

ANYA. Everything. My moods, my bad temper. But it isn't really me, Karl. It's just the illness. You do understand?

KARL. (*With his arm affectionately round her shoulders*) I understand.

(HELEN *half turns her head to look at them, frowns, and turns back to the window.*)

Nothing you say will ever hurt me because I know your heart.

(KARL *claps* ANYA's *hand, they look at each other, and then she kisses his hand.*)

ANYA. Karl, you will be late for your lecture. You must go.

KARL. I wish I didn't have to leave you.

ANYA. Mrs Roper will be back any minute and she will stay with me till Lisa gets back.

HELEN. I'm not going anywhere in particular, I can stay with Mrs Hendryk till Miss Koletzky gets back.

KARL. Would you, Helen?

HELEN. Of course.

KARL. That's very kind of you. (*To* ANYA) Goodbye, darling.

ANYA. Goodbye.

KARL. Thank you, Helen.

(KARL *exits up Centre, closing the door behind him. The daylight starts to fade.*)

HELEN. (*Crossing above the wheelchair to the sofa*) Is Miss Koletzky a relation? (*She sits on the sofa.*)

ANYA. Yes, she's my first cousin. She came to England with us and has stayed with us ever since. This afternoon she has gone to see some friends who are passing through London. They are at the Hotel Russell, not very far away. It is so seldom we see friends from our own country.

HELEN. Would you like to go back?

ANYA. We cannot go back. A friend of my husband's, another professor, fell into disgrace because of his political view – he was arrested.

HELEN. How did that affect Professor Hendryk?

ANYA. His wife and children, you see, were left quite destitute. Professor Hendryk insisted that we should take them into our house. But when the authorities got to hear about it, they forced him to resign his position.

HELEN. Really, it didn't seem worth it, did it?

ANYA. That's what I felt, and I never liked Maria Schultz in the least. She was a most tiresome woman, always carping and criticizing and moaning about something or other. And the children were very badly behaved and very destructive. It seems too bad that because of them we had to leave our nice home and come over here practically as refugees. This will never be home.

HELEN. It does seem rather rough luck on you.

ANYA. Men don't think of that. They only think of their ideas of what is right, or just, or one's duty.

HELEN. I know. Such an awful bore. But men aren't realists like we are.

(*There is a pause as* HELEN *lights a cigarette she has taken from a case in her handbag. A clock outside strikes four.*)

ANYA. (*Looking at her watch*) Lisa never gave me my medicine before she went out. She is very tiresome sometimes the way she forgets things.

HELEN. (*Rising*) Can I do anything?

ANYA. (*Pointing to the shelves on the wall down Right*) It's on the little shelf over there.

(HELEN *moves to the shelves down Right.*)

The little brown bottle. Four drops in water.

(HELEN *stubs out her cigarette in the ashtray on the cupboard Right, and takes the bottle of medicine and a glass from the shelves.*)

It's for my heart, you know. There's a glass over there and a dropper.

(HELEN *moves to the bookshelves Right.*)

Be careful, it's very strong. That's why they keep it out of reach. Sometimes I feel so terribly depressed and I threaten to kill myself, and they think perhaps if I had it near me I'd yield to temptation and take an overdose.

HELEN. (*Taking the dropper-stopper from the bottle*) You often want to, I suppose?

ANYA. (*Complacently*) Oh, yes, one feels so often that one would be better dead.

HELEN. Yes, I can understand that.

ANYA. But, of course, one must be brave and go on.

(HELEN's *back is towards* ANYA. *She throws a quick glance over her shoulder.* ANYA *is not looking her way but is engrossed in her knitting.* HELEN *tilts the bottle and empties all the contents into the glass, adds some water, then takes the glass to* ANYA.)

HELEN. (*Right of* ANYA) Here you are.

ANYA. Thank you, my dear. (*She takes the glass in her left hand and sips.*)

(HELEN *stands up Right of* ANYA.)

It tastes rather strong.

HELEN. Four drops, you said?

ANYA. Yes, that's right. (*She drinks it down quickly, then leans back and puts the glass on her work-table.*)

(HELEN, *tensely strung up, stands watching* ANYA.)

The Professor works much too hard, you know. He takes more pupils than he ought to do. I wish – I wish he could have an easier life.

HELEN. Perhaps some day he will.

ANYA. I doubt it. (*With a little tender smile*) He's so good to everyone. So full of kindness. He is so good to me, so patient. (*She catches her breath*) Ah!

HELEN. What is it?

ANYA. Just – I don't seem to be able to get my breath. You're sure you didn't give me too much?

HELEN. I gave you the right dose.

ANYA. I'm sure – I'm sure you did. I didn't mean – I didn't think . . . (*Her words get slower as she settles back almost as if she is about to go to sleep. Her hand comes up very slowly towards her heart.*) How strange – how very – strange. (*Her head droops sideways on the pillow.*)

(HELEN *moves Right of* ANYA *and watches her. She is now looking frightened. Her hand goes to her face and then down again.*)

HELEN. (*In a low voice*) Mrs Hendryk.

(*There is silence.*)

(*A little louder*) Mrs Hendryk.

(HELEN *moves to Right of* ANYA, *takes her wrist and feels the pulse. When she finds that it has stopped she gasps and flings the hand down in horror, then backs slightly down Right. She moves below the armchair, round it, and stands above the work-table, without taking her eyes off* ANYA. *She stands staring for some moments at* ANYA, *then shakes herself back to reality, sees the glass on the work-table, picks it up and wipes it on her handkerchief, then leans over and puts it carefully into* ANYA'S *left hand. She then goes and leans exhausted over the Left arm of the sofa. Again she pulls herself together, moves to the bookcase Right and picks up the medicine bottle and dropper. She wipes her fingerprints off the bottle and crosses to Right of* ANYA. *She gently presses* ANYA'S *right hand round the bottle, then moves above the work-table, puts the bottle down, takes the dropper out and leaves it beside the bottle. She moves slightly up Centre, looks around, then goes quickly to the sofa for her bag and gloves and moves quickly to the doors up Centre. She stops suddenly and dashes to the shelf for the water jug, wiping it with her handkerchief as she crosses to the work-table, where she puts down the jug. She again goes to the doors up Centre. The sound of a barrel organ is heard off.* HELEN *flings open the Right door and exits in the hall to Right. The front door is heard to slam. There is quite a pause, then the front door is heard opening and closing.* MRS ROPER *pops her head in the doorway up Centre.*)

MRS ROPER. I got the tea.

(MRS ROPER *withdraws her head and disappears to Left. She reappears in the doorway, taking off her hat and coat. These she hangs on a hook off Right of the double doors.*)

And I got the bacon and a dozen boxes of matches. Isn't everything a price these days? I tried to get some kidneys for young Muriel's supper, tenpence each they were, and they looked like little shrunken heads. (*She crosses above the table Right Centre towards the door down Right.*) She'll have to have what the others have and like it. I keep telling her money doesn't grow on trees.

(MRS ROPER *exits down Right. There is a considerable pause, then the front door opens and closes.* LISA *enters up Centre from Right, putting her doorkey into her bag.*)

LISA. (*As she enters*) Have I been long? (*She crosses to the desk, glances at* ANYA *and, thinking she is asleep, smiles, turns to the window and removes her hat. After putting her hat on the desk she turns towards* ANYA *and begins to realize that possibly* ANYA *is more than asleep.*) ANYA? (*She rushes to Right of* ANYA *and lifts her head. She takes her hand away and* ANYA's *head falls again. She sees the bottle on the work-table, moves above the wheelchair, picks up the glass and then the bottle.*)

(MRS ROPER *enters down Right as* LISA *is holding the bottle.*)

MRS ROPER. (*Startled*) Oh, I didn't hear you come in, Miss. (*She moves up Right.*)

LISA. (*Putting the bottle down with a bang; startled by* MRS ROPER's *sudden appearance*) I didn't know you were here, Mrs Roper.

MRS ROPER. Is anything wrong?

LISA. Mrs Hendryk – I think Mrs Hendryk is dead. (*She moves to the telephone, lifts the receiver and dials.*)

(MRS ROPER *moves slowly up Left of* ANYA, *sees the bottle, then turns slowly round to stare at* LISA, *who is waiting impatiently for someone to answer her call. She has her back to* MRS ROPER *and does not see the look. The lights black-out as – the Curtain falls.*)

CURTAIN

ACT TWO

Scene I

SCENE: *The same. Four days later. About midday.*

When curtain rises, the LIGHTS come up. The room is empty. It is much the same as before, except that ANYA'S *wheelchair has gone. The doors are all closed. After a moment,* KARL *enters up Centre, moves down Centre, pauses for a moment and looks where the wheelchair used to be, then sits in the armchair.* LISA *enters up Centre and goes to the desk. She wears outdoor clothes. The* DOCTOR *enters up Centre, looks at the others, then moves below the sofa.* LESTER *enters up Centre and stands rather awkwardly up Centre. They all enter very slowly and are very depressed.*

DOCTOR. (*Rather uncomfortably*) Well, that's over.

LISA. (*Removing her gloves and hat*) I have never been to an inquest in this country before. Are they always like that?

DOCTOR. (*Still a little ill at ease*) Well, they vary, you know, they vary. (*He sits on the sofa at the Right end.*)

LISA. (*After a pause*) It seems so businesslike, so unemotional.

DOCTOR. Well, of course, we don't go in for emotion much. It's just a routine business enquiry, that's all.

LESTER. (*Moving up Left of the sofa; to the* DOCTOR) Wasn't it rather an odd sort of verdict? They said she died from an overdose of stropanthin, but they didn't say how it was administered. I should have thought they'd have said suicide while the balance of the mind was disturbed and have done with it.

(LISA *sits at the desk.*)

KARL. (*Rousing himself*) I cannot believe that Anya committed suicide.

LISA. (*Thoughtfully*) I should not have said so, either.

LESTER. (*Moving Left Centre*) All the same, the evidence was pretty clear. Her fingerprints on the bottle and on the glass.

KARL. It must have been some kind of accident. Her hand shook a great deal, you know. She must have poured in far more than she realized. The curious thing is that I can't remember putting the bottle and glass beside her, yet I suppose I must have done.

(LISA *rises and moves to Left of* KARL. LESTER *sits on the Left arm of the sofa.*)

LISA. It was my fault. I should have given her the drops before I went out.

DOCTOR. It was nobody's fault. Nothing is more unprofitable than accusing oneself of having left undone something one should have done or the opposite. These things happen and they're very sad. Let's leave it at that – (*Under his breath and not to the others*) if we can.

KARL. You don't think Anya took an overdose, deliberately, Doctor?

DOCTOR. (*Slowly*) I shouldn't have said so.

LESTER. (*Rising and moving Left Centre*) She did talk about it, you know. I mean, when she got depressed.

(LISA *moves to the desk.*)

DOCTOR. Yes, yes, nearly all chronic invalids talk about suicide. They seldom commit it.

LESTER. (*After a pause, embarrassed*) I say, I do hope I'm not butting in, coming here. (*He moves Centre.*) I expect you want to be alone. I shouldn't . . .

KARL. No, no, my dear boy, it was kind of you.

LESTER. I just thought perhaps there was something I could do. (*He turns up stage in embarrassment and falls over the chair Left of the table, then moves to Right of* KARL.) I'd do anything – (*He looks devoutly at* KARL.) if only I could do something to help.

KARL. Your sympathy helps. Anya was very fond of you, Lester.

(MRS ROPER *enters up Centre. She wears a rusty black costume and hat. She carries a tray of coffee for four and a plate of sandwiches.* LESTER *goes to the desk.*)

MRS ROPER. (*In a suitably muted voice*) I've made some coffee and some little sandwiches. (*She puts the tray on the table Right Centre. To* KARL) I thought, sir, as you'd need something to keep your strength up.

(LISA *crosses to the tray and pours the coffee.*)

KARL. Thank you, Mrs Roper.

MRS ROPER. (*With conscious virtue*) I hurried back from the inquest as fast as I could, sir – (*She moves Centre.*) so as to have things ready when you come.

KARL. (*Realizing* MRS ROPER's *rather unusual costume of rusty black with a hat*) Did you go to the inquest, then?

MRS ROPER. 'Course I did. I felt I had an interest, like. Poor, dear lady. (*She leans across the sofa to the* DOCTOR.) Low in her spirits, wasn't she? I thought I'd go as a sign of respect, if nothing more. I can't say as it's been very nice, though, having the police here asking questions.

(*During this scene with* MRS ROPER, *the others all avoid looking at her directly in the hope that she will stop talking and leave, but she persists in trying to start a conversation first with one and then the other.*)

DOCTOR. (*Rising*) These routine enquiries have to be made, Mrs Roper. (*He takes a cup of coffee to* KARL, *then goes above* MRS ROPER *to the tray.*)

MRS ROPER. Of course, sir.

DOCTOR. Whenever a certificate cannot be given, there has to be a coroner's enquiry.

MRS ROPER. Oh, yes, sir, I'm sure it's very right and proper, but it's not very nice. That's what I say.

(*The* DOCTOR *takes a cup of coffee for himself, then sits on the sofa.*)

MRS ROPER. It's not what I've been accustomed to. My husband, he wouldn't like it at all if I were to be mixed up in anything of that sort.

LISA. I don't see that you are mixed up in it in any way, Mrs Roper.

MRS ROPER. (*Moving eagerly towards* LISA) Well, they asked me questions, didn't they, as to whether she was low in her spirits and whether she'd ever talked about anything of the kind. (*She moves to Right of* KARL. *Rather significantly*) Oh, quite a lot of questions they asked me.

KARL. Well, that is all over now, Mrs Roper. I don't think you need worry any further.

MRS ROPER. (*Rather squashed*) No, sir, thank you, sir.

(MRS ROPER *exits up Centre, closing the doors behind her.*)

DOCTOR. All ghouls, you know, these women. Nothing they like better than illnesses, deaths, and funerals. An inquest, I expect, is an added joy.

LISA. Lester – coffee?

LESTER. Thanks so much. (*He crosses to the chair Right of the table Right Centre, sits, helps himself to coffee, then becomes engrossed in a book.*)

(LISA *crosses to the desk.*)

KARL. It must have been some kind of accident, it must.

DOCTOR. I don't know. (*He sips his coffee.*) Not quite the same as your coffee, Lisa, my dear.

LISA. (*Crossing below the armchair and sofa and standing down Right*) I expect it's been boiling hard for half an hour.

KARL. It was kindly meant.

LISA. (*Turning to the door down Right, over her shoulder*) I wonder.

(LISA *exits down Right, leaving the door open. The* DOCTOR *rises, takes the plate of sandwiches from the tray and crosses to* KARL.)

DOCTOR. Have a sandwich?

KARL. No, thank you.

DOCTOR. (*Moving to the table Right Centre and putting the sandwiches in front of* LESTER) Finish them up, my boy. Always hungry at your age.

(LESTER, *by now deep in the book, does not look up but automatically helps himself to a sandwich.*)

LESTER. Well, thanks. I don't mind if I do.

LISA. (*Off, calling*) Karl.

KARL. (*Rising and putting his cup on the work-table*) Excuse me a moment. (*He calls and crosses to the door down Right.*) Yes, I am coming.

(KARL *exits Right, closing the door behind him.*)

LESTER. He's terribly cut-up, isn't he, Doctor?

DOCTOR. (*Taking out his pipe*) Yes.

LESTER. It seems odd in a way, at least I don't mean odd, because, I suppose – what I mean is, it's so difficult to understand what other people feel like.

DOCTOR. (*Moving down Centre and lighting his pipe*) Just what are you trying to say, my boy?

LESTER. Well, what I mean is, poor Mrs Hendryk being an invalid and all that, you'd think, wouldn't you, that he'd get a bit impatient with her or feel himself tied.

(*The* DOCTOR *puts the matchstick in the ashtray on the table Right Centre, then sits on the sofa at the Left end.*)

And you'd think that really, underneath, he'd be glad to be free. Not a bit. He loved her. He really loved her.

DOCTOR. Love isn't just glamour, desire, sex appeal – all the things you young people are so sure it is. That's nature's start of the whole business. It's the showy flower, if you like. But love's the root. Underground, out of sight, nothing much to look at, but it's where the life is.

LESTER. I suppose so, yes. But passion doesn't last, sir, does it?

DOCTOR. (*Despairingly*) God give me strength. You young people know nothing about these things. You read in the papers of divorces, of love tangles with a sex angle to everything. Study the columns of deaths sometimes for a change. Plenty of records there of Emily this and John that dying in their seventy-fourth year, beloved wife of So-and-so, beloved husband of someone else. Unassuming records of lives spent together, sustained by the root I've just talked about which still puts out its leaves and its flowers. Not showy flowers, but still flowers.

LESTER. I suppose you're right. I've never thought about it. (*He rises, moves and sits Right of the* DOCTOR *on the sofa.*) I've always thought that getting married is taking a bit of a chance, unless, of course, you meet a girl who . . .

DOCTOR. Yes, yes, that's the recognized pattern. You meet a girl – or you've already met a girl – who's different.

LESTER. (*Earnestly*) But really, sir, she is different.

DOCTOR. (*Good-humouredly*) I see. Well, good luck to you, young fellow.

(KARL *enters down Right. He carries a small pendant. The* DOCTOR *rises.* KARL *crosses to Centre, looking at the pendant.*)

KARL. Will you give this to your daughter, Doctor? It was Anya's and I know she would like Margaret to have it. (*He turns and hands the pendant to the* DOCTOR.)

DOCTOR. (*Moved*) Thank you, Karl. I know Margaret will appreciate the gift. (*He puts the pendant in his wallet, then moves towards the doors up Centre.*) Well, I must be off. Can't keep my surgery patients waiting.

LESTER. (*Rising, and moving up Right Centre; to* KARL) I'll go, too, if you're sure there's nothing I can do for you, sir.

KARL. As a matter of fact there is.

(LESTER *looks delighted.*)

Lisa has been making up some parcels of clothes and things like that – she is sending them to the East London Mission. If you would help her to carry them to the post office . . .

LESTER. Of course I will.

(LESTER *exits down Right.*)

DOCTOR. Goodbye, Karl.

(*The* DOCTOR *exits up Centre.* LESTER *enters down Right. He carries a large box wrapped in brown paper, which he takes to the desk and fastens with Sellotape.* LISA *enters down Right. She carries a brown paper parcel and a small drawer containing papers, letters, etc., and a small trinket box.*)

LISA. (*Moving below the sofa*) If you would look through these, Karl. (*She puts the drawer on the sofa.*) Sit down here and go through these, quietly and alone. It has to be done, and the sooner the better.

KARL. How wise you are, Lisa. One puts these things off and dreads them – dreads the hurt. As you say, it's better to do it and finish.

LISA. I shan't be long. Come along, Lester.

(LISA *and* LESTER *exit up Centre, closing the doors behind them.* KARL *collects the waste-paper basket from the desk, sits on the sofa, puts the drawer on his knee and starts to go through the letters.*)

KARL. (*Reading a letter*) So long ago, so long ago.

(*The front-door bell rings.*)

Oh, go away, whoever you are.

MRS ROPER. (*Off*) Would you come inside, please.

(MRS ROPER *enters up Centre from Right and stands to one side.*)

It's Miss Rollander, sir.

(HELEN *enters up Centre from Right and moves down Centre.* KARL *rises and puts the drawer on the table Right Centre.* MRS ROPER *exits up Centre to Left, leaving the door open.*)

HELEN. I do hope I'm not being a nuisance. I went to the inquest, you see, and afterwards I thought I must come on here and speak to you. But if you'd rather I went away . . .

KARL. No, no, it was kind of you.

(MRS ROPER *enters up Centre from Left, putting on her coat.*)

MRS ROPER. I'll just pop out and get another quarter of tea before he closes. We're right out again.

KARL. (*Fingering the letters in the drawer; far away*) Yes, of course, Mrs Roper.

MRS ROPER. Oh, I see what you're doing, sir. And a sad business it always is. My sister now, she's a widder. Kep' all her husband's letters, she did, what he wrote her from the Middle East. And she'll take them out and cry over them, like as not.

(HELEN, *rather impatient about* MRS ROPER'S *chatter, moves above the armchair.*)

The heart doesn't forget, sir, that's what I say. The heart doesn't forget.

KARL. (*Crossing below the sofa to Right of it*) As you say, Mrs Roper.

MRS ROPER. Must have been a terrible shock to you, sir, wasn't it? Or did you expect it?

KARL. No, I did not expect it.

MRS ROPER. Can't imagine how she came to do such a thing. (*She stares, fascinated, at the place where* ANYA's *chair used to be.*) It don't seem right, sir, not right at all.

KARL. (*Sadly exasperated*) Did you say you were going to get some tea, Mrs Roper?

MRS ROPER. (*Still staring at the wheelchair's place*) That's right, sir, and I must hurry, sir – (*She backs slowly up Centre.*) because that grocer there, he shuts at half past twelve.

(MRS ROPER *exits up Centre, closing the door behind her.*)

HELEN. (*Moving Centre*) I was so sorry to hear . . .

KARL. (*Moving down Right*) Thank you.

HELEN. Of course she'd been ill a long time, hadn't she? She must have got terribly depressed.

KARL. Did she say anything to you before you left her that day?

HELEN. (*Nervously moving above the armchair and round to Left of it*) No, I – I don't think so. Nothing particular.

KARL. (*Moving below the sofa*) But she was depressed – in low spirits?

HELEN. (*Rather grasping at a straw*) Yes. (*She moves below the armchair.*) Yes, she was.

KARL. (*A shade accusingly*) You went away and left her – alone – before Lisa returned.

HELEN. (*Sitting in the armchair; quickly*) I'm sorry about that. I'm afraid it didn't occur to me.

(KARL *moves up Centre.*)

I mean she said she was perfectly all right and she urged me not to stay, and – well, as a matter of fact, I – I thought she really wanted me to go – and so I did. Of course, now . . .

KARL. (*Moving down Right*) No, no. I understand. I can see that if my poor Anya had this in her mind she might have urged you to go.

HELEN. And in a way, really, it's the best thing that could have happened, isn't it?

KARL. (*Moving towards her; angrily*) What do you mean – the best thing that could have happened? (*He moves up Centre.*)

HELEN. (*Rising*) For you, I mean. And for her, too. She wanted to get out of it all, well, now she has. So everything is all right, isn't it? (*She moves up Left Centre, between the armchair and the desk.*)

KARL. (*Moving up Right Centre*) It's difficult for me to believe that she did want to get out of it all.

HELEN. She said so – after all, she couldn't have been happy, could she?

KARL. (*Thoughtfully*) Sometimes she was very happy.

HELEN. (*Circling the armchair*) She couldn't have been, knowing she was a burden on you.

KARL. (*Moving below the sofa; beginning to lose his temper*) She was never a burden to me.

HELEN. Oh, why must you be so hypocritical about it all? I know you were kind to her and good to her, but let's face facts, to be tied to a querulous invalid is a drag on any man. Now, you're free. You can go ahead. You can do anything – anything. Aren't you ambitious?

KARL. I don't think so.

HELEN. But you are, of course you are. I've heard people talk about you, I've heard people say that that book of yours was the most brilliant of the century.

KARL. (*Sitting on the sofa at the Left end*) Fine words, indeed.

HELEN. And they were people who knew. You've had offers, too, to go to the United States, to all sorts of places. Haven't you? You turned them down because of your wife, whom you couldn't leave and who couldn't travel. (*She kneels at the Left end of the sofa.*) You've been tied so long, you hardly know what it is to feel free. Wake up, Karl, wake up. Be yourself. You did the best you could for Anya. Well, now it's over. You can start to enjoy yourself, to live life as it really ought to be lived.

KARL. Is this a sermon you're preaching me, Helen?

HELEN. It's only the present and the future that matter.

KARL. The present and the future are made up of the past.

HELEN. (*Rising and moving Left Centre*) You're free. Why should we go on pretending we don't love each other?

KARL. (*Rising and crossing to the armchair, firmly and almost harshly*) I don't love you, Helen, you must get that into your head. I don't love you. You're living in a fantasy of your own making.

HELEN. I'm not.

KARL. You are. I hate to be brutal, but I've got to tell you now I've no feelings for you of the kind you imagine. (*He sits in the armchair.*)

HELEN. You must have. You must have. (*She moves down Right Centre.*) After what I've done for you. Some people wouldn't have had the courage, but I had. I loved you so much that I couldn't bear to see you tied to a useless querulous woman. You don't know what I'm talking about, do you? I killed her. Now, do you understand? I killed her.

KARL. (*Utterly stupefied*) You killed . . . I don't know what you're saying.

HELEN. (*Moving down Right of* KARL) I killed your wife. I'm not ashamed of it. People who are sick and worn out and useless should be removed so as to leave room for the ones who matter.

KARL. (*Rising and backing away down Left*) You killed Anya?

HELEN. She asked for her medicine. I gave it to her. I gave her the whole bottleful.

KARL. (*Backing further away from her up Left; aghast*) You – you . . .

HELEN. (*Moving Centre*) Don't worry. Nobody will ever know. I thought of everything. (*She speaks rather like a confident, pleased child.*) I wiped off all the fingerprints – (*She moves level with* KARL.) and put her own fingers first round the glass and then round the bottle. So that's all right, you see. (*She moves to Right of him.*) I never really meant to tell you, but I just suddenly felt that I couldn't bear there to be any secrets between us. (*She puts her hands on* KARL.)

KARL. (*Pushing her away*) You killed Anya.

HELEN. If you once got used to the idea . . .

KARL. You – killed – Anya. (*Every time he repeats the words, his consciousness of her act grows greater and his tone more menacing. He seizes her suddenly by the shoulders and shakes her like a rat, then forces her above the Left end of the sofa.*) You miserable immature child – what have you done? Prating so glibly of your courage and your resource. You killed my wife – my Anya. Do you realize what you've done? Talking about things you don't understand, without conscience, without pity. I could take you by the neck and strangle you here and now. (*He seizes her by the throat and starts to strangle her.*)

(HELEN *is forced backwards over the back of the sofa.* KARL *eventually flings her away and she falls face downwards over the Left arm of the sofa, gasping for breath.*)

Get out of here. Get out before I do to you what you did to Anya.

(HELEN *is still gasping for breath and sobbing.* KARL *staggers to the desk chair and leans on the back, near collapse.*)

HELEN. (*Broken and desperate*) Karl.

KARL. Get out. (*He shouts*) Get out, I say.

(HELEN, *still sobbing, rises, staggers to the armchair, collects her handbag and gloves, and, as in a trance, exits up Centre to Right.* KARL *sinks on to the desk chair and buries his head in his hands. There is a pause, then the front door is heard closing.* LISA *enters the hall from Right.*)

LISA. (*Calling*) I'm back, Karl.

(LISA *exits to her bedroom.* KARL *rises, crosses slowly to the sofa and almost collapses on to it.*)

KARL. My poor Anya.

(*There is a pause.* LISA *enters from her bedroom and comes into the room. She is tying an apron on as she enters, and goes to look out of the window.*)

LISA. (*Casually*) I met Helen on the stairs. She looked very strange. Went past me as though she didn't see me. (*She finishes her apron, turns and sees* KARL.) Karl, what has happened? (*She crosses to him.*)

KARL. (*Quite simply*) She killed Anya.

LISA. (*Startled*) What!

KARL. She killed Anya. Anya asked for her medicine and that miserable child gave her an overdose deliberately.

LISA. But Anya's fingerprints were on the glass.

KARL. Helen put them there after she was dead.

LISA. (*A calm, matter-of-fact mind dealing with the situation*) I see – she thought of everything.

KARL. I knew. I always knew that Anya wouldn't have killed herself.

LISA. She's in love with you, of course.

KARL. Yes, yes. But I never gave her any reason to believe that I cared for her. I didn't, Lisa, I swear I didn't.

LISA. I don't suppose you did. She's the type of girl who would assume that whatever she wanted must be so. (*She moves to the armchair and sits.*)

KARL. My poor, brave Anya.

(*There is a long pause.*)

LISA. What are you going to do about it?

KARL. (*Surprised*) Do?

LISA. Aren't you going to report it to the police?

KARL. (*Startled*) Tell the police?

LISA. (*Still calm*) It's murder, you know.

KARL. Yes, it was murder.

LISA. Well, you must report what she said to the police.

KARL. I can't do that.

LISA. Why not? Do you condone murder?

(KARL *rises, paces up Centre, turns slowly to Left, then crosses above the armchair to Left of it.*)

KARL. But I can't let that girl . . .

LISA. (*Restraining herself, calmly*) We've come of our own accord, as refugees, to a country where we live under the protection of its laws. I think we should respect its law, no matter what our own feelings on the subject may be.

KARL. You seriously think I should go to the police?

LISA. Yes.

KARL. Why?

LISA. It seems to me pure common sense.

KARL. (*Sitting at the desk*) Common sense! Common sense! Can one rule one's life by common sense?

LISA. You don't, I know. You never have. You're soft-hearted, Karl. I'm not.

KARL. Is it wrong to feel pity? Can mercy ever be wrong?

LISA. It can lead to a lot of unhappiness.

KARL. One must be prepared to suffer for one's principles.

LISA. Perhaps. That is your business. (*She rises and crosses to Left of the table Right Centre.*) But other people suffer for them as well. Anya suffered for them.

KARL. I know, I know. But you don't understand.

LISA. (*Turning to face* KARL) I understand very well.

KARL. What do you want me to do?

LISA. I have told you. Go to the police. Anya has been murdered. This girl has admitted to murdering her. The police must be told.

KARL. (*Rising and crossing above the armchair to Centre*) You haven't thought, Lisa. The girl is so young. She is only twenty-three.

LISA. Whereas Anya was thirty-eight.

KARL. If she is tried and condemned – what good will it do? Can it bring Anya back? Don't you see, Lisa, revenge can't bring Anya back to life again.

LISA. No. Anya is dead.

KARL. (*Crossing to the sofa and sitting*) I wish you could see it my way.

LISA. (*Moving to Left of the sofa*) I can't see it your way. I loved Anya. We were cousins and friends. We went about as girls together. I looked after her when she was ill. I know how she tried to be brave, how she tried not to complain. I know how difficult life was for her.

KARL. Going to the police won't bring Anya back.

(LISA *does not answer but turns and moves up Right Centre.*)

And don't you see, Lisa, I'm bound to feel responsible myself. I must in some way have encouraged the girl.

LISA. You didn't encourage her. (*She moves to Left of the sofa and kneels, facing* KARL.) Let's speak plainly. She did her utmost to seduce you, and failed.

KARL. No matter how you put it, I feel responsible. Love for me was her motive.

LISA. Her motive was to get what she wanted, as she always has got everything she wanted all her life.

KARL. That's just what has been her tragedy. She has never had a chance.

LISA. And she's young and beautiful.

KARL. (*Sharply*) What do you mean?

LISA. I wonder if you'd be so tender if she were one of your plain girl students.

KARL. (*Rising*) You can't think . . .

LISA. (*Rising*) What can't I think?

KARL. That I want that girl . . .

LISA. (*Moving slowly down Left*) Why not? Aren't you attracted to her? Be honest with yourself. Are you sure you're not really a little in love with the girl?

KARL. (*Crossing to Right of* LISA) You can say that? You? When you know – when you've always known . . .? It's you I love. You! I lie awake at nights thinking about you, longing for you. Lisa, Lisa . . .

(KARL *takes* LISA *in his arms. They embrace passionately. There is a
    shadowy figure in the doorway up Centre. After a pause, the door closes
    with a bang. This makes* KARL *and* LISA *move apart and look at the
    door. They do not see who it was, and the audience are left unaware of the
    identity of the eavesdropper. The* LIGHTS *black-out as* – *the Curtain
    falls.*)

CURTAIN

Scene II

SCENE: *The same. Six hours later. Evening.*

When Curtain rises, the LIGHTS *come up a very little, leaving most of the room
    in darkness.* LISA *is seated on the sofa, at the Right end, smoking. She is
    almost invisible. The front door is heard opening and closing and there is
    the sound of voices in the hall.* KARL *enters up Centre. He has a
    newspaper in his overcoat pocket. The* DOCTOR *follows him on.*

KARL. Nobody's at home. I wonder . . .

(*The* DOCTOR *switches on the lights by the switch Left of the double doors,
    and he and* KARL *see* LISA.)

DOCTOR. Lisa! Why are you sitting here in the dark?

    (KARL *goes to the desk chair and puts his coat over the back of it.*)

LISA. I was just thinking.

            (KARL *sits in the armchair.*)

DOCTOR. I met Karl at the end of the street and we came along
    together. (*He puts his coat on the chair above the table Right Centre.*)
    D'you know what I prescribe for you, Karl? A little alcohol. A
    stiff brandy, eh. Lisa?

            (LISA *makes a slight move.*)

No – I know my way about. (*He goes to the cupboard under the bookcase Right, takes out a bottle of brandy and a glass, and pours a stiff drink.*) He's had a shock, you know. A bad shock.

KARL. I have told him about Helen.

DOCTOR. Yes, he told me.

LISA. It's not been such a shock to you, I gather?

DOCTOR. I've been worried, you know. I didn't think Anya was a suicidal type and I couldn't see any possibility of an accident. (*He crosses to Right of* KARL *and gives him the brandy.*) And then the inquest aroused my suspicions. Clearly the police were behind the verdict. (*He sits Left of* LISA *on the sofa.*) Yes, it looked fishy. The police questioned me fairly closely and I couldn't help seeing what they were driving at. Of course, they didn't actually say anything.

LISA. So you were not surprised?

DOCTOR. No, not really. That young woman thought she could get away with anything. Even murder. Well, she was wrong.

KARL. (*In a low voice*) I feel responsible.

DOCTOR. Karl, take it from me, you weren't responsible in any way. Compared to that young woman you're an innocent in arms. (*He rises and moves up Centre.*) Anyway, the whole thing's out of your hands now.

LISA. You think he should go to the police?

DOCTOR. Yes.

KARL. No.

DOCTOR. Because you insist on feeling partly responsible? You're too sensitive.

KARL. Poor wretched child.

DOCTOR. (*Crossing above the armchair and standing down Left*) Callous, murdering little bitch! That's nearer the mark. And I shouldn't worry before you need. Ten to one it'll never come to an arrest. (*He crosses below* KARL *to Right Centre.*) Presumably she'll deny everything – and there's got to be evidence, you know. The police may be quite sure who's done a thing, but be unable to make out a case. The girl's father is a very important person. One of the richest men in England. That counts.

KARL. There I think you are wrong.

DOCTOR. Oh, I'm not saying anything against the police. (*He moves up Centre.*) If they've got a case they'll go ahead, without fear or favour. All I mean is that they'll have to scrutinize their evidence with extra care. And on the face of it there can't really be much evidence, you know. Unless, of course, she breaks down and confesses the whole thing. And I should imagine she's much too hard-boiled for that.

KARL. She confessed to me.

DOCTOR. That's different. Though as a matter of fact I can't see why she did. (*He moves and sits on the Left arm of the sofa.*) Seems to me a damn silly thing to do.

LISA. Because she was proud of it.

DOCTOR. (*Looking curiously at her*) You think so?

KARL. It is true – that's what is so terrible.

(*The front-door bell rings.*)

Who can that be?

DOCTOR. One of your boys or girls, I expect. (*He rises.*) I'll get rid of them.

(*The* DOCTOR *exits up Centre to Right.* KARL *rises and puts his glass on the desk.*)

OGDEN. (*Off*) Could I see Professor Hendryk, please?

DOCTOR. (*Off*) Would you come this way, please.

(*The* DOCTOR *enters up Centre from Right and stands to one side.*)

It's Inspector Ogden.

(DETECTIVE INSPECTOR OGDEN *and* POLICE SERGEANT PEARCE *enter up Centre from Right.* OGDEN *has a pleasant manner and a poker face. The* SERGEANT *closes the doors, then stands above the table Right Centre.*)

OGDEN. (*Very pleasantly*) I hope we're not disturbing you, Professor Hendryk.

KARL. (*Moving down Left*) Not at all.

OGDEN. Good evening, Miss Koletzky. I expect you didn't think you would see me again – but we have a few more questions to ask. It was an open verdict, you understand. Insufficient evidence as to how the deceased lady came to take the fatal dose.

KARL. I know.

OGDEN. Have your own ideas changed as to that, sir, since we first talked about it?

(KARL *looks quickly at* LISA. OGDEN *and the* SERGEANT *note the look and exchange quick glances. There is a pause.*)

KARL. (*Deliberately*) They have not changed. I still think it must have been some sort of – accident.

(LISA *turns away. The* DOCTOR *almost snorts and turns aside.*)

OGDEN. But definitely not suicide.

KARL. Definitely not suicide.

OGDEN. Well, you're quite right as to that, sir. (*With emphasis*) It was not suicide.

(KARL *and* LISA *turn to* OGDEN.)

LISA. (*Quietly*) How do you know?

OGDEN. By evidence that was not given at the inquest. Evidence as to the fingerprints found on the bottle containing the fatal drug – and on the glass, also.

KARL. You mean . . . But they were my wife's fingerprints, weren't they?

OGDEN. Oh, yes, sir. They were your wife's fingerprints. (*Softly*) But she didn't make them. (*He moves the chair Left of the table Right Centre and sets it Left of the sofa.*)

(*The* DOCTOR *and* KARL *exchange looks.*)

KARL. What do you mean?

OGDEN. It's the sort of thing that an amateur criminal thinks is so easy. To pick up a person's hand and close it round a gun or a bottle or whatever it may be. (*He sits on the chair he has placed Centre.*) But actually it's not so easy to do.

(KARL *sits in the armchair.*)

The position of those fingerprints is such that they couldn't have been made by a living woman grasping a bottle. That means that somebody else took your wife's hand and folded the fingers round the bottle and the glass so as to give the impression that your wife committed suicide. A rather childish piece of reasoning, and done by someone rather cocksure of their own ability. Also, there ought to have been plenty of other prints on the bottle, but there weren't – it had been wiped clean before your wife's were applied. You see what that means?

KARL. I see what it means.

OGDEN. There would be no reason to do such a thing if it was an accident. That only leaves one possibility.

KARL. Yes.

OGDEN. I wonder if you do see, sir. It means – an ugly word – murder.

KARL. Murder.

OGDEN. Doesn't that seem very incredible to you, sir?

KARL. (*More to himself than to* OGDEN) You cannot know how incredible. My wife was a very sweet and gentle woman. It will always seem to me both terrible and unbelievable that anyone should have – killed her.

OGDEN. You, yourself . . .

KARL. (*Sharply*) Are you accusing me?

OGDEN. (*Rising*) Of course not, sir. If I'd any suspicions concerning you, I should give you the proper warning. No, Professor Hendryk, we've checked your story and your time is fully accounted for. (*He resumes his seat.*) You left here in the company of Doctor Stoner and he states that there was no medicine bottle or glass on your wife's table at that time. Between the time you left and the time Miss Koletzky says she arrived here and found your wife dead, every moment of your time is accounted for. You were lecturing to a group of students at the university. No, there is no suggestion of your having been the person to put the fingerprints on the glass.

(*The* DOCTOR *moves down Left.*)

What I am asking you, sir, is whether you have any idea yourself as to who could have done so?

(*There is quite a long pause.* KARL *stares fixedly ahead of him.*)

KARL. (*Presently*) I – (*He pauses.*) cannot help you.

(OGDEN *rises and as he replaces the chair beside the table. He exchanges glances with the* SERGEANT, *who moves to the door down Right.*)

OGDEN. (*Moving Centre*) You will appreciate, of course, that this alters things. I wonder if I might have a look round the flat. Round Mrs Hendryk's bedroom in particular. I can get a search warrant if necessary, but . . .

KARL. Of course. Look anywhere you please. (*He rises.*)

(LISA *rises.*)

My wife's bedroom – (*He indicates the door down Right.*) is through there.

OGDEN. Thank you.

KARL. Miss Koletzky has been sorting through her things.

(LISA *crosses to the door Right and opens it.* OGDEN *and the* SERGEANT *exit down Right.* LISA *turns and looks at* KARL, *then exits down Right, closing the door behind her.*)

DOCTOR. (*Moving up Left of the armchair*) I've known you long enough, Karl, to tell you plainly that you're being a fool.

KARL. (*Moving up Right of the armchair*). I can't be the one to put them on her track. They'll get her soon enough without my help.

DOCTOR. I'm not so sure of that. And it's all high-falutin' nonsense. (*He sits in the armchair.*)

KARL. She didn't know what she was doing.

DOCTOR. She knew perfectly.

KARL. She didn't know what she was doing because life has not yet taught her understanding and compassion. (*He moves above the armchair.*)

(LISA *enters down Right, closing the door behind her.*)

LISA. (*Moving Right Centre; to the* DOCTOR) Have you made him see sense?

DOCTOR. Not yet.

(LISA *shivers.*)

You're cold.

LISA. No – I'm not cold. I'm afraid. (*She moves towards the doors up Centre.*) I shall make some coffee.

(LISA *exits up Centre. The* DOCTOR *rises and moves below the sofa*).

KARL. (*Moving down Left of the armchair*) I wish I could get you and

Lisa to see that revenge will not bring Anya back to life again.

DOCTOR. (*Moving up Left Centre*) And suppose our little beauty goes on disposing of wives that happen to stand in her way?

KARL. I will not believe that.

(*The* SERGEANT *and* OGDEN *enter down Right. The* SERGEANT *stands above the table Right Centre and* OGDEN *stands down Right.*)

OGDEN. I gather some of your wife's clothing and effects have already been disposed of?

KARL. Yes. They were sent off to the East London Mission, I think.

(*The* SERGEANT *makes a note.*)

OGDEN. (*Moving to Right of the sofa*) What about papers, letters?

KARL. (*Crossing to the table Right Centre*) I was going through them this morning. (*He indicates the little drawer.*) Though what you expect to find . . .

OGDEN. (*Evading the issue; vaguely*) One never knows. Some note, a memorandum set down . . .

KARL. I doubt it. Still, look through them, of course, if you must. I don't expect you'll find . . . (*He picks up a bundle of letters tied with ribbon.*) Will you need these? They are the letters I wrote to my wife many years ago.

OGDEN. (*Gently*) I'm afraid I must just look through them. (*He takes the letters from* KARL.)

(*There is quite a pause, then* KARL *turns impatiently towards the doors up Centre.*)

KARL. I shall be in the kitchen if you want me, Inspector Ogden.

(*The* DOCTOR *opens the right half of the doors up Centre.* KARL *exits up Centre. The* DOCTOR *follows him off, closing the door behind him.* OGDEN *moves to Right of the table Right Centre.*)

SERGEANT. Do you think he was in on it?

OGDEN. No, I don't. (*He starts to go through the papers in the drawer.*) Not beforehand. Hadn't the faintest idea, I should say. (*Grimly*) But he knows now – and it's been a shock to him.

SERGEANT. (*Also going through the papers, etc., in the drawer*) He's not saying anything.

OGDEN. No. That would be too much to expect. Doesn't mean to be much here. Not likely to be, under the circumstances.

SERGEANT. If there had been, our Mrs Mop would have known about it. I'd say she was a pretty good snooper. That kind always knows the dirt. And did she enjoy spilling it!

OGDEN. (*With distaste*) An unpleasant woman.

SERGEANT. She'll do all right in the witness box.

OGDEN. Unless she overdoes it. Well, nothing additional here. We'd better get on with the job. (*He moves to the doors up Centre, opens one and calls*) Will you come in here, please. (*He moves below the armchair.*)

(LISA *enters up Centre and moves down Centre. The* DOCTOR *enters up Centre and moves down Right of the sofa.* KARL *enters up Centre and stands up Left of the Sofa. The* SERGEANT *moves to the doors up Centre, closes them and stands in front of them.*)

Miss Koletzky, there are some additional questions I would like to ask you. You understand that you are not forced to answer anything unless you please.

LISA. I do not want to answer any questions.

OGDEN. Perhaps you're wise. Lisa Koletzky, I arrest you on the charge of administering poison to Anya Hendryk on March the fifth last –

(KARL *moves to Right of* LISA.)

– and it is my duty to warn you that anything you say will be taken down and may be used in evidence.

KARL. (*Horror-struck*) What's this? What are you doing? What are you saying?

OGDEN. Please, Professor Hendryk, don't let's have a scene.

KARL. (*Moving behind* LISA *and holding her in his arms*). But you can't arrest Lisa, you can't, you can't. She's done nothing.

LISA. (*Gently pushing* KARL *away; in a loud, clear, calm voice*) I did not murder my cousin.

OGDEN. You'll have plenty of opportunity to say everything you want, later.

(KARL, *losing restraint, advances on* OGDEN, *but the* DOCTOR *holds his arm.*)

KARL. (*Pushing the* DOCTOR *away; almost shouting*) You can't do this. You can't.

OGDEN. (*To* LISA). If you need a coat or a hat . . .

LISA. I need nothing.

(LISA *turns and looks at* KARL *for a moment, then turns and goes up Centre. The* SERGEANT *opens the door.* LISA *exits up Centre.* OGDEN *and the* SERGEANT *follow her off.* KARL *suddenly makes a decision and runs after them.*)

KARL. Inspector Ogden! Come back. I must speak to you.

(*He moves Right Centre.*)

OGDEN. (*Off*) Wait in the hall, Sergeant.

SERGEANT. (*Off*) Yes, sir.

(OGDEN *enters up Centre. The* DOCTOR *crosses to Left Centre.*)

OGDEN. Yes, Professor Hendryk?

KARL. (*Moving to Left of the sofa*) I have something to tell you. I know who killed my wife. It was not Miss Koletzky.

OGDEN. (*Politely*) Who was it, then?

KARL. It was a girl called Helen Rollander. She is one of my pupils. (*He crosses and sits in the armchair.*) She – she formed an unfortunate attachment to me.

(*The* DOCTOR *moves to Left of the armchair.*)

She was alone with my wife on the day in question, and she gave her an overdose of the heart medicine.

OGDEN. (*Moving down Centre*) How do you know this, Professor Hendryk?

KARL. She told me herself, this morning.

OGDEN. Indeed? Were there any witnesses?

KARL. No, but I am telling you the truth.

OGDEN. (*Thoughtfully*) Helen – Rollander. You mean the daughter of Sir William Rollander?

KARL. Yes. Her father is William Rollander. He is an important man. Does that make any difference?

OGDEN. (*Moving below the Left end of the sofa*) No, it wouldn't make any difference – if your story were true.

KARL. (*Rising*) I swear to you that it's true.

OGDEN. You are very devoted to Miss Koletzky, aren't you?

KARL. Do you think I would make up a story just to protect her?

OGDEN. (*Moving Centre*) I think it is quite possible – you are on terms of intimacy with Miss Koletzky, aren't you?

KARL. (*Dumbfounded*) What do you mean?

OGDEN. Let me tell you, Professor Hendryk, that your daily woman, Mrs Roper, came along to the police station this afternoon and made a statement.

KARL. Then it was Mrs Roper who . . .

OGDEN. It is partly because of that statement that Miss Koletzky has been arrested.

KARL. (*Turning to the* DOCTOR *for support*) You believe that Lisa and I . . .

OGDEN. Your wife was an invalid. Miss Koletzky is an attractive young woman. You were thrown together.

KARL. You think we planned together to kill Anya.

OGDEN. No, I don't think you planned it. I may be wrong there, of course.

(KARL *circles the armchair to Centre.*)

I think all the planning was done by Miss Koletzky. There was a prospect of your wife's regaining her health owing to a new treatment. I think Miss Koletzky was taking no chance of that happening.

KARL. But I tell you that it was Helen Rollander.

OGDEN. You tell me, yes. It seems to me a most unlikely story. (*He moves up Centre.*)

(KARL *crosses and stands down Right.*)

It is plausible that a girl like Miss Rollander, who's got the world at her feet and who hardly knows you, would do a thing like that? Making up an accusation of that kind reflects little credit on you, Professor Hendryk – trumping it up on the spur of the moment because you think it cannot be contradicted.

KARL. (*Moving to Right of* OGDEN) Listen. Go to Miss Rollander. Tell her that another woman has been arrested for the murder. Tell her, from me, that I know – know – that with all her faults, she is decent and honest. I swear that she will confirm what I have told you.

OGDEN. You've thought it up very cleverly, haven't you?

KARL. What do you mean?

OGDEN. What I say. But there's no one who can confirm your story.

KARL. Only Helen herself.

OGDEN. Exactly.

KARL. And Doctor Stoner knows. I told him.

ODGEN. He knows because you told him.

DOCTOR. I believe it to be the truth, Inspector Ogden. If you remember, I mentioned to you that when we left Mrs Hendryk that day, Miss Rollander remained behind to keep her company.

OGDEN. A kind offer on her part. (*He crosses to Right of the* DOCTOR.) We interviewed Miss Rollander at the time and I see no reason to doubt her story. She stayed for a short time and then Mrs Hendryk asked her to leave, since she felt tired. (*He moves above the armchair.*)

KARL. Go to Helen now. Tell her what has happened. Tell her what I have asked you to tell her.

OGDEN. (*To the* DOCTOR) Just when did Professor Hendryk tell you that Miss Rollander had killed his wife? Within the last hour, I should imagine.

DOCTOR. That is so.

KARL. We met in the street. (*He moves below the sofa.*)

OGDEN. Didn't it strike you that if this was true, he would have come to us as soon as she admitted to him what she had done?

DOCTOR. He's not that kind of man.

OGDEN. (*Ruthlessly*) I don't think you're really aware what kind of man he is. (*He moves to* KARL's *coat on the desk chair.*) He's a quick and clever thinker, and he's not overscrupulous.

(KARL *starts towards the* INSPECTOR, *but the* DOCTOR *crosses quickly to Left of* KARL *and restrains him.*)

This is your coat and an evening paper, I see. (*He draws the evening paper from the pocket.*)

(KARL *moves down Right of the sofa. The* DOCTOR *moves up Left of the sofa.*)

KARL. Yes, I bought it on the corner, just before I came in. I haven't had time to read it, yet.

OGDEN. (*Moving Centre*) Are you sure?

KARL. Yes – (*He moves Right Centre.*) I am quite sure.

OGDEN. I think you did. (*He reads from the paper*) 'Sir William Rollander's only daughter, Helen Rollander, was the victim of a regrettable accident this morning. In crossing the road she was knocked down by a lorry. The lorry driver claims that Miss Rollander gave him no time to brake. She walked straight into the road without looking right or left, and was killed instantly.'

(KARL *slumps on to the sofa.*)

I think that when you saw that paragraph, Professor Hendryk, you saw a way out to save your mistress by accusing a girl who could never refute what you said – because she was dead.

(*The LIGHTS black-out as – the Curtain falls.*)

CURTAIN

Scene III

SCENE: *The same. Two months later. Late afternoon.*

When Curtain rises, the LIGHTS come up. KARL *is seated on the sofa. The* DOCTOR *is leaning against the table Right Centre, reading the 'Walter Savage Landor'.* LESTER *is pacing up and down Left Centre. The telephone rings. They all start.* LESTER, *who is nearest to the telephone, lifts the receiver.*

LESTER. (*Into the telephone*) Hullo? . . . No. (*He replaces the receiver.*) These reporters never stop. (*He moves down Left.*)

(*The* DOCTOR *crosses and sits in the armchair.* KARL *rises and circles the sofa to Centre.*)

KARL. I wish I had stayed in Court. Why didn't you let me stay?
DOCTOR. Lisa specially asked that you shouldn't remain in Court to hear the verdict. We've got to respect her wish.
KARL. You could have stayed.

DOCTOR. She wanted me to be with you. The lawyers will let us know at once . . .

KARL. They can't find her guilty. They can't. (*He moves up Right.*)

LESTER. (*Moving down Centre*) If you'd like me to go back there . . .

DOCTOR. You stay here, Lester.

LESTER. If I'm any use. If there's anything I could do . . .

DOCTOR. You can answer that damn telephone that keeps ringing.

KARL. (*Moving below the sofa*) Yes, my dear boy. Stay. Your presence here helps me.

LESTER. Does it? Does it, really?

KARL. She must be, she will be acquitted. I can't believe that innocence can go unrecognized. (*He sits on the sofa.*)

(LESTER *moves up Centre.*)

DOCTOR. Can't you? I can. One's seen it often enough. And you've seen it, Karl, time and time again. Mind you, I think she made a good impression on the jury.

LESTER. But the evidence was pretty damning. It's that frightful Roper woman. The things she said. (*He sits Left of the table Right Centre*)

DOCTOR. She believed what she was saying, of course. That's what made her so unshakeable under cross-examination. It's particularly unfortunate that she should have seen you and Lisa embracing each other on the day of the inquest. She did see it, I suppose.

KARL. Yes, she must have seen it. It was true. It's the first time I have ever kissed Lisa.

DOCTOR. And a thoroughly bad time to choose. It's really a thousand pities that snooping woman never saw or heard anything that passed between you and Helen. 'A very nice young lady' – that's all she had to say.

KARL. It is so odd to tell the truth and not be believed.

DOCTOR. All you've done is to bring down a lot of odium on yourself, for cooking up a scurrilous story about a girl who is dead.

KARL. (*Rising and moving up Centre*) If I'd only gone to the police right away, the moment she'd told me . . .

DOCTOR. If only you had. It's particularly unfortunate that you only came out with the story after you'd bought a paper containing the news that she's dead. And your reasons for not going to the police didn't sound credible in the least.

(KARL *moves down Left.*)

Though they are to me, of course, because I know the incredible fool you are. The whole set of circumstances is thoroughly damnable. The Roper woman coming in to find Lisa standing by the body and holding the bottle in gloved fingers. The whole thing has built itself up in the most incredible fashion.

(KARL *crosses and stands down Right. The telephone rings.*)

KARL. Is that . . .? Can it . . .?

(*There is a moment's agonizing pause, then the* DOCTOR *motions to* LESTER, *who rises, goes to the telephone and lifts the receiver.*)

LESTER. (*Into the telephone*) Yes? . . . Hullo? . . . Go to hell! (*He slams the receiver down and stands Right of the desk.*)

DOCTOR. Ghouls, that's what they are, ghouls.

KARL. (*Moving up Right*) If they find her guilty, if they . . .

DOCTOR. Well, we can appeal, you know.

KARL. (*Moving down Centre and then below the sofa*) Why should she have to go through all this? Why should she be the one to suffer? I wish I were in her place.

DOCTOR. Yes, it's always easier when it's oneself.

KARL. After all, I'm partly responsible for what happened . . .

DOCTOR. (*Interrupting*) I've told you that's nonsense.

KARL. But Lisa has done nothing. Nothing. (*He moves down Centre, then goes up Right.*)

DOCTOR. (*After a long pause, to* LESTER) Go and make us some coffee, boy, if you know how.

LESTER. (*Indignantly*) Of course I know how. (*He moves up Centre.*)

(*The telephone rings.* LESTER *makes a move to answer it.*)

KARL. (*Stopping* LESTER) Don't answer it.

(*The telephone goes on ringing.* LESTER *hesitates, then exits up Centre to Left. The telephone goes on ringing solidly.* KARL *eventually rushes to it and picks up the receiver.*)

(*Into the telephone*) Leave me alone, can't you? Leave me alone.

(*He slams down the receiver and sinks into the desk chair.*) I can't bear it. I can't bear it.

DOCTOR. (*Rising and moving to* KARL) Patience, Karl. Courage.

KARL. What good is it saying that to me?

DOCTOR. Not much, but there's nothing else to say, is there? There's nothing that can help you now except courage.

KARL. I keep thinking of Lisa. Of what she must be suffering.

DOCTOR. I know. I know.

KARL. She's so brave. So wonderfully brave.

DOCTOR. (*Moving Centre*) Lisa is a very wonderful person. I have always known that.

KARL. I love her. Did you know I loved her?

DOCTOR. Yes, of course I knew. You've loved her for a long time.

KARL. Yes. Neither of us ever acknowledged it, but we knew. It didn't mean that I didn't love Anya. I did love Anya. I shall always love her. I didn't want her to die.

DOCTOR. I know, I know. I've never doubted that.

KARL. It's strange, perhaps, but one can love two women at the same time.

DOCTOR. Not at all strange. It often happens. (*He moves behind* KARL.) And you know what Anya used to say to me? 'When I'm gone, Karl must marry Lisa.' That's what she used to say. 'You must make him do it, Doctor,' she used to say. 'Lisa will look after him and be good to him. If he doesn't think of it you must put it into his head.' That's what she used to say to me. I promised her that I would.

KARL. (*Rising*) Tell me, really, Doctor. Do you think they'll acquit her? Do you?

DOCTOR. (*Gently*) I think – you ought to prepare yourself . . .

KARL. (*Moving below the armchair*) Even her counsel didn't believe me, did he? He pretended to, of course, but he didn't believe me. (*He sits in the armchair.*)

DOCTOR. No, I don't think he did, but there are one or two sensible people on the Jury – I think. (*He moves down Left.*) That fat woman in the funny hat listened to every word you were saying about Helen, and I noticed her nodding her head in complete agreement. She probably has a husband who went off the rails with a young girl. You never know what queer things influence people.

(The telephone rings.)

KARL. *(Rising)* This time it must be.

(The DOCTOR moves to the telephone and lifts the receiver.)

DOCTOR. *(Into the telephone)* Hullo? . . .

(LESTER enters up Centre from Left, carrying a tray with three cups of coffee on it. The coffee has slopped into the saucers.)

KARL. Well?

LESTER. Is that . . .? *(He puts the tray on the table Right Centre and pours the coffee into the cup from one of the saucers.)*

DOCTOR. *(Into the telephone)* No . . . No, I'm afraid he can't. *(He slams down the receiver.)* Another of the ghouls. *(He crosses to the sofa and sits.)*

KARL. What can they hope to get out of it?

DOCTOR. Increased circulation, I suppose.

LESTER. *(Handing a cup of coffee to KARL)* I hope it's all right. It took me some time to find everything.

KARL. Thank you. *(He crosses to the desk chair and sits.)*

(LESTER hands a cup of coffee to the DOCTOR, then takes his own and stands Right Centre. They sip their coffee. There is quite a pause.)

DOCTOR. Have you ever seen herons flying low over a river bank?

LESTER. No, I don't think I have. Why?

DOCTOR. No reason.

LESTER. What put it into your head?

DOCTOR. I've no idea. Just wishing, I suppose, that all this wasn't true and that I was somewhere else.

LESTER. Yes, I can see that. *(He moves up Centre.)* It's so awful, not being able to do anything.

DOCTOR. Nothing's so bad as waiting.

LESTER. *(After a pause)* I don't believe, you know, that I've ever seen a heron.

DOCTOR. Very graceful birds.

KARL. Doctor, I want you to do something for me.

DOCTOR. *(Rising)* Yes? What is it?

KARL. I want you to go back to the Court.

DOCTOR. (*Crossing to* KARL *and putting his cup on the work-table as he passes*) No, Karl.

KARL. Yes, I know that you promised. But I want you to go back.

DOCTOR. Karl – Lisa . . .

KARL. If the worst happens, I would like Lisa to be able to see you there. And if it isn't the worst – well, then she'll need someone to look after her, to get her away, to bring her here.

(*The* DOCTOR *stares at* KARL *for a moment or two.*)

I know I'm right.

DOCTOR. (*Deciding*) Very well.

LESTER. (*To the* DOCTOR) I can stay and . . .

(KARL *looks at the* DOCTOR *and shakes his head very slightly. The* DOCTOR *is quick to take the hint.*)

DOCTOR. No, you come with me, Lester. (*He moves up Centre.*) There are times when a man has got to be alone. That's right, isn't it, Karl?

KARL. Don't worry about me. I want to stay here quietly with Anya.

DOCTOR. (*Pulling round sharply, as he is on his way to the door*) What did you say? With Anya?

KARL. Did I say that? That's what it seems like. Leave me here. I shan't answer the telephone if it rings. I shall wait now until you come.

(LESTER *exits up Centre. The* DOCTOR *follows him off and closes the door.* KARL *leans back in his chair. The clock chimes six.*)

'While the light lasts I shall remember,
And in the darkness I shall not forget.'

(*There is a pause, then the telephone rings.* KARL *rises, ignores the telephone, takes his coffee cup to the tray, at the same time collecting the* DOCTOR's *cup as he passes the work-table. He then exits with the tray up Centre to Left. While he is off, the telephone stops ringing.* KARL *re-enters and moves down Left, leaving the door open. He pauses for a moment, staring at the work-table, then goes to the record cabinet and takes the Rachmaninov record from it. He goes to the desk and sits, putting the record on the desk in front of him.* LISA *suddenly enters up Centre from Right, shuts the door behind her and leans against it.* KARL *rises and turns.*)

KARL. Lisa! Lisa! (*He goes towards her as though he can hardly believe his eyes.*) Is it true? Is it?

LISA. They found me not guilty.

KARL. (*Attempting to take her in his arms*) Oh, my darling, I'm so thankful. No one shall ever hurt you again, Lisa.

LISA. (*Pushing him away*) No.

KARL. (*Realizing her coldness and aloofness*) What do you mean?

LISA. I've come here to get my things.

KARL. (*Backing above the armchair*) What do you mean – your things?

LISA. Just a few things that I need. Then I am going away.

KARL. What do you mean – going away?

LISA. I'm leaving here.

KARL. But surely – that's ridiculous! D'you mean because of what people would say? Does that matter now?

LISA. You don't understand. I am going away for good.

KARL. Going away – where?

LISA. (*Moving slowly down Centre*) What does it matter? Somewhere. I can get a job. There'll be no difficulty about that. I may go abroad. I may stay in England. Wherever I go I'm starting a new life.

KARL. A new life? You mean – without me?

LISA. Yes. Yes, Karl. That's just what I do mean. Without you.

KARL. (*Backing down Left*) But why? Why?

LISA. (*Up Right of the armchair*) Because I've had enough.

KARL. I don't understand you.

LISA. (*Moving to the sofa*) We're not made to understand each other. We don't see things the same way, and I'm afraid of you.

KARL. How can you be afraid of me?

LISA. Because you're the kind of man who always brings suffering.

KARL. No.

LISA. It's true.

KARL. No.

LISA. I see people as they are. Without malice and without entering into judgement, but without illusions, either. I don't expect people to be wonderful or life to be wonderful, and I don't particularly want to be wonderful myself. If there are fields of amaranth – they can be on the other side of the grave as far as I am concerned.

KARL. Fields of amaranth? What are you talking about?

LISA. I'm talking about you, Karl. You put ideas first, not people. Ideas of loyalty and friendship and pity. And because of that the people who are near, suffer. (*She moves to Right of the arm-chair.*) You knew you'd lose your job if you befriended the Schultzes. And you knew, you must have known, what an unhappy life that would mean for Anya. But you didn't care about Anya. You only cared about your ideas of what was right. But people matter, Karl. They matter as much as ideas. Anya mattered, I matter. Because of your ideas, because of your mercy and compassion for the girl who killed your wife, you sacrificed me. I was the one who paid for your compassion. But I'm not ready to do that any more. I love you, but love isn't enough. You've more in common with the girl Helen than you have with me. She was like you – ruthless. She went all out for the things she believed in. She didn't care what happened to people as long as she got her own way.

KARL. (*Moving towards the armchair*) Lisa, you can't mean what you are saying. You can't.

LISA. I do mean it. I've been thinking it really for a long time. (*She moves below the Left end of the sofa.*) I've thought of it all these days in Court. I didn't really think they'd acquit me. I don't know why they did. The judge didn't seem to think there was much reasonable doubt. But I suppose some of the Jury believed me. There was one little man who kept on looking at me as though he was sizing me up. Just a commonplace ordinary little man – but he looked at me and thought I hadn't done it – or perhaps he thought I was the kind of woman that he'd like to go to bed with and he didn't want me to suffer. I don't know what he thought – but – he was a person looking at another person and he was on my side and perhaps he persuaded the others. And so I'm free. I've been given a second chance to start life again. I'm starting again – alone.

(LISA *exits down Right.* KARL *crosses and sits on the sofa.*)

KARL. (*Pleadingly*) Lisa. You can't mean it. You can't be so cruel. You must listen. Lisa. I implore you.

(LISA *re-enters down Right. She carries a small silver photo frame. She remains down Right, facing* KARL.)

LISA. No, Karl. What happens to the women who love you? Anya loved you and she died. Helen loved you and she's dead. I – have been very near death. I've had enough. I want to be free of you – for ever.

KARL. But where will you go?

(*There is a pause as* LISA *crosses below* KARL *to Centre.*)

LISA. You told me to go away and marry and have children. Perhaps that's what I'll do. If so, I'll find someone like that little man on the jury, someone who'll be human and a person, like me. (*She suddenly cries out*) I've had enough. I've loved you for years and it's broken me. I'm going away and I shall never see you again. Never!

KARL. Lisa!

LISA. (*Moving down Left*) Never!

(*The* DOCTOR *is suddenly heard calling from the hall.*)

DOCTOR. (*Off; calling*) Karl! Karl!

(*The* DOCTOR *enters up Centre from Right and moves towards* KARL, *without noticing* LISA.)

It's all right, my boy. She's acquitted. (*During this he is quite out of breath.*) Do you understand? She's acquitted. (*He suddenly sees* LISA *and crosses to her with outstretched arms.*) Lisa – my dear Lisa. Thank God we've got you safe. It's wonderful. Wonderful!

LISA. (*Trying to respond to him*) Yes, it's wonderful.

DOCTOR. (*Holding her away from him and looking her up and down*) How are you? A little fine drawn – thinner – only natural with all you've been through. But we'll make it up to you. (*He crosses above the armchair to* KARL.) We'll look after you. As for Karl here, you can imagine the state he's been in. Ah, well, thank God that's all over now. (*He turns to* KARL.) What do you say – shall we go out – celebrate? A bottle of champagne – eh? (*He beams expectantly.*)

LISA. (*Forcing a smile*) No, Doctor – not tonight.

DOCTOR. Ah, what an old fool I am. Of course not. You need rest.

LISA. I am all right. (*She moves towards the doors up Centre.*) I must just get my things together.

DOCTOR (*Moving to* LISA) Things?

LISA. I am not – staying here.

DOCTOR. But . . . (*Enlightened*) Oh, I see – well, perhaps that is wise – with people like your Mrs Roper about, with their evil minds and tongues. But where will you go? To an hotel? Better come to us. Margaret will be delighted. It's a very tiny room that we have, but we'll look after you well.

LISA. How kind you are. But I have all my plans made. Tell – tell Margaret that I will come to see her very soon.

(LISA *goes into the hall and exits to her bedroom. The* DOCTOR *turns back to* KARL *and begins to realize that all is not well.*)

DOCTOR (*Moving Centre*) Karl – is anything wrong?

KARL. What should be wrong?

DOCTOR. (*Semi-relieved*) She has been through a terrible ordeal. It takes a little time to – to come back to normal. (*He looks around.*) When I think we sat here – waiting – with that damn telephone ringing all the time – hoping – fearing – and now – all over.

KARL. (*Tonelessly*) Yes – all over.

DOCTOR. (*Robustly*) No decent Jury would ever have convicted her. (*He moves and sits Left of* KARL *on the sofa.*) I told you so. You look half dazed still, Karl. Can't you believe it yet? (*He takes* KARL *affectionately by the shoulder.*) Karl, snap out of it. We've got our Lisa back again.

(KARL *turns sharply away.*)

Oh, I know – I'm clumsy – it takes a little time to get used to the joy.

(LISA *enters from her bedroom and comes into the room. She carries a holdall which she puts on the floor up Centre. She avoids looking at* KARL *and stands up Left Centre.*)

LISA. I'm going now.

DOCTOR. (*Rising*) I'll get a taxi for you.

LISA. (*Sharply*) No – please – I'd rather be alone. (*She turns away Left.*)

(*The* DOCTOR *is slightly taken aback. She relents, moves to the* DOCTOR *and puts her hands on his shoulders.*)

Thank you – for all your kindness – for all you did for Anya – you have been a good friend – I shall never forget.

(LISA *kisses the* DOCTOR, *picks up her holdall, and without once looking at* KARL *exits up Centre to Right.*)

DOCTOR. (*Moving to* KARL) Karl – what does this mean. There is something wrong.

KARL. Lisa is going away.

DOCTOR. Yes, yes – temporarily. But – she is coming back.

KARL. (*Turning to face the* DOCTOR) No, she is not coming back.

DOCTOR. (*Appalled*) What do you mean?

KARL. (*With complete conviction and force*) She – is – not – coming – back.

DOCTOR. (*Incredulously*) Do you mean – you have parted?

KARL. You saw her go – that was our parting.

DOCTOR. But – why?

KARL. She had had enough.

DOCTOR. Talk sense, man.

KARL. It's very simple. She has suffered. She doesn't want to suffer any more.

DOCTOR. Why should she suffer?

KARL. It seems – I am a man – who brings suffering to those who love him.

DOCTOR. Nonsense!

KARL. Is it? Anya loved me and she is dead. Helen loved me and she died.

DOCTOR. Did Lisa say that to you?

KARL. Yes. Am I such a man? Do I bring suffering to those who love me? What did she mean when she talked of fields of amaranth?

DOCTOR. Fields of amaranth. (*He thinks for a moment, then recollects, moves to the table Right Centre, picks up the 'Walter Savage Landor' and gives it to* KARL.) Yes, I was reading there. (*He points to the quotation.*)

KARL. Please leave me.

DOCTOR. I'd like to stay.

KARL. I must get used to being alone.

DOCTOR. (*Moving up Centre, then hesitating and returning to* KARL) You don't think . . .?

KARL. She will not come back.

(*The* DOCTOR *exits reluctantly up Centre to Right.*)

(*He rises, crosses to the desk, switches on the desk light, draws the curtains, then sits at the desk and reads*) 'There are no fields of Amaranth this side of the grave. There are no voices, oh Rhodope, that are not soon mute, however, tuneful: there is no name, with whatever emphasis of passionate love repeated, of which the echo is not faint at last . . .' (*He puts the book gently on the desk, rises, picks up the record, goes to the record player, puts on the record, switches on, then goes slowly to the armchair and sinks into it.*) Lisa – Lisa – how can I live without you? (*He drops his head into his hands.*)

(*The door up Centre opens slowly.* LISA *enters up Centre, moves slowly to Right of* KARL *and puts her hand gently on his shoulder.*)

(*He looks up at* LISA.) Lisa? You've come back. Why?
LISA. (*Kneeling at* KARL's *side*) Because I am a fool.

(LISA *rests her head on* KARL's *lap, he rests his head on hers and the music builds up as – the Curtain falls.*)

CURTAIN

GO BACK FOR MURDER

Presented by Peter Saunders at the Duchess Theatre, London, on 23rd March 1960, with the following cast of characters:

(in the order of their appearance)

JUSTIN FOGG	*Robert Urquhart*
TURNBALL	*Peter Hutton*
CARLA	*Ann Firbank*
JEFF ROGERS	*Mark Eden*
PHILIP BLAKE	*Anthony Marlowe*
MEREDITH BLAKE	*Laurence Hardy*
LADY MELKSHAM	*Lisa Daniely*
MISS WILLIAMS	*Margot Boyd*
ANGELA WARREN	*Dorothy Bromiley*
CAROLINE CRALE	*Ann Firbank*
AMYAS CRALE	*Nigel Green*

The play directed by Hubert Gregg

Décor by Michael Weight

SYNOPSIS OF SCENES

ACT I

London

SCENE 1 A lawyer's office
SCENE 2 A City office
SCENE 3 A room in an hotel suite
SCENE 4 A bed-sitting-room
SCENE 5 A table in a restaurant

ACT II

Alderbury, a house in the West of England
Time: the present. Autumn

AUTHOR'S NOTE

CARLA and her mother, CAROLINE CRALE, are played by the same actress.

As regards the characters in Act II, PHILIP is not greatly changed, but his hair is not grey at the temples, and he is more slender, his manner is less pompous. MEREDITH is less vague, and more alert, his face is less red, and there is no grey in his hair. There is very little change in MISS WILLIAMS, except that she is also not so grey. ANGELA can have plaits, or long hair. ELSA must present the greatest change from LADY MELKSHAM, young, and eager, with her hair on her neck. CAROLINE is distinguishable from CARLA by a different hairstyle, as well as by an older make-up. Her voice, too, must be different, deeper in tone, and her manner more impulsive and intense.

Each scene of Act I represents a small portion of a room. In the original production the scenes were on trucks, but the whole of this Act can be quite simply staged by lighting up different parts of the stage in turn, or by cut-outs.

ACT ONE

Scene I

SCENE: JUSTIN FOGG'S *room in the offices of Fogg, Fogg, Bamfylde and Fogg, Solicitors. An early-autumn afternoon in London.*

The room is rather old-fashioned and cramped for space. The walls are lined with books. An arch up Left Centre leads to the rest of the building, and there is a sash window across the corner up Right. A large desk and swivel chair stand in front of the window. There is a chair Centre for visitors, and a table covered with files is against the wall Left. There is a telephone on the desk.

When Curtain rises, the stage is in darkness, then the LIGHTS come up. JUSTIN FOGG *is seated at the desk, speaking into the telephone. The window is half-open.* JUSTIN *is a young man in the early thirties, sober, staid, but likeable.*

JUSTIN. (*Into the telephone*) I quite see your point, Mrs Ross, but the Law can't be hurried, you know –

(TURNBALL, *an elderly clerk, appears in the archway. He is carrying a file.*)

– we have to wait for their solicitors to reply to our letter . . .

(TURNBALL *coughs.*)

(*To* TURNBALL) Come in, Turnball. (*Into the telephone*) No, it would be *most* inadvisable for you to take *any* steps yourself . . . Yes, we will keep you informed. (*He replaces the receiver.*) Women!

(TURNBALL *places the file on the desk in front of* JUSTIN.)

Miss Le Marchant?
TURNBALL. She's here now, sir.
JUSTIN. Show her in, Turnball. I don't want any interruptions *at*

all. Put anything urgent through to Mr Grimes.

TURNBALL. Very good, sir.

(TURNBALL *exits.* JUSTIN *rises, crosses to the table Left, selects a file, returns to his desk, sits, and puts* TURNBALL'*s file in the desk drawer.* TURNBALL *re-enters and stands to one side.*)

(*He announces*) Miss Le Marchant.

(CARLA *enters. She is aged twenty-one, pretty, and determined. She wears a coat and carries bag and gloves. She speaks with a Canadian accent.* TURNBALL *exits.*)

JUSTIN. (*Rising, moving to* CARLA *and offering his hand*) How do you do?

CARLA. How do you do, Mr Fogg? (*She looks at him in dismay, ignoring his outstretched hand.*) But you're *young!*

(JUSTIN *looks at* CARLA *for a moment, amused, although still formal.*)

JUSTIN. Thank you. But I can assure you I'm a fully qualified solicitor.

CARLA. I'm sorry – it's just – that I expected you to be – rather old.

JUSTIN. Oh, you expected my father? He died two years ago.

CARLA. I see. I'm sorry. It was stupid of me. (*She offers him her hand.*)

(JUSTIN *shakes hands with* CARLA.)

JUSTIN. (*Indicating the chair Centre*) Do sit down.

(CARLA *sits Centre.*)

(*He returns to his desk and sits at it.*) Now, tell me what I can do for you.

(*There is a pause whilst* CARLA *looks at* JUSTIN, *a little uncertain how to begin.*)

CARLA. Do you know who I am?

JUSTIN. Miss Carla Le Marchant of Montreal.

CARLA. (*Looking away*) My name isn't really Le Marchant.

JUSTIN. Oh, yes, it is. Legally.

CARLA. (*Leaning forward*) So – you *do* know all about me?

JUSTIN. We have acted for Mr Robert Le Marchant over a number of years.

CARLA. All right, then, let's get down to it. My name may be legally
Le Marchant by adoption – or deed poll – or habeas corpus –
or whatever the legal jargon is. (*She removes her gloves.*) But I was
born – (*She pauses.*) Caroline Crale. Caroline was my mother's
name, too. My father was Amyas Crale. Sixteen years ago my
mother stood her trial for poisoning my father. They found her
– guilty. (*She takes a deep breath. Defiantly*) That's right, isn't it?

JUSTIN. Yes, those are the facts.

CARLA. I only learned them six months ago.

JUSTIN. When you came of age?

CARLA. Yes. I don't think they wanted me to know. Uncle Robert
and Aunt Bess, I mean. They brought me up believing my
parents were killed in an accident when I was five years old.
But my mother left a letter for me – to be given me when I was
twenty-one, so they had to tell me all about it.

JUSTIN. Unfortunate.

CARLA. Do you mean you think they ought not to have told me?

JUSTIN. No, no, I don't mean that at all. I meant it was unfortunate
for *you* – it must have been a bad shock.

CARLA. Finding out that my father was murdered and that my
mother did it?

JUSTIN. (*After a pause; kindly*) There were – extenuating circumstances, you know.

CARLA. (*Firmly*) It's not extenuating circumstances I'm interested
in. It's facts.

JUSTIN. Yes, facts. Well, you've got your facts. Now – you can put
the whole thing behind you. (*He smiles encouragingly.*) It's your
future that matters now, you know, not the past. (*He rises and
crosses above the desk to the table Left.*)

CARLA. I think, before I can go forward – I've got to – go back.

(JUSTIN, *arrested and puzzled, turns to* CARLA.)

JUSTIN. I beg your pardon?

CARLA. It's not as simple as you make it sound. (*She pauses.*) I'm
engaged – or I was engaged – to be married.

(JUSTIN *picks up the cigarette box from the table Left and offers it to* CARLA,
who takes a cigarette.)

JUSTIN. I see. And your fiancé found out about all this?

CARLA. Of course, I told him.

JUSTIN. And he – er – reacted unfavourably? (*He replaces the box on the table.*)

CARLA. (*Without enthusiasm*) Not at all. He was perfectly splendid. Said it didn't matter at all.

JUSTIN. (*Puzzled*) Well, then?

CARLA. (*Looking up at* JUSTIN) It isn't what a person *says* . . . (*She leaves it at that.*)

JUSTIN. (*After a moment*) Yes, I see. (*He lights* CARLA*'s cigarette with the lighter from the table Left.*) At least, I think I do.

CARLA. Anyone can *say* things. It's what they *feel* that matters.

JUSTIN. Don't you think that perhaps you're super-sensitive?

CARLA. (*Firmly*) No.

JUSTIN. But, my dear girl . . .

CARLA. Would *you* like to marry the daughter of a murderess? (*She looks at* JUSTIN.)

(JUSTIN *looks down.*)

(*Quietly*) You see, you wouldn't.

JUSTIN. You didn't give me time to answer. I wouldn't particularly *want* to marry the daughter of a murderer, or of a drunkard or of a dope-fiend or of anything else unpleasant. (*He picks up the cigarette box, crosses above* CARLA *to the desk and puts the lighter and cigarette box on it.*) But what the hell, if I loved a girl, she could be the daughter of Jack the Ripper for all I cared.

CARLA. (*Looking around the room*) I don't believe you would mind as much as Jeff does. (*She shivers.*)

JUSTIN. Do you find it cold?

CARLA. I think your central heating's kind of low.

JUSTIN. It's kind of non-existent, I'm afraid. (*He smiles.*) I mean, we haven't any. Shall I get them to light the fire for you?

CARLA. No, please.

(JUSTIN *looks at the window, sees it is open, quickly closes it, then leans over the desk to* CARLA.)

JUSTIN. This Mr – er . . . This Jeff . . .?

CARLA. You'll see him. He's coming to call for me, if you don't mind. (*She looks at her wrist-watch.*) Hell, I'm wasting time. I didn't come to consult you about my love life. (*Struck*) At least, I suppose I did. I've got to find out the truth, you see.

JUSTIN. I told you just now that there were extenuating circumstances. Your mother was found guilty, but the Jury made a strong recommendation to mercy. Her sentence was commuted to imprisonment.

CARLA. And she died in prison three years later.

JUSTIN. (*Sitting at the desk*) Yes.

CARLA. In her letter, my mother wrote that she wanted me to know definitely that she was innocent. (*She looks defiantly at* JUSTIN.)

JUSTIN. (*Unimpressed*) Yes.

CARLA. You don't believe it?

JUSTIN. (*Carefully finding his words*) I think – a devoted mother – might want to do the best she could for her daughter's peace of mind.

CARLA. No, no, *no*! She wasn't like that. She never told lies.

JUSTIN. How can you know? You were a child of five when you saw her last.

CARLA. (*Passionately*) I do know. My mother didn't tell lies. When she took a thorn out of my finger once, she said it would hurt. And going to the dentist. All those things. She was never one to sugar the pill. What she said was always *true*. (*She rises quickly, and turns up Left.*) And if she says she was innocent then she *was* innocent. You don't believe me – but it's *so*. (*She takes a handkerchief from her bag and dabs her eyes.*)

JUSTIN. (*Rising*) It's better, always, to face the truth.

CARLA. (*Turning to him*) That is the truth.

JUSTIN. (*Shaking his head, quietly*) It isn't the truth.

CARLA. How can you be so sure? Does a Jury never make a mistake?

JUSTIN. There are probably several guilty people walking around free, yes, because they've been given the benefit of the doubt. But in your mother's case – there wasn't any doubt.

CARLA. You weren't there. It was your father who attended the case . . .

JUSTIN. (*Interrupting*) My father was the solicitor in charge of the defence, yes.

CARLA. Well – *he* thought her innocent, didn't he?

JUSTIN. Yes. (*Embarrassed*) Yes, of course. You don't quite understand these things . . .

CARLA. (*Cynically*) You mean that it was *technical* only?

(JUSTIN *is slightly at a loss how to explain.*)

(*She moves Centre, in front of her chair.*) But he himself, personally – what did *he* think?

JUSTIN. (*Stiffly*) Really, I've no idea.

CARLA. Yes, you have. He thought she was guilty. (*She turns and faces Left.*) And you think so, too. (*She pauses, then turns to* JUSTIN.) But how is it that you remember it all so well?

JUSTIN. (*Looking steadily at her*) I was eighteen – just going up to Oxford – not in the firm, yet – but – interested. (*Remembering*) I was in Court every day.

CARLA. What did you think? Tell me. (*She sits Centre. Eagerly*) I have to know.

JUSTIN. Your mother loved your father desperately – but he gave her a raw deal – he brought his mistress into the house – subjected your mother to humiliation and insult. Mrs Crale endured more than any woman could be expected to endure. He drove her too far. The means were to hand – try and understand. Understand and forgive. (*He crosses above the desk and stands down Left.*)

CARLA. I don't need to forgive. She didn't do it.

JUSTIN. (*Turning to her*) Then who the devil did?

(CARLA, *taken aback, looks up at* JUSTIN.)

(*He crosses below* CARLA *to Right.*) Well, that's the point, isn't it? Nobody else had the slightest motive. If you were to read up the reports of the case . . .

CARLA. I have. I've gone to the files. I've read up every single detail of the trial.

(JUSTIN *crosses behind the desk and goes through the file he put on it.*)

JUSTIN. Well, then, take the facts. Aside from your mother and father, there were five people in the house that day. There were the Blakes – Philip and Meredith, two brothers, two of your father's closest friends. There was a girl of fourteen, your mother's half-sister – Angela Warren, and her governess – Miss – something or other, and there was Elsa Greer, your father's mistress – and there wasn't the least suspicion against any of them – and besides, if you'd seen . . . (*He breaks off.*)

CARLA. (*Eagerly*) Yes – go on . . .

JUSTIN. (*Turning to the window, with feeling*) If you'd seen her standing there in the witness box. So brave, so polite – bearing it all so patiently, but never – for one moment – fighting. (*He looks at* CARLA.) You're like her, you know, to look at. It might *be* her sitting there. There's only one difference. You're a fighter. (*He looks in the file.*)

CARLA. (*Looking out front, puzzled*) She didn't fight – why?

JUSTIN. (*Crossing down Left*) Montagu Depleach led for the defence. I think now that may have been a mistake. He had an enormous reputation, but he was – theatrical. His client had to play up. But your mother didn't play up.

CARLA. Why?

JUSTIN. She answered his questions with all the right answers – but it was like a docile child repeating a lesson – it didn't give old Monty his chance. He built up to the last question – 'I ask you, Mrs Crale, *did* you kill your husband?' And she said: 'No – er – no, really I d-didn't.' She stammered. It was a complete anticlimax, utterly unconvincing.

CARLA. And then what happened?

JUSTIN. (*Crossing above* CARLA *to the desk*) Then it was Asprey's turn. He was Attorney-General, later. Quiet, but quite deadly. Logic – after old Monty's fireworks. He made mincemeat of her. Brought out every damning detail. I – I could hardly bear it . . .

CARLA. (*Studying him*) You remember it all very well.

JUSTIN. Yes.

CARLA. Why?

JUSTIN. (*Taken aback*) I suppose . . .

CARLA. Yes?

JUSTIN. I was young, impressionable.

CARLA. You fell in love with my mother.

(JUSTIN *forces a laugh and sits at the desk.*)

JUSTIN. Something of the kind – she was so lovely – so helpless – she'd been through so much – I – I'd have died for her. (*He smiles.*) Romantic age – eighteen.

CARLA. (*Frowning*) You'd have died for her – but you thought her guilty.

JUSTIN. (*Firmly*) Yes, I did.

(CARLA *is really shaken. She bends her head, fighting back her tears.* TURN-
BALL *enters and moves to Left of the desk.*)

TURNBALL. A Mr Rogers is here, sir, asking for Miss Le Marchant.
(*He looks at* CARLA.)

CARLA. Jeff. (*To* TURNBALL) Please – ask him to wait.

TURNBALL. Certainly, Miss Le Marchant.

(TURNBALL *looks closely at* CARLA *for a moment, then exits.*)

CARLA. (*Looking after* TURNBALL) He looked at me . . . (*She breaks
off.*)

JUSTIN. Turnball was at your mother's trial. He's been with us for
nearly forty years.

CARLA. Please, ask him back.

(JUSTIN *rises and moves to the arch.*)

JUSTIN. (*Calling*) Turnball. (*He returns to Right of the desk.*)

(TURNBALL *enters.*)

TURNBALL. Yes, sir?

(JUSTIN *motions to* CARLA. TURNBALL *moves down Left of* CARLA.)

CARLA. Mr Turnball – I'm Carla Crale. I believe you were at my
mother's trial.

TURNBALL. Yes, Miss Crale, I was. Er – I knew at once who you
were.

CARLA. Because I'm so like my mother?

TURNBALL. The dead spit of her, if I may put it so.

CARLA. What did you think – at the trial? Did you think she was
guilty?

(TURNBALL *looks at* JUSTIN. JUSTIN *nods for* TURNBALL *to
answer.*)

TURNBALL. (*Kindly*) You don't want to put it that way. She was a
sweet, gentle lady – but she'd been pushed too far. As I've
always seen it, she didn't rightly know what she was doing.

CARLA. (*To herself; ironically*) Extenuating circumstances. (*She looks at*
JUSTIN.)

(JUSTIN *sits at the desk. After a while,* CARLA *looks back at* TURN-BALL.)

TURNBALL. (*After a pause*) That's right. The other woman – that Elsa Greer – she was a hussy if ever there was one. Sexy, if you'll excuse the word. And your father was an artist – a really great painter; I understand some of his pictures are in the Tate Gallery – and you know what artists are. That Greer girl got her hooks into him good and proper – a kind of madness it must have been. Got him so he was going to leave his wife and child for her. Don't ever blame your mother, Miss Crale. Even the gentlest lady can be pushed too far.

JUSTIN. Thank you, Turnball.

(TURNBALL *looks from* CARLA *to* JUSTIN, *then exits.*)

CARLA. He thinks as you do – guilty.

JUSTIN. A gentle creature – pushed too far.

CARLA. (*Acquiescing*) I – suppose so – yes. (*With sudden energy*) No! I don't believe it. I won't believe it. You – you've got to help me.

JUSTIN. To do what?

CARLA. Go back into the past and find out the truth.

JUSTIN. You won't believe the truth when you hear it.

CARLA. Because it *isn't* the truth. The defence was suicide, wasn't it?

JUSTIN. Yes.

CARLA. It *could* have been suicide. My father *could* have felt that he'd messed up everything, and that he'd be better out of it all.

JUSTIN. It was the only defence possible – but it wasn't convincing. Your father was the last man in the world to take his own life.

CARLA. (*Doubtfully*) Accident?

JUSTIN. Conine – a deadly poison, introduced into a glass of beer by accident?

CARLA. All right, then. There's only one answer. Someone else.

(JUSTIN *begins to thumb through the file on his desk, which contains separate sheafs of notes on each person connected with the case.*)

JUSTIN. One of the five people there in the house. Hardly Elsa Greer. She'd got your father besotted about her, and he was going to get a divorce from his wife and marry her. Philip

Blake? He was devoted to your father and always had been.

CARLA. (*Weakly*) Perhaps *he* was in love with Elsa Greer, too.

JUSTIN. He certainly was not. Meredith Blake? He was your father's friend, too, one of the most amiable men that ever lived. Imagination boggles at the thought of his murdering anyone.

CARLA. All right. All right. Who else do we have?

JUSTIN. Angela Warren, a schoolgirl of fourteen? And the governess, Miss Whoever her name is.

CARLA. (*Quickly*) Well, what about Miss Whoever her name was?

JUSTIN. (*After a slight pause*) I see the way your mind is working. Frustration, lonely spinster, repressed love for your father. Let me tell you that Miss – Williams – (*He looks in the file.*) yes, that was her name – Williams – wasn't like that, at all. She was a tartar, a woman of strong character, and sound common sense. (*He closes the file.*) Go and see her for yourself if you don't believe me.

CARLA. That's what I'm going to do.

JUSTIN. (*Looking up*) What?

CARLA. (*Stubbing out her cigarette in the ashtray on the desk*) I'm going to see them *all*. (*She rises.*) That's what I want you to do for me. Find out where they all are. Make appointments for me with them.

JUSTIN. With what reason?

CARLA. (*Crossing to Left*) So that I can ask them questions, make them remember.

JUSTIN. What can they remember that could be useful after sixteen years?

CARLA. (*Putting on her gloves*) Something, perhaps, that they never thought of at the time. Something that wasn't evidence – not the sort of thing that would come out in court. It will be like patchwork – a little piece of this and a little piece of that. And in the end, who knows, it might add up to something.

JUSTIN. Wishful thinking. You'll only give yourself more pain in the end. (*He puts the file in the desk drawer.*)

CARLA. (*Defiantly*) My mother was innocent. I'm starting from there. And you're going to help me.

JUSTIN. (*Stubbornly*) That's where you're wrong. (*He rises.*) I'm not going to help you to chase a will-o'-the-wisp.

(CARLA *and* JUSTIN *stare at each other.*)

(JEFF ROGERS *suddenly strides in.* TURNBALL, *indignantly protesting, follows him on.* JEFF *is a big, slick, self-satisfied man of thirty-five, good-looking and insensitive to others. He wears an overcoat and carries a hat, which he throws on to the desk.*)

JEFF. (*Standing above the desk*) Sorry to bust in, but all this sitting around in waiting-rooms gives me claustrophobia. (*To Carla*) Time means nothing to you, honey. (*To Justin*) I take it you're Mr Fogg? Pleased to meet you.

(JEFF *and* JUSTIN *shake hands.*)

TURNBALL. (*In the archway; to Justin*) I'm extremely sorry, sir. I was – er – quite unable to restrain this – gentleman.
JEFF. (*Cheerily*) Forget it, Pop. (*He slaps Turnball on the back.*)

(TURNBALL *winces.*)

JUSTIN. It's quite all right, Turnball.

(TURNBALL *exits.*)

JEFF. (*Calling*) No hard feelings, Turnball. (*To Carla*) Well, I suppose you haven't finished your business, Carla?
CARLA. But I have. I came to ask Mr Fogg something – (*Coldly*) and he's answered me.
JUSTIN. I'm sorry.
CARLA. All right, Jeff. Let's go. (*She moves to the arch.*)
JEFF. Oh, Carla—

(CARLA *stops and turns.*)

– I rather wanted to have a word with Mr Fogg, myself – about some affairs of mine here. Would you mind? I'll only be a few minutes.

(CARLA *hesitates.*)

CARLA. I'll go and soothe Mr Turnball's feelings. He was absolutely horrified by your behaviour.

(CARLA *exits.*)

JEFF. (*Moving to the arch and calling*) That's right, darling. Tell him

I'm an overseas hick who knows no better. (*He laughs loudly and turns.*) That old boy's like something out of Dickens.

JUSTIN. (*Dryly*) Come in, Mr – er . . . (*He looks unsuccessfully for Jeff's name on the band inside his hat.*)

JEFF. (*Not listening*) I wanted to have a word with you, Mr Fogg. (*He moves down Centre.*) It's this business about Carla's mother. The whole thing's given her a bit of a jolt.

JUSTIN. (*Very cold and legal*) Not unnaturally.

JEFF. It's a shock to learn suddenly that your mother was a cold-blooded poisoner. I don't mind telling you that it was a bit of a jolt to *me*, too.

JUSTIN. Indeed!

(JEFF *moves and sits on the up-stage end of the desk.*)

JEFF. There I was, all set to marry a nice girl, uncle and aunt some of the nicest people in Montreal, a well-bred girl, money of her own, everything a man could want. And then – out of the blue– *this*.

JUSTIN. It must have upset you.

JEFF. (*With feeling*) Oh, it did.

JUSTIN. (*Quietly*) Sit down, Mr – er . . .

JEFF. What?

JUSTIN. (*Nodding towards the chair Centre.*) On the chair.

(JEFF *looks at the chair Centre, then rises, moves to the chair and sits on it.*)

JEFF. Oh, I'll admit that, just at first, I thought of backing out – you know, kids – things like that?

JUSTIN. You have strong views about heredity?

JEFF. You can't do any cattle breeding without realizing that certain strains repeat themselves. 'Still', I said to myself, 'it isn't the girl's fault. She's a fine girl. You can't let her down. You've just got to go through with it.'

(JUSTIN *picks up the box of cigarettes and lighter and crosses above* JEFF *to Left of him.*)

JUSTIN. Cattle breeding.

JEFF. So I told her it made no difference at all. (*He takes a packet of American cigarettes and a lighter from his pocket.*)

JUSTIN. But it does?

JEFF. (*Taking a cigarette from his packet*) No, no, I've put it behind me. But Carla's got some morbid idea in her head of raking the whole thing up. That's got to be stopped. (*He offers* JUSTIN *a cigarette.*)

JUSTIN. Yes? No. (*He puts the cigarette box quickly on the table Left.*)

JEFF. She'll only upset herself. Let her down lightly – but let your answer be '*No*'. See?

(JEFF *lights his cigarette. At the same moment,* JUSTIN *flicks the lighter he holds, sees* JEFF *has his own, so extinguishes it quickly, and puts it on the table Left.*)

JUSTIN. I see.

JEFF. Of course – I suppose making all these enquiries would be quite – er – good business for your firm. You know, fees, expenses, all that . . .

JUSTIN. (*Crossing below* JEFF *to Right*) We are a firm of solicitors, you know, not enquiry agents.

JEFF. Sorry, must have explained myself clumsily.

JUSTIN. Yes.

JEFF. What I want to say is – I'll stump up the necessary – but drop it.

JUSTIN. (*Moving behind the desk*) You will excuse me, Mr – er . . . but Miss Le Marchant is my client.

JEFF. (*Rising*) Yep, well, if you're acting for Carla, you must agree that it's best for her not to go harrowing herself raking up the past. Make her give it up. Once we're married, she'll never think of it again.

JUSTIN. And will you never think of it again?

JEFF. That's a good question. Yes, I daresay I'll have one or two nasty moments.

JUSTIN. If the coffee should taste bitter . . .?

JEFF. That sort of thing.

JUSTIN. Which won't be very pleasant for her.

JEFF. (*Cheerily*) Well, what can a man do? You can't undo the past. Glad to have met you, Fogg. (*He offers his hand.*)

(JUSTIN *looks at* JEFF's *hand, then picks up* JEFF's *hat from the desk and puts it in the outstretched hand.* JEFF *exits.* JUSTIN *turns to the window, opens it wide, then lifts the telephone receiver.*)

JUSTIN. (*Into the telephone*) Has Miss Le Marchant left yet? . . . Well, ask her to come back for a minute. I shan't keep her long. (*He replaces the receiver, crosses to the table Left, takes a cigarette from the box, lights it, then returns to Right of the desk.*)

(CARLA *enters.*)

CARLA. (*Looking coldly at* JUSTIN) Yes?

JUSTIN. I've changed my mind.

CARLA. (*Startled*) What?

JUSTIN. That's all. I've changed my mind. I will fix up an appointment for you to see Mr Philip Blake here. I will let you know when.

(CARLA *smiles.*)

Go on. Don't keep Mr – er . . . don't keep him waiting. He wouldn't be pleased. You'll be hearing from me. (*He ushers* CARLA *to the arch.*)

(CARLA *exits.*)

(*He goes to the desk and lifts the receiver. Into the telephone*) Get me Kellway, Blake and Leverstein, will you? I want to speak to Mr Philip Blake personally. (*He replaces the receiver.*) Cattle breeding!

The LIGHTS dim to black-out

Scene II

SCENE: *Philip Blake's office*

It is a very handsome room. A door up Right leads to the outer office. Up Left is a cupboard for drinks, let into the wall. A large and ornate desk is Left with a damask-covered swivel chair behind it. A chair, to match, for visitors is down Right. There are shaded, electric wall-brackets Right and Left. On the desk there is an intercom in addition to the telephone.

When the LIGHTS come up, PHILIP BLAKE is sitting at the desk, smoking *and reading the 'Financial Times'. He is a good-looking man of fifty odd, grey at the temples, with a slight paunch. He is self-important, with traces of nervous irritability. He is very sure of himself. The intercom buzzes.* PHILIP *presses the switch.*

PHILIP. (*Into the intercom*) Yes?

VOICE. (*Through the intercom*) Miss Le Marchant's here, Mr Blake.

PHILIP. Ask her to come in.

VOICE. Yes, Mr Blake.

(PHILIP *releases the switch, frowns, folds his newspaper and lays it on the desk, rises, moves down Left of the desk, turns and faces the door. He shows slight traces of uneasiness while he waits.* CARLA *enters. She wears a different coat, and carries different gloves and handbag.*)

PHILIP. Good Lord.

(PHILIP *and* CARLA *look at each other for a moment, then* CARLA *closes the door and moves down Centre.*)

Well, so it's Carla. (*He recovers himself and shakes hands with her.*) Little Carla! (*With rather forced geniality*) You were – what – five years old when I saw you last.

CARLA. Yes. I must have been just about. (*She screws up her eyes.*) I don't think I remember you . . .

PHILIP. I was never much of a children's man. Never knew what to say to them. Sit down, Carla.

(CARLA *sits on the chair down Right and places her handbag on the floor beside the chair.*)

(*He offers the box of cigarettes from the desk.*) Cigarette?

(CARLA *declines.*)

(*He replaces the box on the desk, moves behind the desk and looks at his watch.*) I haven't much time, but . . . (*He sits at the desk.*)

CARLA. I know you're a terribly busy person. It's good of you to see me.

PHILIP. Not at all. You're the daughter of one of my oldest and closest friends. You remember your father?

CARLA. Yes. Not very clearly.

PHILIP. You should. Amyas Crale oughtn't to be forgotten. (*He pauses.*) Now, what's this all about? This lawyer chap – Fogg – son of old Andrew Fogg, I suppose –

(CARLA *nods.*)

– wasn't very clear about why you wanted to see me. (*There is a trace of sarcasm in his voice during the following sentence.*) But I gathered that it wasn't just a case of looking up your father's old friends?

CARLA. No.

PHILIP. He told me that you'd only recently learnt the facts about your father's death. Is that right?

CARLA. Yes.

PHILIP. Pity, really, you ever had to hear about it at all.

CARLA. (*After a pause; firmly*) Mr Blake, when I came in just now you were startled. You said 'Good Lord!' Why?

PHILIP. Well, I . . .

CARLA. Did you think, just for the moment, that it was my mother standing there?

PHILIP. There is an amazing resemblance. It startled me.

CARLA. You – you didn't like her?

PHILIP. (*Drily*) Could you expect me to? She killed my best friend.

CARLA. (*Stung*) It *could* have been suicide.

PHILIP. Don't run away with that idea. Amyas would never have killed himself. He enjoyed life far too much.

CARLA. He was an artist, he could have had temperamental ups and downs.

PHILIP. He didn't have that kind of temperament. Nothing morbid or neurotic about Amyas. He had his faults, yes – he chased women, I'll admit – but most of his affairs were quite short-lived. He always went back to Caroline.

CARLA. What fun that must have been for her!

PHILIP. She'd known him since she was twelve years old. We were all brought up together.

CARLA. I know so little. Tell me.

PHILIP. (*Sitting back comfortably in his chair*) She used to come and stay at Alderbury for the holidays with the Crales. My family had the big house next door. We all ran wild together. Meredith, my elder brother, and Amyas were much of an age. I was a year or two younger. Caroline had no money of her own, you know. I was a younger son, out of the running, but both Meredith and Amyas were quite good catches.

CARLA. How cold-blooded you make her sound.

PHILIP. She *was* cold-blooded. Oh, she appeared impulsive, but behind it there was a cold calculating devil. And she had a wicked temper. You know what she did to her baby half-sister?

CARLA. (*Quickly*) No?

PHILIP. Her mother had married again, and all the attention went to the new baby – Angela. Caroline was jealous as hell. She tried to kill the baby.

CARLA. No!

PHILIP. Went for her with a pair of scissors, I believe. Ghastly business. The child was marked for life.

CARLA. (*Outraged*) You make her sound a – a monster!

PHILIP. (*Shrugging*) Jealousy is the devil.

CARLA. (*Studying him*) You hated her – didn't you?

PHILIP. (*Startled*) That's putting it rather strongly.

CARLA. No, it's true.

PHILIP. (*Stubbing out his cigarette*) I suppose I'm bitter. (*He rises, moves to Right of the desk and sits on the down-stage corner of it.*) But it seems to me that you've come over here with the idea in your head that your mother was an injured innocent. That isn't so. There's Amyas's side of it, too. He was your father, girl, and he loved life . . .

CARLA. I know. I know all that.

PHILIP. You've got to see this thing as it was. Caroline was no good. (*He pauses.*) She poisoned her husband. And what I can't forget, and never will forget, is that *I* could have saved him.

CARLA. How?

PHILIP. My brother Meredith had a strange hobby. He used to fiddle about with herbs and hemlock and stuff and Caroline had stolen one of his patent brews.

CARLA. How did you know that it was *she* who had taken it?

PHILIP. (*Grimly*) I knew all right. And I was fool enough to hang about waiting to talk it over with Meredith. Why I hadn't the sense to realize that *Caroline* wouldn't wait, I can't think. She'd pinched the stuff to use – and by God, she used it at the first opportunity.

CARLA. You *can't* be sure it was she who took it.

PHILIP. My dear girl, she *admitted* taking it. Said she'd taken it to do away with herself.

CARLA. That's possible, isn't it?

PHILIP. Is it? (*Caustically*) Well, she *didn't* do away with herself.

(CARLA *shakes her head. There is a silence.*)

(*He rises and makes an effort to resume a normal manner.*) Have a glass of sherry? (*He moves below and Left of the desk to the cupboard up Left, takes out a decanter of sherry and a glass and puts them on the desk.*) Now, I suppose I've upset you? (*He pours a glass of sherry.*)

CARLA. I've got to find out about things.

PHILIP. (*Crossing and handing the glass to* CARLA) There was a lot of sympathy for her at the trial, of course. (*He moves behind the desk.*) Amyas behaved badly, I'll admit, bringing the Greer girl down to Alderbury. (*He replaces the decanter in the cupboard.*) And she *was* pretty insolent to Caroline.

CARLA. Did you like her?

PHILIP. (*Guardedly*) Young Elsa? Not particularly. (*He turns to the cupboard, takes out a bottle of whisky and a glass and puts them on the desk.*) She wasn't my type, damnably attractive, of course. Predatory. Grasping at everything she wanted. (*He pours whisky for himself.*) All the same, I think she'd have suited Amyas better than Caroline did. (*He replaces the bottle in the cupboard.*)

CARLA. Weren't my mother and father happy together?

PHILIP. (*With a laugh*) They never stopped having rows. His married life would have been one long *hell* if it hadn't been for the way of escape his painting gave him. (*He squirts soda into his drink and sits at the desk.*)

CARLA. How did he meet Elsa?

PHILIP. (*Vaguely*) Some Chelsea party or other. (*He smiles.*) Came along to me – told me he'd met a marvellous girl – absolutely different from any girl he'd met before. Well, I'd heard *that* often enough. He'd fall for a girl like a ton of bricks, and a month later, when you mentioned her, he'd stare at you and wonder who the hell you were talking about. But it didn't turn out that way with Elsa. (*He raises his glass.*) Good luck, m'dear. (*He drinks.*)

(CARLA *sips her sherry.*)

CARLA. She's married now, isn't she?

PHILIP. (*Drily*) She's run through three husbands. A test pilot who crashed himself, some explorer chap whom she got bored with. She's married now to old Lord Melksham, a dreamy peer who writes mystical poetry. I should say she's about had *him* by now. (*He drinks.*)

CARLA. Would she have gotten tired of my father, I wonder?

PHILIP. Who knows?

CARLA. I must meet her.

PHILIP. Can't you let things go?

CARLA. (*Rising and putting her glass on the desk*) No, I've got to understand.

PHILIP. (*Rising*) Determined, aren't you?

CARLA. Yes, I'm a fighter. But my mother – wasn't.

(*The intercom buzzes.* CARLA *turns and picks up her bag.*)

PHILIP. Where did you get that idea? Caroline was a terrific fighter. (*He presses the switch. Into the intercom*) Yes?

VOICE. (*Through the intercom*) Mr Foster's here, Mr Blake.

PHILIP. Tell him I won't keep him a moment.

VOICE. Yes, sir.

(PHILIP *releases the switch.*)

CARLA. (*Struck*) Was she? Was she really? But – she didn't fight at her trial.

PHILIP. No.

CARLA. Why didn't she?

PHILIP. Well, since she knew she was guilty . . . (*He rises.*)

CARLA. (*Angrily*) She wasn't guilty!

PHILIP. (*Angrily*) You're obstinate, aren't you? After all I've told you!

CARLA. You still hate her. Although she's been dead for years. Why?

PHILIP. I've told you . . .

CARLA. Not the real reason. There's something else.

PHILIP. I don't think so.

CARLA. You hate her – now why? I shall have to find out. Goodbye, Mr Blake. Thank you.

PHILIP. Goodbye.

(CARLA *moves to the door and exits, leaving the door open.*)

(*He stares after her for a moment, slightly perplexed, then he closes the door, sits at the desk and presses the intercom switch. Into the intercom*) Ask Mr Foster to come in.

VOICE. (*Through the intercom*) Yes, sir.

PHILIP *sits back in his chair and picks up his drink as the LIGHTS dim to black-out*

Scene III

SCENE: *The sitting-room of an hotel suite.*

There is an arch back Centre leading to a small entrance hall with a door Left. There is a long window Right. A French settee stands Left with an armchair to match Right. In front of the settee there is a long stool, and a small table with a house telephone stands under the window. There are electric wall-brackets Right and Left of the arch. In the hall there is a console table and a row of coathooks on the wall Right.

When the LIGHTS come up, JUSTIN *is by the armchair, placing some files in his briefcase. His coat is on the settee.* CARLA *enters the hall from Left, puts her gloves and handbag on the hall table, removes her coat and hangs it on the hooks.*

CARLA. Oh, I'm so glad you're here.

JUSTIN. (*Surprised and pleased*) Really? (*He puts his briefcase on the armchair and moves down Right.*) Meredith Blake will be here at three o'clock.

CARLA. Good! What about Lady Melksham?

JUSTIN. She didn't answer my letter.

CARLA. Perhaps she's away?

JUSTIN. (*Crossing to Left of the arch*) No, she's not away. I took steps to ascertain that she's at home.

CARLA. I suppose that means that she's going to ignore the whole thing.

JUSTIN. Oh, I wouldn't say that. She'll come all right.

CARLA. (*Moving Centre*) What makes you so sure?

JUSTIN. Well, women usually . . .

CARLA. (*With a touch of mischief*) I see – you're an authority on women.

JUSTIN. (*Stiffly*) Only in the legal sense.

CARLA. And – strictly in the legal sense . . .?

JUSTIN. Women usually want to satisfy their curiosity.

(CARLA *sees* JUSTIN's *coat on the settee, crosses and picks it up.*)

CARLA. I really do like you – you make me feel much better. (*She moves towards the hooks.*)

(*The telephone rings.*)

(*She thrusts the coat at* JUSTIN, *crosses and lifts the telephone receiver. Into the telephone*) Hullo? . . .

(JUSTIN *hangs his coat in the hall.*)

Oh, ask him to come up, will you? (*She replaces the receiver and turns to* JUSTIN.) It's Meredith Blake. Is he like his hateful brother?

JUSTIN. (*Moving Centre*) A very different temperament, I should say. Do you need to feel better?

CARLA. What?

JUSTIN. You said just now I made you feel better. Do you need to feel better?

CARLA. Sometimes I do. (*She gestures to him to sit on the settee.*)

(JUSTIN *sits on the settee.*)

I didn't realize what I was letting myself in for.

JUSTIN. I was afraid of that.

CARLA. I could still – give it all up – go back to Canada – forget. Shall I?

JUSTIN. (*Quickly*) No! No – er – not now. You've got to go on.

CARLA. (*Sitting in the armchair*) That's not what you advised in the first place.

JUSTIN. You hadn't started then.

CARLA. You still think – that my mother was guilty, don't you?

JUSTIN. I can't see any other solution.

CARLA. And yet you want me to go on?

JUSTIN. I want you to go on until *you* are satisfied.

(*There is a knock on the hall door.* CARLA *and* JUSTIN *rise.* CARLA *goes to the hall, opens the door and steps back.* JUSTIN *crosses to Right of the armchair and faces the hall.* MEREDITH BLAKE *enters the hall from Left. He is a pleasant, rather vague man with a thatch of grey hair. He gives the impression of being rather ineffectual and irresolute. He wears country tweeds with hat, coat and muffler.*)

MEREDITH. Carla. My dear Carla. (*He takes her hands.*) How time flies. May I? (*He kisses her.*) It seems incredible that the little girl I knew should have grown up into a young lady. How like your mother you are, my dear. My word!

CARLA. (*Slightly embarrassed; gesturing to* JUSTIN) Do you know Mr Fogg?

MEREDITH. My word, my word! (*He pulls himself together.*) What? (*To* JUSTIN) Ah, yes, I knew your father, didn't I? (*He steps into the room.*)

(CARLA *closes the door, then moves into the room and stands Left of the arch.*)

JUSTIN. (*Moving to Right of* MEREDITH) Yes, sir. (*He shakes hands.*) May I take your coat?

MEREDITH. (*Unbuttoning his coat; to* CARLA) And now – tell me all about yourself. You're over from the States –

(JUSTIN *takes* MEREDITH's *hat.*)

– thank you – no, Canada. For how long?

CARLA. I'm not quite sure – yet.

(JUSTIN *eyes* CARLA.)

MEREDITH. But you are definitely making your home overseas?

CARLA. Well – I'm thinking of getting married.

MEREDITH. (*Removing his coat*) Oh, to a Canadian?

CARLA. Yes.

(MEREDITH *hands his coat and muffler to* JUSTIN, *who hangs them with the hat, in the hall.*)

MEREDITH. Well, I hope he's a nice fellow and good enough for you, my dear.

CARLA. Naturally *I* think so. (*She gestures to* MEREDITH *to sit in the armchair.*)

(MEREDITH *goes to sit in the armchair, sees* JUSTIN*'s briefcase and picks it up.* JUSTIN *moves above the armchair.*)

MEREDITH. Good. If you're happy, then I'm very happy for you. And so would your mother have been.

CARLA. (*Sitting on the settee at the up-stage end*) Do you know that my mother left a letter for me in which she said she was innocent?

MEREDITH. (*Turning and looking at* CARLA; *sharply*) Your mother wrote *that?*

CARLA. Does it surprise you so much?

(JUSTIN *sees* MEREDITH *is uncertain what to do with the briefcase and offers to take it.*)

MEREDITH. Well, I shouldn't have thought Caroline . . . (*He hands the briefcase to* JUSTIN.)

(JUSTIN *puts the briefcase on the table Right.*)

I don't know – I suppose she felt – (*He sits in the armchair.*) it would distress you less . . .

CARLA. (*Passionately*) It doesn't occur to you that what she wrote me might be true?

MEREDITH. Well, yes – of course. If she solemnly wrote that when she was dying – well, it stands to reason that it must be true – doesn't it? (*He looks up at* JUSTIN *for support.*)

(*There is a pause.*)

CARLA. What a rotten liar you are. (*She rises.*)
MEREDITH. (*Shocked*) Carla!

(CARLA *goes into the hall and picks up her handbag.*)

CARLA. Oh, I know it was meant to be kind. But kindness doesn't really help. I want you to tell me all about it. (*She steps into the room and searches in her bag.*)
MEREDITH. You know the facts – (*To* JUSTIN) doesn't she?
JUSTIN. (*Crossing down Left*) Yes, sir, she does.
MEREDITH. Going over them will be painful – and quite un-

profitable. Better let the whole thing rest. You're young and pretty and engaged to be married and that's all that really matters.

(JUSTIN *sees* CARLA *searching in her bag, takes out his cigarette case and offers it to her.* MEREDITH *takes a snuff-box from his waistcoat pocket.*)

JUSTIN. (*To* CARLA) You looking for one of these?

MEREDITH. (*Offering the snuff-box to* CARLA) Have a pinch of . . . No, I don't suppose you do, but I'll . . . (*He offers the box to* JUSTIN.) Oh, will you?

(JUSTIN *declines.* CARLA *takes a cigarette from* JUSTIN, *who also takes one.*)

CARLA. I've asked your brother Philip, you know. (*She puts her bag on the stool.*)

(JUSTIN *lights the cigarettes with his lighter.*)

MEREDITH. Oh – Philip! You wouldn't get much from him. Philip's a busy man. So busy making money, that he hasn't time for anything else. If he did remember anything, he'd remember it all wrong. (*He sniffs the snuff.*)

CARLA. (*Sitting on the settee at the up-stage end*) Then *you* tell me.

(JUSTIN *sits on the settee at the down-stage end.*)

MEREDITH. (*guardedly*) Well – you'd have to understand a bit about your father – first.

CARLA. (*Matter-of-fact*) He had affairs with other women and made my mother very unhappy.

MEREDITH. Well – er – yes – (*He sniffs*) but these affairs of his weren't really important until Elsa came along.

CARLA. He was painting her?

MEREDITH. Yes, my word – (*He sniffs*) I can see her now. Sitting on the terrace where she posed. Dark – er – shorts and a yellow shirt. 'Portrait of a girl in a yellow shirt', that's what he was going to call it. It was one of the best things Amyas ever did. (*He puts his snuff-box in his pocket.*)

CARLA. What happened to the picture?

MEREDITH. I've got it. I bought it with the furniture. I bought the house, too. Alderbury. It adjoins my property, you know. I didn't want it turned into a building estate. Everything was sold by the executors and the proceeds put in trust for you. But you know that, I expect.

CARLA. I didn't know you'd bought the house.

MEREDITH. Well, I did. It's let to a Youth Hostel. But I keep one wing just as it was, for myself. I sold off most of the furniture . . .

CARLA. But you kept the picture. Why?

MEREDITH. (*As though defending himself*) I tell you, it was the best thing Amyas ever did. My word, yes! It goes to the nation when I die. (*He pauses.*)

(CARLA *stares at* MEREDITH.)

Well, I'll try to tell you what you want to know. Amyas brought Elsa down there – ostensibly because he was painting her. She hated the pretence. She – she was so wildly in love with him and wanted to have it out with Caroline then and there. She felt in a false position. I – I understood her point of view.

CARLA. (*Coldly*) You sound most sympathetic towards her.

MEREDITH. (*Horrified*) Not at all. My sympathies were all with Caroline. I'd always been – well, in love with Caroline. I asked her to marry me – but she married Amyas instead. Oh, I can understand it – he was a brilliant person and very attractive to women, but he didn't look after her the way *I'd* have looked after her. I remained her friend.

CARLA. And yet you believe she committed murder?

MEREDITH. She didn't really know what she was doing. There was a terrific scene – she was overwrought . . .

CARLA. Yes?

MEREDITH. And that same afternoon she took the conine from my laboratory. But I swear there was no thought of murder in her mind when she took it – she had some idea of – of – doing away with herself.

CARLA. But as your brother Philip said, 'She *didn't* do away with herself.'

MEREDITH. Things always look better the next morning. And there was a lot of fuss going on, getting Angela's things ready for school – that was Angela Warren, Caroline's half-sister. She was a real little devil, always scrapping with someone, or playing tricks. She and Amyas were forever fighting, but he was very fond of her – and Caroline adored her.

CARLA. (*Quickly*) After once trying to kill her?

MEREDITH. (*Looking at* CARLA; *quickly*) I've always been sure that that story was grossly exaggerated. Most children are jealous of the new baby.

CARLA. (*After puffing at her cigarette*) My father was found dead – after lunch, wasn't he?

MEREDITH. Yes. We left him on the terrace, painting. He often wouldn't go into lunch. The glass of beer that Caroline had brought him was there by his side – empty. I suppose the stuff was already beginning to work. There's no pain – just a slow – paralysis. Yes. When we came out after lunch – he was dead. The whole thing was a nightmare.

CARLA. (*Rising, upset*) A nightmare . . .

MEREDITH. (*Rising*) I'm sorry, my dear. I didn't want to talk about it to you. (*He looks at* JUSTIN.)

CARLA. If I could go down there – to where it happened. Could I?

MEREDITH. Of course, my dear. You've only to say the word.

CARLA. (*Moving Centre and turning to face* JUSTIN) If we could go over it there – all of us . . .

MEREDITH. What do you mean by all of us?

CARLA. (*Turning to face* MEREDITH) Your brother Philip and you, and the governess, and Angela Warren, and – yes – even Elsa.

MEREDITH. I hardly think Elsa would come. She's married, you know.

CARLA. (*Wryly*) Several times, I hear.

MEREDITH. She's changed very much. Philip saw her at a theatre one night.

CARLA. Nothing lasts. You loved my mother once – but *that* didn't last, did it? (*She stubs out her cigarette in the ashtray on the stool.*)

MEREDITH. What?

CARLA. (*Crossing down Left*) Everything's different from what I thought it would be. I can't seem to find my way.

(JUSTIN *rises.*)

If I could go down to Alderbury . . .

MEREDITH. You're welcome at any time, my dear. Now, I'm afraid I must . . .

(CARLA *gazes out front.*)

JUSTIN. (*Moving to the hall*) I'll get your coat, sir. (*He sees* CARLA *is in a brown study.*) Carla's most grateful to you, sir. (*He takes* MEREDITH's *coat, hat and muffler from the hooks.*)

CARLA. (*Recollecting herself*) Oh, yes. Yes, thank you for coming.

(MEREDITH *goes to the hall, where* JUSTIN *helps him on with his coat.*)

MEREDITH. Carla, the more I think of it all . . .

CARLA. Yes?

MEREDITH. (*Moving Centre*) I believe, you know, that it's quite possible Amyas did commit suicide. He may have felt more remorseful than we know. (*He looks hopefully at* CARLA.)

CARLA. (*Unconvinced*) It's a nice thought.

MEREDITH. Yes, yes – well, goodbye, my dear.

CARLA. Goodbye.

MEREDITH. (*Taking his hat from* JUSTIN) Goodbye, Mr Fogg.

JUSTIN. (*Opening the door*) Goodbye, sir.

MEREDITH. (*Mumbling*) Goodbye. Goodbye.

(MEREDITH *exits.* JUSTIN *closes the door and moves Centre.*)

CARLA. Well!

JUSTIN. Well!

CARLA. What a fool!

JUSTIN. Quite a nice kindly fool.

(*The telephone rings.*)

CARLA. (*Crossing to the telephone*) He doesn't believe anything of the sort. (*She lifts the receiver.*) Why does he say so? (*Into the telephone*) Yes? . . . Yes. I see. (*She replaces the receiver. Disappointed*) She's not coming.

JUSTIN. Lady Melksham?

CARLA. Yes. Unavoidably prevented.

(JUSTIN *goes into the hall and collects his coat.*)

JUSTIN. Don't worry, we'll think of something.

CARLA. (*Looking out of the window*) I've got to see her, she's the hub of it all.

JUSTIN. (*Moving Centre and putting on his coat*) You're going to take tea with Miss Williams, aren't you?

CARLA. (*Flatly*) Yes.

JUSTIN. (*Rather eagerly*) Want me to come with you?

CARLA. (*Without interest*) No, there's no need.

JUSTIN. Maybe there'll be a letter from Angela Warren in tomorrow's post. I'll phone you if I may?

CARLA. (*Still looking through the window*) Please.

JUSTIN. (*After a pause*) What a fool your father was.

(CARLA *turns.*)

Not to recognize quality when he had it.

CARLA. What do you mean?

JUSTIN. Elsa Greer was pretty brash, you know, crude allure, crude sex, crude hero worship.

CARLA. Hero worship?

JUSTIN. Yes. Would she have made a dead set at your father if he hadn't been a celebrated painter? Look at her subsequent husbands. Always attracted by a somebody – a big noise in the world – never the man himself. But Caroline, your mother, would have recognized quality in a – (*He pauses and self-consciously gives a boyish smile*) well – even in a solicitor.

(CARLA *picks up* JUSTIN's *briefcase and looks at him with interest.*)

CARLA. I believe you're still in love with my mother. (*She holds out the briefcase.*)

JUSTIN. Oh, no. (*He takes the briefcase and smiles.*) I move with the times, you know.

(CARLA *is taken aback, but is pleased and smiles.*)

Goodbye.

(JUSTIN *exits.* CARLA *looks after him, taking in what he has said. The telephone rings.* CARLA *lifts the receiver. The light starts to dim as twilight falls.*)

CARLA. (*Into the telephone*) Hullo? . . . Yes . . . Oh, it's you, Jeff . . . (*She takes the whole instrument and sits in the armchair with it, tucking one leg under her.*) It may be a silly waste of time, but it's my time and if I . . . (*She straightens the seam of her stocking.*) What? . . . (*Crossly*) You're quite wrong about Justin. He's a good friend – which is more than you are . . . All right, so I'm quarrelling . . . No, I don't want to dine with you . . . I don't want to dine with you anywhere.

(ELSA MELKSHAM *enters the hall from Left, quietly closes the door and stands in the hall, looking at* CARLA. ELSA *is tall, beautiful, very made-up and extremely smart. She wears hat and gloves, and a red velvet coat over a black dress, and carries her handbag.*)

At the moment your stock is pretty low with me. (*She bangs the receiver down, rises and puts the instrument on the table Right.*)

ELSA. Miss Le Marchant – or do I say 'Miss Crale'?

(CARLA, *startled, turns quickly.*)

CARLA. So you've come after all?

ELSA. I always meant to come. I just waited until your legal adviser had faded.

CARLA. You don't like lawyers?

ELSA. I prefer, occasionally, to talk woman to woman. Let's have some light. (*She switches on the wall-brackets by the switch Left of the arch, then moves down Centre and looks hard at* CARLA.) Well, you don't look very much like the child I remember.

CARLA. (*Simply*) I'm like my mother.

ELSA. (*Coldly*) Yes. That doesn't particularly prejudice me in your favour. Your mother was one of the most loathsome women I've ever known.

CARLA. (*Hotly*) I've no doubt she felt the same about you.

ELSA. (*Smiling*) Oh, yes, the feeling was mutual. (*She sits on the settee at the up-stage end.*) The trouble with Caroline was that she wasn't a very good loser.

CARLA. Did you expect her to be?

ELSA. (*Removing her gloves; amused*) Really, you know, I believe I did. I must have been incredibly young, and naïve. Because I myself couldn't understand clinging on to a man who didn't want me, I was quite shocked that she didn't feel the same. But I never dreamt that she'd *kill* Amyas rather than let me have him.

CARLA. She didn't kill him.

ELSA. (*Without interest*) She killed him all right. She poisoned him more or less in front of my eyes – in a glass of iced beer. And I never dreamed – never guessed . . . (*With a complete change of manner*) You think at the time that you will never forget – that the pain will always be there. And then – it's all gone – gone – like that. (*She snaps her fingers.*)

CARLA. (*Sitting in the armchair*) How old were you?

ELSA. Nineteen. But I was no injured innocent. Amyas Crale didn't seduce a trusting young girl. It wasn't like that at all. I met him at a party and I fell for him right away. I knew he was the only man in the world for me. (*She smiles.*) I think he felt the same.

CARLA. Yes.

ELSA. I asked him to paint me. He said he didn't do portraits. I said what about the portrait he'd done of Marna Vadaz, the dancer. He said special circumstances had led to that. I knew they'd had an affair together. I said, 'I *want* you to paint me.' He said, 'You know what'll happen? I shall make love to you.' I said, 'Why not?' And he said, 'I'm a married man, and I'm very fond of my wife.' I said that now we'd got that settled, when should we start the sittings? He took me by the shoulders and turned me towards the light and looked me over in a considering sort of way. Then he said, 'I've often thought of painting a flight of outrageously coloured Australian macaws alighting on St Paul's Cathedral. If I painted you in your flamboyant youth against a background of nice traditional English scenery, I believe I'd get the same effect.' (*She pauses. Quickly*) So it was settled.

CARLA. And you went down to Alderbury.

(ELSA *rises, removes her coat, puts it on the down-stage end of the settee and moves Centre.*)

ELSA. Yes. Caroline was charming. She could be, you know. Amyas was very circumspect. (*She smiles.*) Never said a word to me his wife couldn't have overheard. I was polite and formal. Underneath, though, we both knew . . . (*She breaks off.*)

CARLA. Go on.

ELSA. (*Putting her hands on her hips*) After ten days he told me I was to go back to London.

CARLA. Yes?

ELSA. I said, 'The picture isn't finished.' He said, 'It's barely begun. The truth is I can't paint you, Elsa.' I asked him why, and he said that I knew very well 'why' and that's why I'd got to clear out.

CARLA. So – you went back to London?

ELSA. Yes, I went. (*She moves up Centre and turns.*) I didn't write to him. I didn't answer his letters. He held out for a week. And then – he came. I told him that it was fate and it was no use struggling against it, and he said, 'You haven't struggled much, have you, Elsa?' I said I hadn't struggled at all. It was wonderful and more frightening than mere happiness. (*She frowns.*) If only we'd kept away – if only we hadn't gone back.

CARLA. Why did you?

ELSA. The unfinished picture. It haunted Amyas. (*She sits on the settee at the up-stage end.*) But things were different this time – Caroline had caught on. I wanted to have the whole thing on an honest basis. All Amyas would say was, 'To hell with honesty. I'm painting a picture.'

(CARLA *laughs.*)

Why do you laugh?

CARLA. (*Rising and turning to the window*) Because I know just how he felt.

ELSA. (*Angrily*) How should *you* know?

CARLA. (*Simply*) Because I'm his daughter, I suppose.

ELSA. (*Distantly*) Amyas's daughter. (*She looks at* CARLA *with a new appraisement.*)

CARLA. (*Turning and crossing above the armchair to Centre*) I've just begun to know that. I hadn't thought about it before. I came over because I wanted to find out just what happened sixteen years ago. I am finding out. I'm beginning to know the people – what they felt, what they are like. The whole thing's coming alive, bit by bit.

ELSA. Coming alive? (*Bitterly*) I wish it would.

CARLA. My father – you – Philip Blake – Meredith Blake. (*She crosses down Left.*) And there are two more. Angela Warren . . .

ELSA. Angela? Oh, yes. She's quite a celebrity in her way – one of those tough women who travel to inaccessible places and write books about it. She was only a tiresome teenager then.

CARLA. (*Turning*) How did *she* feel about it all?

ELSA. (*Uninterested*) I don't know. They hustled her away, I think. Some idea of Caroline's that contact with murder would damage her adolescent mind – though I don't know why Caroline should have bothered about damage to her mind when she had already damaged her face for her. When I heard that story I ought to have realized what Caroline was capable of, and when I actually *saw* her take the poison . . .

CARLA. (*Quickly*) You *saw* her?

ELSA. Yes. Meredith was waiting to lock up his laboratory. Caroline was the last to come out. I was just before her. I looked over my shoulder and saw her standing in front of a shelf with a small bottle in her hand. Of course, she might only have been looking at it. How was I to know?

CARLA. (*Crossing to Centre*) But you suspected?

ELSA. I thought she meant it for herself.

CARLA. Suicide? And you didn't *care*?

ELSA. (*Calmly*) I thought it might be the best way out.

CARLA. (*Crossing above the armchair to the window*) Oh, no . . .

ELSA. Her marriage to Amyas had been a failure from the start – if she'd really cared for him as much as she pretended, she'd have given him a divorce. There was plenty of money – and she'd probably have married someone else who would have suited her better.

CARLA. How easily you arrange other people's lives. (*She moves down Right.*) Meredith Blake says I may come down to Alderbury. I want to get everyone there. Will you come?

ELSA. (*Arrested, but attracted by the idea*) Come down to Alderbury?

CARLA. (*Eagerly*) I want to go over the whole thing on the spot. I want to see it as though it were happening all over again.

ELSA. Happening all over again . . .

CARLA. (*Politely*) If it's too painful for you . . .

ELSA. There are worse things than pain. (*Harshly*) It's forgetting that's so horrible – it's as though you were dead yourself. (*Angrily*) You – stand there so damned young and innocent – what do you know about loving a man? I loved Amyas. (*With fire*) He was so alive, so full of life and vigour, such a man. And she put an end to all that – your mother. (*She rises.*) She put an end to Amyas so that *I* shouldn't have him. And they didn't even hang her. (*She pauses. In an ordinary tone*) I'll come to Alderbury. I'll join your circus. (*She picks up her coat and holds it out to* CARLA.)

(CARLA *crosses to* ELSA *and helps her on with her coat.*)

Philip, Meredith – Angela Warren – all four of us.

CARLA. Five.

ELSA. Five?

CARLA. There was a governess.

ELSA. (*Collecting her bag and gloves from the settee*) Oh, yes, the governess. *Very* disapproving of me and Amyas. Devoted to Caroline.

CARLA. Devoted to my mother – *she'll* tell me. I'm going to see her next. (*She goes into the hall and opens the door.*)

ELSA. (*Moving to the hall*) Perhaps you'll get your legal *friend* to telephone me, will you?

(ELSA *exits.* CARLA *closes the door and moves Centre.*)

CARLA. The governess!

The LIGHTS dim to black-out

Scene IV

SCENE: *Miss Williams's bed-sitting-room.*

It is an attic room with a small window in the sloping roof Left. The door is presumed to be in the 'fourth wall'. There is a fireplace, fitted with a gas fire, back Centre. There is a divan with cover and cushions Right. A gate-legged table stands under the window. A small table with a table-lamp on it is Right of the fireplace. Upright chairs stand Left of the fireplace and down Left, and there is an old-fashioned armchair with a footstool under it, Centre. An electric kettle is plugged into the skirting, Right of the fireplace.

When the LIGHTS come up, the lamp is on, but the window curtains are not yet closed. A tray of tea for two is on the table Left. The kettle is steaming and the teapot is beside it. The gas fire is lit. MISS WILLIAMS is seated in the armchair Centre. She is sixty odd, intelligent, with clear enunciation and a pedagogic manner. She wears a tweed skirt and blouse, with a *cardigan and a scarf round her shoulders.* CARLA *is seated on the divan, looking through a photograph album. She wears a brown dress.*

CARLA. I *do* remember you. It's all coming back. I didn't think I did.

MISS WILLIAMS. You were only five years old.

CARLA. You looked after me?

MISS WILLIAMS. No, you were not my responsibility. I was in charge of Angela. Ah, the kettle's boiling. (*She rises, picks up the teapot and makes the tea.*) Now, are you going to be happy there, dear?

CARLA. I'm fine, thanks.

MISS WILLIAMS. (*Pointing to the album*) That's Angela – you were only a baby when that was taken.

CARLA. What was she like?

MISS WILLIAMS. (*Putting down the kettle*) One of the most interesting pupils I ever had. Undisciplined, but a first-class brain. She took a first at Somerville and you may have read her book on the rock paintings of the Hazelpa?

CARLA. Um?

MISS WILLIAMS. It was very well reviewed. Yes, I'm very proud of Angela. (*She puts the teapot on the tray Left.*) Now, we'll just let that stand a minute, shall we?

CARLA. (*Putting the album on the up-stage end of the divan*) Miss Williams, you know why I've come?

MISS WILLIAMS. Roughly, yes. (*She moves to the fireplace.*) You have just learnt the facts about the tragedy that ended your father's life, and you want fuller information about the whole matter. (*She switches off the kettle.*)

CARLA. And, I suppose, like everybody else, you think I ought to forget the whole thing?

MISS WILLIAMS. Not at all. It appears to be perfectly natural that you should want to understand. Then, and only then, can you forget about it.

CARLA. Will you tell me everything?

MISS WILLIAMS. Any questions you like to put to me I will answer to the full extent of my knowledge. Now, where's my little footstool? I have a little footstool somewhere. (*She turns the armchair to face the divan and looks around for the footstool.*)

CARLA. (*Rising and drawing the footstool out from under the armchair*) Here we are.

MISS WILLIAMS. Thank you, dear. (*She seats herself comfortably in the armchair and puts her feet on the footstool.*) I like to keep my feet off the ground.

CARLA. I think – first – that I'd like to know just what my father and mother were like – what *you* thought they were like, I mean. (*She sits on the divan.*)

MISS WILLIAMS. Your father, as you know, has been acclaimed as a great painter. I, of course, am not competent to judge. I do not, myself, admire his paintings. The drawing seems to me faulty and the colouring exaggerated. However, that may be, I have never seen why the possession of what is called the artistic temperament should excuse a man from ordinary decent behaviour. Your mother had a great deal to put up with where he was concerned.

CARLA. And she minded?

MISS WILLIAMS. She minded very much. Mr Crale was not a faithful husband. She put up with his infidelities and forgave him for them – but she did not take them meekly. She remonstrated – and with spirit.

CARLA. You mean they gave each other hell?

MISS WILLIAMS. (*Quietly*) That would not be my description. (*She rises and crosses below the armchair to the table Left.*) There were quarrels, yes, but your mother had dignity, and your father was in the wrong. (*She pours the tea.*)

CARLA. Always?

MISS WILLIAMS. (*Firmly*) Always. I was – very fond of Mrs Crale. And very sorry for her. She had a lot to bear. If I had been Mr Crale's wife, I should have left him. No woman should submit to humiliation at her husband's hands.

CARLA. You didn't like my father?

MISS WILLIAMS. (*Tight-lipped*) I disliked him – very much.

CARLA. But he was really fond of my mother?

(MISS WILLIAMS *picks up a cup of tea and the sugar bowl and crosses to* CARLA.)

MISS WILLIAMS. I believe honestly that he cared for her – but men . . .! (*She sniffs, then hands the cup of tea to* CARLA.)

CARLA. (*Slightly amused*) You don't think much of men?

MISS WILLIAMS. (*With slight fanaticism*) Men still have the best of this world. I hope it will not always be so. (*She thrusts the sugar bowl at* CARLA.) Sugar?

CARLA. I don't take it, thanks. And then Elsa Greer came along?

(MISS WILLIAMS *crosses to the table, puts down the sugar bowl and picks up her cup of tea.*)

MISS WILLIAMS. (*With distaste*) Yes. Ostensibly to have her portrait painted; they made poor progress with the picture. (*She crosses to Centre.*) Doubtless they had other things to talk about. It was obvious that Mr Crale was infatuated with the girl and that she was doing nothing to discourage him. (*She sniffs, then sits in the armchair.*)

CARLA. What did *you* think of her?

MISS WILLIAMS. I thought she was good-looking, but stupid. She had had, presumably, an adequate education, but she never opened a book, and was quite unable to converse on any intellectual subject. All she ever thought about was her own personal appearance – and men, of course.

CARLA. Go on.

MISS WILLIAMS. Miss Greer went back to London, and very pleased we were to see her go. (*She pauses and sips her tea.*) Then Mr Crale went away and I knew, and so did Mrs Crale, that he had gone after the girl. They reappeared together. The *sittings* were to be continued, and we all knew what that meant. The girl's manner became increasingly insolent, and she finally came out into the open with some outrageous remarks about what *she* would do at Alderbury when she was mistress there.

CARLA. (*Horrified*) Oh, no!

MISS WILLIAMS. Yes, yes, yes. (*She pauses and sips her tea.*) Mr Crale came in, and his wife asked him outright if it was true that he planned to marry Elsa. There he stood, a great giant of a man, looking like a naughty schoolboy. (*She rises, goes to the table Left, puts down her cup, picks up a plate of biscuits and crosses to* CARLA.) My blood boiled. I really could have killed him. Do have one of these biscuits, they're Peek Frean's.

CARLA. (*Taking a biscuit*) Thank you. What did my mother do?

MISS WILLIAMS. I think she just went out of the room. I know I – I tried to say something to her of what I felt, but she stopped me. 'We must all behave as usual,' she said. (*She crosses and puts the plate on the table Left.*) They were all going over to tea with Mr Meredith Blake that afternoon. Just as she was going, I remember she came back and kissed me. She said, 'You're such a comfort to me.' (*Her voice breaks a little.*)

CARLA. (*Sweetly*) I'm sure you were.

MISS WILLIAMS. (*Crossing to the fireplace, picking up the kettle and unplugging it*) Never blame her for what she did, Carla. It is for you, her daughter, to understand and forgive.

CARLA. (*Slowly*) So even you think she did it.

MISS WILLIAMS. (*Sadly*) I *know* she did it.

CARLA. Did she *tell* you she did it?

MISS WILLIAMS. (*Taking the kettle to the table Left*) Of course not. (*She refills the teapot.*)

CARLA. What *did* she say?

MISS WILLIAMS. She took pains to impress upon me that it must be suicide.

CARLA. You didn't – believe her?

MISS WILLIAMS. I said, 'Certainly, Mrs Crale, it *must* have been suicide.'

CARLA. But you didn't believe what you were saying.

MISS WILLIAMS. (*Crossing to the fireplace and replacing the kettle*) You have got to understand, Carla, that I was entirely on your mother's side. My sympathies were with *her* – not with the police. (*She sits in the armchair.*)

CARLA. But murder . . . (*She pauses.*) When she was charged, you wanted her acquitted?

MISS WILLIAMS. Certainly.

CARLA. On any pretext?

MISS WILLIAMS. On any pretext.

CARLA. (*Pleading*) She *might* have been innocent.

MISS WILLIAMS. No.

CARLA. (*Defiantly*) She *was* innocent.

MISS WILLIAMS. No, my dear.

CARLA. She was – she *was*. She wrote it to me. In a letter she wrote when she was dying. She said I could be *sure* of that.

(*There is a stunned silence.*)

MISS WILLIAMS. (*In a low voice*) That was wrong – very wrong of her. To write a lie – and at such a solemn moment. I should not have thought that Caroline Crale would have done a thing like that. She was a truthful woman.

CARLA. (*Rising*) It could be the truth.

MISS WILLIAMS. (*Definitely*) No.

CARLA. You can't be positive. You *can't!*

MISS WILLIAMS. I *can* be positive. Of all the people connected with the case, I *alone* can be *sure* that Caroline Crale was guilty. Because of something I saw. I withheld it from the police – I have never told anyone. (*She rises.*) But you must take it from me, Carla, quite definitely, that your mother *was* guilty. Now, can I get you some more tea, dear? We'll both have some, shall we? It sometimes gets rather chilly in this room. (*She takes* CARLA's *cup and crosses to the table Left.*)

CARLA *looks distracted and bewildered as – the LIGHTS dim to black-out*

Scene V

SCENE: *A table in a restaurant.*
The table is in an alcove decorated in delicate Oriental style, equipped with three banquettes.

When LIGHTS come up, CARLA *is seated Right of the table and* ANGELA WARREN *is seated above and Centre of it. They are just finishing lunch.* CARLA *is wearing a mink-trimmed coat.* ANGELA *is a tall woman of thirty, of distinguished appearance, well-dressed in a plain suit with a mannish hat. There is a not too noticeable scar on her left cheek.*

ANGELA. (*Putting down her brandy glass*) Well, now that we've finished our meal, Carla, I'm prepared to talk. I should have been sorry if you'd gone back to Canada without our being able to meet. (*She offers* CARLA *a cigarette from a leather case.*)

(CARLA *declines and takes a cigarette from an American pack on the table.*)

(*She takes one of her own cigarettes.*) I wanted to fix it before, but I've had a hundred and one things to do before leaving tomorrow. (*She lights* CARLA's *cigarette and then her own with a lighter which matches her case.*)

CARLA. I know how it is. You're going by sea?

ANGELA. Yes, much easier when you're carting out a lot of equipment.

CARLA. I told you I saw Miss Williams?

ANGELA. (*Smiling*) Dear Miss Williams. What a life I used to lead her. Climbing trees and playing truant, and plaguing the life out of everyone all round me. I was jealous, of course.

CARLA. (*Startled*) Jealous?

ANGELA. Yes – of Amyas. I'd always come first with Caroline and I couldn't bear her to be absorbed in him. I played all sorts of tricks on him – put – what was it, now – some filthy stuff – valerian, I think, in his beer, and once I put a hedgehog in his bed. (*She laughs.*) I must have been an absolute menace. How right they were to pack me off to school. Though, of course, I was furious at the time.

CARLA. How much do you remember of it all?

ANGELA. Of the actual happening? Curiously little. We'd had lunch – and then Caroline and Miss Williams went into the garden room, and then we all came in and Amyas was dead and there was telephoning, and I heard Elsa screaming somewhere – on the terrace, I think with Caroline. I just wandered about, getting in everyone's way.

CARLA. I can't think why *I* don't remember anything. After all, I was five. Old enough to remember *something*.

ANGELA. Oh, you weren't there. You'd gone away to stay with your godmother, old Lady Thorpe, about a week before.

CARLA. Ah!

ANGELA. Miss Williams took me into Caroline's room. She was lying down, looking very white and ill. I was frightened. She said I wasn't to think about it – I was to go to Miss Williams's sister in London, and then on to school in Zurich as planned. I said I didn't want to leave her – and then Miss Williams chipped in and said in that authoritative way of hers – (*She mimics Miss Williams*) 'The best way you can help your sister,

Angela, is to do what she wants you to do without making any fuss.' (*She sips her brandy.*)

CARLA. (*Amused*) I know just what you mean. There's something about Miss Williams which makes you feel you've just got to go along with her.

ANGELA. The police asked me a few questions, but I didn't know why. I just thought there had been some kind of accident, and that Amyas had taken poison by mistake. I was abroad when they arrested Caroline, and they kept it from me as long as they could. Caroline wouldn't let me go and see her in prison. She did everything she could to keep me out of it all. That was just like Caroline. She always tried to stand between me and the world.

CARLA. She must have been very fond of you.

ANGELA. It wasn't that. (*She touches her scar.*) It was because of this.

CARLA. That happened when you were a baby.

ANGELA. Yes. You've heard about it. It's the sort of thing that happens – an older child gets mad with jealousy and chucks something. To a sensitive person, like Caroline, the horror of what she had done never quite left her. Her whole life was one long effort to make up to me for the way she had injured me. Very bad for *me*, of course.

CARLA. Did you ever feel vindictive about it?

ANGELA. Towards Caroline? Because she had spoiled my beauty? (*She laughs.*) I never had much to spoil. No, I never gave it a second thought.

(CARLA *picks up her bag from the seat beside her, takes out a letter and hands it to* ANGELA.)

CARLA. She left a letter for me – I'd like you to read it.

(*There is a pause as* ANGELA *reads the letter.* CARLA *stubs out her cigarette.*)

I'm so confused about her. Everyone seems to have seen her differently.

ANGELA. She had a lot of contradictions in her nature. (*She turns a page and reads*) '. . . want you to know that I did not kill your father.' Sensible of her. You might have wondered. (*She folds the letter and puts it on the table.*)

CARLA. You mean – you believe she *wasn't* guilty?

ANGELA. Of course she wasn't guilty. Nobody who knew Caroline could have thought for one moment that she was guilty.

CARLA. (*Slightly hysterical*) But they do – they all do – except you.

ANGELA. More fool they. Oh, the evidence was damning enough, I grant you, but anybody who knew Caroline well should know that she couldn't commit murder. She hadn't got it in her.

CARLA. What about . . .?

ANGELA. (*Pointing to her scar*) This? How can I explain? (*She stubs out her cigarette.*) Because of what she did to me, Caroline was always watching herself for violence. I think she decided that if she was violent in speech she would have no temptation to violence in action. She'd say things like, 'I'd like to cut So-and-so in pieces and boil him in oil.' Or she'd say to Amyas, 'If you go on like this, I shall *murder* you.' Amyas and she had the most fantastic quarrels, they said the most outrageous things to each other. They both loved it.

CARLA. They *liked* quarrelling?

ANGELA. Yes. They were that kind of couple. Living that way, with continual rows and makings up, was their idea of fun.

CARLA. (*Sitting back*) You make everything sound different. (*She picks up the letter and puts it in her bag.*)

ANGELA. If only *I* could have given evidence. But I suppose the sort of thing I could have said wouldn't count as evidence. But you needn't worry, Carla. You can go back to Canada and be quite sure that Caroline *didn't* murder Amyas.

CARLA. (*Sadly*) But then – who did?

ANGELA. Does it matter?

CARLA. Of course it matters.

ANGELA. (*In a hard voice*) It must have been some kind of accident. Can't you leave it at that?

CARLA. No, I can't.

ANGELA. Why not?

(CARLA *does not answer.*)

Is it a man? (*She sips her brandy.*)

CARLA. Well – there is a man, yes.

ANGELA. Are you engaged?

(CARLA, *slightly embarrassed, takes a cigarette from her packet.*)

CARLA. I don't know.

ANGELA. He minds about this?

CARLA. (*Frowning*) He's very magnanimous.

ANGELA. (*Appreciatively*) How bloody! I shouldn't marry him.

CARLA. I'm not sure that I want to.

ANGELA. Another man? (*She lights* CARLA's *cigarette.*)

CARLA. (*Irritably*) Must everything be a man?

ANGELA. Usually seems to be. I prefer rock paintings.

CARLA. (*Suddenly*) I'm going down to Alderbury tomorrow. I want all the people concerned to be there. I wanted you as well.

ANGELA. Not me. I'm sailing tomorrow.

CARLA. I want to re-live it – as though I were my mother and not myself. (*Strongly*) *Why* didn't she fight for her life? *Why* was she so defeatist at her trial?

ANGELA. I don't know.

CARLA. It wasn't like her, was it?

ANGELA. (*Slowly*) No, it wasn't like her.

CARLA. It *must* have been one of those four other people.

ANGELA. How persistent you are, Carla.

CARLA. I'll find out the truth in the end.

ANGELA. (*Struck by* CARLA's *sincerity*) I almost believe you will. (*She pauses.*) I'll come to Alderbury with you. (*She picks up her brandy glass.*)

CARLA. (*Delighted*) You will? But your boat sails tomorrow.

ANGELA. I'll take a plane instead. Now, are you sure you won't have some brandy? I'm going to have some more if I can catch his eye. (*She calls*) Waiter!

CARLA. I'm *so* glad you're coming.

ANGELA. (*Sombrely*) Are you? Don't hope for too much. Sixteen years. It's a long time ago.

(ANGELA *drains her glass as the LIGHTS dim to black-out and – the Curtain falls.*)

CURTAIN

ACT TWO

SCENE: *Alderbury, a house in the West of England.*

The scene shows a section of the house, with the Garden Room Right and the terrace Left with communicating French windows between them. The room is at an angle, so that the terrace extends and tapers off below it to Right. Doors back Centre, in the room, and at the up-stage end of the terrace, lead to the house. An exit, at the up-stage end of a vine-covered pergola Left, leads to the garden. There is another door down Right in the room. Above this door is a small alcove with shelves for decorative plates and ornaments. A console table stands under the shelves. There is a table Left of the door Centre, on which there is a telephone and a carved wooden head. On the wall above the table is the portrait of Elsa, painted by Amyas. There is a sofa Right of the door Centre, with a long stool in front of it. Armchairs stand Right and Left, and there is an occasional table Left of the armchair Right. There is a stone bench Centre of the terrace.

When Curtain rises, the stage is in darkness, then the LIGHTS come up to show the house shrouded in darkness and the terrace bathed in moonlight. The long stool is on the sofa, and both are covered with a dust sheet. The armchairs are also covered with dust sheets. The window curtains are closed. After a few moments, voices are heard off up Centre.

CARLA. (*Off*) Which way do we go?

MEREDITH. (*Off*) This way, mind that little step. (*He is heard to stumble.*) I always used to fall over it.

JUSTIN. (*Off; stumbling*) Good heavens! Shall I leave the door?

MEREDITH. (*Off*) Few things as depressing as an unlived-in house. I do apologize.

(MEREDITH *enters up Centre and the LIGHTS on the room snap up. He wears an overcoat, and has an old fishing hat, pulled down. He moves down Right.* CARLA *follows* MEREDITH *on. She wears a loose coat and a headscarf. She moves Left.* JUSTIN *enters last. He carries his bowler hat. He moves down Centre, turns and looks around the room.*)

This is what we call the garden room. Cold as a morgue. Looks like a morgue, too, doesn't it? (*He laughs and rubs his hands.*) Not that I've ever seen the inside of a – hum . . . I'll just remove these. (*He goes to the sofa and removes the dust sheet.*)

JUSTIN. Let me help you. (*He moves to Left of the sofa and takes the dust sheet from* MEREDITH.)

(CARLA *moves to the armchair Left and removes the dust sheet, which she gives to* JUSTIN.)

MEREDITH. This bit of the house has been shut up, you see, ever since . . . (*He indicates the long stool on the sofa.*) Ah, that's an old friend. (*He takes the stool from the sofa.*) Let me see, I think it went somewhere there. (*He places the stool Right Centre.*) It's sad, somehow. It was so alive, once, and now it's dead.

(CARLA *sits on the Left end of the stool and looks at the portrait.*)

CARLA. Is that the picture?

MEREDITH. What? Yes. Girl in a yellow shirt.

CARLA. You left it here?

MEREDITH. Yes. I – somehow couldn't bear to look at it. It reminded me too much . . . (*He recollects himself, crosses to the French windows and opens the curtains.*)

CARLA. How she's changed.

MEREDITH. (*Turning*) You've seen her?

CARLA. Yes.

MEREDITH. (*Crossing to the armchair Right and removing the dust sheet*) I haven't seen her for years.

CARLA. She's beautiful still. But not like that. So alive and triumphant – and young. (*She draws a breath and faces front.*) It's a wonderful portrait.

MEREDITH. Yes – (*He points Left.*) and that is where he painted her – out there on the terrace. Well, I'll just dispose of these – (*He takes the dust sheets from* JUSTIN) in the next room, I think.

(MEREDITH *exits Right.* CARLA *rises, goes to the French windows, unlocks them and moves on to the terrace.* JUSTIN *looks at her, then follows and stands on the step just outside the windows.*)

CARLA. Justin – do you think this scheme of mine is quite crazy? Jeff thinks I'm mad.

JUSTIN. (*Crossing to the exit above the pergola and looking off*) I shouldn't let that worry you.

(MEREDITH *enters down Right and crosses to the French windows.*)

CARLA. (*Sitting on the bench*) I don't.

MEREDITH. I'll just go and meet the others.

(MEREDITH *exits up Centre.*)

CARLA. You understand, don't you, just what I want done?

JUSTIN. (*Crossing to Right*) You want to reconstruct in your mind's eye what happened here sixteen years ago. You want each witness in turn to describe the scene in which they participated. Much of it may be trivial and irrelevant, but you want it in full. (*He moves to her.*) Their recollections, of course, will not be exact. In a scene where more than one witness was present, the two accounts may not agree.

CARLA. That might be helpful.

JUSTIN. (*Doubtfully*) It might – but you must not build too much on it. People do recollect things differently. (*He moves up stage and looks around.*)

CARLA. What I'm going to do is to make-believe I *see* it all happening. I shall imagine my mother and my father . . . (*She suddenly breaks off.*) You know, I think my father must have been great fun.

JUSTIN. (*Moving behind* CARLA) What?

CARLA. I think I should have liked him a lot.

JUSTIN. (*Turning and peering off down Left; drily*) Women usually did.

CARLA. It's odd – I feel sorry for Elsa. In that picture in there she looks so young and alive – and now – there's no life left in her. I think it died when my father died.

JUSTIN. (*Sitting below* CARLA *on the bench*) Are you casting her as Juliet?

CARLA. You don't?

JUSTIN. No. (*He smiles.*) I'm your mother's man.

CARLA. You're very faithful, aren't you? Too faithful, maybe.

(JUSTIN *looks at* CARLA.)

JUSTIN. (*After a pause*) I don't really quite know what we're talking about.

CARLA. (*Rising; matter-of-fact*) Let's get back to business. Your part is to look hard for discrepancies – flaws – you've got to be very legal and astute.

JUSTIN. Yes, ma'am.

(*Voices of the others arriving can be heard off up Centre, with* MEREDITH *greeting them.*)

(*He rises.*) Here they are.

CARLA. I'll go and meet them.

(CARLA *goes into the room and exits Centre. The LIGHTS slowly dim to black-out,* JUSTIN *moves down Left, then a spotlight comes up revealing his face. He acts as compere.*)

JUSTIN. Now, are we all ready? I will just impress on you once more why we are all here. We want to reconstruct, as far as we can, the happenings of sixteen years ago. We shall endeavour to do this, by asking each person or persons to recount in turn their own part in what went on, and what they saw, or over-heard. This should make an almost continuous picture. Sixteen years ago. We shall start on the afternoon of the sixteenth of August, the day before the tragedy took place, with a conver-sation that Mr Meredith Blake had with Caroline Crale in the garden room. Out here on the terrace, Elsa Greer was posing for Amyas Crale, who was painting her. From that we shall go on to Elsa Greer's narrative, to the arrival of Philip Blake, and so on. Mr Meredith Blake, will you begin?

(*The spotlight fades.* MEREDITH'*s voice can be heard in the darkness.*)

MEREDITH. It was the afternoon of the sixteenth of August, did you say? Yes, yes, it was. I came over to Alderbury. Stopped in on my way to Framley Abbott. Really to see if I could pick any of them up later to give them a lift – they were coming over to me for tea. Caroline had been cutting roses, and when I opened the door into the garden room . . .

(*The LIGHTS come up. It is a glorious, hot summer's day.* CAROLINE CRALE *is standing in the French windows looking on to the terrace. She carries a trug with roses, etc., and wears gardening gloves. On the terrace,* ELSA *poses on the bench, facing Centre. She wears a yellow shirt and black shorts.* AMYAS CRALE *is seated on a stool Centre, facing Left, before his easel, painting* ELSA. *His paintbox is on the ground below him. He is a big, handsome man, wearing an old shirt and paint-stained slacks. There is a trolley Left of the terrace with various bottles and glasses, including a bottle of beer in an ice-bucket. In the room, a landscape now hangs in place of the portrait.* MEREDITH *enters up Centre.*)

Hullo, Caroline.

CAROLINE. (*Turning*) Merry! (*She crosses to the stool, puts the trug on it, removes her gloves and puts them in the trug.*)

MEREDITH. (*Closing the door*) How's the picture going? (*He crosses to the French windows and looks out.*) It's a nice pose. (*He moves to Left of the stool and takes a rose from the trug.*) What have we here? 'Ena Harkness'. (*He smells the rose.*) My word, what a beauty.

CAROLINE. Merry, do you think Amyas really cares for that girl?

MEREDITH. No, no, he's just interested in painting her. You know —what Amyas is.

CAROLINE. (*Sitting in the armchair Right*) This time I'm afraid, Merry. I'm nearly thirty, you know. We've been married over six years, and in looks, I can't hold a candle to Elsa.

MEREDITH. (*Replacing the rose in the trug and moving above the stool to Left of* CAROLINE) That's absurd, Caroline. You know that Amyas is really devoted to you and always will be.

CAROLINE. Does one ever know with men?

MEREDITH. (*Close to her and bending over her*) I'm still devoted to you, Caroline.

CAROLINE. (*Affectionately*) Dear Merry. (*She touches his cheek.*) You're so sweet.

(*There is a pause.*)

I long to take a hatchet to that girl. She's just helping herself to my husband in the coolest manner in the world.

MEREDITH. My dear Caroline, the child probably doesn't realize in the least what she's doing. She's got an enormous admiration and hero worship for Amyas and she probably doesn't understand at all that he's maybe falling in love with her.

(CAROLINE *looks pityingly at him.*)

CAROLINE. So there really are people who can believe six impossible things before breakfast.

MEREDITH. I don't understand.

CAROLINE. (*Rising and crossing to Left of the stool*) You live in a nice world all your own, Merry, where everybody is just as nice as you are. (*She looks at the roses. Cheerfully*) My 'Erythina Christo Galli' is in wonderful bloom this year. (*She crosses to the French windows and goes on to the terrace.*)

(MEREDITH *follows* CAROLINE *on to the terrace.*)

Come and see it before you go into Framley Abbott. (*She crosses to the up-stage end of the pergola.*)

MEREDITH. Just you wait till you see my 'Tecoma Grandiflora'. (*He moves to* CAROLINE.) It's magnificent.

(CAROLINE *puts her fingers to her lips to quieten* MEREDITH.)

CAROLINE. Ssh!

MEREDITH. What? (*He looks through one of the arches of the pergola at* ELSA *and* AMYAS.) Oh, man at work.

(CAROLINE *and* MEREDITH *exit by the up-stage end of the pergola.*)

ELSA. (*Stretching herself*) I *must* have a break.

AMYAS. No – no, wait. There – oh, well, if you must.

(ELSA *rises.*)

(*He takes a cigarette from a packet in the paintbox, and lights it.*)

Can't you stay still for more than five minutes?

ELSA. Five minutes! Half an hour. (*She moves down Left.*) Anyway, I've got to change.

AMYAS. Change? Change what?

ELSA. Change out of this. (*She crosses above* AMYAS *and stands behind him.*) We're going out to tea, don't you remember? With Meredith Blake.

AMYAS. (*Irritably*) What a damned nuisance. Always something.

ELSA. (*Leaning over* AMYAS *and putting her arms around his neck*) Aren't you sociable!

AMYAS. (*Looking up at her*) My tastes are simple. (*As though quoting*) A pot of paint, a brush and thou beside me, not able to sit still for five minutes . . .

(*They both laugh.* ELSA *snatches* AMYAS's *cigarette and straightens up.*)

ELSA. (*Drawing on the cigarette*) Have you thought about what I said?
AMYAS. (*Resuming painting*) What did you say?
ELSA. About Caroline. Telling her about us.
AMYAS. (*Easily*) Oh, I shouldn't worry your head about that just yet.
ELSA. But, Amyas . . .

(CAROLINE *enters down Left.*)

CAROLINE. Merry's gone into Framley Abbott for something, but he's coming back here. (*She crosses below the bench towards the French windows.*) I must change.
AMYAS. (*Without looking at her*) You look all right.
CAROLINE. I must do something about my hands, they're filthy. I've been gardening. Are you going to change, Elsa?

(ELSA *returns the cigarette to* AMYAS.)

ELSA. (*Insolently*) Yes. (*She moves to the French windows.*)

(PHILIP *enters up Centre.*)

CAROLINE. (*Moving into the room*) Philip! The train must have been on time for once.

(ELSA *comes into the room.*)

This is Meredith's brother Philip – Miss Greer.
ELSA. Hullo. I'm off to change.

(ELSA *crosses and exits up Centre.*)

CAROLINE. Well, Philip, good journey? (*She kisses him.*)
PHILIP. Not too bad. How are you all?
CAROLINE. Oh – fine. (*She gestures towards the terrace.*) Amyas is out there on the terrace. I must clean up, forgive me. We're going over to Merry's to tea.

(CAROLINE *smiles and exits up Centre.* PHILIP *closes the door after her, then wanders on to the terrace and stands in front of the bench.*)

AMYAS. (*Looking up and smiling*) Hullo, Phil. Good to see you. What a summer. Best we've had for years.

PHILIP. (*Crossing below* AMYAS *to Right*) Can I look?

AMYAS. Yes. I'm on the last lap.

PHILIP. (*Looking at the painting*) Wow!

AMYAS. (*Stubbing out his cigarette*) Like it? Not that you're any judge, you old Philistine.

PHILIP. I buy pictures quite often.

AMYAS. (*Looking up at him*) As an investment? To get in on the ground floor? Because somebody tells you So-and-so is an up-and-coming man? (*He grins.*) I know you, you old money hog. Anyway, you can't buy this. It's not for sale.

PHILIP. She's quite something.

AMYAS. (*Looking at the portrait*) She certainly is. (*Suddenly serious*) Sometimes I wish I'd never seen her.

PHILIP. (*Taking a cigarette from his case*) D'you remember when you first told me you were painting her? 'No personal interest in her,' you said. Remember what I said? (*He grins.*) 'Tell that to the Marines.'

AMYAS. (*Overlapping*) 'Tell that to the Marines.' All right – all right. So you were clever, you cold-blooded old fish. (*He rises, crosses to the trolley, takes the bottle of beer from the ice-bucket, and opens it.*) Why don't *you* get yourself a woman? (*He pours the beer*)

PHILIP. No time for 'em. (*He lights his cigarette.*) And if I were you, Amyas, I wouldn't get tied up with any more.

AMYAS. It's all very well for you to talk. I just can't leave women alone. (*He grins suddenly.*)

PHILIP. How about Caroline? Is she cutting up rough?

AMYAS. What do you think? (*He takes his glass, crosses to the bench and sits on the down-stage end.*) Thank the Lord you've turned up, Phil. Living in this house with four women on your neck is enough to drive any man to the loony bin.

PHILIP. Four?

AMYAS. There's Caroline being bloody to Elsa in a well-bred, polite sort of way. Elsa being just plain bloody to Caroline.

(PHILIP *sits on the easel stool*)

There's Angela, hating my guts because at last I've persuaded Caroline to send her to boarding-school. She ought to have gone years ago. She's a nice kid, really, but Caroline spoils her, and she's inclined to run wild. She put a hedgehog in my bed last week.

(PHILIP *laughs*)

Oh, yes, very funny – but you wait till *you* ram your feet down on a lot of ruddy prickles. And then lastly, but not leastly, there's the governess. Hates me like poison. Sits there at meals with her lips set together, oozing disapproval.

MISS WILLIAMS. (*Off, down Left*) Angela, you must get changed.

ANGELA. (*Off*) Oh, I'm all right.

PHILIP. They seem to have got you down a bit.

MISS WILLIAMS. (*Off*) You're not all right. You can't go out to tea with Mr Blake in those jeans.

AMYAS. *Nil desperandum!* (*He drinks.*)

(ANGELA *enters down Left.*)

ANGELA. (*As she enters*) Merry wouldn't mind. (*She crosses to* PHILIP *and pulls him to his feet.*) Hullo, Philip.

(MISS WILLIAMS *enters down Left and crosses above the bench to the French windows.*)

MISS WILLIAMS. Good afternoon, Mr Blake. I hope you had a good journey down from London?

PHILIP. Quite good, thank you.

(MISS WILLIAMS *goes into the room, sees the trug on the stool, picks it up, returns to the terrace and exits by the garden door up Left.*)

ANGELA. (*Crossing to left of* AMYAS) You've got paint on your ear.

AMYAS. (*Rubbing a painty hand on his other ear*) Eh?

ANGELA. (*Delighted*) Now you've got paint on both ears. He can't go out to tea like that, can he?

AMYAS. I'll go out to tea with ass's ears if I like.

ANGELA. (*Putting her arms around* AMYAS*'s neck from behind and mocking him*) Amyas is an ass! Amyas is an ass!

AMYAS. (*Chanting*) Amyas is an ass.

(MISS WILLIAMS *enters up Left and moves to the French windows.*)

MISS WILLIAMS. Come along, Angela.

(ANGELA *jumps over the bench and runs to the easel.*)

ANGELA. You and your stupid painting. (*Vindictively*) I'm going to write 'Amyas is an ass' all over your picture in scarlet paint. (*She bends down, grabs a brush and proceeds to rub it in the red paint on the palette.*)

(AMYAS *rises quickly, puts his glass down stage of the bench, crosses to* ANGELA *and grabs her hand before she has time to damage the picture.*)

AMYAS. If you ever tamper with any picture of mine – (*Seriously*) I'll kill you. Remember that. (*He picks up a piece of rag and cleans the brush.*)

ANGELA. You're just like Caroline – she's always saying, 'I'll kill you' to people – but she never does, why, she won't even kill wasps. (*Sulkily*) I wish you'd hurry up and finish painting Elsa – then she'd go away.

PHILIP. Don't you like her?

ANGELA. (*Snappily*) No. I think she's a terrible bore. (*She crosses to Left and turns.*) I can't imagine why Amyas has her here.

(PHILIP *and* AMYAS *exchange looks.* AMYAS *crosses to* ANGELA.)

I suppose she's paying you a terrible lot of money for painting her, is she, Amyas?

AMYAS. (*Putting his arm around* ANGELA*'s shoulders and guiding her towards the French windows.*) Go and finish your packing. Four-fifteen train tomorrow, and good riddance. (*He gives her a playful shove and turns down stage.*)

(ANGELA *hits* AMYAS *on the back. He turns and collapses on the bench, and she pommels his chest.*)

ANGELA. I hate you – I hate you. Caroline would never have sent me away to school if it wasn't for you.

PHILIP. Mind the beer. (*He crosses to the bench, picks up the glass and puts it on the trolley.*)

ANGELA. You just want to get rid of me. You wait – I'll get even with you – I'll – I'll . . .

MISS WILLIAMS. (*With sharp authority*) Angela! Angela, come along.

ANGELA. (*Near to tears; sulkily*) Oh, all right.(*She runs into the room.*)

(MISS WILLIAMS *follows* ANGELA *into the room.* ELSA *enters up Centre. She has changed into a dress and looks ravishing.* ANGELA *gives* ELSA *a venomous look and runs out up Centre.* MISS WILLIAMS *follows* ANGELA *off, and closes the door.*)

AMYAS. (*Sitting up*) Wham! Why didn't you stand up for me? I'm black and blue..

PHILIP. (*Leaning against the down-stage end of the pergola*) Black and blue? You're all the colours of the rainbow.

(ELSA *wanders on to the terrace and moves down Centre, beside the easel.*)

You've got enough paint on you to . . . (*He breaks off as he sees* ELSA.)

AMYAS. Hullo, Elsa. All dolled up? You'll knock poor old Merry all of a heap.

PHILIP. (*Drily*) Yes – I – I've been admiring the picture. (*He crosses below the easel to Right of it and looks at the portrait.*)

ELSA. I shall be glad when it's finished. I *loathe* having to sit still. Amyas grunts and sweats and bites his brushes and doesn't hear you when you speak to him.

AMYAS. (*Playfully*) All models should have their tongues cut out.

(ELSA *crosses and sits below* AMYAS *on the bench.*)

(*He looks appraisingly at her.*) Anyway, you can't walk across the fields to Merry's in those shoes.

ELSA. (*Turning her foot this way and that; demurely*) I shan't need to. He's coming to fetch me in his car.

AMYAS. Preferential treatment, eh? (*He grins.*) You've certainly got old Merry going. How do you do it, you little devil?

ELSA. (*Playfully*) I don't know what you mean.

(AMYAS *and* ELSA *are immersed in each other.* PHILIP *crosses to the French windows.*)

PHILIP. (*As he passes them*) I'll go and have a wash.

AMYAS. (*Not hearing* PHILIP; *to* ELSA) Yes, you do. You know damn well what I mean. (*He moves to kiss* ELSA'*s ear, realizes* PHILIP *has said something and turns to him.*) What?

PHILIP. (*Quietly*) A wash.

(PHILIP *goes into the room and exits up Centre, closing the door behind him.*)

AMYAS. (*Laughing*) Good old Phil.

ELSA. (*Rising and crossing below the easel to Right*) You're very fond of him, aren't you?

AMYAS. Known him all my life. He's a great guy.

ELSA. (*Turning and looking at the portrait*) I don't think it's a bit like me.

AMYAS. Don't pretend you've any artistic judgement, Elsa. (*He rises.*) You know nothing at all.

ELSA. (*Quite pleased*) How rude you are. Are you going out to tea with all that paint on your face?

(AMYAS *crosses to the paintbox, takes up a piece of rag and moves to* ELSA.)

AMYAS. Here, clean me off a bit.

(ELSA *takes the rag and rubs his face.*)

Don't put the turps in my eye.

ELSA. Well, hold still. (*After a second she puts both her arms around his waist.*) Who do you love?

AMYAS. (*Not moving; quietly*) Caroline's room faces this way – so does Angela's.

ELSA. I want to talk to you about Caroline.

AMYAS. (*Taking the rag and sitting on the stool*) Not now. I'm not in the mood.

ELSA. It's no good putting it off. She's got to know *sometime*, hasn't she?

AMYAS. (*Grinning*) We could go off Victorian fashion and leave a note on her pin-cushion.

ELSA. (*Moving between* AMYAS *and the easel*) I believe that's just what you'd like to do. But we've got to be absolutely fair and above-board about the whole thing.

AMYAS. Hoity-toity!

ELSA. Oh, do be serious.

AMYAS. *I am* serious. I don't want a lot of fuss and scenes and hysterics. Now, mind yourself. (*He pushes her gently aside.*)

ELSA. (*Moving Right*) I don't see why there should be scenes and hysterics. Caroline should have too much dignity and pride for that. (*She pivots around.*)

AMYAS. (*Absorbed in painting*) Should she? You don't know Caroline.

ELSA. When a marriage has gone wrong, it's only sensible to face the fact calmly.

AMYAS. (*Turning to look at her*) Advice from our marriage counsellor. Caroline loves me and she'll kick up the hell of a row.

ELSA. (*Moving down Right*) If she *really* loved you, she'd want you to be happy.

AMYAS. (*Grinning*) With somebody else? She'll probably poison you and stick a knife into me.

ELSA. Don't be ridiculous!

AMYAS. (*Wiping his hands and nodding at the picture*) Well, that's that. Nothing doing until tomorrow morning. (*He drops the rag, rises and moves to* ELSA.) Lovely, lovely Elsa. (*He takes her face in his hands.*) What a lot of bloody nonsense you talk. (*He kisses her.*)

(ANGELA *rushes in up Centre, runs on to the terrace and exits down Left.* ELSA *and* AMYAS *break apart.* MISS WILLIAMS *enters up Centre, goes on to the terrace and looks off Left.*)

MISS WILLIAMS. (*Calling*) Angela!

AMYAS. (*Crossing down Left*) She went this-a-way. Shall I catch her for you?

MISS WILLIAMS. (*Moving down Left Centre*) No, it's all right. She'll come back of her own accord as soon as she sees nobody is paying any attention to her.

(ELSA *goes into the room, picks up a magazine from the sofa and sits in the armchair Right.*)

AMYAS. There's something in that.

MISS WILLIAMS. She's young for her age, you know. Growing up is a difficult business. Angela is at the prickly stage.

AMYAS. (*Moving up Left*) Don't talk to me of prickles. Reminds me too much of that ruddy hedgehog.

MISS WILLIAMS. That was very naughty of Angela.

AMYAS. (*Moving to the French windows*) Sometimes I wonder how you can stick her.

MISS WILLIAMS. (*Turning to face* AMYAS) I can see ahead. Angela will be a fine woman one day, and a distinguished one.

AMYAS. I still say Caroline spoils her. (*He goes into the room and crosses to Centre of it.*)

(MISS WILLIAMS *moves to the French windows and listens.*)

ELSA. (*In a whisper*) Did she see us?

AMYAS. Who can say? I suppose I've got lipstick on my face now as well as paint.

(AMYAS *glances off Left and exits quickly up Centre.* MISS WILLIAMS *comes into the room and moves above the stool, uncertain whether to go or not. She decides to stay.*)

MISS WILLIAMS. You haven't been over to Mr Blake's house yet, have you, Miss Greer?

ELSA. (*Flatly*) No.

MISS WILLIAMS. It's a delightful walk there. You can go by the shore or through the woods.

(CAROLINE *and* PHILIP *enter up Centre.* CAROLINE *glances around the room, then goes to the French windows and looks on to the terrace.* PHILIP *closes the door and looks at the carved head on the table up Left Centre.*)

CAROLINE. Are we all ready? Amyas has gone to clean the paint off himself.

ELSA. He needn't. Artists aren't like other people.

(CAROLINE *pays no attention to* ELSA.)

CAROLINE. (*Moving to the armchair Left; to* PHILIP) You haven't been down here since Merry started on his lily pond, have you, Phil? (*She sits.*)

PHILIP. Don't think so.

ELSA. People in the country talk of nothing but their gardens.

(*There is a pause.* CAROLINE *takes her spectacles from her handbag and puts them on.* PHILIP *looks at* ELSA, *and then sits on the stool facing the head.*)

CAROLINE. (*To* MISS WILLIAMS) Did you ring up the vet about Toby?

MISS WILLIAMS. Yes, Mrs Crale. He'll come first thing tomorrow.

CAROLINE. (*To* PHILIP) Do you like that head, Phil? Amyas bought it last month.

PHILIP. Yes. It's good.

CAROLINE. (*Searching in her handbag for her cigarettes*) It's the work of a young Norwegian sculptor, Amyas thinks very highly of him. We're thinking of going over to Norway next year to visit him.

ELSA. That doesn't seem to me very likely.

CAROLINE. Doesn't it, Elsa? Why?

ELSA. You know very well.

CAROLINE. (*Lightly*) How very cryptic. Miss Williams, would you mind – my cigarette case – (*She indicates the table Right Centre.*) it's on that little table.

(MISS WILLIAMS *goes to the table Right Centre, picks up the cigarette case, opens it and offers a cigarette to* CAROLINE. PHILIP *takes out his cigarettes, rises and offers them to* CAROLINE.)

(*She takes a cigarette from her own case.*) I prefer these – do you mind?

(MISS WILLIAMS *moves to the table up Left Centre and puts the case on it.* PHILIP *lights* CAROLINE's *cigarette, then takes one of his own and lights it.*)

ELSA. (*Rising and moving below the stool*) This would be quite a good room if it was properly fixed. All this litter of old-fashioned stuff cleared out.

(*There is a pause.* PHILIP *looks at* ELSA.)

CAROLINE. We like it as it is. It holds a lot of memories.

ELSA. (*Loudly and aggressively*) When *I'm* living here I shall throw all this rubbish out.

(PHILIP *crosses to* ELSA *and offers her a cigarette.*)

No, thank you.

(PHILIP *crosses to Right.*)

Flame-coloured curtains, I think – and one of those French wall-papers. (To PHILIP) Don't you think that would be rather striking?

CAROLINE. (*Evenly*) Are you thinking of buying Alderbury, Elsa?

ELSA. It won't be necessary for me to buy it.

CAROLINE. What do you mean?

ELSA. Must we pretend? (*She moves Centre.*) Come now, Caroline, you know perfectly well what I mean.

CAROLINE. I assure you I've no idea.

ELSA. (*Aggressively*) Oh, don't be such an ostrich, burying your head in the sand and pretending you don't know all about it. (*She turns, moves to Right of the stool, tosses the magazine on to the armchair Right and moves up Right.*) Amyas and I love each other. It's his house, not yours.

(ANGELA *runs on down Left, crosses to the French windows, stops outside and listens.* PHILIP *and* MISS WILLIAMS *are frozen.*)

And after we're married I shall live here with him.

CAROLINE. (*Angrily*) I think you must be crazy.

ELSA. Oh, no, I'm not. (*She sits on the sofa at the Left end.*) It will be much simpler if we're honest about it. There's only one decent thing for you to do – give him his freedom.

CAROLINE. Don't talk nonsense!

ELSA. Nonsense, is it? Ask *him*.

(AMYAS *enters up Centre.* ANGELA, *unseen, exits by the door up Left.*)

CAROLINE. I will. Amyas, Elsa says you want to marry her. Is it true?

AMYAS. (*After a slight pause; to* ELSA) Why the devil couldn't you hold your tongue?

CAROLINE. Is it true?

(AMYAS, *leaving the door open, crosses to the armchair Right, picks up the magazine and sits.*)

AMYAS. We don't have to talk about it now. (*He looks at the magazine.*)

CAROLINE. But we *are* going to talk about it now.

ELSA. It's only fair to Caroline to tell her the truth.

CAROLINE. (*Icily*) I don't think you need bother about being fair to me. (*She rises and crossses to* AMYAS.) Is it true, Amyas?

(AMYAS *looks hunted and glances from* ELSA *to* CAROLINE.)

AMYAS. (*To* PHILIP) Women.

CAROLINE. (*Furiously*) Is it true?

AMYAS. (*Defiantly*) All right. It's true enough.

(ELSA *rises, triumphant.*)

But I don't want to talk about it now.

ELSA. You see? It's no good your adopting a dog-in-the-manger attitude. These things happen. It's nobody's fault. One just has to be rational about it. (*She sits on the stool, facing up stage.*) You and Amyas will always be good friends, I hope.

CAROLINE. (*Crossing to the door up Centre*) Good friends! Over his dead body.

ELSA. What do you mean?

CAROLINE. (*Turning in the open doorway*) I mean that I'd kill Amyas before I'd give him up to you.

(CAROLINE *exits up Centre. There is a frozen silence.* MISS WILLIAMS *sees* CAROLINE'*s bag on the armchair Left, picks it up and exits hurriedly up Centre.*)

AMYAS. (*Rising and crossing to the French windows*) Now you've done it. We'll have scenes and ructions and God knows what.

ELSA. (*Rising*) She had to know some time.

AMYAS. (*Moving on to the terrace*) She needn't have known till the picture was finished.

(ELSA *moves to the French windows.*)

(*He stands behind the bench.*) How the hell can a man paint with a lot of women buzzing about his ears like wasps?

ELSA. You think nothing's important but your painting.

AMYAS. (*Shouting*) Nothing is to me.

ELSA. Well, I think it matters to be honest about things.

(ELSA *rushes angrily out up Centre.* AMYAS *comes into the room.*)

AMYAS. Give me a cigarette, Phil.

(PHILIP *offers his cigarettes and* AMYAS *takes one.*)

(*He sits astride the stool.*) Women are all alike. Revel in scenes. Why the devil couldn't she hold her tongue? I've got to finish that picture, Phil. It's the best thing I've ever done. And a couple of damn women want to muck it up between them. (*He takes out his matches and lights his cigarette.*)

PHILIP. Suppose she refuses to give you a divorce?

AMYAS. (*Abstracted*) What?

PHILIP. I said – suppose Caroline refuses to divorce you. Suppose she digs her toes in.

AMYAS. Oh, that. Caroline would never be vindictive. (*He tosses the spent match out of the French windows.*) You don't understand, old boy.

PHILIP. And the child. There's the child to consider.

AMYAS. Look, Phil, I know you mean well, but don't go on croaking like a raven, I can manage my own affairs. Everything will turn out all right, you'll see.

PHILIP. Optimist!

(MEREDITH *enters up Centre, closing the door behind him.*)

MEREDITH. (*Cheerily*) Hullo, Phil. Just got down from London? (*To* AMYAS) Hope you haven't forgotten you're all coming over to me this afternoon. I've got the car here. I thought Caroline and Elsa might prefer it to walking this hot weather. (*He crosses to Left Centre*)

AMYAS. (*Rising*) Not Caroline *and* Elsa. If Caroline drives, Elsa will walk, and if Elsa rides, Caroline will walk. Take your pick. (*He goes on to the terrace, sits on the stool and busies himself with painting.*)

MEREDITH. (*Startled*) What's the matter with him? Something happened?

PHILIP. It's just come out.

MEREDITH. What?

PHILIP. Elsa broke the news to Caroline that she and Amyas planned to marry. (*Maliciously*) Quite a shock for Caroline.

MEREDITH. No! You're joking!

(PHILIP *shrugs, moves to the armchair Right, picks up the magazine, sits and reads.*)

(*He goes on to the terrace and turns to* AMYAS.) Amyas! You – this – it can't be true?

AMYAS. I don't know yet what you're talking about. What can't be true?

MEREDITH. You and Elsa. Caroline . . .

AMYAS. (*Cleaning his brush*) Oh, that.

MEREDITH. Look here, Amyas, you can't just for the sake of a sudden infatuation, break up your whole married life. I know Elsa's very attractive . . .

AMYAS. (*Grinning*) So you've noticed that, have you?

MEREDITH. (*Crossing below* AMYAS *to Right; much concerned*) I can quite understand a girl like Elsa bowling any man over, yes, but think of her – she's very young, you know. She might regret it bitterly later on. Can't you pull yourself together? For little Carla's sake? Make a clean break here and now, and go back to your wife.

(AMYAS *looks up thoughtfully.*)

(*He crosses to the bench and turns.*) Believe me, it's the right thing. I know it.

AMYAS. (*After a pause; quietly*) You're a good chap, Merry. But you're too sentimental.

MEREDITH. Look at the position you've put Caroline in by having the girl down here.

AMYAS. Well, I wanted to paint her.

MEREDITH. (*Angrily*) Oh, damn your pictures!

AMYAS. (*Hotly*) All the neurotic women in England can't do that.

MEREDITH. (*Sitting on the bench*) It's disgraceful the way you've always treated Caroline. She's had a miserable life with you.

AMYAS. I know – I know. I've given Caroline one hell of a life – and she's been a saint about it. (*He rises and moves down Right.*) But she always knew what she was letting herself in for. Right from the start I told her what an egotistic loose-living bastard I was. (*He turns.*) But this is different.

MEREDITH. (*Quickly*) This is the first time you've brought a woman into the house and flaunted her in Caroline's face.

AMYAS. (*Crossing to the trolley*) What you don't seem to understand, Meredith, is that when I'm painting, nothing else matters – least of all a pair of jealous, quarrelling women. (*He turns to the trolley and picks up the glass of beer.*)

(ANGELA *enters by the door up Left and moves slowly to easel. She is now clean and tidy, in a cotton frock.*)

Don't worry, Merry, everything's going to be all right, you'll see. (*He sips the beer.*) Oh, it's warm. (*He turns and sees* ANGELA.) Hullo, Angy, you're looking remarkably clean and tidy.

ANGELA. (*Abstracted*) Oh – yes. (*She crosses to* AMYAS.) Amyas, why does Elsa say she's going to marry you? She couldn't. People can't have two wives. It's bigamy. (*Confidentially*) You can go to prison for it.

(AMYAS *glances at* MEREDITH, *puts his glass on the trolley, puts an arm around* ANGELA*'s shoulder and leads her to Right Centre.*)

AMYAS. Now, where did you hear that?

ANGELA. I was out here. I heard it through the window.

AMYAS. (*Sitting on the stool by the easel*) Then it's time you got out of the habit of eavesdropping.

(ELSA *enters up Centre with her bag and gloves, which she puts on the table up Left Centre.*)

ANGELA. (*Hurt and indignant*) I wasn't – I couldn't *help* hearing. Why did Elsa say that?

AMYAS. It was a kind of joke, darling.

(CAROLINE *enters by the door up Left and moves down Left.*)

CAROLINE. It's time we started. Those of us who are going to walk.

MEREDITH. (*Rising*) I'll drive you.

CAROLINE. I'd rather walk.

(ELSA *comes on to the terrace.*)

Take Elsa in the car. (*She crosses below* AMYAS *to* ANGELA.)

ELSA. (*Moving to Right of* MEREDITH) Don't you grow herbs and all sorts of exciting things?

CAROLINE. (*To* ANGELA) That's better. You won't be able to wear jeans at school, you know.

ANGELA. (*Crossing angrily down Left*) School! I wish you wouldn't keep on about *school*.

MEREDITH. (*Continuing to* ELSA) I make cordials and potions. I have my own little laboratory.

ELSA. It sounds fascinating. You must show me.

(CAROLINE *crosses to* ANGELA, *looking at* ELSA *on the way. She straightens* ANGELA*'s pig-tails.*)

MEREDITH. I shall probably deliver a lecture. I'm terribly enthusiastic about my hobby.

ELSA. Doesn't one pick certain herbs by the light of the moon?

CAROLINE. (*To* ANGELA) You'll like school, you know, once you get there.

MEREDITH. (*To* ELSA) That was the old-fashioned superstition.

ELSA. You don't go as far as that?

MEREDITH. No.

ELSA. Are they *dangerous*?

MEREDITH. Some of them are.

CAROLINE. (*Turning*) Sudden death in a little bottle. Belladonna. Hemlock.

(ANGELA *runs between* ELSA *and* MEREDITH *and puts her arms around his waist.*)

ANGELA. You read us something once – about Socrates – and how he died.

MEREDITH. Yes, conine – the active principle of hemlock.

ANGELA. It was wonderful. It made me want to learn Greek.

(*They all laugh.* AMYAS *rises and picks up his paintbox.*)

AMYAS. We've talked enough. Let's get started. (*He moves towards the door up Left.*) Where's Phil? (*He glances in the French windows and calls*) Phil.

PHILIP. Coming.

(AMYAS *exits by the door up Left.* PHILIP *rises and puts down the magazine.* ELSA *goes into the room and collects her gloves and bag.*)

ANGELA. (*Moving to Right of* CAROLINE) Caroline – (*She whispers anxiously*) it isn't possible, is it, for Elsa to marry Amyas?

(CAROLINE *replies calmly, overheard only by* MEREDITH.)

CAROLINE. Amyas will only marry Elsa after I am dead.

ANGELA. Good. It *was* a joke.

(ANGELA *runs off down Left.*)

MEREDITH. (*Moving to Right of* CAROLINE) Caroline – my dear – I can't tell you . . .

CAROLINE. Don't . . . Everything's finished – I'm finished . . .

(PHILIP *comes on to the terrace.*)

PHILIP. The lady's waiting to be driven.

MEREDITH. (*Slightly at a loss*) Oh.

(MEREDITH *goes into the room and escorts* ELSA *off up Centre.* MISS WILLIAMS *enters up Centre and looks off after* MEREDITH *and* ELSA. *She stands in the room, uncertain for a moment, then goes to the French windows and overhears the last of the conversation between* PHILIP *and* CAROLINE.)

CAROLINE. (*To* PHILIP; *brightly*) We'll go by the wood path, shall we?

PHILIP. (*Moving to Right of* CAROLINE) Caroline – is it in order for me to offer my condolences?

CAROLINE. Don't.

PHILIP. Perhaps you realize, now, that you made a mistake.

CAROLINE. When I married him?

PHILIP. Yes.

CAROLINE. (*Looking* PHILIP *straight in the eye*) However it may turn out – I made no mistake. (*She resumes her light manner*) Let's go.

(CAROLINE *exits down Left.* PHILIP *follows her off.* MISS WILLIAMS *comes on to the terrace.*)

MISS WILLIAMS. (*Calling*) Mrs Crale. (*She moves below the bench.*) Mrs Crale.

(CAROLINE *re-enters down Left.*)

CAROLINE. Yes, Miss Williams?

MISS WILLIAMS. I'm going into the village. Shall I post the letters that are on your desk?

CAROLINE. (*Turning to go*) Oh, yes, please. I forgot them.

MISS WILLIAMS. Mrs Crale –

(CAROLINE *turns.*)

– if I could do anything – anything at all to help . . .

CAROLINE. (*Quickly*) Please. We must go on as usual – just behave as usual.

MISS WILLIAMS. (*Fervently*) I think you're wonderful.

CAROLINE. Oh, no, I'm not. (*She moves to Left of* MISS WILLIAMS.) Dear Miss Williams. (*She kisses her.*) You've been such a comfort to me.

(CAROLINE *exits quickly down Left.* MISS WILLIAMS *looks after her, then sees the empty beer bottle and glass on the trolley. She picks up the bottle, looks at it for a moment, and then looks off after* CAROLINE. *She puts the bottle in the ice-bucket, picks up the ice-bucket and glass and crosses below the bench to the French windows. As she does so, the LIGHTS slowly dim to black-out. A spotlight comes up on* JUSTIN *down Left.*)

JUSTIN. We come now to the next morning, the morning of the seventeenth. Miss Williams?

(*The spotlight fades,* MISS WILLIAMS*'s voice can be heard in the darkness.*)

MISS WILLIAMS. I'd been going through Angela's school list with Mrs Crale. She looked tired and unhappy but she was very composed. The telephone rang, and I went into the garden room to answer it.

(*The LIGHTS come up. A clean glass and a fresh bottle of beer, not in an ice-bucket, is on the trolley.* PHILIP *is seated on the bench on the terrace reading a Sunday paper. The telephone rings.* MISS WILLIAMS *enters up Centre, goes to the telephone and lifts the receiver. She carries a school list.* CAROLINE *follows* MISS WILLIAMS *on, with her spectacles in her hand. She looks towards the telephone, then crosses wearily above the stool to the armchair Right and sits.*)

(*Into the telephone*) Yes? . . . Oh, good morning, Mr Blake . . . Yes, he's here. (*She looks through the French windows to* PHILIP *and calls*) Mr Blake, it's your brother, he'd like to have a word with you. (*She holds out the receiver.*)

(PHILIP *rises, folds his paper, tucks it under his arm, comes into the room and takes the receiver.*)

PHILIP. (*Into the telephone*) Hullo, Philip here . . .

MISS WILLIAMS. (*Crossing above the stool to Right of it; to* CAROLINE) That completes the school list, Mrs Crale. I wonder if you would like to give it a final check? (*She sits on the Right end of the stool.*)

CAROLINE. (*Taking the list*) Let me see. (*She puts on her spectacles and studies the list.*)

PHILIP. (*Into the telephone*) What? . . . What do you say? . . . Good
Lord – are you sure? . . . (*He looks round at* CAROLINE *and*
MISS WILLIAMS.) Well, I can't talk now . . . Yes, better come
along here. I'll meet you . . . Yes – we'll talk it over – discuss
what's best to be done . . .

CAROLINE. (*To* MISS WILLIAMS) What about these?

MISS WILLIAMS. (*Looking at the list*) Those items are optional.

PHILIP. (*Into the telephone*) No, I can't, now – it's difficult . . . You
are sure? Yes, but you're a bit vague sometimes. It could have
got mislaid . . . All right – if you're sure . . . Be seeing you. (*He
replaces the receiver, gives a worried look at the others, goes on the terrace
and paces up and down.*)

CAROLINE. (*Giving the list to* MISS WILLIAMS) I do hope I'm doing
the right thing about Angela. (*She removes her spectacles.*)

MISS WILLIAMS. I think you can be quite certain of that,
Mrs Crale.

CAROLINE. I want so terribly to do what's best for her. You know
why.

MISS WILLIAMS. Believe me, you have nothing to reproach yourself with where Angela is concerned.

CAROLINE. I – disfigured her for life. She'll always have that scar.

(PHILIP *looks off Left through the pergola.*)

MISS WILLIAMS. One cannot alter the past.

(PHILIP *exits up Left, above the pergola.*)

CAROLINE. No. It taught me what a wicked temper I have. I've
been on my guard ever since. But you *do* see, don't you, why
I've always spoilt her a little?

MISS WILLIAMS. School life will suit her. She needs the contacts of
other minds – minds of her own age. (*She rises.*) You're doing
the right thing – I'm sure of that. (*In a businesslike way*) I'd better
get on with her packing – I don't know whether she wants to
take any books with her.

(MISS WILLIAMS *exits up Centre, closing the door behind her.* CARO-
LINE *sinks wearily back into her chair.* PHILIP *enters down Left and
stands looking off Left.* AMYAS *enters by the door up Left, carrying his
paintbox.*)

AMYAS. (*To* PHILIP; *irritably*) Where is that girl? (*He moves to his stool.*) Why can't she get up in the morning.

(PHILIP, *looking off Left, does not answer.*)

(*He sits, puts his paintbox on the ground beside him and arranges his gear.*) Have you seen her, Phil? What's the matter with you? Has nobody given you any breakfast?

PHILIP. (*Turning*) Eh? Oh, yes, of course. I – I'm waiting for Merry. He's coming over. (*He looks at his watch.*) I wonder which way he'll come – I forgot to ask him. Upper or lower path. I could go along and meet him.

AMYAS. Lower path's the shorter one. (*He rises and goes into the room.*) Where the devil is that girl? (*To* CAROLINE) Have you seen Elsa? (*He goes to the door up Centre.*)

CAROLINE. I don't think she's up yet.

(AMYAS *is about to open the door.*)

Amyas, come here, I want to talk to you.

AMYAS. (*Opening the door*) Not now.

CAROLINE. (*Firmly*) Yes, now.

(AMYAS *looks sheepish, but closes the door.* PHILIP *moves below the bench.* ELSA *enters down Left, dressed in shorts and shirt.*)

PHILIP. (*To* ELSA) You're late on parade. You look on top of the world this morning.

ELSA. (*Radiant*) Do I? I feel it.

(PHILIP *exits down Left.* ELSA *goes to the bench and sits facing the pergola, basking in the sun.*)

AMYAS. (*Moving above the stool*) Caroline, I've told you I don't want to discuss this. I'm sorry Elsa blew her top. I told her not to.

CAROLINE. You didn't want a scene until you'd finished your picture, is that it?

AMYAS. (*Moving to* CAROLINE) Thank the Lord you understand.

CAROLINE. I understand you very well.

(ELSA *swings her legs over the bench and faces front. After a moment she hears raised voices, rises and goes to the French windows to listen.*)

AMYAS. Good. (*He bends down to kiss* CAROLINE.)

CAROLINE. I may understand, but that doesn't mean that I'm taking this lying down. (*She turns to him.*) Do you really mean you want to marry this girl?

AMYAS. (*Moving to her*) Darling, I'm very fond of you – and of the child. You know that. I always shall be. (*Roughly*) But you've got to understand this. I'm damned well going to marry Elsa and nothing shall stop me.

CAROLINE. (*Facing front*) I wonder.

AMYAS. (*Moving up Right of the stool*) If you won't divorce me, we'll live together and she can take the name of Crale by deed poll.

(PHILIP *enters down Left, sees* ELSA *listening, and unseen, lounges against the down-stage pillar of the pergola.*)

CAROLINE. You've thought it all out, haven't you?

AMYAS. (*Moving Right*) I love Elsa – and I mean to have her.

CAROLINE. (*Trembling*) Do as you please – I'm warning you.

AMYAS. (*Turning*) What do you mean by that?

CAROLINE. (*Turning suddenly on him*) I mean you're mine – and I don't mean to let you go.

(AMYAS *moves to* CAROLINE.)

Sooner than let you go to that girl, I'll . . .

AMYAS. Caroline, don't be a fool.

CAROLINE. (*Near to tears*) You and your women! You don't deserve to live.

AMYAS. (*Trying to embrace her*) Caroline . . .

CAROLINE. I mean it. (*She pushes him away.*) Don't touch me. (*She crosses to the door down Right in tears.*) It's too cruel – it's too cruel.

AMYAS. Caroline . . .

(CAROLINE *exits down Right.* AMYAS *gives a hopeless gesture, turns and crosses towards the French windows.* ELSA *turns quickly away, sees* PHILIP *and quickly looks nonchalant.*)

(*He goes on the terrace.*) Oh, there you are at last. (*He moves to his stool and sits.*) What do you mean by wasting half the morning? *Get* into the pose.

ELSA. (*Looking at* AMYAS *over the top of the easel*) I'll have to get a pullover. It's quite a chilly wind.

AMYAS. Oh, no, you don't. It'll change all the tones of the skin.

ELSA. I've got a yellow one like this shirt – and, anyway, you're painting my hands this morning, you said so.

(ELSA *pouts and runs off by the door up Left.*)

AMYAS. (*Shouting after* ELSA) You don't know what I'm painting. Only I know that. Oh, hell! (*He squeezes paint from a tube on to his palette and mixes the paint.*)

PHILIP. Trouble with Caroline?

AMYAS. (*Looking up*) Heard some of it, did you?

(PHILIP *crosses below* AMYAS *to Right.*)

I knew just what would happen. Elsa had to open her big mouth. Caroline gets hysterical and won't listen to reason.

PHILIP. (*Turning*) Poor Caroline! (*He does not say it with pity, instead there is a trace of satisfaction in his tone.*)

(AMYAS *looks sharply at* PHILIP.)

AMYAS. Caroline is all right. Don't waste your pity on her.

PHILIP. (*Crossing to Left Centre*) Amyas, you're incredible. I don't know that I'd really blame Caroline if she took a hatchet to you.

AMYAS. (*Irritably*) Do stop pacing, Phil. You're putting me off. I thought you were going to meet Merry.

PHILIP. (*Moving to the up-stage end of the pergola*) I was afraid of missing him.

AMYAS. What's the big hurry? You saw him yesterday.

PHILIP. (*Crossly*) Since I seem to annoy you, I'll take myself off.

(PHILIP *exits up Left, above the pergola.* ELSA *enters by the door up Left, with a pullover draped over her arm.*)

AMYAS. (*Looking up*) At last! Now, get me some beer, will you, I'm thirsty. What on earth you want with a pullover on a day like this I don't know. I'm boiling. You'll be wanting snow boots next, and a hot-water bottle to sit on.

(ELSA *drops her pullover on the bench, goes to the trolley and pours a glass of beer.*)

(*He rises, goes down Right, turns and looks at his painting.*) This is the best thing I've ever done. (*He moves to the painting and bends down to it.*) Do you think Da Vinci knew what he'd done when he'd finished La Giaconda?

(ELSA *crosses with the glass of beer and holds it out over the easel.*)

ELSA. La – what?

AMYAS. (*Taking the glass*) La Gia – the Mona Lisa, you ignorant bitch – oh, never mind. (*He drinks.*) Pah! It's warm. Isn't there a bucket of ice?

ELSA. (*Sitting on the bench*) No. (*She takes up her pose.*)

AMYAS. Somebody's always forgetting something. (*He crosses above the bench and looks off Left.*) I loathe hot beer. (*He calls*) Hi, Angela!

ANGELA. (*Off Left; calling*) What?

AMYAS. Go and get me a bottle of beer from the refrigerator.

(ANGELA *enters down Left.*)

ANGELA. Why should I?

AMYAS. Common humanity. (*He crosses to his stool.*) Come on, now, be a sport.

ANGELA. Oh, all right.

(ANGELA *sticks her tongue out at* AMYAS *and runs off by the door up Left.*)

AMYAS. Charming little girl. (*He sits on his stool.*) Your left hand's wrong – up a bit.

(ELSA *moves her left hand.*)

That's better. (*He sips some beer.*)

(MISS WILLIAMS *enters up Centre and goes on to the terrace.*)

MISS WILLIAMS. (*To* AMYAS) Have you seen Angela?

AMYAS. She's just gone into the house to get me some beer. (*He paints.*)

MISS WILLIAMS. Oh.

(MISS WILLIAMS *seems surprised. She turns and exits quickly by the door up Left.* AMYAS *whistles as he works.*)

ELSA. (*After a few moments*) Must you whistle?

AMYAS. Why not?

ELSA. That particular tune?

AMYAS. (*Not understanding*) What? (*He sings*) 'When we are married, why what shall we do?' (*He grins.*) Not very tactful.

(CAROLINE *enters by the door up Left, carrying a bottle of beer.*)

CAROLINE. (*Moving down Centre; coldly*) Here's your beer. I'm sorry the ice was forgotten.

AMYAS. Oh, thank you, Caroline. Open it for me, will you? (*He holds out his glass.*)

(CAROLINE *takes the glass, crosses to the trolley, and with her back to the audience, opens the bottle and pours the beer.* AMYAS *begins to whistle the same tune, realizes this, and checks himself.* CAROLINE *takes the bottle and the glass of beer to* AMYAS.)

CAROLINE. Here's your beer.

AMYAS. (*Taking the glass*) And you hope it chokes me. (*He grins.*) Here's to hoping! (*He drinks.*) Phew, this tastes worse than the other. Still, it *is* cold.

(CAROLINE *places the bottle beside the paintbox, goes into the room and exits up Centre.* AMYAS *resumes painting.* MEREDITH *enters breathlessly down Left.*)

MEREDITH. Is Phil about?

AMYAS. He went to meet you.

MEREDITH. Which path?

AMYAS. Lower one.

MEREDITH. I came by the other.

AMYAS. Well, you can't go on chasing each other. Better hang on and wait.

MEREDITH. (*Taking out his handkerchief and wiping his brow*) I'm hot. I'll go inside. It's cooler. (*He crosses to the French windows.*)

AMYAS. Get yourself a cold drink. Get one of the women to get it for you.

(MEREDITH *goes into the room, and hesitates, uncertain what to do.*)

(*He looks at* ELSA.) You've wonderful eyes, Elsa. (*He pauses.*) I'll leave the hands – concentrate on the eyes. I haven't quite got them.

(MEREDITH *moves to the French windows and looks out to the terrace.*)

Move your hands as much as you like – I'm getting it. Now for God's sake don't move or talk.

(MEREDITH *turns and crosses in the room to Right Centre.*)

ELSA. I don't want to talk.

AMYAS. That's a change.

(ANGELA *enters up Centre, carrying a tray with a jug of iced lemonade and two glasses, which she places on the table Right.*)

ANGELA. Refreshments!

MEREDITH. Oh, thank you, Angela. (*He moves to the tray and pours a glass of lemonade.*)

ANGELA. (*Crossing to the French windows*) We aim to please. (*She goes on to the terrace. To* AMYAS) Did you get your beer all right?

AMYAS. Sure I did. You're a great gal.

ANGELA. (*Laughing*) Very kind, aren't I? Ha, ha. You wait and see.

(ANGELA *runs into the room and exits up Centre, closing the door behind her.* MEREDITH *sips his lemonade.*)

AMYAS. (*Suspicious*) That kid's up to something. (*He rubs his right shoulder.*) That's funny.

ELSA. What's the matter?

AMYAS. I'm very stiff this morning. Rheumatism, I suppose.

ELSA. (*Mocking*) Poor creaking old man.

(PHILIP *enters down Left.*)

AMYAS. (*Chuckling*) Creaking with age. Hullo, Phil. Merry's inside waiting for you.

PHILIP. Good. (*He crosses and goes into the room.*)

(MEREDITH *puts his glass on the tray and meets* PHILIP *at Centre.* AMYAS *resumes painting.*)

MEREDITH. Thank goodness you've come. I didn't know what to do.

PHILIP. What is all this? Caroline and the governess were in the room when you rang up.

MEREDITH. (*In a low voice*) There's a bottle missing from my lab.

PHILIP. So you told me. But what's in it?

MEREDITH. Conine.

PHILIP. Hemlock?

MEREDITH. Yes, conine's the pure alkaloid.

PHILIP. Dangerous?

MEREDITH. Very.

PHILIP. And you've no idea whatsoever who could have taken it?

MEREDITH. No. I always keep the door locked.

PHILIP. You locked it yesterday?

MEREDITH. You know I did. You saw me.

PHILIP. You're sure about this – you haven't just mislaid the bottle – shoved it away somewhere? (*He crosses to Right.*)

MEREDITH. I showed it them all yesterday. And then I put it back in its place on the shelf.

PHILIP. (*Turning, sharply*) Who came out of the room last?

MEREDITH. (*Unwillingly*) Caroline – I waited for her.

PHILIP. But you weren't watching her?

MEREDITH. No.

PHILIP. (*With decision*) Well, then Caroline took it.

MEREDITH. You really think so?

PHILIP. (*Crossing above* MEREDITH *to Left*) So do you, or you wouldn't be in such a state.

MEREDITH. That's what she had in mind yesterday – when she said everything was finished for her. She meant to do away with herself. (*He sinks on to the stool, and faces up stage.*)

PHILIP. Well, cheer up, she hasn't done away with herself yet.

MEREDITH. You've seen her this morning. Is she all right?

PHILIP. Seems just the same as usual to me.

MEREDITH. What are we going to do?

PHILIP. You'd better tackle her.

MEREDITH. I don't know – how shall I go about it?

PHILIP. I should just say straight out – 'You pinched my conine yesterday. Hand it back, please.'

MEREDITH. (*Doubtfully*) Like that?

PHILIP. (*Crossing above* MEREDITH *to Right*) Well, what do you want to say?

MEREDITH. I don't know. (*He brightens.*) We've got plenty of time, I imagine. She wouldn't take the stuff until she goes to bed, would she?

PHILIP. (*Drily*) Probably not. If she means to take it at all.

MEREDITH. You think she doesn't?

PHILIP. (*Crossing below* MEREDITH *to Left*) She may want it to make a theatrical scene with Amyas. Give up that girl or I'll swallow this and kill myself.

MEREDITH. That wouldn't be like Caroline.

PHILIP. Well – you know her best. (*He moves up Left Centre.*)

MEREDITH. You're always bitter about Caroline. You used to be crazy about her once – don't you remember? (*He rises.*)

PHILIP. (*Turning; annoyed*) A brief attack of calf love. It wasn't serious.

MEREDITH. And then – you turned against her.

PHILIP. (*Exasperated*) Let's stick to the present, shall we?

MEREDITH. Yes. Yes, of course.

(CAROLINE *enters up Centre.*)

CAROLINE. Hullo, Merry, stay to lunch, won't you? It'll be ready in a moment. (*She moves to the French windows.*)

MEREDITH. Well, thanks.

(CAROLINE *goes on to the terrace and stands by the easel, looking at* AMYAS)

ELSA. (*To* AMYAS; *as* CAROLINE *comes out*) I shall have a break.

AMYAS. (*Rather indistinctly*) Stop where you are, damn you.

MEREDITH. (*To* PHILIP) After lunch, I'll take Caroline out in the garden and tackle her. All right?

(PHILIP *nods, closes the door up Centre and moves to the French windows.* ELSA *rises and stretches.* MEREDITH *moves to the table Right and picks up his half-finished lemonade.*)

CAROLINE. (*Urgently*) Amyas . . .

PHILIP. (*Moving on to the terrace*) You seem very preoccupied this morning, Caroline.

CAROLINE. (*To* PHILIP; *over her shoulder*) I? Oh, yes, I'm very busy getting Angela off. (*To* AMYAS. *Very urgently*) You will do it, Amyas. You *must*. This afternoon.

(PHILIP *moves above the bench.* AMYAS *passes his hand over his forehead. He has lost control of clear speech.*)

AMYAS. All ri-right. I'll see – her packing . . .

CAROLINE. (*Turning to the French windows*) We – we do want Angela to get off without too much fuss. (*She goes into the room and stands above the stool.*)

(PHILIP *crosses to the French windows.* ELSA *sits on the bench.* AMYAS *shakes his head to try and clear his brain.*)

PHILIP. (*To* CAROLINE) You spoil that brat.

CAROLINE. (*Plumping cushions on the sofa*) We shall miss her terribly when she's gone.

PHILIP. (*Stepping into the room*) Where's little Carla?

(MEREDITH *crosses to the armchair Left with his drink, and sits.*)

CAROLINE. She's gone to stay with her godmother for a week. She'll be home the day after tomorrow.

MEREDITH. What's Miss Williams going to do with herself when Angela's gone?

CAROLINE. She's got a post at the Belgian Embassy. I shall miss her.

(*A dinner gong sounds off in the hall.*)

Lunch.

(ANGELA *bursts in up Centre.*)

ANGELA. (*As she enters*) I'm starving. (*She runs on to the terrace. To* ELSA *and* AMYAS) Lunch, you two.

(MISS WILLIAMS *appears in the doorway up Centre.* CAROLINE *crosses to the table Right Centre and picks up her cigarette case.*)

ELSA. (*Rising and picking up her pullover*) Coming.

(ANGELA *goes into the room.*)

(*To* AMYAS) Lunch?

AMYAS. I – ah!

MISS WILLIAMS. Do try not to shout so, Angela, it really isn't necessary.

ANGELA. I'm not shouting.

(ANGELA *exits up Centre.* MISS WILLIAMS *follows her off.*)

CAROLINE (*Moving to the door up Centre; to* MEREDITH) I should bring that in with you.

(MEREDITH *rises.*)

PHILIP. (*Looking at* MEREDITH) What – lemonade?

CAROLINE. (*To* PHILIP) For you, we've got a lovely bottle of . . .

PHILIP. Châteauneuf du Pape? Good! Hasn't Amyas finished it yet?

CAROLINE. (*To* MEREDITH) What a nice surprise to see you.

MEREDITH. I really came over to see Philip, but I'm always happy to stay to lunch.

(CAROLINE *and* PHILIP *exit up Centre.* ELSA *comes into the room.*)

(*He turns to* ELSA) Amyas?

ELSA. (*Crossing to the door up Centre*) There's something he wants to finish.

(ELSA *exits up Centre.* MEREDITH *follows her off.*)

ANGELA. (*Off*) He hates stopping for lunch.

(*The paintbrush drops from* AMYAS's *hand. THE LIGHTS slowly dim to black-out. A spotlight comes up on* JUSTIN *down Left.*)

JUSTIN. They all went in to lunch, leaving Amyas painting on the terrace. After lunch, Miss Williams and Mrs Crale went out with coffee. Miss Williams?

(*The spotlight fades.* MISS WILLIAMS's *voice can be heard in the darkness.*)

MISS WILLIAMS. Mr Crale often refused lunch and went on painting. It was nothing out of the ordinary. He liked a cup of coffee brought to him, though. I poured it and Mrs Crale took it out to him, and I followed. At the trial I told what we found. But there was something else – something I have not told anyone. I think it right that I should tell it now.

(*The LIGHTS come up.* AMYAS *lies prostrate on the ground below the easel.* CAROLINE *and* MISS WILLIAMS *are in the room, standing at the stool, on which there is a tray of coffee.* MISS WILLIAMS *is Right of the stool, pouring out a cup of coffee, which she gives to* CAROLINE. CAROLINE *takes the coffee on to the terrace.*)

CAROLINE. (*As she goes on to the terrace*) Amyas. (*She sees* AMYAS *on the ground. Horrified*) Amyas! (*She stands for a moment, puts the coffee-cup on the bench, rushes to* AMYAS, *kneels beside him and picks up his hand.*)

(MISS WILLIAMS *comes quickly on to the terrace and moves to Left of* CAROLINE.)

He's – I think he's dead. (*She is distracted.*) Well, go on. Quick. Telephone for a doctor or something.

(MISS WILLIAMS *goes quickly into the room. As soon as* MISS WILLIAMS *reaches the French windows,* CAROLINE *gives a furtive look round, takes out her handkerchief, picks up the beer bottle, wipes it, then presses* AMYAS*'s hand round it.* MEREDITH *enters up Centre.*)

MISS WILLIAMS. (*To* MEREDITH) Get Doctor Fawcett, quickly. It's Mr Crale. He's been taken ill.

(MEREDITH *stares at* MISS WILLIAMS *for a moment, then moves to the telephone and lifts the receiver.* MISS WILLIAMS *goes on to the terrace in time to see* CAROLINE *pressing* AMYAS*'s fingers round the bottle.* MISS WILLIAMS *freezes.* CAROLINE *rises, crosses quickly to the trolley, puts the bottle on it, then stands facing Left.* MISS WILLIAMS *turns slowly and goes into the room.*)

MEREDITH. (*Into the telephone*) Four-two, please . . . Doctor Faw-cett? . . . This is Alderbury . . . Can you come at once? Mr Crale has been taken seriously ill . . .

MISS WILLIAMS. He's . . .

MEREDITH. (*To* MISS WILLIAMS) What? (*Into the telephone*) Just a moment. (*To* MISS WILLIAMS) What did you say?

(ELSA *enters up Centre.* PHILIP *follows her on. They are laughing and joking.*)

MISS WILLIAMS. (*In a clear voice*) I said he's dead.

(MEREDITH *replaces the receiver.*)

ELSA. (*Staring at* MISS WILLIAMS) What did you say? Dead? Amyas? (*She rushes on to the terrace and stares down at* AMYAS.) Amyas! (*She draws in her breath, runs and kneels above* AMYAS *and touches his head.*)

(CAROLINE *turns. The others are motionless.*)

(*Quietly*) Amyas!

(*There is a pause.* PHILIP *runs on to the terrace and stands below the bench.* MISS WILLIAMS *comes on to the terrace and stands below the French windows.* MEREDITH *follows her on and stands up Left of the bench.*)

(*She looks up at* CAROLINE) You've killed him. You said you'd kill him, and you've done it. Sooner than let me have him, you've killed him. (*She jumps up and goes to throw herself at* CAROLINE.)

(PHILIP *moves quickly, stops* ELSA *and propels her round to* MISS WILLIAMS. ELSA *is hysterical and screams.* ANGELA *enters up Centre and stands beside the sofa.*)

MISS WILLIAMS. Be quiet. Control yourself.
ELSA. (*In a frenzy*) She killed him. She killed him.
PHILIP. Take her inside – get her to lie down.

(MEREDITH *takes* ELSA *into the room.*)

CAROLINE. Miss Williams, don't let Angela come – don't let her see.

(MEREDITH *takes* ELSA *off up Centre.* MISS WILLIAMS *looks at* CAROLINE *for a moment, then sets her lips firmly and goes into the room.* PHILIP *kneels beside* AMYAS *and feels his pulse.*)

ANGELA. Miss Williams, what is it? What's happened?
MISS WILLIAMS. Come to your room, Angela. There's been an accident.

(MISS WILLIAMS *and* ANGELA *exit up Centre.*)

PHILIP. (*Looking up at* CAROLINE) It's murder.
CAROLINE. (*Shrinking back, suddenly indecisive*) No. No – he did it himself.
PHILIP. (*Quietly*) You can tell that story – to the police.

(*The LIGHTS slowly dim to black-out. A spotlight comes up on* JUSTIN *down Left.*)

JUSTIN. In due course the police arrived. They found the missing phial of conine in a drawer in Caroline's room. It was empty.

She admitted taking it – but denied using it and swore she had no idea *why* it should be empty. No fingerprints but Meredith's and her own were found on it. On the terrace, a small eye-dropper was found crushed underfoot. It contained traces of conine and shows how the poison was introduced into the beer. Angela Warren told how she got a fresh bottle of beer from the refrigerator. Miss Williams took it from her and Caroline took it from Miss Williams, opened it and gave it to Amyas, as you have just heard. Neither Meredith nor Philip Blake touched it or went near it. A week later Caroline Crale was arrested on a charge of murder.

(*The spotlight fades. After a moment, the LIGHTS come up showing the scene as it was at the beginning of the Act. The coffee, lemonade, trolley, easel, etc., have been removed. The picture on the wall is again that of* ELSA. PHILIP *stands Right of the sofa.* MEREDITH *is seated on the sofa at the Left end.* ANGELA *is seated on the Left arm of the sofa.* ELSA *stands in front of the door up Centre.* MISS WILLIAMS *is seated on the Right end of the stool.* CARLA *is seated in the armchair Right.* JUSTIN *is just inside the French windows with a notebook in his hand. They are all dressed for outdoors with coats and hats.* ELSA *is in mink. She appears excited.* MEREDITH *is crushed and miserable.* PHILIP *is aggressive.* MISS WILLIAMS *sits with lips set firm.* ANGELA *is upright, interested and thoughtful.*)

PHILIP. (*Irritably*) Well, we've been through this extraordinary performance which must have been most painful to some of us. (*He crosses above the stool to Right of* JUSTIN.) And what have we learnt? Nothing that we did not know before. (*He glares at* JUSTIN.)

(JUSTIN *smiles.* PHILIP *goes on to the terrace, stands by the bench and lights a cigarette.* MISS WILLIAMS *rises and moves Right.*)

JUSTIN. (*Thoughtfully*) I wouldn't say that.

MEREDITH. It's brought it all back – just as though it happened yesterday. Most painful.

ELSA. (*Crossing to the sofa and sitting on it, Right of* MEREDITH) Yes, it brought it all back. It brought *him* back.

ANGELA. (*To* JUSTIN) What have you learned that you did not know before?

JUSTIN. We shall go into that.

(PHILIP *comes into the room and crosses to Centre.*)

PHILIP. May I point out something that does not seem to be recognized by anybody? (*He moves to Right of* JUSTIN.) What we have been listening to – and supplying – can only be recollections, and probably faulty ones at that.

JUSTIN. As you say.

PHILIP. And therefore quite useless as evidence. (*He turns away up Left Centre.*) We haven't heard *facts* at all, only people's vague recollections of facts.

JUSTIN. (*Moving to Left of* PHILIP) What we have heard has no evidential value as such – but it *has* a value, you know.

PHILIP. In what way?

JUSTIN. Shall we say, in what people choose to remember? Or, alternatively, choose to forget.

PHILIP. Very clever – but fanciful.

ANGELA. (*To* PHILIP) I don't agree. I . . .

PHILIP. (*Overriding* ANGELA) And I will point out something else. (*He crosses below the stool and stands between* MISS WILLIAMS *and* ELSA.) It's not just a question of what people remember, or do not remember. It might be a question of deliberate lying.

JUSTIN. Of course.

ANGELA. That's just the point, I rather imagine. (*She rises and moves Centre.*) Or am I wrong?

JUSTIN. You are thinking on the right lines, Miss Warren.

(ANGELA *crosses to the armchair Left.*)

PHILIP. (*Exasperated*) Look here, what is all this? If somebody is deliberately lying – why then . . .

ANGELA. (*Sitting in the armchair Left*) Exactly.

PHILIP. (*Crossing to* JUSTIN; *angrily*) Do you mean you have got us here with the idea – the preposterous idea that one of us could be guilty of murder?

ANGELA. Of course he has. Have you only just realized it?

PHILIP. I never heard such offensive nonsense in my life.

ANGELA. If Amyas didn't kill himself, and if his wife didn't murder him, then one of us must have done so.

PHILIP. But it has already been made perfectly clear, in the course of what we've heard, that nobody but Caroline *could* have killed him.

JUSTIN. I don't think we can be as certain as all that.

PHILIP. (*Crossing below the stool to Right*) Oh, God!

JUSTIN. (*Not heeding*) There is the question you yourself raised, the question of lying.

(*There is a slight pause.* PHILIP *sits on the Right end of the stool, with his back to the audience.*)

When one person's evidence is corroborated or acquiesced in by another person — (*He moves down Centre.*) then it can be regarded as checked. But some of what we have heard is vouched for by only one person. (*He crosses below the stool and moves up Centre.*) For instance, at the very beginning, we had to rely solely on Mr Meredith Blake here for what passed between him and Caroline Crale.

MEREDITH. (*Indignantly*) But, really . . .

JUSTIN. (*Quickly*) Oh, I'm not disputing the authenticity of what you told us. I only point out that the conversation *could* have been an entirely different one.

MEREDITH. (*Rising*) It was as accurate as anything could be after a lapse of sixteen years.

JUSTIN. Quite. (*He crosses to the French windows and goes on to the terrace.*) But remember the fine weather and the open windows. This means that most of the conversations, even those that were apparently *tête-à-têtes*, could be and probably were, overheard from either inside or outside the room. (*He comes into the room and stands up Left Centre*) But that is not so for all of them.

MEREDITH. (*Moving Left*) Are you getting at me?

(*There is pause.* JUSTIN *looks at his notebook.*)

JUSTIN. Not necessarily. I singled you out because you started the ball rolling.

MISS WILLIAMS. (*Moving to Right of the stool*) I would like to state here and now that any account I have given of *my* part in the affair is true. There is no witness who saw what I saw — Caroline Crale wiping fingerprints off that bottle — but I solemnly swear that is exactly what I saw her do. (*She turns to* CARLA.) I am sorry, for Carla's sake, I have to tell you this, but Carla is, I hope, courageous enough to face the truth.

ANGELA. Truth is what she asked for.

JUSTIN. And truth is what will help her. (*He crosses below the stool to* MISS WILLIAMS.) What you don't realize, Miss Williams, is that what you have told us goes a long way towards proving Caroline Crale's *innocence*, not her guilt.

(*There are general exclamations from the others.* PHILIP *rises and moves to Left of the stool.*)

MISS WILLIAMS. What do you mean?

JUSTIN. You say you saw Caroline Crale take a handkerchief, wipe the beer bottle, and then press her husband's fingers on it?

MISS WILLIAMS. Yes.

JUSTIN. (*After a pause, quietly*) The beer *bottle*?

MISS WILLIAMS. Certainly. The bottle.

JUSTIN. But the poison, Miss Williams, was not found in the bottle – not a trace of it. The conine was in the *glass*.

(*There are general exclamations from the others.*)

ANGELA. You mean . . .?

JUSTIN. (*Moving up Centre*) I mean that if Caroline wiped the bottle, she thought the conine had been in the bottle. But if she had been the poisoner, she would have *known* where the conine was. (*He turns to* CARLA.)

(MISS WILLIAMS *moves to the sofa.* MEREDITH, *bewildered, moves Right.*)

CARLA. (*On a very soft sigh*) Of course.

(*There is a pause.*)

JUSTIN. (*Moving to* CARLA) We all came here today to satisfy one person. Amyas Crale's daughter. Are you satisfied, Carla?

(*There is a pause.* CARLA *rises and moves above the stool.* JUSTIN *sits in the armchair Right*)

CARLA. Yes. I'm satisfied. I know now – oh, I know now such a lot of things.

PHILIP. What things?

CARLA. (*Moving Left Centre*) I know that you, Philip Blake, fell violently in love with my mother, and that when she turned you down and married Amyas, you never forgave her. (*To* MEREDITH) You thought you still loved my mother – but really it was Elsa you loved.

(MEREDITH *looks at* ELSA, *who smiles triumphantly.*)

But all that doesn't matter – what does matter is that I know now what made my mother behave so oddly at her trial.

(MISS WILLIAMS *sits on the sofa at the Left end.*)

I know what she was trying to hide. (*She crosses above the stool to* JUSTIN.) And I know just why she wiped those fingerprints off the bottle. Justin, do you know what I mean?

JUSTIN. I'm not quite sure.

CARLA. There's only one person Caroline would have tried to shield – (*She turns to* ANGELA) you.

ANGELA. (*Sitting up*) Me?

CARLA. (*Crossing to* ANGELA) Yes. It's all so clear. You'd played tricks on Amyas, you were angry with him – vindictive because you blamed him for sending you to school.

ANGELA. He was quite right.

CARLA. But you didn't think so at the time. You were angry. It was you who went and fetched a bottle of beer for him, although it was my mother who took it to him. And, remember, you'd tampered with his beer once before. (*She moves above the stool and kneels upon it.*) When Caroline found him dead with the beer bottle and glass beside him, all that flashed into her mind.

ANGELA. She thought I'd murdered him?

CARLA. She didn't think you meant to. She thought you'd just played a trick, that you meant to make him sick, but that you had miscalculated the dose. Whatever you'd done, you'd killed him and she had to save you from the consequences. Oh, don't you see, it all fits in? The way she got you hustled off to Switzerland, the pains she took to keep you from hearing about the arrest and the trial.

ANGELA. She must have been mad.

CARLA. She had a guilt complex about you, because of what she'd done to you as a child. So, in her way, she paid her debt.

ELSA. (*Rising and crossing below the stool to* ANGELA) So, it was you.

ANGELA. Don't be absurd. Of course it wasn't. Do you mean to say you believe this ridiculous story?

CARLA. Caroline believed it.

JUSTIN. Yes, Caroline believed it. It explains so much.

ANGELA. (*Rising and crossing below the stool to* CARLA) And you, Carla? Do you believe it?.

CARLA. (*After a pause*) No.

ANGELA. Ah! (*She moves to the sofa and sits on it at the Right end.*)

CARLA. But then, there's no other solution.

(ELSA *sits in the armchair Left.*)

JUSTIN. Oh, yes, I think there might be. (*He rises and crosses to Left Centre.*) Tell me, Miss Williams, would it be natural or likely for Amyas Crale to have helped Angela by packing her clothes for her?

MISS WILLIAMS. Certainly not. He'd never dream of doing such a thing.

JUSTIN. And yet you, Mr Philip Blake, overheard Amyas Crale say, 'I'll see to her packing.' I think you were wrong.

PHILIP. Now look here, Fogg, have you got the nerve to insinuate that I was lying?

(*The LIGHTS dim to black-out.*)

JUSTIN. I'm not insinuating anything. But let me remind you that the picture we now have is built up from remembered conversations.

(*The spotlight comes up on* JUSTIN *down Left.*)

Memory is the only thread that hangs this picture together – it is a fragile thread and uncertain. I suggest one conversation we've heard about went quite differently. Let's suppose it went something like this.

(*The spotlight fades and after a moment the LIGHTS come up to reveal the house and terrace as it was sixteen years previously.* CAROLINE *is seated in the armchair Right, and* AMYAS *is about to open the door up Centre to go out. Instead he turns towards* CAROLINE.)

AMYAS. I've told you, Caroline, I don't want to discuss this.

CAROLINE. You didn't want a scene until you'd finished your picture. That's it, isn't it?

(AMYAS *crosses and leans over* CAROLINE.)

Oh, I understand you very well.

(AMYAS *is about to kiss her.*)

(*She rises quickly and crosses to Left.*) And what you're doing is monstrous. You're going to treat this girl the same way as you've treated all the others. You were in love with her, but you're not now. All you want is to string her along so that you can finish that picture.

AMYAS. (*Smiling*) All right, then. That picture matters.

CAROLINE. So does she.

AMYAS. She'll get over it.

CAROLINE. (*Partly pleading*) Oh, you! You've got to tell her. Now – today. You can't go on like this, it's too cruel.

AMYAS. (*Crossing to* CAROLINE) All right, I'll send her packing. But the picture . . .

CAROLINE. Damn the picture! You and your women. You don't deserve to live.

AMYAS. Caroline. (*He tries to embrace her.*)

CAROLINE. I mean it. No, don't touch me. (*She crosses down Right.*) It's too cruel – it's too cruel.

AMYAS. Caroline!

(CAROLINE *exits down Right. The LIGHTS dim to black-out. The spotlight comes up on* JUSTIN *down Left.*)

JUSTIN. Yes, that's how that conversation went. Caroline pleaded, but not for herself. Philip Blake didn't hear Amyas say, 'I'll see to her packing' – what he in fact heard was the voice of a dying man struggling to say, 'I'll *send* her packing.'

(*The spotlight fades on* JUSTIN. *The LIGHTS come up. Everyone is back in the same positions as they were before the black-out.*)

A phrase he'd no doubt used before of other mistresses, but this time he spoke of you – (*He turns to* ELSA) didn't he, Lady

Melksham? The shock of that conversation was terrific, wasn't it? And straight away you acted. You'd seen Caroline take that phial of conine the day before. You found it at once when you went upstairs for a pullover. You handled it carefully, filled an eye-dropper from it, came down again, and when Amyas asked you for beer, you poured it into the glass, added the conine, and brought the beer to him. You resumed your pose. You watched him as he drank. Watched him feel the first twinges, the stiffness of the limbs, and the slow paralysis of the speech. You sat there and watched him die. (*He gestures to the portrait.*) That's the portrait of a woman who watched the man she loved die.

(ELSA *rises quickly and stands looking at the portrait.*)

And the man who painted it didn't know what was happening to him. But it's there, you know – in the eyes.

ELSA. (*In a hard voice*) He deserved to die. (*She looks at* JUSTIN.) You're a clever man, Mr Fogg. (*She moves to the door up Centre and opens it.*) But there isn't a damn thing you can do about it.

(ELSA *exits up Centre. There is a stunned silence, then gradually everyone starts to speak together.* CARLA *goes on to the terrace and stands below the bench.*)

PHILIP. There – there must be *something* we can do.

MEREDITH. I can't believe it, I simply can't believe it.

ANGELA. (*Rising*) It stares one in the face – how blind we've been.

PHILIP. What can we do, Fogg – what the hell can we do?

JUSTIN. In law, I'm afraid, nothing.

PHILIP. Nothing – what do you mean – nothing? (*He goes to the door up Centre.*) Why, the woman practically admitted . . . I'm not so sure you're right about that.

(PHILIP *exits up Centre.*)

ANGELA. (*Moving to the door up Centre.*) It's ridiculous, but true.

(ANGELA *exits up Centre.*)

MISS WILLIAMS. (*Moving to the door up Centre*) It's incredible, it's incredible! I can't believe it.

(MISS WILLIAMS *exits up Centre.* PHILIP *re-enters up Centre.*)

PHILIP. (*To* JUSTIN) I'm not so sure you're right about that. I'll get my fellow on to it in the morning.

(PHILIP *exits up Centre.*)

MEREDITH. (*Moving to the door up Centre*) Elsa of all people, it seems absolutely impossible. Caroline's dead, Amyas is dead, there's no-one to bear witness – (*he turns in the doorway*) is there?

(MEREDITH *shakes his head and exits up Centre. The babel dies down.* CARLA *sits on the up-stage end of the bench.* JUSTIN *looks out of the French windows for a moment at* CARLA, *then goes on to the terrace.*)

JUSTIN. What do you want done, Carla?

CARLA. (*Quietly*) Nothing. She's been sentenced already, hasn't she?

JUSTIN. (*Puzzled*) Sentenced?

CARLA. To life imprisonment – inside herself. (*She looks at him.*) Thank you.

JUSTIN. (*Crossing above the bench to Left; embarrassed*) You'll go back to Canada, now, and get married. There's no legal proof, of course, but we can satisfy your Jeff. (*He crosses below* CARLA *to Centre and looks at his notes.*)

CARLA. We don't need to satisfy him. I'm not going to marry him. I've already told him so.

JUSTIN. (*Looking up*) But – why?

CARLA. (*Thoughtfully*) I think I've – well – grown out of him. And I'm not going back to Canada. After all, I do belong here.

JUSTIN. You may be – lonely.

CARLA. (*With a mischievous smile*) Not if I marry an English husband. (*Gravely*) Now, if I could induce *you* to fall in love with me . . .

JUSTIN. (*Turning to her*) *Induce* me? Why the devil do you think I've done all this?

CARLA. (*Rising*) You've been mixing me up with my mother. But I'm Amyas's daughter, too. I've got a lot of the devil in me. I want you to be in love with *me*.

JUSTIN. Don't worry. (*He smiles, moves to her and takes her in his arms.*)

CARLA. (*Laughing*) I don't.

(*They kiss.* MEREDITH *enters up Centre.*)

MEREDITH. (*As he enters*) May I suggest a drink at my house before
. . . (*He realizes the room is empty, goes to the French windows and looks out.*) Oh! (*He smiles.*) My word!

(MEREDITH *exits up Centre and the LIGHTS dim to black-out as – the Curtain falls.*)

CURTAIN

ALSO BY AGATHA CHRISTIE

The Mousetrap and Selected Plays

The first-ever publication in book form of The Mousetrap, the longest-running play in the history of London's West End, plus three other Christie thrillers.

The Mousetrap
A homicidal maniac terrorizes a group of snowbound guests to the refrain of 'Three Blind Mice'. . .

And Then There Were None
Ten guilty people, brought together on an island in mysterious circumstances, await their sentence . . .

Appointment With Death
The suffocating heat of an exotic Middle-Eastern setting provides a backdrop for murder . . .

The Hollow
A set of friends convene at a country home where their convoluted relationships mean that any one of them could be a murderer . . .

Christie's plays are as compulsive as her novels. Their colourful characters and ingenious plots provide yet more evidence of her mastery of the detective thriller.

ISBN: 0 00 649618 0

ALSO BY AGATHA CHRISTIE
ADAPTED BY CHARLES OSBORNE

Spider's Web

Clarissa, the wife of a Foreign Office diplomat, is given to daydreaming. 'Supposing I were to come down one morning and find a dead body in the library, what should I do?' she muses.

Clarissa has her chance to find out when she discovers a body in her drawing-room. Desperate to dispose of it before her husband comes home with an important foreign politician, Clarissa attempts to persuade her three house guests to become accessories and accomplices. As the search begins for the murderer in their midst, the house party is interrupted by the arrival of a police inspector, who needs convincing that there has been no murder at all . . .

Written in 1954 specifically for Margaret Lockwood, *Spider's Web* became one of three successful Agatha Christie plays running simultaneously in London that Christmas, alongside *The Mousetrap* and *Witness for the Prosecution*. Now, following his acclaimed *Black Coffee* and *The Unexpected Guest* play novelisations, Charles Osborne brings Agatha Christie's elusive mystery to a new legion of fans.

Published in hardback September 2000

ISBN: 0 00 226198 7

ALSO BY AGATHA CHRISTIE
ADAPTED BY CHARLES OSBORNE

Black Coffee

Sir Claud Amory has discovered the formula for a new
powerful explosive, which is stolen by one of the large
household of relatives and friends. Locking everyone in
the library, Sir Claud switches off the lights to allow the
thief to replace the formula on the table, no questions
asked. When the lights come on, he is dead, and Hercule
Poirot – with assistance from Hastings and Inspector Japp
– has to unravel a tangle of family feuds, old flames and
suspicious foreigners to find the killer and prevent a global
catastrophe.

Black Coffee was Agatha Christie's first playscript, origi-
nally performed in 1930 and made into a now rarely-seen
film the following year. Now Charles Osborne, author of
The Life and Crimes of Agatha Christie, has adapted the play
into a full-length novel. Combining her typically beguiling
plot and sparkling dialogue with his own faithful narrative,
he has produced a novel that will endure for as long as any
of Agatha Christie's books.

'A lively and light-hearted read which will give pleasure to
all those who have long wished that there was just one
more Christie to devour'

ANTONIA FRASER, *Sunday Telegraph*

ISBN: 0 00 651137 6

ALSO BY AGATHA CHRISTIE
ADAPTED BY CHARLES OSBORNE

The Unexpected Guest

When a stranger runs his car into a ditch in dense fog near the South Wales coast, and makes his way to an isolated house, he discovers a woman standing over the dead body of her wheelchair-bound husband, gun in her hand. She admits to murder, and the unexpected guest offers to help her concoct a cover story.

But is it possible that Laura Warwick did *not* commit the murder after all? If so, who is she shielding? The victim's retarded young half-brother or his dying matriarchal mother? Laura's lover? Perhaps the father of a little boy killed in an accident for which Warwick was responsible? The house seems full of possible suspects . . .

The Unexpected Guest is considered to be one of the finest of Agatha Christie's mysteries, hailed as 'another *Mousetrap*' when it opened as a play in the West End in 1958. Now Charles Osborne's novelisation finally brings her superb story to a new legion of fans.

'Like a martini – crisp, dry, sophisticated, habit-forming – will satisfy all devotees of Christie's neat plotting.'

Booklist

ISBN: 0 00 651368 9

ALSO BY AGATHA CHRISTIE

Come, Tell Me How You Live

Agatha Christie was already well known as a crime writer when she accompanied her husband, Max Mallowan, to Syria and Iraq in the 1930s. She took enormous interest in all his excavations, and when friends asked what her strange life was like, she decided to answer their questions in this delightful book.

First published in 1946, *Come, Tell Me How You Live* gives a charming picture of Agatha Christie herself, while also giving insight into some of her most popular novels, including *Murder in Mesopotamia* and *Appointment with Death*. It is, as Jacquetta Hawkes concludes in her introduction, 'a pure pleasure to read'.

'Perfectly delightful . . . colourful, lively and occasionally touching and thought-provoking.'
CHARLES OSBORNE, *Books & Bookmen*

'Good and enjoyable . . . she has a delightfully light touch.'
MARGHANITA LASKI, *Country Life*

ISBN: 0 00 653114 8

ALSO BY AGATHA CHRISTIE
WRITING AS 'MARY WESTMACOTT'

Absent in the Spring

'The one book that has satisfied me completely'
Agatha Christie

Returning from a visit to her daughter in Iraq, Joan
Scudamore finds herself unexpectedly alone and stranded
in an isolated rest house by flooding of the railway tracks.
This sudden solitude compels Joan to assess her life for the
first time ever and face up to many of the truths about
herself. Looking back over the years, Joan painfully re-
examines her attitudes, relationships and actions and
becomes increasingly uneasy about the person who is
revealed to her . . .

'I've not been so emotionally moved by a story since the
memorable *Brief Encounter* . . . *Absent in the Spring* is a *tour
de force* which should be recognized as a classic.'
New York Times

ISBN: 0 00 649947 3

ALSO BY AGATHA CHRISTIE

While the Light Lasts and Other Stories

Like many of her contemporaries, Agatha Christie wrote stories for magazines in the 1920s and '30s, and most eventually found their way into her books of short stories. Now detective work worthy of Christie herself has unearthed seven 'new' stories, plus early magazine versions of two Poirot short stories which she later extended for book publication.

The House of Dreams is the first story Agatha Christie ever wrote and recounts the effects of a macabre recurring dream on a man's life. **The Actress** tells of a woman who turns the tables on her blackmailer, **The Edge** is a gripping tale of jealousy and infidelity, and in **Christmas Adventure** Poirot is caught up in some unseasonal mayhem. **The Lonely God** is an unlikely love story about two lost souls who meet in the British Museum, while in **Manx Gold** two young heroes race against time to discover buried treasure. **Within a Wall** tells of a tragic love triangle between a portrait painter, his wife and his daughter's godmother, and after **The Mystery of the Baghdad Chest**, another early Poirot story which Agatha Christie would later rework, the book concludes with **While the Light Lasts**, where a Rhodesian tobacco plantation is the setting for an unexpected visitor from beyond the grave . . .

ISBN: 0 00 651018 3

ALSO AVAILABLE
BY CHARLES OSBORNE

The Life and Crimes of Agatha Christie

Agatha Christie was the author of over 100 plays, short story collections and novels which have been translated into 103 languages; she is outsold only by the Bible and Shakespeare. Many have tried to copy her but none has succeeded. Attempts to capture her personality on paper, to discover her motivations or the reasons for her popularity, have usually failed. Charles Osborne, a lifelong student of Agatha Christie, has approached this most private of people above all through her books, and the result is a fascinating companion to her life and work.

This 'professional life' of Agatha Christie provides authoritative information on each book's provenance, on the work itself and on its contemporary critical reception set against the background of the major events in the author's life. Illustrated with many rare photographs, this comprehensive guide to the world of Agatha Christie has been fully updated to include details of all the publications, films and TV adaptations in the 25 years since her death.

ISBN: 0 00 257033 5 Hardback
ISBN: 0 00 653097 4 Paperback

ALSO AVAILABLE
BY ANNE HART

Agatha Christie's
Miss Marple

*'I have had a lot of experience in solving different little problems
that have arisen.'*

Most of the 'little problems' tackled by Miss Marple
occurred in the pretty rural village of St Mary Mead and
came in the shape of murder, robbery and blackmail. In
the 40 years of her career, she even solved cases as far
afield as London and the Caribbean. But though she
usually masqueraded as 'everybody's favourite great aunt',
what was she *really* like?

In this authorized biography of the world's most famous
female sleuth, Anne Hart combs through the 12 novels
and 20 short stories in which Miss Marple appeared,
uncovering clue after clue and amassing all the evidence to
solve the most difficult case of them all – the mystery of
Miss Marple.

'A great treat for Agatha Christie addicts'   *Daily Mail*

ISBN: 0 00 649956 2

ALSO AVAILABLE
BY ANNE HART

Agatha Christie's
Hercule Poirot

'My name is Hercule Poirot and I am probably the greatest detective in the world.'

The dapper, moustache-twirling little Belgian with the egg-shaped head, curious mannerisms and inordinate respect for his own 'little grey cells' has solved some of the most puzzling crimes of the century. Yet despite being familiar to millions, Poirot himself has remained an enigma - until now.

From his first appearance in 1920 to his last in 1975, from country-house drawing-rooms to opium dens in Limehouse, from Mayfair to the Mediterranean, Anne Hart stalks the legendary sleuth, unveiling the mysteries that surround him. Sifting through 33 novels and 56 short stories, she examines his origins, tastes, relationships and peculiarities, revealing a character as fascinating as the books themselves.

'Thorough and perceptive . . . a genuinely studious (but thoroughly readable) work'   *Daily Mail*

ISBN: 0 00 649957 0